The series Lecture Notes in Computer Science (LNCS), including its subseries Lecture Notes in Artificial Intelligence (LNAI) and Lecture Notes in Bioinformatics (LNBI), has established itself as a medium for the publication of new developments in computer science and information technology research, teaching, and education.

LNCS enjoys close cooperation with the computer science R & D community, the series counts many renowned academics among its volume editors and paper authors, and collaborates with prestigious societies. Its mission is to serve this international community by providing an invaluable service, mainly focused on the publication of conference and workshop proceedings and postproceedings. LNCS commenced publication in 1973.

Yang Xiang · Jian Shen
Editors

Machine Learning for Cyber Security

7th International Conference, ML4CS 2025
Hangzhou, China, December 12–14, 2025
Proceedings

Springer

Editors
Yang Xiang
Swinburne University of Technology
Melbourne, VIC, Australia

Jian Shen
Zhejiang Sci-Tech University
Hangzhou, Zhejiang, China

ISSN 0302-9743 ISSN 1611-3349 (electronic)
Lecture Notes in Computer Science
ISBN 978-981-95-7819-1 ISBN 978-981-95-7820-7 (eBook)
https://doi.org/10.1007/978-981-95-7820-7

This Springer imprint is published by the registered company Springer Nature Singapore Pte Ltd.
The registered company address is: 152 Beach Road, #21-01/04 Gateway East, Singapore 189721, Singapore

Preface

The Seventh International Conference on Machine Learning for Cyber Security (ML4CS 2025) was held in Hangzhou, China, during December 12–14, 2025. ML4CS is a well-recognized annual international forum for AI-driven security researchers to exchange ideas and present their work. This volume contains papers presented at ML4CS 2025. The conference received 97 submissions. The committee accepted 18 regular papers, with each accepted paper receiving at least 2 double-blind reviews. The proceedings contain revised versions of the accepted papers. While revisions were expected to take the referees' comments into account, this was not enforced, and the authors bear full responsibility for the content of their papers.

ML4CS 2025 was organized by the School of Information Science and Engineering (School of Cyber Science and Technology), Zhejiang Sci-Tech University. Furthermore, ML4CS 2025 was supported by Zhejiang Provincial Key Laboratory of Digital Fashion and Data Governance, Zhejiang Key Laboratory of Artificial Intelligence of Things (AIoT) Network and Data Security, and Zhejiang Provincial International Cooperation Base for Science and Technology on Cloud Computing Security and Data Aggregation. The conference would not have been such a success without the support of these organizations, and we sincerely thank them for their continued assistance and support.

We would also like to thank the authors who submitted their papers to ML4CS 2025, and the conference attendees for their interest and support. We thank the Organizing Committee for their time and effort dedicated to arranging the conference. This allowed us to focus on the paper selection and deal with the scientific program. We thank the Program Committee members and the external reviewers for their hard work in reviewing the submissions; the conference would not have been possible without their expert reviews. Finally, we thank the EasyChair system and its operators, for making the entire process of managing the conference convenient.

December 2025

Yang Xiang
Jian Shen

Organization

Honorary Chairs

Jianfeng Ma	Xidian University, China
Wanlei Zhou	City University of Macau, China
Yang Xiang	Swinburne University of Technology, Australia

General Chair

Jian Shen	Zhejiang Sci-Tech University, China
Willy Susilo	University of Wollongong, Australia
Aniello Castiglione	University of Salerno, Italy

Program Chairs

Xiaofeng Chen	Xidian University, China
Xinyi Huang	Jinan University, China
Zilong Jin	Zhejiang Sci-Tech University, China

Publication Chairs

Weizhi Meng	Lancaster University, UK
Yebo Feng	Nanyang Technological University, Singapore
Fei Gao	Beijing University of Posts and Telecommunications, China

Publicity Co-Chairs

Zakirul Alam Bhuiyan	Fordham University, USA
Vijayakumar Pandi	JJ College of Engineering and Technology, India
Debiao He	Wuhan University, China

Web Chairs

Chunhua Su	University of Aizu, Japan
Tianqi Zhou	Zhejiang Sci-Tech University, China

Organization Chairs

Shouling Ji	Zhejiang University, China
Bin Wang	Hikvision, China
Xiaolin Liu	Zhejiang University, China
Huijie Yang	Zhejiang Sci-Tech University, China

PC Members

Silvio Barra	University of Salerno, Italy
M. Z. Alam Bhuiyan	Guangzhou University, China
Carlo Blundo	University of Salerno, Italy
Yiqiao Cai	Huaqiao University, China
Luigi Catuogno	University of Salerno, Italy
Xiaofeng Chen	Xidian University, China
Zhe Chen	Singapore Management University, Singapore
Frngapor Cuppens	École Polytechnique de Montréal, Canada
Changyu Dong	Newcastle University, UK
Mohammed EI-Abd	American University of Kuwait, Kuwait
Dieter Gollmann	Hamburg University of Technology, Germany
Mengmeng Ge	Monash University, Australia
Saeid Hosseini	Sohar University, Oman
Chingfang Hsu	Huazhong University of Science and Technology, China
Jin Hong	University of Western Australia, Australia
Haibo Hu	Hong Kong Polytechnic University, China
Xinyi Huang	Fujian Normal University, China
Lutful Karim	Seneca Polytechnic, Canada
Hadis Karimipour	University of Calgary, Canada
Abigail Koay	University of the Sunshine Coast, Australia
Sokratis Katsikas	Open University of Cyprus, Cyprus
Wei Kong	Zhejiang Sci-Tech University, China
Neeraj Kumar	Thapar Institute of Engineering and Technology, India
Kangshun Li	South China Agricultural University, China

Kaitai Liang	University of Turku, Finland/TU Delft, The Netherlands
Shigang Liu	Swinburne University of Technology, Australia
Hui Liu	University of Calgary, Canada
Wei Lu	Sun Yat-sen University, China
Tianhao Liu	Beijing Jiaotong University, China
Dengzhi Liu	Jiangsu Ocean University, China
Chao Lin	Fujian Normal University, China
Hongbo Li	South China Agricultural University, China
Xiaobo Ma	Xi'an Jiaotong University
Fabio Martinelli	IIT-CNR, Italy
Ficco Massimo	University of Salerno, Italy
Weizhi Meng	Lancaster University, UK
Nour Moustafa	UNSW Canberra, Australia
Yuantian Miao	University of New Castle, Australia
Vincenzo Moscato	University of Naples Federico II, Italy
Francesco Palmieri	University of Salerno, Italy
Umberto Petrillo	Sapienza University of Rome, Italy
Lianyong Qi	Qufu Normal University, China
Shahryar Rahnamayan	Brock University, Canada
Hao Ren	Sichuan University, China
Khaled Riad	Zagazig University, Egypt/King Faisal University, Saudi Arabia
Shifeng Sun	Shanghai Jiao Tong University, China
Yi Li	Swinburne University of Technology, Australia
Jun Shen	Shanghai University, China
Shuai Shang	University of Electronic Science and Technology of China, China
Haowen Tan	Zhejiang Sci-Tech University, China
Zhiyuan Tan	Edinburgh Napier University, UK
Chen Wang	Zhejiang Sci-Tech University, China
Ding Wang	Peking University, China
Derek Wang	Data61, CSIRO, Australia
Feng Wang	Wuhan University, China
Yunling Wang	Xi'an University of Posts and Telecommunications, China
Hui Wang	Nanchang Institute of Technology, China
Jianfeng Wang	Xidian University, China
Jin Wang	Soochow University, China
Licheng Wang	Beijing University of Posts and Telecommunications, China
Lingyu Wang	University of British Columbia Okanagan, Canada

Contents

Blockchain-Based Cross-Domain Data Auditing Scheme for E-Commerce AI 1
Meiqin Tang, Wei Chen, and Chaoping Chang

DFI-GNN: A Dual-Feature Interaction Graph Neural Network Model for Multimodal Medical Image Classification 16
Meng Yu, Lijuan Sun, Yutong Gao, Gaohu Li, Jingchen Wu, and Xu Wu

A Fast-Verifiable Threshold BLS Signature Scheme 33
Suliu Yang, Tianqi Zhou, Meijia Guo, and Yuluo Zeng

Cracking Passwords with LLMs by Exploiting Linguistic Features 52
Tianyu Zuo, Wenying Zhang, and Dewen Ding

AgentGuard: An Active Threat Discovery System for Package Confusion Using Multi-agent Collaboration 69
Wei Ma, Yu Li, Zhi Chen, Ye Liu, Lingxiao Jiang, Qiang Hu, and Junyi Tao

Parallelizable Oblivious Non-equi-Joins in Trusted Execution Environments 84
Xingquan Li, Sen Zhao, Guohua Tian, and Meixia Miao

Blockchain-Based Anonymous Aggregate Signature Scheme for Medical Internet of Things 105
Lifeng Zhou, Xinchun Yin, Su Jia, and Hongbin Zhou

A Structured Chinese Encoding Framework for Multi-field Encrypted Fuzzy Query with Non-bootstrapping CKKS 124
Shutong Liu, Liping Zhuang, Jin Peng, Yuying Lin, and Zheng Gong

Evidential Deep Fusion for Multi-channel Analysis Against Public-Key Cryptosystems 139
Zeli Chen, Yuhan Qian, Jing Gao, Jing Yu, Yaoling Ding, Xuexin Zheng, and An Wang

Token-Efficient Binary Vulnerability Prioritization via Function Pre-filtering with LLMs 154
Zhuoyuan Niu, Chen Wang, and Wei Wu

A Prefix-Based Homomorphic Encryption Protocol for Efficient Secure Comparison 166
Shutong Li, Baodong Qin, and Xiao Deng

A Verifiable Data Possession Scheme for Distributed Computing 180
Wenying Zheng, Zelin Ni, Yahui Zhu, and Tianqi Zhou

Entropy-Aware Watermarking for Code Generation Models 193
Ying Shi, Siyuan Bao, Hanzhou Wu, Jingyu Ye, and Xinpeng Zhang

A Verifiable and Privacy-Preserving Federated Learning Framework via Homomorphic Encryption 207
Chun Fang, Shengmin Xu, Xiaoguo Li, and Jinhua Ma

Empirical Study on Adversarial Robustness Degradation in Image Classification via Unlearning 221
Natchapol Shinno, Haibo Zhang, and Takeshi Saitoh

P^2FR-VFL: Privacy-Enhanced Vertical Federated Learning Framework via P^2FR-PSI and Homomorphic Encryption 236
Huizhong Zhao, Shengmin Xu, Jianchang Lai, and Zhongsheng Tan

Performance Evaluation of Parallel Inference Pipeline for Multi-model Processing on Edge Devices 251
So-Yeon Lee, Tae-Jun Yoon, and Dae-Young Kim

Multi-authority Attribute-Based Access Control with Dynamic Policy Updates for Federated Learning 261
Jialu Wang, Huijie Yang, Jingang Li, and Wenying Zheng

Author Index 283

Blockchain-Based Cross-Domain Data Auditing Scheme for E-Commerce AI

Meiqin Tang, Wei Chen(✉), and Chaoping Chang

School of Integrated Circuits, Wuxi Vocational College of Science and Technology, Wuxi 214028, China
18961759130@163.com

Abstract. The rapid proliferation of artificial intelligence (AI) systems has led to the generation of massive amounts of valuable data, which can be leveraged to enhance analytical capabilities and support intelligent decision-making. Since the quality of such decision-making is fundamentally determined by the AI models trained on these data, it is crucial to perform periodic audits to verify and maintain data integrity. However, traditional data auditing solutions encounter significant challenges due to the reluctance of different domains to share data. To this end, we propose a Blockchain-based Cross-Domain Data Auditing (BCDDA) scheme designed for trustworthy AI systems. BCDDA employs a Chameleon Hash-based mechanism to efficiently construct audit metadata, thereby reducing the computational overhead on domain servers. Furthermore, it adopts a parallel data auditing architecture, in which audit tags are recorded on the main blockchain, while AI data are redundantly stored across multiple domain servers to ensure recoverability even if a shard is compromised. In addition, BCDDA supports dynamic operations on AI data, such as insertion, deletion, and modification, without regenerating audit tags, thereby enhancing system flexibility. Experimental evaluations conducted with four shard consensus nodes demonstrate that the proposed BCDDA scheme achieves high efficiency in audit tag generation and shard consensus processes. The results confirm that BCDDA provides a secure, reliable, and scalable solution for cross-domain AI data auditing in decentralized environments.

Keywords: Data auditing · E-commerce AI · Blockchain · Distributed system

1 Introduction

The consumer electronics such as smartphones, tablets, and other smart devices, generate vast amounts of consumer data [27,32]. E-commerce platforms can leverage AI techniques to analyze this data, predict trends, and plan future business strategies. With the large number of consumer electronic devices in use today, the volume of data generated is immense. On promotional days, the amount of data produced is even more staggering. To manage this, e-commerce platforms typically divide their operations into multiple regions,

Y. Xiang and J. Shen (Eds.): ML4CS 2025, LNCS 16456, pp. 1–15, 2026.
https://doi.org/10.1007/978-981-95-7820-7_1

deploying regional servers nearby to handle data collection and storage for each area. However, due to transmission issues and unexpected failures, data can be lost or corrupted, significantly impacting data analysis and decision-making for e-commerce business strategies [20,22]. Therefore, periodic integrity verification of consumer electronic data, or data auditing, is necessary.

Sharding blockchain is a technology that improves overall processing capability and scalability by dividing the network into multiple independent shards, each of which independently processes and stores a portion of the transactions [7]. It is designed to address the performance bottlenecks in traditional blockchain systems, where all nodes must process all data. Due to the distributed and parallel nature of sharding blockchain, it is particularly well-suited for multi-domain e-commerce networks. By deploying a shard within each domain to handle the auditing of consumer electronic data, the concurrent performance of data auditing processes on e-commerce platforms can be significantly enhanced.

However, the data auditing within a domain relies entirely on the trustworthiness of the shard's nodes. If the nodes within a shard are compromised, it could lead to malicious activities in the data auditing process for that domain. While transferring data within a domain to other domains for consensus on data integrity across multiple shards could enhance security, this approach may face resistance, as domains may belong to different departments that are unwilling to share their data with each other [18,19,21]. The challenge we aim to address is how to accelerate data auditing efficiency using sharding blockchain without requiring the sharing of data between domain servers. To this end, we propose the blockchain-based cross-domain data auditing scheme (BCDDA), with the following main contributions:

- We designed a Chameleon Hash-based method for constructing audit metadata. The e-commerce server pre-generates audit tags and auxiliary parameters using the public keys of the various domain servers. Subsequently, the domain servers can use their private keys to generate auxiliary parameters that match the local data and tags, thereby reducing the computational overhead on the domain servers and better handling sudden data processing demands.
- We constructed a parallel data auditing architecture based on sharding blockchain. The audit tags adopted by the domain servers are stored on the main chain, which is maintained by all domain servers. The auditing of consumer electronic data within each shard/domain is managed by the consensus nodes within the respective shard chains. This includes the design of the block structure and consensus process for both the main chain and the shard chains. Additionally, the domain server applies a random mask to its local data and generates new auxiliary data, which is then sent to other domain servers for storage. This approach prevents issues that could arise from a single shard's consensus node being compromised.
- Additionally, BCDDA supports dynamic operations such as adding, deleting, and modifying data on the domain servers, allowing consumer electronic data updates without the need to generate new data audit tags. We also validated

BCDDA in an experimental environment with four shard consensus nodes, and the results demonstrate that the generation of audit tags and the shard consensus process in BCDDA are acceptable.

2 Related Work

Utilizing collected consumer electronics data for AI applications to support prediction and automated production has become a very common practice. Depending on the application's objectives, these can generally be categorized into recommendation and prediction [1,8–10,24,33,37], intelligent manufacturing [5,11,12,26,28,30], and system security [6,23,25,34–36]. Research on auditing consumer electronics data is still in its early stages. However, with the emergence and maturation of distributed frameworks like edge computing and blockchain, research on data auditing is increasingly trending towards distributed approaches. Most of these studies focus on multi-replica and cross-server data auditing.

Multi-replica data integrity verification refers to the practice of users backing up their data on multiple cloud servers and performing integrity verification on these backups simultaneously. Li et al. designed an integrity verification method for edge-cached data by constructing a consensus mechanism for collaboration among edge servers [4,14]. This method prevents data corruption or loss in geographically distributed and resource-constrained edge servers. Subsequently, Li et al. proposed a blockchain-based decentralized scheme capable of withstanding Byzantine faults, offering higher accuracy and efficiency in data integrity verification [15]. Li et al. also introduced a lightweight collaborative integrity auditing scheme for cloud data with multiple replicas and multiple cloud service providers, eliminating the need for third-party auditors and tag generation [16]. Shen et al. proposed an integrity verification protocol for outsourced data backups, achieving public verification through user-friendly backup algorithms and non-interactive succinct proofs, thus reducing the cost of generating and uploading replicas on the client side [29].

Cross-server data integrity verification involves dividing user data into multiple parts and storing them across different servers using cross-server encoding to enhance the robustness of the auditing process. Chen et al. proposed a blockchain-based decentralized system that utilizes incentive mechanisms and privacy-enhancing technologies to achieve proofs of data retrievability and replication [3]. Li et al. introduced a blockchain-based synchronously provable data possession scheme for digital twin environments, ensuring the security and reliability of data in the virtual space through time-state verification and data integrity checks [17]. Su et al. proposed a decentralized self-auditing scheme for multi-cloud storage environments, where data integrity verification is achieved through interactions among distributed cloud servers [31].

However, the aforementioned studies do not address the issue of data auditing in multi-domain environments, and they fail to support the computational demands of large-scale concurrent data auditing. Additionally, existing blockchain-based data auditing protocols require the participation of all blockchain nodes in the consensus process, which significantly reduces the overall throughput of the data auditing system. To address these challenges, we designed BCDDA based on a sharding blockchain architecture.

3 Preliminaries

This section begins by presenting the system architecture of BCDDA, followed by an analysis of its potential threats and corresponding security model.

3.1 System Model

Within the BCDDA architecture, three core components are defined: the E-commerce Server, the Domain Server, and the Blockchain Node, as described in the following section.

- *E-commerce Server:* Acting as the legitimate custodian of consumer electronic information, this component conducts analytical and predictive processing to inform future strategic decisions. To maintain data reliability, it periodically inspects the integrity of the records preserved on the Domain Server. It is further presumed to behave in an honest and trustworthy fashion.
- *Domain Servers:* These are the actual storage locations for consumer electronics data. Due to unexpected situations or system failures, they may cause damage to the stored data, requiring them to periodically respond to data audit requests. Additionally, they may be curious about the data stored by other Domain Servers. They are considered to be honest but curious.
- *Blockchain Nodes:* These nodes are responsible for the periodic auditing of data stored on the Domain Servers, reaching consensus on the audit results, and recording them on the shard chain. These nodes may be malicious, but the proportion of malicious nodes does not exceed half. Moreover, they will only engage in malicious behavior if it benefits them. They are considered to be malicious but rational.

Next, the framework of BCDDA is summarized in Definition 1.

Definition 1. *BCDDA contains seven algorithms:*

- ***Setup****: In the system initialization phase, the E-commerce Server first derives and disseminates the required system parameters according to a predefined security parameter. Each participating entity, including the E-commerce Server, Domain Servers, and Blockchain Nodes, then independently establishes its own public and private key pairs and exchanges the public keys for mutual authentication. The processes of blockchain sharding and subsequent management are also completed at this stage.*
- ***InitGen****: Given the audit tag generation requirements of different Domain Servers, the E-commerce Server first generates initial tags and supporting data, and then sends them to the respective Domain Servers.*

- ***TagGen:*** *Given the initial tags and supporting data, the Domain Server first generates the replica and sends to another Domain Server. Then, the Domain Server generates corresponding supporting data based on its stored data and replica to match the initial tags, and then submits them for consensus on the main chain and storage.*
- ***Challenge:*** *With the audit period and the number of challenge data blocks determined, Blockchain Nodes independently generate two random seeds and deliver them to the Domain Servers that belong to the same shard.*
- ***Proof:*** *Based on the received random seeds and the designated number of challenge data blocks, the Domain Server constructs a proof utilizing its locally maintained dataset and subsequently transmits the result to the Blockchain Nodes.*
- ***Consensus:*** *Based on the proof provided by the Domain Server, the Blockchain Nodes perform verification, execute a consensus protocol to ensure collective agreement, and then create a shard block, which is appended to their respective local ledgers.*
- ***DynamicOp:*** *Based on the defined dynamic operation types, such as data insertion, removal, and modification, each Domain Server performs the necessary updates on its local dataset and regenerates the associated metadata, ensuring that the tags maintained on the main chain remain intact.*

3.2 System Threats and Security Model

Intuitively, BCDDA faces the following threats. A Domain Server might lose or tamper with stored data due to system failures. A Domain Server may be curious about the data contents of other Domain Servers. Blockchain Nodes might skip the verification of audit data and falsely report that the data is intact, motivated by the desire to earn rewards. Even if only a small portion of the data on a Domain Server is compromised, it should still be detectable. Based on these threats, we propose the following security model, which is formalized via the following definitions.

The BCDDA framework is exposed to multiple potential adversarial behaviors. Specifically, Domain Servers may suffer data corruption or loss arising from internal faults, or they may attempt to access or infer information belonging to other domains. Likewise, Blockchain Nodes can exhibit selfish behavior by bypassing the verification of audit results and misreporting data integrity to obtain additional rewards. The proposed design ensures that even minor data corruption within any Domain Server remains detectable. On the basis of these identified threats, a corresponding security model is constructed and rigorously defined through the subsequent formal descriptions.

Definition 2 (Correctness): The BCDDA protocol achieves correctness provided that the E-commerce Server, Domain Server, and Blockchain Nodes perform their respective procedures honestly and as specified. Under this condition, the integrity proof generated by the protocol must be verifiable and successfully validated through the Consensus process.

Definition 3 (Privacy): The BCDDA protocol is said to preserve privacy provided that no Domain Server can feasibly recover or derive the original data of any other Domain Server, except with a negligible probability under the defined security assumptions.

Definition 4 (Unforgeability): The BCDDA protocol is said to achieve unforgeability if, under circumstances where a consumer electronics replica is compromised or damaged, the likelihood that a Domain Server can fabricate or reconstruct a fraudulent integrity proof that passes the verification process is negligible within the defined security parameters.

Definition 5 (Recovery): The BCDDA protocol is said to achieve recovery provided that, in the presence of data corruption or loss, the system can restore the original data from its redundant replica residing in an alternative shard within the blockchain network.

Definition 6 (Detectability): The BCDDA protocol is said to achieve detectability provided that, in scenarios where merely a small subset of the data maintained by the Domain Servers becomes corrupted or altered, the Blockchain Nodes can still identify such inconsistencies with a non-negligible probability under the defined security assumptions.

4 BCDDA Construction

To facilitate a comprehensive understanding of the proposed system, this section initially discusses the underlying design rationale of BCDDA and then provides an in-depth exposition of its core architectural and functional features.

4.1 Overview

The overview of BCDDA is depicted in Fig. 1. First, the E-commerce Server generates initial tags and supporting data based on the requirements of the Domain Servers and sends them to the Domain Servers. The initial tags and supporting data are, in fact, Chameleon hashes. The Domain Servers then use their private keys to generate Chameleon hashes that match the local data. Next, the Blockchain Nodes issue challenges to the Domain Servers within the shard and verify the proofs returned by the Domain Servers, reaching consensus based on the results. Finally, the Domain Servers can perform dynamic operations on local data without modifying the tags on the main chain.

4.2 Concrete Protocol

This subsection summarizes the concrete construction of BCDDA.

Setup(λ) → (SK, PK): Let g be the generator of a cyclic group $\mathcal{G}$ of order p, where p is a sufficiently large prime determined by the security parameter λ. The E-commerce Server specifies a pseudo-random number generator $PN(\cdot)$

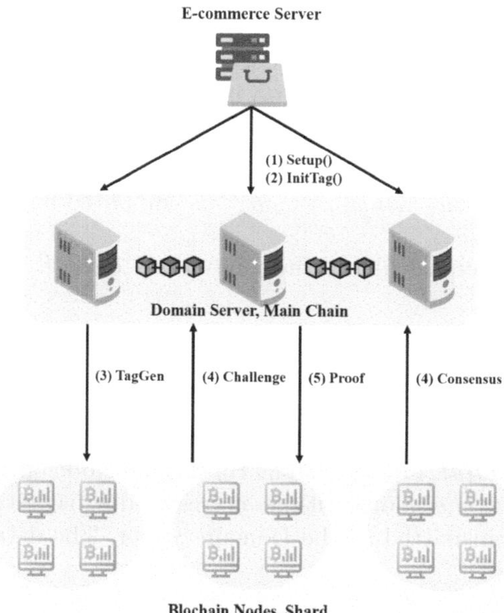

Fig. 1. Overview of BCDDA

together with a hash function $H(\cdot)$. By seeding $PN(\cdot)$ with a random input, a sequence of pseudo-random values $rn_1, rn_2, rn_3, \ldots$ is produced. The server randomly selects a private key $x \in \mathcal{Z}_p^*$ and derives its corresponding public key as $X = g^x$. Likewise, each Domain Server independently chooses a private key y_i and computes the associated public key $Y_i = g^{y_i}$. The collection of secret keys is represented as $SK = x, y$, whereas the public key set is denoted by $PK = \mathcal{G}, g, p, X, Y, PRNG(\cdot), H(\cdot)$.

InitTag(rq) $\boldsymbol{\rightarrow}$ ***(Tag, sd$_1$, sd$_2$):*** When the E-commerce Server receives a Tag generation request rq from the Domain Servers, it selects two random number seeds and generates parameters that match the Tag. The specific execution process for a single Domain Server is as follows:

- The Domain Server generates a tag computation request rq, which includes the number of tags (n) to be computed and the Domain Server's ID (ID).
- The E-commerce Server randomly chooses two seed values, denoted as sd_1 and sd_2, which are utilized to generate the supporting data r_i' and the corresponding random data blocks m_i'.
- The E-commerce Server generates the tag set $Tag = T_1, T_2, \cdots, T_n$, where each tag is computed as $T_i = g^{m_i'} \times Y^{r_i'} \times H(ID||i)$.
- The E-commerce Server transmits the Tag, sd_1, and sd_2 to the Domain Server.

TagGen(Tag, sd₁, sd₂, m) → (m^{rep}, R, R^{rep}): After receiving the Tag, sd_1, sd_2, and m from the E-commerce Server, the Domain Server first generates a backup m^{rep}, which will be stored on other Domain Servers, as well as the initial file and backup's supporting data R and R^{rep} that match the Tag. The specific execution steps are as follows:

- The replica $m^{rep} = m_1^{rep}, m_2^{rep}, \cdots, m_n^{rep}$ is computed by a random seed sd_3. $m_i^{rep} = m_i + PN(sd_3)_i$.
- The Domain Server calculates the supporting data $R = \{r_1, r_2, \cdots, r_n\}$, where $r_i = \frac{m_i' + y \times r' - m_i}{y}$.
- The Domain Server calculates the supporting data $R^{rep} = \{r_1^{rep}, r_2^{rep}, \cdots, r_n^{rep}\}$, where $r_i^{rep} = \frac{m_i' + y \times r' - m_i^{rep}}{y}$.
- The Domain Server sends the m^{rep}, R^{rep} to another Domain Server.

Challenge(·) → (chal, chal^{sig}): The Blockchain Node initiates the challenge process by producing $chal$ along with its corresponding signature $chal^{sig}$, which are subsequently transmitted to the Domain Server. The detailed procedure is described as follows:

- The Blockchain Node first specifies the number of data blocks to be audited, denoted as c.
- It subsequently generates a random value sd^{ind}, which is employed to determine the indices of the data blocks selected for auditing.
- Another random value, sd^{fac}, is then produced to compute the weighting factors corresponding to these selected data blocks.
- The challenge $chal$ is formulated as a tuple c, sd^{ind}, sd^{fac}.
- Finally, the Blockchain Node signs $chal$ to obtain $chal^{sig}$ and transmits both $chal$ and $chal^{sig}$ to the Domain Server.

Proof(chal, chal^{sig}) → (P, P^{sig}): Upon receiving the $chal$, the Domain Server constructs a proof P utilizing the locally stored data and transmits it to the Blockchain Nodes. The detailed procedure is presented as follows:

- The Domain Server first derives the index set $IND = \{PN(sd^{ind})_1, PN(sd^{ind})_2, \cdots, PN(sd^{ind})_c\}$ and the coefficient set $FAC = \{a_1, a_2, \cdots, a_c\}$, where each coefficient is defined as $a_i = PN(sd_i^{fac})$, according to the received $chal$.
- The Domain Server then computes the proof $P = \prod_{i \in IND} g^{a_i \times m_i} \times Y^{a_i \times r_i} = g^{\sum_{i \in IND} a_i \times m_i} \times Y^{\sum_{i \in IND} a_i \times r_i}$.
- Finally, the Domain Server generates the signature P^{sig} and transmits both P and P^{sig} to the Blockchain Node.

Consensus(chal, P, P^{sig}) → (Block^{new}): When all blockchain nodes receive P and P^{sig}, they first verify the P returned by the Domain Server using the Tag on the main chain. After verification, the nodes sign the verification results and send them to the block generation node. The block generation node then creates a block containing the verification results for the current time period and sends it to the other blockchain nodes. Once the other blockchain nodes verify the block, they update their local blockchain.

- According to $chal$, the Blockchain Node computes the IND and FAC.
- According to Tag stored on main chain, the Blockchain Node computes $\sigma = \prod_{i \in IND} Tag_i^{a_i}$.
- Blockchain Node verify $\sigma \stackrel{?}{=} P$. If they are equal, return True; if not, return False.
- The Blockchain Node signs P, $chal$, and σ, then sends them to the current block-producing node.
- The block-producing node verifies the signatures from the other Blockchain Nodes, then packages them into a block and sends it to the other nodes. The block structure is shown in Fig. X.
- The remaining Blockchain Nodes verify the packaged block, and if it is correct, they update their local blockchain.

DynamicOp(op) $\rightarrow$ ***($m_{i-update}, m_{i-update}^{rep}$):*** If the Domain Server needs to perform dynamic operations on the data, it only needs to generate supporting data that matches the new data, allowing dynamic operations to be carried out without modifying the tags on the main chain. The operations for add, delete, and modify are as follows:

- add: $op = \{(ADD, n+1), m_{i-update}\}$, Domain Server has to add a data block to the file. It first generates $m_{i-update}^{rep} = m_{i-update} + PN(sd_{n+1}^{n})$. Then, it calculates $r_i = \frac{m_i' + y \times r' - m_{i-update}}{y}$, $r_i^{rep} = \frac{m_i' + y \times r' - m_{i-update}^{rep}}{y}$, where $i = n+1$.
- delete: $op = \{(DEL, ind), m_{i-update} = \emptyset)\}$, Domain Server has to delete a data block to the file. It first generates $m_{i-update}^{rep} = \emptyset + PN(sd_{n+1}^{n})$. Then, it calculates $r_i = \frac{m_i' + y \times r' - m_{i-update}}{y}$, $r_i^{rep} = \frac{m_i' + y \times r' - m_{i-update}^{rep}}{y}$.eon hash of data block $dA_j^{mp_i}$ is $(b_j^{mp_i}, X_j', r_j^{mp_i})$, where $i = ind$
- modify: $op = \{(MOD, ind), m_{i-update})\}$, Domain Server has to modify a data block to the file. It first generates $m_{i-update}^{rep} = m_{i-update} + PN(sd_{n+1}^{n})$. Then, it calculates $r_i = \frac{m_i' + y \times r' - m_{i-update}}{y}$, $r_i^{rep} = \frac{m_i' + y \times r' - m_{i-update}^{rep}}{y}$, where $i = ind$

5 Security Analysis

The security of BCDDA relies on the underlying security of the chameleon hash function [13] and the pseudo-random number generator [2]. The chameleon hash possesses the property of public collision resistance, implying that an adversary without access to the private key can produce a valid hash collision for a properly generated hash only with a negligible probability δ. Likewise, an adversary lacking the seed of the pseudo-random number generator can correctly reproduce the corresponding random numbers with a negligible probability η.

5.1 Correctness

Theorem 1: *If the E-commerce Server, Domain Server, and Blockchain Nodes execute the BCDDA protocol faithfully, the integrity proof generated by the Domain Server will always be successfully validated by the Blockchain Nodes during verification.*

Proof: The integrity proof corresponding to the challenged data blocks is denoted as σ. The TPO must verify whether the equation $\prod_{i\in IND} H(FN||i)^{a_i}$ $(X^{r'_i}), \sigma \stackrel{?}{=} \delta$ holds. The verification process is illustrated as follows:
$\prod_{i\in IND}(H(FN||i)^{a_i} X^{r'_i a_i})\sigma$
$= \prod_{i\in IND}(H(FN||i)^{a_i} X^{r'_i a_i}) \prod_{i\in IND}(g^{a_i m'_i}))$
$= \prod_{i\in IND}(H(FN||i)^{a_i}) \prod_{i\in IND}(g^{a_i(xr'_i+m'_i)})$
$= \prod_{i\in IND}(H(FN||i)^{a_i}) \prod_{i\in IND}(g^{a_i(r_i x+m_i)})$
$= \prod_{i\in IND}(H(FN||i)^{a_i})(g^{\sum_{i\in IND} a_i(r_i x+m_i)})$
$= \prod_{i\in IND}(Tag_i^{a_i})$
$= \sigma$
Therefore, BCDDA satisfies the property of correctness. ■

5.2 Privacy

Theorem 2: *The probability that a Domain Server can access or reconstruct another Domain Server's original file is negligible.*

Proof: Each Domain Server can only obtain the replicas of data from other Domain Servers, where $m_i^{rep} = m_i + PN(sd_3)_i$. To retrieve the original data m_i, a Domain Server would need to obtain the random number without knowing the random seed sd_3, which would require breaking the security of the pseudo-random number generator. The probability of this occurring is η, which is negligible. ■

5.3 Unforgebility

Theorem 3: *In the event of consumer electronics data corruption, the probability that a Domain Server can forge or reconstruct a valid integrity proof enabling the replica to pass verification is negligible.*

Proof: To produce a valid integrity proof for the replica, the Domain Server must create a new r'_i for the corrupted m_i^{rep} to pass verification by other Domain Servers. However, without access to the private key x, the chance of successfully generating a new r'_i is δ, which is negligible. ■

5.4 Recovery

Theorem 4: *In the event of data corruption on a Domain Server, the system can recover the original consumer electronics data from its corresponding replica with a non-negligible probability.*

Proof: Since $m_i^{rep} = m_i + PN(sd_3)_i$, the Domain Server can recovery the $m_i = m_i^{rep} - PN(sd_3)_i$. The situation where recovery is impossible occurs when the same data block is corrupted in both the original data and the replica. The probability of this happening is $\frac{1}{n}$, which is negligible. ■

5.5 Detectability

Theorem 5: *Even when merely a small fraction of the consumer electronics data maintained by a Domain Server becomes corrupted, the Blockchain Node is capable of identifying this abnormality with a non-negligible probability.*

Proof: Suppose an edge server deletes k data blocks from a file containing n blocks. Let c denote the number of challenged blocks. The probability of detecting the missing data blocks, represented as $P_{detected}$, can be expressed as $P_d = 1 - P_{ud} = 1 - \frac{n-k}{n} \times \frac{n-k-1}{n-1} \times \frac{n-k-2}{n-2} \times \cdots \times \frac{n-k-c+1}{n-c+1}$. Since $\frac{n-i-k}{n-i} > \frac{n-i-1-k}{n-i-1}$, it follows that $1 - \left(\frac{n-k}{n}\right)^c < P_d < 1 - \left(\frac{n-k-c+1}{n-c+1}\right)$. This probability remains non-negligible. Intuitively, when approximately 1% of the data is corrupted, auditing about 4.6% of the total data blocks can yield a detection probability exceeding 99%. ■

6 Performance Analysis

We implemented the BCDDA protocol using Python programming on virtual machines. Six virtual machine nodes were set up, simulating one E-commerce Server, one Domain Server, and four sharded blockchain nodes. The security strength was set to 1024 bits.

As shown in Fig. 2(a), the time required to generate backups is relatively unaffected by changes in block size. This is because the backup involves adding a random mask of the same size as the block. While larger block sizes result in fewer data blocks, the time required to generate the mask for each block increases. This leads to minimal fluctuation in the backup generation time relative to block size for the same file size. Additionally, it is straightforward to understand that the larger the file size, the longer it takes to generate the replica.

As illustrated in Fig. 2(b), the time required to generate the initial tag increases exponentially with block size. This occurs because the process of generating the initial tag is conducted modulo p, resulting in relatively consistent time consumption across different block sizes. Consequently, the total time expenditure is directly linked to the number of data blocks, which increases exponentially, leading to an overall exponential growth in time overhead. Additionally, larger file sizes further contribute to increased time consumption.

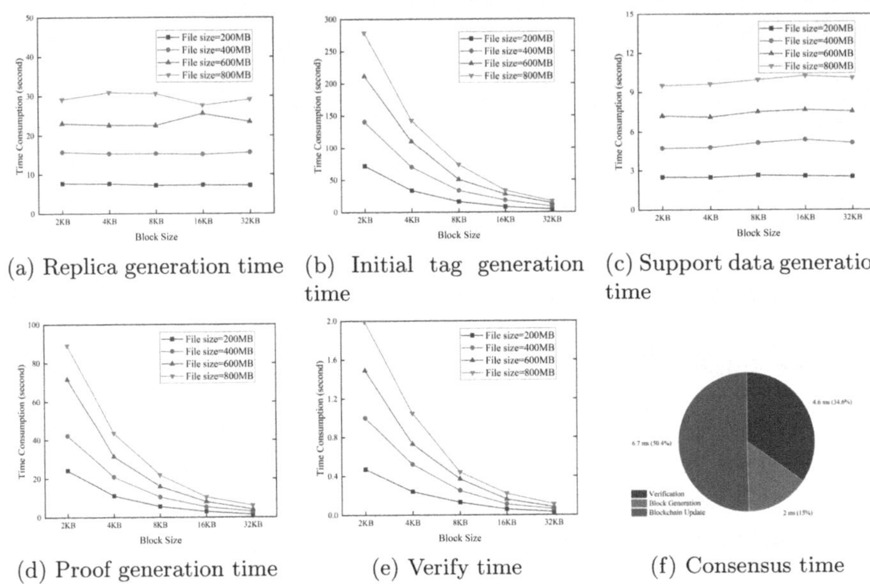

(a) Replica generation time (b) Initial tag generation time (c) Support data generation time

(d) Proof generation time (e) Verify time (f) Consensus time

Fig. 2. Performance analysis of Different Phases

As seen in Fig. 2(c), the time required for the Domain Server to generate support data shows little variation with changes in block size. The reason for this is similar to that in Fig. 2(a): the reduction in the number of data blocks and the increase in the time required to generate support data for each block counterbalance each other, resulting in minimal overall time overhead fluctuation. Clearly, the larger the file size, the greater the time overhead.

As shown in Fig. 2(d) and (e), both the generation of the proof and the verification of the proof exhibit an exponential change in time overhead with respect to block size for the same file size. This is because the sampling ratio is fixed, meaning the number of data blocks that need to be processed is directly proportional to the total number of data blocks. Since the processing of each data block's proof and verification is conducted modulo p, the time overhead is relatively consistent, leading to the exponential trend observed in Fig. 2(d) and (e). Similarly, larger file sizes result in longer processing times.

Figure 2(f) shows that the overall consensus time for the four shard blockchain nodes is 13.3 ms, which is relatively low. Among the three steps, the local blockchain updates between nodes account for half of the time, as this involves communication and coordination between multiple nodes. The remaining time is spent on block generation and signature verification, which take relatively less time. Overall, the time overhead for the consensus process is acceptable.

7 Conclusion

To address the issue of multi-domain data auditing in e-commerce, we proposed a sharding blockchain-based solution. In this approach, a Domain Server is designated in each shard to manage the storage of consumer electronics data within the respective domain. Additionally, local data is backed up on another Domain Server using a random masking technique, ensuring the recoverability of consumer electronics data. The audit data structure is constructed using Chameleon Hash to guarantee the security of the scheme. Finally, experimental results demonstrate that the time overhead for audit metadata generation, the auditing process, and the blockchain consensus process is all within acceptable limits. In future work, we plan to focus on developing consensus protocols that are better suited for data auditing.

References

1. Alzahrani, A., Asghar, M.Z.: Maintaining user security in consumer electronics-based online recommender systems using federated learning. IEEE Trans. Consum. Electron. **70**(1), 2657–2665 (2023)
2. Blum, L., Blum, M., Shub, M.: A simple unpredictable pseudo-random number generator. SIAM J. Comput. **15**(2), 364–383 (1986)
3. Chen, D., Yuan, H., Hu, S., Wang, Q., Wang, C.: Bossa: a decentralized system for proofs of data retrievability and replication. IEEE Trans. Parallel Distrib. Syst. **32**(4), 786–798 (2020)
4. Chen, X., et al.: Android HIV: a study of repackaging malware for evading machine-learning detection. IEEE Trans. Inf. Forensics Secur. **15**, 987–1001 (2019)
5. Deng, Z., et al.: AI agents under threat: a survey of key security challenges and future pathways. ACM Comput. Surv. (2025). https://doi.org/10.1145/3716628
6. Ding, F., Zhu, G., Alazab, M., Li, X., Yu, K.: Deep-learning-empowered digital forensics for edge consumer electronics in 5G HetNets. IEEE Consum. Electron. Maga. **11**(2), 42–50 (2020)
7. Djenouri, Y., Yazidi, A., Srivastava, G., Lin, J.C.W.: Blockchain: applications, challenges, and opportunities in consumer electronics. IEEE Consum. Electron. Maga. **13**(2), 36–41 (2023)
8. Dong, R., et al.: One mutation fits all: exploring universal library fuzzing based on exogenous mutation. IEEE Trans. Dependable Secure Comput. **22**, 6580–6591 (2025)
9. Doulani, K., Rajput, A., Hazra, A., Adhikari, M., Singh, A.K.: Explainable AI for communicable disease prediction and sustainable living: implications for consumer electronics. IEEE Trans. Consum. Electron. **70**(1), 2460–2467 (2023)
10. Feng, X., Zhu, X., Han, Q.L., Zhou, W., Wen, S., Xiang, Y.: Detecting vulnerability on iot device firmware: a survey. IEEE/CAA J. Automatica Sinica **10**(1), 25–41 (2022)
11. Goh, Y., Jung, D., Hwang, G., Chung, J.M.: Consumer electronics product manufacturing time reduction and optimization using AI-based PCB and VLSI circuit designing. IEEE Trans. Consum. Electron. **69**(3), 240–249 (2023)
12. Kim, T., et al.: AI-empowered database management platform for new materials discovery for consumer electronics. In: Proceeding of the 2023 IEEE 20th Consumer Communications & Networking Conference, pp. 929–930. IEEE, Las Vegas (2023)

13. Krawczyk, H., Rabin, T.: Chameleon hashing and signatures. Cryptology ePrint Archive (1998)
14. Li, B., et al.: Cooperative assurance of cache data integrity for mobile edge computing. IEEE Trans. Inf. Forensics Secur. **16**, 4648–4662 (2021)
15. Li, B., He, Q., Yuan, L., Chen, F., Lyu, L., Yang, Y.: Edgewatch: collaborative investigation of data integrity at the edge based on blockchain. In: Proceedings of the 28th ACM SIGKDD Conference on Knowledge Discovery and Data Mining, pp. 3208–3218 (2022)
16. Li, T., Chu, J., Hu, L.: Cia: a collaborative integrity auditing scheme for cloud data with multi-replica on multi-cloud storage providers. IEEE Trans. Parallel Distrib. Syst. **34**(1), 154–162 (2022)
17. Li, T., Wang, H., He, D., Yu, J.: Synchronized provable data possession based on blockchain for digital twin. IEEE Trans. Inf. Forensics Secur. **17**, 472–485 (2022)
18. Li, Y., Shen, J., Ji, S., Lai, Y.H.: Blockchain-based data integrity verification scheme in aiot cloud–edge computing environment. IEEE Trans. Eng. Manag. (2023)
19. Li, Y., Shen, J., Ji, S., Wen, S., Zhu, T., Xiang, Y.: Collusion-resistant multi-replica data auditing with optimized metadata generation. IEEE Trans. Depend. Secure Comput. (2025)
20. Li, Y., Shen, J., Obaidat, M.S., Vijayakumar, P., Selvaradjou, S., Hsiao, K.F.: Chameleon hash based collaborative time-series data integrity monitoring. ACM Trans. Auton. Adapt. Syst. (2025)
21. Li, Y., Shen, J., Vijayakumar, P., Lai, C.F., Sivaraman, A., Sharma, P.K.: Next-generation consumer electronics data auditing scheme towards cloud-edge distributed and resilient machine learning. IEEE Trans. Consum. Electron. **70**(1), 2244–2256 (2024)
22. Li, Y., Zheng, W., Pandi, V., Bhuiyan, M.Z.A., Thamilarasi, C.: Parallel and batch multiple replica auditing protocol for edge computing. In: 2023 IEEE International Conference on Parallel & Distributed Processing with Applications, Big Data & Cloud Computing, Sustainable Computing & Communications, Social Computing & Networking (ISPA/BDCloud/SocialCom/SustainCom), pp. 254–261. IEEE (2023)
23. Lin, Q., Jiang, S., Zhen, Z., Chen, T., Wei, C., Lin, H.: Fed-PEMC: a privacy-enhanced federated deep learning algorithm for consumer electronics in mobile edge computing. IEEE Trans. Consum. Electron. **70**(1), 4073–4086 (2024)
24. Liu, P., Jiang, L., Lin, H., Hu, J., Garg, S., Alrashoud, M.: Federated multimodal learning for privacy-preserving driver break recommendations in consumer electronics. IEEE Trans. Consum. Electron. **70**(1), 4564–4573 (2023)
25. Patole, R., Singh, N., Adhikari, M., Singh, A.K.: Multi-view ensemble federated learning for efficient prediction of consumer electronics applications in fog networks. IEEE Trans. Consum. Electron. **70**(1), 4597–4604 (2023)
26. Prist, M., et al.: Machine learning-as-a-service for consumer electronics fault diagnosis: a comparison between Matlab and Azure ML. In: Proceedings of the 2020 IEEE International Conference on Consumer Electronics, pp. 1–5. IEEE, Las Vegas (2020)
27. Sai, S., Goyal, D., Chamola, V., Sikdar, B.: Consumer electronics technologies for enabling an immersive metaverse experience. IEEE Consum. Electron. Maga. **13**(3), 16–24 (2023)

28. Shafiq, M., Yadav, R., Javed, A.R., Mohsan, S.A.H.: CoopGBFS: a federated learning and game-theoretic-based approach for personalized security, recommendation in 5G beyond IoT environments for consumer electronics. IEEE Trans. Consum. Electron. **70**(1), 2648–2656 (2023)
29. Shen, J., Chen, X., Huang, X., Xiang, Y.: Public proofs of data replication and retrievability with user-friendly replication. IEEE Trans. Dependable Secure Comput. **21**(4), 2057–2067 (2023)
30. Sheng, C., Zhou, W., Ma, W., Zhu, X., Wen, S., Xiang, Y.: Network traffic fingerprinting for iiot device identification: a survey. IEEE Trans. Ind. Inf. (2025). https://doi.org/10.1109/TII.2025.3534441
31. Su, Y., Li, Y., Yang, B., Ding, Y.: Decentralized self-auditing scheme with errors localization for multi-cloud storage. IEEE Trans. Dependable Secure Comput. **19**(4), 2838–2850 (2021)
32. Velikic, G.: Diversity of consumer electronics. IEEE Consum. Electron. Maga. **12**(5), 22–23 (2023)
33. Wu, Y., Tang, S., Zhang, L., Fan, L., Lei, X., Chen, X.: Resilient machine learning-based semantic-aware MEC networks for sustainable next-G consumer electronics. IEEE Trans. Consum. Electron. **70**(1), 2188–2199 (2023)
34. Xie, H., Wang, Y., Ding, Y., Yang, C., Zheng, H., Qin, B.: Verifiable federated learning with privacy-preserving data aggregation for consumer electronics. IEEE Trans. Consum. Electron. **70**(1), 2696–2707 (2023)
35. Zhou, W., et al.: The security of using large language models - a survey with emphasis on chatgpt. IEEE/CAA J. Automatica Sinica **12**(1), 1–26 (2025). https://doi.org/10.1109/JAS.2024.124983
36. Zhu, X., Wen, S., Camtepe, S., Xiang, Y.: Fuzzing: a survey for roadmap. ACM Comput. Surv. **54**(11s), 1–36 (2022). https://doi.org/10.1145/3512345
37. Zhu, X., et al.: When software security meets large language models: a survey. IEEE/CAA J. Automatica Sinica **12**(2), 317–334 (2025)

DFI-GNN: A Dual-Feature Interaction Graph Neural Network Model for Multimodal Medical Image Classification

Meng Yu[1,2], Lijuan Sun[1,3], Yutong Gao[1,4,5](✉), Gaohu Li[1], Jingchen Wu[1], and Xu Wu[1,2]

[1] Key Laboratory of Trustworthy Distributed Computing and Service (BUPT), Ministry of Education, Beijing 100876, China
{yumeng,sunlijuan,lgh,lulu,wux}@bupt.edu.cn

[2] School of Cyberspace Security, Beijing University of Posts and Telecommunications, Beijing 100876, China

[3] National Library of China, Beijing 100876, China

[4] Key Laboratory of Ethnic Language Intelligent Analysis and Security Governance, Ministry of Education, Minzu University of China, Beijing 100876, China

[5] Hainan International College of Minzu University of China, Li'an International Education Innovation pilot Zone, Hainan 572499, China
ytgao92@muc.edu.cn

Abstract. Multimodal classification in medical imaging faces two key challenges in cross-modal feature fusion: significant semantic gaps between modalities often cause loss of critical pathological information during fusion, and existing diagnostic models generally process cases individually without leveraging population-level diagnostic knowledge. To address these issues, we propose the Dual-Feature Interaction Graph Neural Network (DFI-GNN). Our approach integrates feature interaction fusion, collective knowledge mining, and collaborative optimization. Specifically, we first introduce a dual-feature interaction fusion module that preserves original discriminative features through differentiable regularization constraints and residual feature backpropagation. Second, we construct patient association graphs based on multimodal feature similarity to mine population-level diagnostic knowledge via graph attention networks. Finally, a multimodal-graph collaborative learning strategy jointly optimizes multimodal loss, graph relational loss, and fusion regularization loss, enhancing single-modal discriminability, collective knowledge relevance, and cross-modal fusion robustness. Extensive experiments on multiple benchmarks show that DFI-GNN achieves superior performance in multimodal feature learning, offering a more reliable solution for medical image diagnosis.

Keywords: Multimodal Learning · Graph Neural Network · Medical Imaging · Dual-Feature Interactive Graph Neural Network · Cross-Modal Fusion

Y. Xiang and J. Shen (Eds.): ML4CS 2025, LNCS 16456, pp. 16–32, 2026.
https://doi.org/10.1007/978-981-95-7820-7_2

1 Introduction

In modern medical diagnosis, the accurate judgment of diseases often relies on the comprehensive analysis of multi-source heterogeneous sensitive data. Such data not only comes from diverse sources and has heterogeneous formats but also bears strict privacy protection requirements and high sensitivity due to its association with core information such as patients' personal health status and physiological characteristics. For instance, the visual features of lesions provided by medical images (including images of patients' private body parts) and the semantic information (e.g., patients' symptoms and medical history) recorded in electronic medical records (EMRs) and diagnostic texts are all privacy-sensitive data subject to strict legal and ethical constraints. Together, they form the core basis for diagnostic decisions. However, under the premise of ensuring data security and compliant use, multimodal classification in medical imaging still faces two core challenges:

Information Loss in Cross-Modal Fusion. Medical images and clinical texts exhibit fundamental differences across multiple dimensions: in terms of data structure, medical images are represented as pixel matrices conveying continuous visual features, whereas texts consist of discrete vocabulary forming structured descriptions; in terms of semantic expression, medical images rely on spatial correlations of visual features to transmit information, while texts employ combinations of professional terminology to articulate pathological attributes; in terms of information density, medical images contain massive redundant data, whereas texts concentrate on key points through condensed language. These disparities make direct fusion prone to feature distortion, and during the transformation from low-level to high-level representations, the original modal features often fail to be adequately preserved, resulting in the loss of critical information.

Missing Group Associations. The essence of medical diagnosis lies in the accumulation of knowledge and the transmission of experience. Patients with the same type of disease exhibit similar patterns, and the sensitive health information contained in these similar cases is crucial for improving diagnostic accuracy. Current models rely solely on single-case data for inference, rendering them susceptible to individual noise interference and failing to uncover the latent cross-modal associations within the patient population. As a result, it is difficult to extract robust diagnostic features from the commonalities of cases, which limits the generalization performance of the models.

Early studies mostly focused on single-modal feature enhancement or simple feature concatenation, failing to address the representation gap caused by modal heterogeneity. Although existing cross-modal attention mechanisms can establish inter-modal correlations, they still suffer from the loss of critical diagnostic sensitive information and lack the integration of population-level sensitive knowledge. Notably, with the rapid development of graph neural networks in the

M. Yu and L. Sun—Contributed equally to this research.

field of relationship mining, recent studies have begun to explore the construction of case association networks, which provides a new technical path for solving the key problem of collaborative optimization between individual features and population knowledge (Fig. 1).

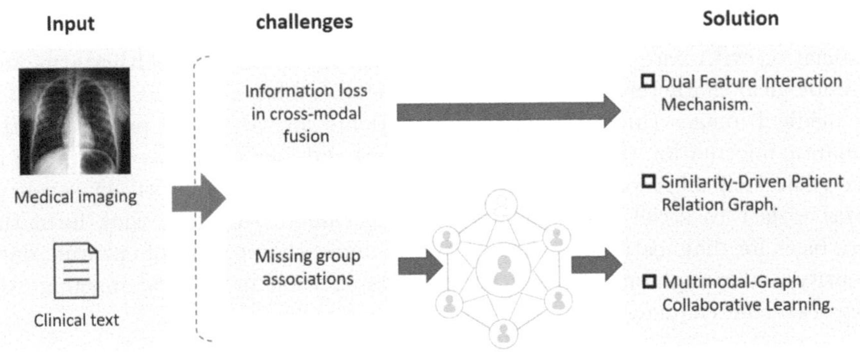

Fig. 1. Problem overview.

To address these challenges, this paper proposes A Dual-Feature Interaction Graph Neural Network Model (DFI-GNN). The model first employs a dual feature interaction fusion mechanism—leveraging regularized fusion to balance the complementarity of multimodal sensitive features while preserving critical raw sensitive information through original feature reinjection, thereby solving the problem of sensitive information loss in cross-modal fusion. Building upon this, we construct a patient relation graph based on feature similarity and utilize graph neural networks to uncover population-level diagnostic patterns, achieving a leap from individual diagnosis to collective knowledge reasoning. Additionally, we innovatively propose a multimodal-graph collaborative learning mechanism by jointly optimizing the multimodal contrastive loss and graph relational loss. We achieve accurate alignment of cross-modal features while enhancing semantic consistency in population-level associations. Our main contributions are as follows:

Dual-Feature Interaction Mechanism. By integrating regularization and raw feature feedback, a balance is established between fully excavating complementary information among heterogeneous modalities and maximizing the retention of the discriminative ability of the original features of each modality. This effectively addresses the critical issue of diagnostic information loss that is prevalent in cross-modal fusion.

Similarity-Driven Patient Relation Graph. We construct a patient association graph based on multimodal feature similarity between patients, transforming scattered individual case data into a structured population knowledge network. This design enables the model to simulate the reasoning logic of referring to similar cases in clinical diagnosis and further uncover implicit population-level diagnostic patterns.

Multimodal-Graph Collaborative Learning. Through the joint optimization of multiple losses including multimodal contrastive loss and graph relational loss, cross-modal feature alignment is achieved while enhancing the ability to mine potential associations between patients. Ultimately, this realizes the coordinated improvement of intra-modal feature discriminability, inter-modal feature consistency, and population knowledge relevance.

2 Related Work

2.1 Multimodal Fusion

Multimodal fusion improves task performance via heterogeneous data integration and cross-modal information mining. In medical applications, fusing CT/MRI visual features and EHR semantic data reveals sensitive pathological correlations, mitigates single-modal bias, and supports clinical decision-making [1,2].

Current multimodal fusion methods are primarily categorised into three types: early fusion, mid-stage fusion, and late fusion [3]. Early fusion directly integrates raw or shallow-level features during the feature extraction stage. Whilst this approach boasts a simple architecture, it exhibits high sensitivity to cross-modal differences and is susceptible to data issues [4]. Mid-stage fusion (feature-level fusion) first independently extracts high-level features from each modality before performing cross-modal integration, exemplified by approaches such as multimodal Transformers and cross-modal attention networks. Li et al.'s longitudinal multimodal Transformer effectively models temporal dependencies and cross-modal relationships in lung nodule classification by integrating sequential imaging features with latent clinical features from electronic health records [5]. Liangli et al. designed a deep supervision-based cross-modal retrieval framework based on mid-stage fusion [6]. Overall, mid-stage fusion supports multi-level feature extraction and integration, effectively capturing complex cross-modal relationships, but incurs higher computational costs.

Late-stage fusion first processes each modality independently to generate preliminary decisions, subsequently aggregating these outcomes through weighted voting or probabilistic fusion methods. Xiang et al. applied this strategy to thyroid ultrasound image diagnosis, enhancing diagnostic accuracy by integrating decision outcomes from fused ultrasound image features and clinical text features [7]. Whilst late-stage fusion preserves modality independence and avoids early feature distortion, it fails to model deep semantic interactions between modalities.

In recent years, multimodal fusion techniques have advanced primarily along two key directions: firstly, balancing performance and efficiency through hybrid model architectures; secondly, achieving deep semantic alignment via cross-modal pre-training.

Regarding hybrid model architectures, research has predominantly focused on integrating the strengths of different fusion stages. For instance, the MATR method employs a multi-scale visual encoder and a shared-parameter Transformer architecture, combined with cross-attention, to learn multi-scale representations of lesion features [8]. CDDFuse proposes a dual-branch Transformer-CNN architecture, establishing a synergistic relationship between shared and unique features through correlation-driven loss: low-frequency features are encoded by the Transformer, while high-frequency details are preserved by an Invertible Neural Network (INN), thereby achieving the fusion objective of 'global integration and detail retention' [9].

In cross-modal pre-training, Zhang et al. drew upon natural language supervision methods such as CLIP [10], introducing contrastive learning techniques to process medical visual representations. They enhanced cross-modal alignment by integrating paired image and text data [11]. The Moon team further developed a visual-linguistic pre-training model, unifying medical image comprehension with text generation to achieve end-to-end fusion of imaging data and diagnostic reports [12]. Wang et al.'s TieNet text-image embedding network demonstrates the value of post-processing semantic fusion by classifying thoracic diseases through integrating chest X-ray features with report text [13].

While these fusion approaches balance strengths across different stages to some extent, they still lack effective mechanisms to mobilise collective-level clinical knowledge—a crucial dimension for simulating real-world diagnostic reasoning processes.

2.2 Graph Neural Networks

Graph neural networks(GNN), by modelling data as nodes and edges, can efficiently capture complex relationships between data points. Consequently, they demonstrate extensive application value in medical research, spanning disease diagnosis, biomarker identification, medical imaging analysis, and other domains. This offers novel technical pathways for addressing complex medical challenges.

In the field of brain disease research, GNN have emerged as vital tools for uncovering functional brain connectivity and identifying disease-associated biomarkers. STGC-GCAM employs GNN to identify key brain regions and functional connectivity markers for Alzheimer's disease from multi-region fMRI data [14]; Zhang et al. utilised inductive GNN and feature importance analysis to pinpoint brain regions associated with autism spectrum disorder (ASD) [15]. Furthermore, the multi-relational MedGraphNet employs information embeddings from existing textual knowledge to initialise nodes, enabling precise inference of associations between drugs, genes, diseases, and phenotypes. This approach has demonstrated significant efficacy in Alzheimer's disease research [16].

In medical image analysis, GNN significantly enhance disease analysis accuracy by structurally modelling image data (e.g., treating lung nodules as nodes and spatial relationships as edges). Specific applications include: the UG-GAT framework achieving precise classification of three-dimensional medical images [17]; Li et al.'s MSA-GCN first constructs a graph based on breast tumour features, then employs graph convolutional techniques to aggregate inter-tumour relational information, ultimately achieving efficient tumour grading [18]; in Alzheimer's disease detection, Tang et al.'s CSAGP method effectively captures latent correlations between multimodal images through graph pooling and a dual transformer architecture [19].

GNN also play a significant role in fundamental biomedical research and clinical decision-making. DeepGraphGO achieves precise prediction of protein functions by constructing protein association graphs [20]; in clinical settings, heterogeneous graphs built from patient records reveal hidden comorbidity patterns [21], while GraphCare enhances capabilities in medical prediction tasks by constructing personalised knowledge graphs [22].

Overall, these graph theory-based GNN methods effectively transform fragmented individual case data into structured knowledge networks, offering novel analytical perspectives for medical research. However, it should be noted that most current GNN approaches remain limited in their focus on unimodal data, failing to fully integrate the complementary strengths of heterogeneous modalities (such as medical imaging, textual data, and electronic health records). This represents a key breakthrough direction for the future advancement of GNN within the medical field.

3 Model

3.1 Model Architecture

The DFI-GNN model primarily accomplishes its cross-modal learning objectives through four interconnected modules: feature extraction, dual-feature interactive fusion, graph neural network construction, and multimodal-graph collaborative learning. The model architecture is as follows (Fig. 2):

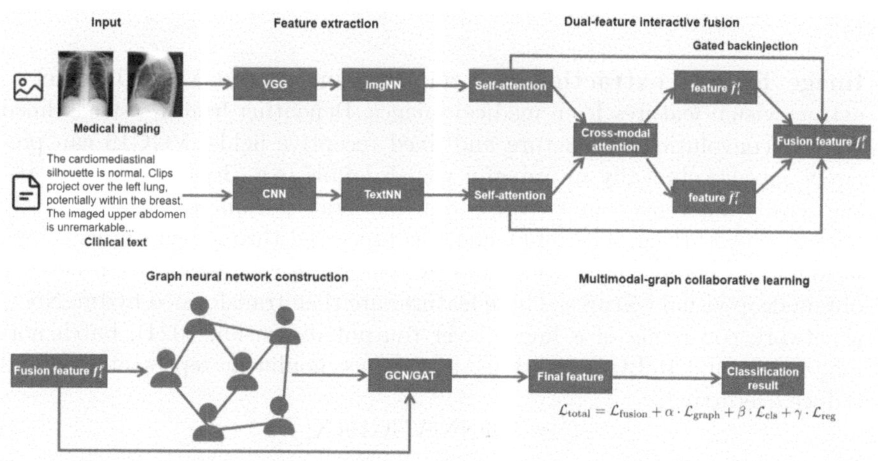

Fig. 2. DFI-GNN Model Architecture

First, within the feature extraction module, the VGG network is employed to extract medical image features while a CNN extracts clinical text features. An independent encoder is utilised (incorporating batch normalisation to stabilise the training process, alongside Dropout to suppress noise interference) to unify the dimensionality of image and text features.

Secondly, the dual-feature interaction fusion module employs self-attention mechanisms to enhance key information expression within each modality, while cross-modal attention facilitates bidirectional interaction between modalities. This module further integrates regularised fusion layers and gated fusion layers: regularised fusion layers balance modal weights to prevent model bias towards any single modality; while the gated fusion layer dynamically adjusts the feedback proportion of fused information to the original features, ultimately yielding a fused representation that effectively combines the complementary strengths of both modalities.

Thirdly, within the GNN construction module, a block-wise optimisation strategy is employed to construct a similarity-based adjacency matrix, circumventing memory overflow issues caused by direct computation of large-scale similarity matrices. This module treats the multimodal features obtained from the interaction fusion module as nodes, feeding them into a graph convolutional network with GCN or GAT as the backbone architecture. This captures sample correlations and outputs graph aggregation features.

Finally, the multimodal-graph collaborative learning module optimizes the entire fusion and collaboration process via a multi-task loss function, effectively boosting the model's task performance.

3.2 Feature Extraction Module

The core objective of the feature extraction module is to extract discriminative basic features from heterogeneous medical data (medical images and clinical texts).

- **Image feature extraction**. We employ a pre-trained VGG19 model to extract visual features from medical images. Benefiting from its streamlined stacked convolutional structure and fixed receptive fields, VGG19 can precisely capture clinically meaningful visual details (e.g., lesion edges and tissue density differences) in X-rays, and its moderate parameter scale effectively alleviates overfitting. The input image is processed through VGG19's convolutional and pooling layers, followed by removal of the classification head to obtain deep visual features. These features are then transformed by ImgNN—a network consisting of a linear layer (output dimension 1024), batch normalization, and ReLU activation—to enhance nonlinear representation and reduce overfitting.

$$\mathbf{f}_i^I = \mathrm{ImgNN}(\mathrm{VGG19}(\mathbf{X}_i^I)) \tag{1}$$

- **Text feature extraction**. Clinical texts are encoded using a pre-trained CNN model, whose lightweight architecture enables efficient capture of core semantic information of diagnostic keywords via local convolution kernels while effectively controlling computing and memory overhead, thus achieving computational balance with the image feature extraction module. The derived semantic features are then projected into a 1024-dimensional space that aligns with image features via TextNN. Mirroring the structure of ImgNN, TextNN integrates a linear layer, batch normalization, and ReLU activation. The process is defined as:

$$\mathbf{f}_i^T = \text{TextNN}(\text{CNN}(\mathbf{X}_i^T)) \tag{2}$$

3.3 Dual-Feature Interactive Fusion

The core objective of the dual-feature interaction fusion module is to achieve effective alignment between modalities while preserving the discriminative power of original features. Its key steps include self-attention enhancement, cross-modal interaction, regularized fusion, and gated feedback.

- **Self-attention enhancement**. Enhancing the discriminative power of unimodal features through self-attention mechanisms. For image features, it captures internal feature dependencies to highlight clinically critical regions; for text features, it focuses on semantic correlations between diagnostic keywords to strengthen core clinical information representation.

$$\begin{gathered}\mathbf{q}_i^T = \mathbf{W}_q^T \cdot \mathbf{f}_i^T, \quad \mathbf{k}_i^T = \mathbf{W}_k^T \cdot \mathbf{f}_i^T, \quad \mathbf{v}_i^T = \mathbf{W}_v^T \cdot \mathbf{f}_i^T \\ \alpha_i^T = \text{Softmax}\left(\frac{\mathbf{q}_i^T \cdot (\mathbf{k}_i^T)^T}{\sqrt{d}}\right) \\ \mathbf{f}_i^T = \alpha_i^T \cdot \mathbf{v}_i^T + \mathbf{f}_i^T\end{gathered} \tag{3}$$

  Here, d denotes feature dimension and the residual connection preserves original features. Image features are enhanced similarly, yielding $\hat{\mathbf{f}}_i^I$.
- **Cross-modal attention**. The interaction of features is achieved through cross-modal attention. Image features focus on the key semantics in the text, while text features focus on the key visual information in the image:

$$\begin{aligned}\hat{\mathbf{f}}_i^I &= \text{CrossAttn}(\hat{\mathbf{f}}_i^I, \hat{\mathbf{f}}_i^T) \\ \hat{\mathbf{f}}_i^T &= \text{CrossAttn}(\hat{\mathbf{f}}_i^T, \hat{\mathbf{f}}_i^I)\end{aligned} \tag{4}$$

  Among them, the q of cross-attention comes from the current modal, while k and v come from another mode, and the calculation method is consistent with that of self-attention.
- **Regularization fusion**. The regularization fusion module achieves feature fusion and modal alignment by attention-weighted fusion of bimodal features.

$$\begin{aligned}\mathbf{a}_i &= \text{Softmax}\left(\text{MLP}\left(\hat{\mathbf{f}}_i^I \oplus \hat{\mathbf{f}}_i^T\right)\right) \\ f_i^F &= a_i^I \cdot \hat{\mathbf{f}}_i^I + a_i^T \cdot \hat{\mathbf{f}}_i^T\end{aligned} \tag{5}$$

  Here, $\mathbf{a}_i = [a_i^I, a_i^T]$ represents the modal attention weights, and $\oplus$ indicates feature concatenation.
- **Gated back injection**. This mechanism dynamically regulates the proportion of feedback from the fused features to the original features, selectively integrating effective information from the fused features while preserving the

discriminative power of the original features. The formula is as follows, and g_i^I, $g_i^T \in [0,1]$ is the gated weight.

$$\begin{aligned} g_i^I &= \text{Sigmoid}\left(\text{MLP}\left(\hat{\mathbf{f}}_i^I \oplus \mathbf{f}_i^F\right)\right), \tilde{\mathbf{f}}_i^I = \hat{\mathbf{f}}_i^I + g_i^I \cdot \mathbf{f}_i^F \\ g_i^T &= \text{Sigmoid}\left(\text{MLP}\left(\hat{\mathbf{f}}_i^T \oplus \mathbf{f}_i^F\right)\right), \tilde{\mathbf{f}}_i^T = \hat{\mathbf{f}}_i^T + g_i^T \cdot \mathbf{f}_i^F \end{aligned} \tag{6}$$

3.4 Graph Neural Networks Construction

Based on the correlation of multimodal features, we construct a patient association network and mine population diagnostic knowledge through GNN. The adjacency matrix is built by fusing cosine similarities between image features $\tilde{\mathbf{f}}_i^I$ and text features $\tilde{\mathbf{f}}_i^T$ across samples. And the k-nearest neighbor strategy is adopted to construct the adjacency matrix A.

$$\begin{aligned} s_{i,j}^I &= \frac{\tilde{\mathbf{f}}_i^I \cdot \tilde{\mathbf{f}}_j^I}{\|\tilde{\mathbf{f}}_i^I\| \cdot \|\tilde{\mathbf{f}}_j^I\|}, \quad s_{i,j}^T = \frac{\tilde{\mathbf{f}}_i^T \cdot \tilde{\mathbf{f}}_j^T}{\|\tilde{\mathbf{f}}_i^T\| \cdot \|\tilde{\mathbf{f}}_j^T\|} \\ s_{i,j} &= \frac{s_{i,j}^I + s_{i,j}^T}{2}, \quad A_{i,j} = \begin{cases} 1 & \text{if } j \in \text{Top-}k(s_{i,:}) \\ 0 & \text{otherwise} \end{cases} \end{aligned} \tag{7}$$

We support two GNN architectures: GCN and GAT. GCN aggregates neighboring node features to propagate group knowledge, using a two-layer convolutional structure. GAT employs an attention mechanism to dynamically compute weights between nodes, emphasizing more relevant neighbors through multi-head attention. Both architectures enhance the representation of multimodal features by incorporating population-level relational information.

3.5 Multimodal-Graph Collaborative Learning

The objective function of DFI-GNN integrates multimodal loss, graph structure loss, classification loss and regularization loss to form multi-objective constraints, and its mathematical expression is:

$$\mathcal{L}_{\text{total}} = \mathcal{L}_{\text{fusion}} + \alpha \cdot \mathcal{L}_{\text{graph}} + \beta \cdot \mathcal{L}_{\text{cls}} + \gamma \cdot \mathcal{L}_{\text{reg}}$$

Among them, α,β andγ are the hyperparameters for balancing each loss term, These hyperparameters are determined through a grid search strategy on the validation set to ensure optimal model performance on the target task. The specific definition of each loss term is given as follows:

- **Multimodal fusion loss.** Multimodal fusion loss achieves deep collaborative learning of cross-modal data through joint optimization from three dimensions: feature representation, distribution alignment, and semantic association. The three aspects respectively conduct multi-level integration at the sample level, distribution level and task level, jointly promoting multimodal representation.

$$\mathcal{L}_{\text{fusion}} = \mathcal{L}_{\text{sim}} + \mathcal{L}_{\text{consis}} + \mathcal{L}_{\text{infoNCE}} \tag{8}$$

- In the feature dimension, the Similarity Loss constrains the matching graphic and text samples to approach each other in the embedding space, enhancing the local discriminability between modalities.

$$\mathcal{L}_{\text{sim}} = E\left[\log(1 + e^{\theta_{i,j}}) - S_{i,j} \cdot \theta_{i,j}\right] \tag{9}$$

where $\theta_{i,j} = \frac{1}{2}\left(\cos(\tilde{\mathbf{f}}_i^I, \tilde{\mathbf{f}}_j^I) + \cos(\tilde{\mathbf{f}}_i^T, \tilde{\mathbf{f}}_j^T)\right)$ denotes the average feature similarity between samples i and j across modalities, $S_{i,j}$ represents label similarity.

- In the distribution dimension, the Modality Consistency Loss achieves global modal alignment by minimizing the difference in the feature distribution between the image and the text:

$$\mathcal{L}_{\text{consis}} = E\left[\left\|\hat{\mathbf{f}}_i^I - \hat{\mathbf{f}}_i^T\right\|_2^2\right] \tag{10}$$

- In the semantic dimension, the InfoNCE loss is based on the contrastive learning mechanism to maximize the mutual information of positive sample pairs, thereby establishing higher-order semantic associations.

$$\mathcal{L}_{\text{infoNCE}} = -E\left[\log \frac{\exp\left(\cos(\mathbf{f}_i^I, \mathbf{f}_i^T)/\tau\right)}{\sum_{j=1}^{N} \exp\left(\cos(\mathbf{f}_i^I, \mathbf{f}_j^T)/\tau\right)}\right] \tag{11}$$

– **Graph structure loss**. Graph structure loss is used to optimize the structural rationality of the patient association network and ensure the effective mining of group knowledge, mainly through the joint constraints of three sub-losses:

$$\mathcal{L}_{\text{graph}} = \text{Tr}\left(\mathbf{H}^T\mathbf{L}\mathbf{H}\right) + \|\deg(A) - k\|_2^2 + \|A\|_1 \tag{12}$$

- $\mathcal{L}_{\text{smooth}} = \text{Tr}\left(\mathbf{H}^T\mathbf{L}\mathbf{H}\right)$ is used to constrain the smoothness of graph features and ensure that the feature representations of adjacent nodes remain consistent;
- $\mathcal{L}_{\text{degree}} = \|\deg(A) - k\|_2^2$ is used to constrain the number of connections of each node (i.e., node degree) to approach the preset value k, thereby controlling the sparse density of the graph;
- $\mathcal{L}_{\text{sparsity}} = \|A\|_1$ is used to constrain the sparsity of the adjacency matrix, reduce redundant connections, and highlight the key associations between nodes.

- **Classification loss**. Classification loss is employed to constrain the predicted results of bimodal features to align with the true labels. For multi-class datasets and multi-label classification datasets, the loss functions are respectively as follows:

$$\begin{aligned}\mathcal{L}_{\text{cls}}^{(1)} &= \text{CE}\left(\text{output}(\hat{\mathbf{f}}_i^I), y_i\right) + \text{CE}\left(\text{output}(\hat{\mathbf{f}}_i^T), y_i\right) \\ \mathcal{L}_{\text{cls}}^{(2)} &= \text{BCEWithLogitsLoss}\left(\text{output}(\hat{\mathbf{f}}_i^I), \mathbf{y}_i\right) + \\ &\quad \text{BCEWithLogitsLoss}\left(\text{output}(\hat{\mathbf{f}}_i^T), \mathbf{y}_i\right)\end{aligned} \tag{13}$$

- **Regularization loss**. Regularization loss is used to balance the weights of the two modes during fusion, avoiding the dominance of the single mode.

$$\mathcal{L}_{\text{reg}} = E\left[(a_i^I - 0.5)^2 + (a_i^T - 0.5)^2\right] \tag{14}$$

4 Experiment

4.1 DataSet

To comprehensively verify the effectiveness and generalization ability of the DFI-GNN model in multimodal medical image classification tasks, this study selected three representative public datasets.

- **MIMIC-CXR** [23]. This dataset contains 377,110 chest X-ray images and corresponding radiology reports from 159,477 ICU patients at Beth Israel Deaconess Medical Center (2011–2016). It includes 14 pathology labels, which were extracted using CheXpert and validated by radiologists. The dataset is split into 70% for train, 15% for validation, and 15% for test.
- **IU-Xray** [24]. This dataset comprises 7,470 chest X-ray images and 3,955 structured reports from outpatient records at Indiana University Hospital. Each patient has an average of 2.2 images and one report. It includes annotations for 2 types of pathologies. The dataset is split into 70% for train, 15% for validation, and 15% for test.
- **Pascal Science** [25]. This dataset is derived from PASCAL VOC 2008 and consists of 1,000 natural images, each annotated with 5 descriptive sentences. It covers 20 object categories. The dataset is split into 80% for train, 10% for validation, and 10% for test (Table 1).

Table 1. Statistical Overview of Datasets

Dataset	Images	Category	Modality
MIMIC-CXR	377,110	14	X-ray + reports
IU-Xray	7,470	2	X-ray + reports
Pascal Science	1,000	20	Natural image + caption

4.2 Comparative Experiment

To validate the effectiveness of this approach, two prevailing state-of-the-art methods were selected for comparison in the experiments, with mean average precision (mAP) serving as the evaluation metric. mAP is a widely adopted indicator in information retrieval for assessing classification and ranking quality, comprehensively evaluating a model's performance across categories in terms of accuracy and recall.

Specifically, the experiment selected MMGL [26] and DSCMR [6] as benchmark models, both of which demonstrate outstanding performance and widespread recognition in multimodal medical data fusion tasks: MMGL excels at capturing graph-based structural correlations between modalities, while DSCMR focuses on cross-modal feature alignment (Table 2).

Table 2. mAP Performance Comparison with Benchmark Models on Medical Datasets

Model	MIMIC-CXR	IU-Xray
MMGL	85.97	88.74
DSCMR	80.34	70.78
DFI-GNN	94.35	95.33

Experimental results demonstrate that our model achieves superior performance to both DSCMR and MMGL on the two medical datasets. On the MIMIC-CXR dataset, which possesses the largest sample size and most abundant pathological labels, DFI-GNN's mAP exceeds that of DSCMR by 14.01% and surpasses MMGL by 8.38%. On the smaller IU-Xray dataset, DFI-GNN also maintained a significant lead, demonstrating robustness to variations in sample size. This advantage stems from its dual-feature interaction mechanism: whilst MMGL constructs static graphs based on predefined relationships and DSCMR relies on fixed cross-modal mappings, DFI-GNN dynamically updates graph structures through multimodal self-attention and cross-attention, thereby capturing fine-grained semantic associations between medical images and text.

4.3 Ablation Experiment

Analysis of Feature Fusion Strategies. In feature fusion tasks, different fusion strategies exert a significant influence on model performance. This experiment compared three feature fusion methods: direct concatenation, regularised fusion (without injecting raw features), and dual-feature interaction (injecting raw features via a gating mechanism), employing mAP as the evaluation metric (Table 3).

The experimental results show that there are differences in the mAP index among the three fusion strategies, and the dual-feature interaction scheme exhibits the best performance. Although the direct concatenation method is

Table 3. mAP Performance Comparison of Different Feature Fusion Strategies

Fusion solution	MIMIC-CXR	IU-Xray	Pascal Science
Direct Concat	92.34	93.75	73.80
Regularized fusion	92.45	94.15	73.98
DFI	94.35	95.33	77.00

straightforward to implement, model performance is constrained by scale discrepancies and redundant information between different features. Regularised fusion mitigates feature scale inconsistencies through L2 regularisation, yielding a modest mAP improvement. However, its reliance solely on transformed features and insufficient retention of original detail information limits its adaptability to challenging samples, resulting in an mAP metric still inferior to the dual-feature interaction approach.

Experimental results conclusively validate the significant value of incorporating original features during feature fusion. As the foundational information carriers of medical sensitive data, original features not only preserve pixel-level native image details and word-level fundamental semantics but also provide critical support for subsequent advanced feature transformations. Reintroducing original features through a gating mechanism not only enriches the information available to the model and reduces information loss during feature transformation but also ensures feature diversity.

Analysis of Graph Neural Network Architecture. To validate the effectiveness of graph structures for collective knowledge learning and compare the performance differences between different GNN architectures, this study systematically evaluated three modeling methods: no graph structure, GCN based on feature similarity, and GAT based on feature similarity. The experimental results are shown in Table 4. The results in Table 4 demonstrate that graph structures can precisely capture the complex associations between samples, effectively addressing the shortcomings of traditional models in relational information mining. Among these graph-based models, GAT further enhances the capability of capturing key relationships through its unique attention mechanism.

Table 4. mAP Performance Comparison of Different GNN Architecture

GNN Architecture	MIMIC-CXR	IU-Xray	Pascal Science
no graph	70.26	72.30	77.00
GCN	91.60	94.43	76.87
GAT	94.35	95.33	76.64

In contrast, on the Pascal Science natural image dataset, the mAP values of all three methods hovered around 76%, with negligible differences. This indicates that when explicit semantic associations between samples are absent, graph structures struggle to provide additional information gain. These comparative results conclusively demonstrate that feature similarity-based graph modelling can effectively capture complex cross-modal associations and latent relationships between medical cases.

It should be specifically noted that the results exhibited a certain degree of fluctuation during repeated experiments. The reason for this mainly lies in the block graph construction strategy of large-scale datasets: to avoid memory overflow caused by the construction of a full data graph, the experiment adopts the method of calculating sample similarity in blocks and generating an adjacency matrix. Due to discrepancies between local and global similarity computations, sample associations at block boundaries may introduce noise, compromising graph structural consistency and ultimately causing unstable model performance fluctuations.

Analysis of Variant Models of the Loss Function. To investigate the impact of different loss functions on the DFI-GNN model for multimodal classification tasks of medical images, we compared the performance of five variant models based on the IU-Xray and MIMIC datasets (Table 5).

Table 5. Comparison of mAP Performance with Different Loss Functions (%).

Variant Models	MIMIC-CXR	IU-Xray
DFI-GNN-fusion	92.84	93.79
DFI-GNN-graph	80.35	77.52
DFI-GNN-cls	84.51	92.61
DFI-GNN-reg	55.30	58.38
DFI-GNN-total	94.35	95.33

Experiments demonstrate that different loss functions exert a significant influence on the performance of the DFI-GNN model. The DFI-GNN fusion model exhibits outstanding multimodal fusion capabilities but lacks structural constraints; DFI-GNN-graph takes graph structure optimization as its primary goal. Therefore, it is highly sensitive to the graph construction quality of different datasets, which in turn leads to fluctuations in the mAP index of the model; DFI-GNN-reg primarily suppresses overfitting through regularisation mechanisms but fails to support model learning for core tasks, resulting in the lowest performance. Although DFI-GNN-cls focuses on classification objectives and performs relatively well under a single loss function, it still has room for improvement in multi-label tasks.

In contrast, the proposed model employing a joint loss function achieves notable improvements across all evaluation metrics, thereby validating the effectiveness of multi-objective collaborative optimization. Specifically, $\mathcal{L}_{\text{fusion}}$ ensures deep semantic-level alignment of multimodal features, providing high-quality input for subsequent graph construction; $\mathcal{L}_{\text{graph}}$ imposes constraints on the structural rationality of dynamic patient association graphs, enhancing the reliability of group knowledge mining; $\mathcal{L}_{\text{cls}}$ directly optimizes the classification objective, ensuring the task-oriented nature of the model; and $\mathcal{L}_{\text{reg}}$ mitigates overfitting through regularization, thereby improving model generalization. These four components achieve a balanced regulation through the joint loss function, preventing performance bias caused by the dominance of any single objective and enabling the model to achieve synergistic gains across the three core stages: feature fusion, graph structure learning, and classification prediction (Fig. 3).

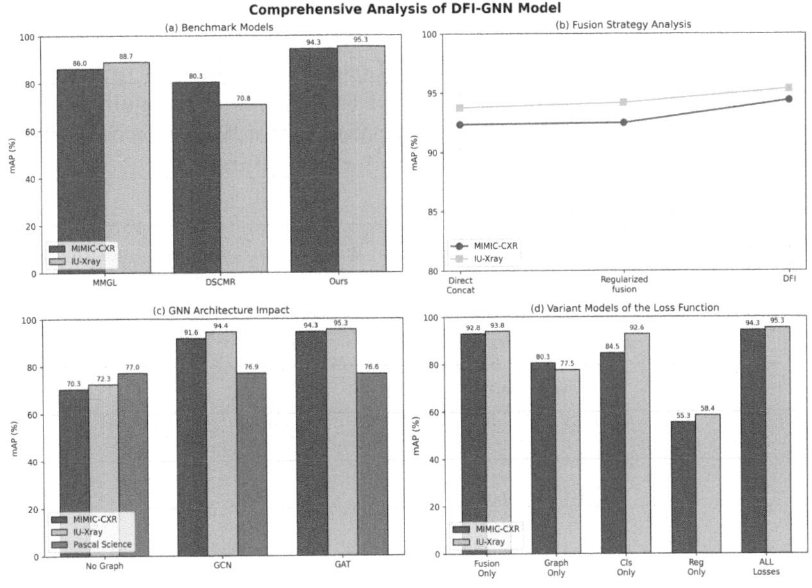

Fig. 3. Comprehensive experimental analysis of the DFI-GNN model. (a) Benchmark comparison; (b) Fusion strategy analysis; (c) GNN architecture impact; (d) Variant Models of the Loss Function.

5 Conclusion

In the fusion of multimodal medical data, there exist problems such as the information loss in cross-modal fusion and missing group associations, which prompts us to propose a multimodal model for medical images based on the dual-feature interaction graph neural network (DFI-GNN). This model can achieve the deep integration of medical images and texts through a bimodal feature interaction mechanism, the construction of dynamic patient association graphs, and a multi-objective contrast loss function, while effectively mining group diagnostic patterns. The experimental results show that DFI-GNN exhibits outstanding performance in medical image multi-label classification tasks, achieving significantly higher mAP across multiple public datasets compared to existing methods. Thus, it provides valuable reference basis for the diagnosis and classification of diseases and contributes to the efficiency and scientificity of clinical decision-making.

Acknowledgments. This work is supported by the Major Projects of National Natural Science Foundation of China (Grant No.72293580/72293583).

References

1. Krones, F., Marikkar, U., Parsons, G., Szmul, A., Mahdi, A.: Review of multimodal machine learning approaches in healthcare. Inf. Fusion **114**, 102690 (2025)
2. Kumar, S., Rani, S., Sharma, S., Min, H.: Multimodality fusion aspects of medical diagnosis: a comprehensive review. Bioengineering **11**(12), 1233 (2024)
3. Teoh, J.R., Dong, J., Zuo, X., Lai, K.W., Hasikin, K., Wu, X.: Advancing healthcare through multimodal data fusion: a comprehensive review of techniques and applications. PeerJ Comput. Sci. **10**, e2298 (2024)
4. Stahlschmidt, S.R., Ulfenborg, B., Synnergren, J.: Multimodal deep learning for biomedical data fusion: a review. Brief. Bioinf. **23**(2), bbab569 (2022)
5. Li, T.Z., et al.: Longitudinal multimodal transformer integrating imaging and latent clinical signatures from routine ehrs for pulmonary nodule classification. In: International Conference on Medical Image Computing and Computer-Assisted Intervention, pp. 649–659. Springer, Heidelberg (2023). https://doi.org/10.1007/978-3-031-43895-0_61
6. Zhen, L., Hu, P., Wang, X., Peng, D.: Deep supervised cross-modal retrieval. In: Proceedings of the IEEE/CVF Conference on Computer Vision and Pattern Recognition, pp. 10394–10403 (2019)
7. Xiang, Z., et al.: Self-supervised multi-modal fusion network for multi-modal thyroid ultrasound image diagnosis. Comput. Biol. Med. **150**, 106164 (2022)
8. Tang, W., He, F., Liu, Y., Duan, Y.: Matr: multimodal medical image fusion via multiscale adaptive transformer. IEEE Trans. Image Process. **31**, 5134–5149 (2022)
9. Zhao, Z., et al.: Cddfuse: correlation-driven dual-branch feature decomposition for multi-modality image fusion. In: Proceedings of the IEEE/CVF Conference on Computer Vision and Pattern Recognition, pp. 5906–5916 (2023)
10. Radford, A., et al.: Learning transferable visual models from natural language supervision. In: International Conference on Machine Learning, pp. 8748–8763. PmLR (2021)
11. Zhang, Y., Jiang, H., Miura, Y., Manning, C.D., Langlotz, C.P.: Contrastive learning of medical visual representations from paired images and text. In: Machine Learning for Healthcare Conference, pp. 2–25. PMLR (2022)
12. Wang, X., Peng, Y., Lu, L., Lu, Z., Summers, R.M.: Tienet: text-image embedding network for common thorax disease classification and reporting in chest x-rays. In: Proceedings of the IEEE Conference on Computer Vision and Pattern Recognition, pp. 9049–9058 (2018)

13. Moon, J.H., Lee, H., Shin, W., Kim, Y.H., Choi, E.: Multi-modal understanding and generation for medical images and text via vision-language pre-training. IEEE J. Biomed. Health Inf. **26**(12), 6070–6080 (2022)
14. Zhang, Y., et al.: A novel spatiotemporal graph convolutional network framework for functional connectivity biomarkers identification of alzheimer's disease. Alzheimer's Res. Therapy **16**(1), 60 (2024)
15. Zhang, J., Guo, J., Lu, D., Cao, Y.: Asd-swnet: a novel shared-weight feature extraction and classification network for autism spectrum disorder diagnosis. Sci. Rep. **14**(1), 13696 (2024)
16. Macaulay, O., et al.: Medgraphnet: leveraging multi-relational graph neural networks and text knowledge for biomedical predictions. In: bioRxiv, pp. 2024–09 (2024)
17. Hao, J., et al.: Uncertainty-guided graph attention network for parapneumonic effusion diagnosis. Med. Image Anal. **75**, 102217 (2022)
18. Li, K., et al.: Msa-gcn: a multi-information selection aggregation graph convolutional network for breast tumor grading. IEEE J. Biomed. Health Inf. **27**(12), 5994–6005 (2023)
19. Tang, C., et al.: Csagp: detecting alzheimer's disease from multimodal images via dual-transformer with cross-attention and graph pooling. J. King Saud Univ.-Comput. Inf. Sci. **35**(7), 101618 (2023)
20. You, R., Yao, S., Mamitsuka, H., Zhu, S.: Deepgraphgo: graph neural network for large-scale, multispecies protein function prediction. Bioinformatics **37**(Supplement_1), i262–i271 (2021)
21. Liu, F.: The application of artificial intelligence to chest medical image analysis. Intell. Med. **1**(3), 104–117 (2021)
22. Jiang, P., Xiao, C., Cross, A., Sun, J.: Graphcare: enhancing healthcare predictions with personalized knowledge graphs. arXiv preprint arXiv:2305.12788 (2023)
23. Johnson, A.E., et al.: Mimic-cxr-jpg, a large publicly available database of labeled chest radiographs. arXiv preprint arXiv:1901.07042 (2019)
24. Demner-Fushman, D., et al.: Preparing a collection of radiology examinations for distribution and retrieval. J. Am. Med. Inf. Assoc. **23**(2), 304–310 (2015)
25. Zisserman, A.: The pascal visual object classes challenge 2008 (voc2008) results. In: VOC/voc2008/Workshop/Index. html (2008)
26. Zheng, S., et al.: Multi-modal graph learning for disease prediction. IEEE Trans. Med. Imaging **41**(9), 2207–2216 (2022)

A Fast-Verifiable Threshold BLS Signature Scheme

Suliu Yang[1,2,3], Tianqi Zhou[1,2,3](✉), Meijia Guo[1,2,3], and Yuluo Zeng[1,2,3]

[1] School of Information Science and Engineering (School of Science and Technology), Zhejiang Sci-Tech University, Hangzhou 310018, China
tq_zhou@126.com

[2] Zhejiang Provincial Key Laboratory of Digital Fashion and Data Governance, Zhejiang Sci-Tech University, Hangzhou 310018, Zhejiang, China

[3] Zhejiang Provincial Innovation Center of Advanced Textile Technology, Shaoxing 312000, Zhejiang, China

Abstract. BLS signature scheme is widely employed in blockchain systems due to its compact signature size and non-interactive aggregation capability. However, the standard BLS threshold signature faces critical bottlenecks. First, the verification process needs computationally expensive bilinear pairing operations. Second, the distributed key generation requires multiple communication rounds. This work introduces a novel fast-verifiable threshold BLS signature scheme. We design a non-interactive key generation protocol that integrates program obfuscation with pseudorandom functions. It enables participants to deterministically derive threshold keys for dynamic groups through a single registration, which eliminates interactive rounds. Second, we develop an efficient verification algorithm by embedding Chaum-Pedersen proofs, which bypasses the conventional bilinear pairing verification. It can shifts computational overhead to more efficient elliptic curve operations. Third, we provide formal security proofs in the random oracle model under standard cryptographic assumptions, including the co-CDH hardness assumption. It demonstrates existential unforgeability against chosen message attacks.

Experimental results demonstrate that our scheme achieves over 50% faster verification compared to standard threshold BLS while preserving all essential features including signature aggregation and threshold security. The performance advantage becomes particularly pronounced in large-scale committee scenarios. The moderate overhead introduced during key generation and signing phases ensures superior overall performance in verification-intensive applications such as blockchain systems.

Keywords: Threshold signature · Distributed key generation · BLS signature · Fast verification

1 Introduction

With the rapid development of blockchain technology and distributed systems, traditional centralized trust models are facing unprecedented challenges.

Y. Xiang and J. Shen (Eds.): ML4CS 2025, LNCS 16456, pp. 33–51, 2026.
https://doi.org/10.1007/978-981-95-7820-7_3

Distributed systems require secure key management and signature operations in the absence of trusted third parties. This makes threshold cryptography a research hotspot in the cryptographic field in recent years. As an important branch of threshold cryptography, threshold signatures can distribute signing power among multiple participants, which can effectively prevent single points of failure and key leakage risks. They have broad application prospects in areas such as digital currency wallets, blockchain consensus mechanisms, and distributed identity authentication.

The BLS (Boneh-Lynn-Shacham) signature scheme was proposed by Boneh et al. in 2001 [1]. Using bilinear mappings, the construction naturally achieves short signature length and native aggregation capabilities. Compared to traditional ECDSA signatures, BLS signatures reduce the signature length by approximately 50%. And it can aggregates multiple signatures into a single signature through simple group operations. These characteristics make BLS signatures particularly suitable for resource-constrained distributed environments. However, the original BLS signature scheme is a single-point signature and cannot directly meet the security requirements of distributed environments, which has prompted researchers to explore threshold variants of BLS signatures [2].

Early threshold signature schemes primarily relied on trusted third parties for key generation and distribution. For instance, the distributed key generation protocol proposed by Pedersen in 1991 [3] assumed that all participants were honest. This strong trust assumption is often difficult to satisfy in practical applications, as deploying a trusted third party itself introduces a single point of failure risk. With the continuous expansion of distributed system scales, eliminating the trusted third party has become a key challenge for the practical application of threshold signatures.

Driven by blockchain applications, research on threshold BLS signatures has made significant progress.The scheme by Gennaro et al. [4] is a foundational work in non-interactive threshold signatures. They were the first to systematically construct a practical non-interactive threshold BLS signature scheme. The primary advantage of this scheme lies in its milestone contribution âĂŞ it explicitly established an implementation framework for "non-interactivity," enabling participants' local signature fragments to be aggregated into a complete signature without multiple communication rounds, significantly enhancing the practicality of threshold signatures. However, its notable drawback lies in performance bottlenecks: the verification phase still requires two expensive bilinear pairing operations, and its security relies on non-standard and computationally complex "knowledge assumptions," posing challenges to its practical deployment efficiency and theoretical simplicity.Addressing the verification efficiency bottleneck of the aforementioned scheme, Kuchta et al. [5] proposed significant optimizations. Their core advantage is the innovative aggregation technique that reduces the number of bilinear pairing operations required for signature verification from being dependent on the threshold parameter to a constant level (only 2 pairings), removing a key performance barrier for large-scale, resource-constrained IoT applications. However, this optimization introduces new drawbacks: in pursuit of maximum efficiency, their security model fails to adequately protect against public key manipulation attacks by malicious participants, and its security relies on another non-standard q-MSDH assumption, raising concerns about its robustness under open adversary models.During approximately the same period, the work by Boneh and Drijvers et al. [6] advanced the field from another dimension âĂŞ security foundations and functional extensions. The foremost advantage of this scheme is its proven security under standard cryptographic assumptions, with explicit design to resist the aforementioned public key manipulation attacks, thereby providing stronger security guarantees. Additionally, a breakthrough functional advantage is the introduction of a "proxy re-secret" mechanism, enabling the signing committee to dynamically and securely rotate signing authority without executing a completely new distributed key generation process âĂŞ a feature crucial for dynamic systems like blockchain. Naturally, the drawback of this scheme is the cost paid for achieving strong security and dynamic functionality: relatively complex design, increased implementation difficulty, and elevated state management overhead. In the exploration of optimizing BLS signature verification efficiency, researchers have proposed solutions at multiple levels. In fact, As early as the batch verification work [7], researchers proposed methods to simultaneously verify multiple signatures using random linear combinations, thereby amortizing the pairing cost per verification at the system level.To completely overcome the bottleneck of pairing operations, researchers have explored construction methods based on different mathematical hard problems. In 2023, Zhang et al. [8] proposed a pairing-free lightweight certificateless aggregate signature scheme for Vehicular Ad-Hoc Networks (VANETs). The notable advantage of this scheme lies in its extremely lightweight nature: it entirely eliminates computationally expensive bilinear pairing operations, relying only on more efficient elliptic curve scalar multiplications, thereby achieving orders of magnitude improvement in signature generation and verification speed, making it highly suitable for latency-sensitive VANET environments. Simultaneously, its certificateless property avoids the certificate management overhead of traditional Public Key Infrastructure (PKI) and the key escrow issues of Identity-Based Cryptography (IBC). However, this optimization comes with corresponding drawbacks: by abandoning pairing operations, the scheme cannot achieve the natural and concise aggregation mechanism inherent to BLS signatures; the computational complexity of its aggregation process and the size of the final aggregate signature are generally inferior to ideal BLS aggregation, and its overall efficiency advantage may diminish in large-scale aggregation scenarios. On the other hand, the efficiency of Distributed Key Generation (DKG) protocols has consistently been a critical bottleneck hindering the large-scale adoption of threshold signatures. Gennaro et al. [9] introduced a landmark work. The core advantage of their scheme is that it was the first DKG protocol provably secure under standard cryptographic assumptions, capable of rigorously resisting active adversaries, thereby elevating the security standard of DKG to a new level. However, achieving this stronger security came at the cost of increased complexity, including more communication rounds and greater bandwidth overhead.

This made its practical deployment efficiency fall short of theoretical expectations, rendering it difficult to apply in latency-sensitive or resource-constrained environments. Facing the challenge of inefficient secure schemes, the research community began exploring performance optimization without sacrificing core security, with "static initialization" emerging as a key direction. The work by Kate and Goldberg [10] was a significant step in making DKG practical in this context. Their key contribution lies in systematically discussing the challenges of deploying DKG in real-world internet environments and explicitly proposing the concept of using long-term keys. This enabled "static initialization," where a single DKG execution supports long-term, multiple signing sessions, drastically reducing the operational costs associated with frequent initializations. However, a drawback of this scheme and many subsequent static initialization techniques is that, in pursuit of efficiency, some compromises in the security model are sometimes necessary. Furthermore, when dealing with extremely large-scale, highly dynamic networks, their communication complexity remains an unresolved challenge.

The main technical challenges currently faced by threshold BLS signatures include: First, how to reduce the number of bilinear pairing operations in the verification process while ensuring security; Second, how to design efficient DKG protocols to support large-scale participant scenarios; Finally, how to achieve secure system initialization without introducing strong trust assumptions. Solving these problems is of great significance for promoting the application of threshold signatures in practical distributed systems.

Addressing the technical challenges outlined in the research background above, the main contributions of this paper include:

- **Static DKG Initialization Mechanism:** Designed a DKG protocol that is executed once and used multiple times. By combining an improved Pedersen DKG protocol with a proof-of-ownership mechanism, it significantly reduces system operational overhead while ensuring security. Compared to traditional DKG protocols, our scheme reduces the communication complexity in the initialization phase, making it particularly suitable for deployment in large-scale distributed systems.
- **Protocol of Fast Verification :** Based on the randomized verification idea of the CPABLS scheme [7], we extended it to the threshold signature scenario and proposed a fast verification algorithm specifically designed for threshold BLS signatures. Through equation transformation, this algorithm reduces the number of required bilinear pairing operations for threshold signature verification from 2 to 1, while maintaining security equivalent to standard verification.
- **Complete System Architecture:** Provided a complete protocol design encompassing system initialization, distributed key generation, threshold signing, and fast verification. The scheme includes rigorous security proofs and detailed efficiency analysis, ensuring the unity of theoretical soundness and practical feasibility. We specifically designed a signature share verifica-

tion mechanism based on DLEQ (Discrete Logarithm Equality) to effectively prevent malicious participants from submitting invalid signature shares.
- **Practical Optimizations:** Proposed multiple optimization techniques tailored for practical deployment needs, including precomputation of Lagrange coefficients, caching mechanisms for aggregate public keys, and batch verification of signature shares. Experiments show that these optimization techniques can further enhance system performance, enabling the scheme to maintain efficient operation even in resource-constrained environments.

The scheme proposed in this paper significantly improves system performance while maintaining the security properties of threshold signatures, providing a more practical security solution for application scenarios such as blockchain consensus, distributed asset management, and secure multi-party computation.

2 Related Works

2.1 Threshold Signatures and Distributed Key Generation

Threshold signatures enhance system security and robustness by distributing signing power among multiple participants. Traditional threshold signature schemes rely on complex interactive distributed key generation protocols. Such protocols not only require multiple communication rounds, introducing significant latency and overhead, but are also prone to failure due to participant dropout, posing challenges in practical deployment.

To simplify key management, the academic community has explored non-interactive key derivation methods. Recent advances in cryptographic primitives such as program obfuscation and constrained pseudorandom functions have opened new possibilities for this direction [11,12]. These techniques enable keys to be derived non-interactively using only a set of public parameters and identity markers. Our scheme innovatively combines obfuscated programs, constrained PRFs, and pseudorandom generators to construct a static non-interactive distributed key generation mechanism [13,14]. This approach completely eliminates interaction rounds: participants only need to register during system initialization, after which any group can generate threshold keys through local computation. This offers significant practical advantages for large-scale distributed systems.

2.2 Verifiable Aggregate Signature Schemes

Signature aggregation is a key technology for improving system scalability. Within the BLS framework, most aggregation schemes still cannot avoid the time-consuming pairing operations during verification. Some research efforts have attempted to improve efficiency through batch verification, i.e., verifying multiple signatures simultaneously, but the performance gains are limited and the applicable scenarios are restricted.

In the domain of verification optimization, discrete logarithm equality proofs, such as the Chaum-Pedersen proof [15], have been employed to construct verifiable signature shares, ensuring the correctness of each share during the aggregation process. This approach has been applied in Schnorr multi-signature schemes like that of Maxwell et al. [16].

However, our scheme advances a step further by elevating this proof mechanism from mere "correctness verification" to the "core of the verification process." We design a sophisticated randomized verification equation that enables the verifier to confirm signature validity by verifying a zero-knowledge proof embedded within the signature [17], without directly computing the traditional pairing-based verification equation. This design removes the most computationally expensive operations from the verification process, serving as the key to achieving the "fast verification" objective.

3 Preliminaries

3.1 Bilinear Groups

Our scheme is constructed over Type III asymmetric bilinear groups, formally defined as follows.

Let $\mathbb{G}_1$, $\mathbb{G}_2$, and $\mathbb{G}_T$ be three multiplicative cyclic groups of large prime order p. Let g_1 be a generator of $\mathbb{G}_1$, and g_2 be a generator of $\mathbb{G}_2$. A non-degenerate bilinear map defined over $\mathbb{G}_1$ and $\mathbb{G}_2$ is denoted as $e : \mathbb{G}_1 \times \mathbb{G}_2 \rightarrow \mathbb{G}_T$.

This bilinear map satisfies the following three fundamental properties:

Bilinearity: For any elements $A \in \mathbb{G}_1$, $B \in \mathbb{G}_2$, and any scalars $y, z \in \mathbb{Z}_p^*$, it holds that:

$$e(A^y, B^z) = e(A, B)^{yz}$$

Non-degeneracy: The map e does not send all input pairs to the identity element. Specifically:

$$e(g_1, g_2) \neq 1_{\mathbb{G}_T}$$

where $1_{\mathbb{G}_T}$ is the identity element of the target group $\mathbb{G}_T$. This ensures that $e(g_1, g_2)$ is a generator of $\mathbb{G}_T$.

Computability: For any given pair of elements $(A, B) \in \mathbb{G}_1 \times \mathbb{G}_2$, there exists an efficient polynomial-time algorithm to compute the result of the bilinear map $e(A, B)$.

3.2 Pseudorandom Generator, (PRG)

A deterministic function $\mathsf{PRG} : \{0,1\}^\lambda \rightarrow \{0,1\}^{2\lambda}$ is a secure pseudorandom generator if for any PPT distinguisher $\mathcal{D}$, its advantage in distinguishing the following two distributions is negligible:

- $\{y : s \xleftarrow{\$} \{0,1\}^\lambda, y \leftarrow \mathsf{PRG}(s)\}$

- $\{y : y \xleftarrow{\$} \{0,1\}^{2\lambda}\}$

  The advantage of $\mathcal{D}$ is defined as:

$$\mathsf{Adv}_{\mathcal{D}}^{\mathsf{PRG}}(\lambda) = \left| \Pr[\mathcal{D}(y) = 1 \mid y \leftarrow \mathsf{PRG}(s)] - \Pr[\mathcal{D}(y) = 1 \mid y \xleftarrow{\$} \{0,1\}^{2\lambda}] \right| \leq \mathsf{negl}(\lambda)$$

where the probabilities are taken over the random choices of s and y, and the random coins of $\mathcal{D}$.

3.3 Pseudorandom Function, (PRF)

A function family $F : \mathcal{K} \times \mathcal{W} \rightarrow \mathcal{Y}$ is a secure pseudorandom function if no probabilistic polynomial-time (PPT) adversary $\mathcal{A}$ can achieve more than a negligible advantage in the following security experiment:

1. The challenger pics a random bit $a \xleftarrow{\$} \{0,1\}$ and $P \xleftarrow{\$} \mathcal{K}$.
2. The adversary $\mathcal{A}$ may adaptively submit queries $w \in \mathcal{W}$ to the challenger.
3. If $a = 0$, the challenger returns $F(P, w)$.
4. If $a = 1$, the challenger returns $\mathcal{R}(w)$.
5. $\mathcal{A}$ outputs a bit a'.

The adversary's advantage is defined as:

$$\mathbf{Adv}_{\mathcal{A}}^{\mathrm{PRF}}(\lambda) = \left| \Pr[a' = a] - \frac{1}{2} \right|.$$

Constrained Pseudorandom Function, (CPRF): A constrained PRF is an enhanced variant of a PRF that allows the master key holder to derive a "constrained key" which can compute the PRF output on some constrained set S, while the PRF values remain pseudorandom for inputs outside S. The proposed scheme conceptually leverages the determinism of PRF to ensure that the same set of inputs always produces the same output.

3.4 Indistinguishability Obfuscator, (iO)

A uniform PPT algorithm iO is called an indistinguishability obfuscator if it satisfies the following conditions:

- **Functional Preservation:** For every circuit C and every input x,

$$\Pr[iO(C)(x) = C(x)] = 1.$$

- **Indistinguishability:** For any two circuits C_0 and C_1 of the same size and functionality, the following two distributions are computationally indistinguishable:
  - $\{iO(C_0)\}$

- $\{iO(C_1)\}$

That is, for any PPT distinguisher $\mathcal{D}$,

$$|\Pr[\mathcal{D}(iO(C_0)) = 1] - \Pr[\mathcal{D}(iO(C_1)) = 1]| \leq \mathsf{negl}(\lambda).$$

In this work, iO is used to obfuscate the program PKE that contains a fixed PRF key. Even though the program is made public, the internal PRF key remains hidden, while allowing any user to execute the program and obtain the PRF output by providing the correct credentials.

3.5 Zero-Knowledge Proofs

The proposed scheme employs the Chaum-Pedersen discrete logarithm equality proof protocol.

Definition 1 (Discrete Logarithm Equality Proof (DLEQ)). *A DLEQ protocol enables a prover to convince a verifier that for public group elements $(g, h, u, v) \in \mathbb{G}^2$ (where $\mathbb{G}$ is a cyclic group of order p), the relation $\log_g(u) = \log_h(v)$ holds, without revealing the discrete logarithm value s.*

The standard non-interactive Chaum-Pedersen protocol is as follows:

Proof Generation. $\mathsf{Prove}_{\mathsf{DLEQ}}(g, h, u, v, s)$:

1. Select a random $k \xleftarrow{\$} \mathbb{Z}_p$.
2. Compute $R_1 = g^k$, $R_2 = h^k$.
3. Compute the challenge $c = H_{\mathsf{dleq}}(g, h, u, v, R_1, R_2)$, where H_{dleq} is a random oracle.
4. Compute the response $s_k = k - c \cdot s \mod p$.
5. Output the proof $\pi = (c, s_k)$.

Verification. $\mathsf{Verify}_{\mathsf{DLEQ}}(g, h, u, v, \pi)$:

1. Compute $R_1' = g^{s_k} \cdot u^c$, $R_2' = h^{s_k} \cdot v^c$.
2. Verify $c \stackrel{?}{=} H_{\mathsf{dleq}}(g, h, u, v, R_1', R_2')$.
3. If equal, output 1 (accept); otherwise output 0 (reject).

This protocol satisfies completeness, special soundness, and zero-knowledge. In this work, the protocol is used to generate correctness proofs for signature shares, specifically to prove that $\log_{g_1}(\mathsf{pk}_{i,1}) = \log_{H_{\mathsf{msg}}(m)}(\sigma_i)$.

4 System Model and Design Goal

This system model establishes a decentralized validator committee to deliver efficient and secure authentication for critical data requiring blockchain recording. At its core, the model employs threshold signature schemes to enable distributed consensus formation and collective signature generation by the committee. This approach produces cryptographically undeniable validity proofs that support efficient verification while being permanently anchored on the blockchain.

4.1 System Model

This paper proposes a blockchain data verification system based on threshold signatures, which achieves trusted authentication of off-chain data through a decentralized committee. The system model comprises the following core components:

Data: Raw information that requires on-chain recording and authentication. This can encompass any information needing trusted verification, such as STATE roots for cross-chain transactions, market data provided by decentralized oracles, or computational result commitments.

Committee: A decentralized network comprising a fixed number of pre-selected, trusted nodes. The committee collectively maintains an aggregate public key for a threshold signature scheme, which serves as its unique public identifier and is registered on the blockchain.

Participating Members: For a specific data authentication request, at least t (meeting a predefined threshold) members from the committee must participate. Each participating member uses their private key share to generate a partial signature for the data, thereby endorsing its validity.

Signature Aggregation: After collecting at least t valid partial signatures, they are combined into a single compact aggregate signature using a specific aggregation algorithm. This signature, comparable in size to an individual signature, serves as proof of collective authorization by the entire committee.

Smart Contract: Automated verification and execution logic deployed on the blockchain. It stores the committee's aggregate public key and exposes a verification function. Any combination of data and aggregate signature must be submitted to this contract for validation.

Blockchain: Functions as the ultimate trust anchor and state machine. Once the smart contract successfully verifies the data and signature, the data is confirmed and recorded on the immutable ledger.

Transaction Rollback: If the smart contract fails to verify the data signature, a transaction rollback mechanism is triggered. The entire transaction (including data submission) is reverted, no state changes occur, and gas fees are consumed to deter spam attacks (Fig. 1).

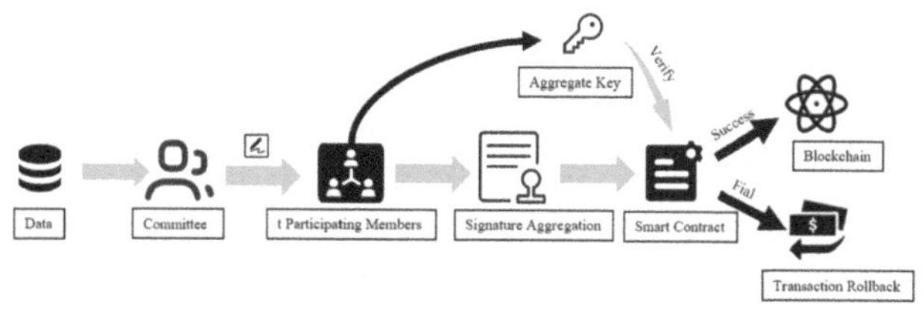

Fig. 1. The system model.

Algorithm 1. Construction of the program PKE

Require: : $\hat{x}_1, \ldots, \hat{x}_G \in \{0,1\}^{2\lambda}$, $i \in [G]$, $s \in \{0,1\}^\lambda$
Ensure: : Output or $\perp$
1: **Constants:** PRF, PRG
2: **if** $\hat{x}_i \neq \mathsf{PRG}(s)$ **then**
3: **return** $\perp$
4: **else**
5: **return** $\mathsf{PRF}(\hat{x}_1, \ldots, \hat{x}_G)$
6: **end if**

4.2 Design Goals

Based on the aforementioned system model and security requirements, our scheme aims to achieve the following design objectives:

Decentralization: To achieve a fully decentralized threshold signature mechanism that operates without relying on any trusted third party or centralized service provider. By employing non-interactive key generation and distributed signature verification, we eliminate single points of failure and enhance system robustness and censorship resistance.

Efficient Aggregation: To fully leverage the inherent homomorphic properties of BLS signatures, supporting efficient aggregation of both signatures and public keys. This not only significantly reduces storage and transmission overhead but also substantially improves system scalability, making it suitable for high-throughput blockchain environments.

Fast Verification: : To optimize the verification algorithm by shifting core computations to the more efficient $\mathbb{G}_1$ group and employing randomized verification equations. This approach maintains security while achieving faster verification speeds compared to standard BLS verification, a crucial feature for applications requiring frequent signature verification.

5 The Proposed Scheme

1. Setup$(1^\lambda) \to pp$: Create three cyclic groups $\mathbb{G}_1$, $\mathbb{G}_2$, and $\mathbb{G}_T$ of prime order p. Select generators $g_1 \in \mathbb{G}_1$ and $g_2 \in \mathbb{G}_2$, and define an efficiently computable bilinear map $e : \mathbb{G}_1 \times \mathbb{G}_2 \to \mathbb{G}_T$. The scheme employs the following cryptographic hash functions: H_{msg}:Hash-to-curve function, $H_{\mathsf{msg}} : \{0,1\}^* \to \mathbb{G}_1$, used for mapping arbitrary messages to group elements.
H_{pop}: Proof-of-possession hash function, $H_{\mathsf{pop}} : \{0,1\}^* \to \mathbb{G}_1$, employed for demonstrating ownership of private keys. H_{dleq}: DLEQ proof hash function, $H_{\mathsf{dleq}} : \{0,1\}^* \to \mathbb{Z}_p$, utilized in Chaum-Pedersen discrete logarithm equality proofs. Select a random key for the constrained PRF: $K \xleftarrow{\$} \{0,1\}^\lambda$.

Select a pseudorandom generator: $\mathsf{PRG} : \{0,1\}^{\lambda} \rightarrow \{0,1\}^{2\lambda}$. Select a random value: $x_0 \xleftarrow{\$} \{0,1\}^{2\lambda}$. Construct the program PKE, as shown below in Algorithm 1 and pad it to the appropriate length. Compute the obfuscated program: $\mathsf{PiO} \leftarrow iO(\mathsf{PKE})$. Output the public parameters:

$$\mathsf{pp} = (\mathbb{G}_1, \mathbb{G}_2, \mathbb{G}_T, p, e, g_1, g_2, H_{\mathsf{msg}}, H_{\mathsf{pop}}, H_{\mathsf{dleq}}, \mathsf{PiO}, x_0, \mathsf{PRG})$$

2. KeyGen$(\mathsf{pp}, i, t, n) \rightarrow (\mathsf{sk}_i, \mathsf{pk}_i, \pi_{\mathsf{pop},i})$: For each participant $i \in [N]$:
   - Choose its random secret value a_i, and construct a polynomial $f_i(z) = a_0 + a_1 z + \cdots + a_{t-1} z^{t-1}$.

   All x_i values are collected and stored in public storage. Participant P_i can compute the private key shares as shown in Algorithm 2:

Algorithm 2. Compute Private Key Share

1: For each participant $i \in [N]$:
2: **for** $i \leftarrow 1$ to n **do**
3: **if** $j = i$ **then**
4: $(f_i(j)) = PRF(x_j) = PiO.evaluate(x_i = j, input = j)$
5: $\mathrm{sk}_j \leftarrow \sum_{i=1, i \neq j}^{n} (f_i(j))$
6: **end if**
7: **end for**
8: **return** sk_j

   - Public key share:

$$pk_i = sk_i \cdot g$$

   - Master public key: $PK = sk \cdot g = \sum_{i=1}^{n} pk_i$.
   - Proof of possession:
     - Each participant generates proof:

$$\pi_{\mathsf{pop},i} = \mathsf{sk}_i \cdot H_{\mathsf{pop}}(\mathsf{pk}_i)$$

     - Publicly reveal pk_i and $\pi_{\mathsf{pop},i}$.
3. **Signing** $(\mathsf{pp}, \mathsf{sk}i, m) \rightarrow (\sigma_i, \pi\mathsf{dleq}, i)$: Each participant P_i computes:
   - Partial signature:

$$\sigma_i = \mathsf{sk}_i \cdot H_{\mathsf{msg}}(m)$$

   - Generate Chaum-Pedersen proof components:

$$\pi_{dleq,i} \leftarrow Prove_{dleq}(g_1, H_{\mathsf{msg}}(m), pk_i, \sigma_i, sk_i)$$

   which proves the discrete logarithm equality:

$$log_{g_1}(pk_i) = log_{H_{msg}(m)}(\sigma_i)$$

   - Output signature share: $(\sigma_i, \pi_{dleq,i})$
4. **Combination** $(\mathsf{pp}, (\sigma_i, \pi_{dleq,i})_{i \in S}) \rightarrow \sigma$:

- Verify the validity of each $\pi_{dleq,i}$.
- For signature shares that pass verification, apply Lagrange interpolation:

$$\sigma = \sum_{i \in S} L_i \cdot \sigma_i$$

where L_i are Lagrange coefficients.
- Generate Chaum-Pedersen proof components:

$$\pi_{dleq} \leftarrow Prove_{dleq}(g_1, H_{\mathsf{msg}}(m), pk, \sigma, sk)$$

which proves the discrete logarithm equality:

$$log_{g_1}(pk_1) = log_{H_{msg}(m)}(\sigma)$$

- Output the aggregated signature (σ, π_{dleq}).

5. **Verify** $(\mathsf{pp}, PK, m, \sigma) \rightarrow 0/1$:
   - Verify the validity of π_{dleq}. If π_{dleq} is valid, it outputs 1; otherwise, it outputs 0.

6 Security Analysis

For signature schemes, the core security objective is *unforgeability* – that no computationally bounded adversary can forge a valid signature. We adopt the standard cryptographic security model of *existential unforgeability under chosen message attacks* (EUF-CMA) to evaluate our scheme. In this model, the adversary is permitted to adaptively query the system for signatures on arbitrary messages from honest participants. The adversary's ultimate goal is to successfully forge a valid signature for a message that was not previously queried.

To precisely describe the security threats and security goals faced by our scheme, we formally define the following security game. This game is conducted between a challenger and an adversary, where the challenger simulates the real execution environment of the scheme, while the adversary attempts to break the scheme's security. The workflow of this security game is precisely described by the following Algorithm 3:

Definition 2 (EUF-CMA Security). *A threshold signature scheme $\mathcal{TS}$ is* EUF-CMA secure *if for all probabilistic polynomial time (PPT) adversaries $\mathcal{A}$, its advantage is negligible:*

$$\mathsf{Adv}_{\mathcal{TS},\mathcal{A}}^{\mathsf{EUF-CMA}}(\lambda) = \Pr\left[\mathsf{Game}_{\mathcal{TS},\mathcal{A}}^{\mathsf{EUF-CMA}}(1^\lambda) = 1\right] \leq \mathsf{negl}(\lambda)$$

We define a sequence of hybrid games Hyb_0 to Hyb_6, where Hyb_0 is the original game, and each subsequent game modifies one component while preserving computational indistinguishability via cryptographic assumptions. Let $\epsilon = \mathsf{Adv}_{\mathcal{TS},\mathcal{A}}^{\mathsf{EUF-CMA}}(\lambda)$ be the advantage of $\mathcal{A}$ in Hyb_0.

Algorithm 3 . EUF-CMA Security Game for Threshold Signatures $\mathsf{Game}^{\mathsf{EUF-CMA}}_{\mathcal{TS},\mathcal{A}}(1^\lambda)$

1: **Initialization:**
2: Challenger $\mathcal{C}$ runs $\mathsf{pp} \leftarrow \mathsf{Setup}(1^\lambda, n, t)$ to generate public parameters.
3: $\mathcal{C}$ generates $(\{\mathsf{sk}_i\}_{i=1}^n, \mathsf{PK}) \leftarrow \mathsf{KeyGen}(\mathsf{pp})$, where:
4: $\mathsf{sk}_i \in \mathbb{Z}_p$ is the private share of party i
5: $\mathsf{PK} = g_1^\alpha \in \mathbb{G}_1$ with $\alpha = \sum_{i=1}^n \lambda_i \mathsf{sk}_i$ (Lagrange coefficients λ_i)
6: $\mathcal{C}$ sends $\mathsf{pp}, \mathsf{PK}, \{\mathsf{pk}_i = g_1^{\mathsf{sk}_i}\}_{i=1}^n$ to adversary $\mathcal{A}$
7: **Query Phase:** $\mathcal{A}$ adaptively issues queries (polynomially bounded in λ):
8: • Corrupt(i): $\mathcal{C}$ returns sk_i (restriction: $|\mathcal{C}| \leq t-1$ where $\mathcal{C}$ is corrupted set)
9: • Sign(S, m): For $S \subseteq [n], |S| \geq t$, and $|S \setminus \mathcal{C}| \geq 1$:
10: $\mathcal{C}$ computes $\sigma_i = H_{\mathsf{msg}}(m)^{\mathsf{sk}_i}$ for $i \in S$
11: $\mathcal{C}$ combines via $\mathsf{Combine}(\{\sigma_i\}_{i\in S}) = \prod_{i\in S} \sigma_i^{\lambda_i^S}$
12: $\mathcal{C}$ returns signature σ with CP ZK proof π
13: **Forgery:**
14: $\mathcal{A}$ outputs (m^*, σ^*, S^*) where $|S^*| \geq t$ and $|S^* \cap \mathcal{C}| \leq t-1$
15: $\mathcal{A}$ wins if and only if:
16: 1. $\mathsf{Verify}(\mathsf{pp}, \mathsf{PK}, m^*, \sigma^*) = 1$ (i.e., $e(\sigma^*, g_2) = e(H_{\mathsf{msg}}(m^*), \mathsf{PK})$)
17: 2. m^* was never queried to Sign (for any S with $|S| \geq t$ and $|S \setminus \mathcal{C}| \geq 1$)
18: 3. S^* is not a subset of $\mathcal{C}$

Game Hyb_0: Original Game Identical to $\mathsf{Game}^{\mathsf{EUF-CMA}}_{\mathcal{TS},\mathcal{A}}$. By definition:

$$\Pr[\mathsf{Hyb}_0 = 1] = \epsilon$$

Game Hyb_1: Guess Target Message m^*

At initialization, challenger $\mathcal{C}$ guesses m^* (the adversary's forgery message) from the set of Q_H possible queries $\mathcal{A}$ will make to H_{msg} (since $\mathcal{A}$ must query $H_{\mathsf{msg}}(m^*)$ to forge a valid signature in ROM). If $\mathcal{A}$ outputs m^* not in the guessed set, $\mathcal{C}$ aborts.

Indistinguishability: $\mathcal{A}$'s view in Hyb_1 is identical to Hyb_0 until the guess is verified. The probability of correct guess is $1/Q_H$, thus:

$$\Pr[\mathsf{Hyb}_1 = 1] = \frac{1}{Q_H} \cdot \Pr[\mathsf{Hyb}_0 = 1] = \frac{\epsilon}{Q_H}$$

Justification: $\mathcal{A}$ cannot distinguish Hyb_1 from Hyb_0 because the guess is made in secret; the only difference is aborting on incorrect guesses.

Game Hyb_2: Guess Target Signing Set $\mathbf{S}^*$

$\mathcal{C}$ additionally guesses a t-size subset $S^* \subseteq [n]$ (the signing set for $\mathcal{A}$'s forgery). If $\mathcal{A}$ outputs S^* with $|S^*| \neq t$ or S^* not equal to the guessed set, $\mathcal{C}$ aborts.

Indistinguishability: The number of possible t-size subsets is $\binom{n}{t}$. The guess is uniform and secret, so:

$$\Pr[\mathsf{Hyb}_2 = 1] = \frac{1}{\binom{n}{t}} \cdot \Pr[\mathsf{Hyb}_1 = 1] = \frac{\epsilon}{Q_H \cdot \binom{n}{t}}$$

Justification: Forgery requires $|S^*| \geq t$, but any S^* with $|S^*| > t$ can be reduced to a t-size subset via Lagrange interpolation.

Game Hyb_3: Embed S^* into Obfuscated PKE Program (iO Security)

The scheme uses obfuscated program PKE to manage key share distribution. $\mathcal{C}$ constructs modified program PKE' that:

- Hardcodes guessed S^* and public values $\{x_i = \mathsf{pk}_i\}_{i \in S^*}$
- For input $(\hat{x}_1, \ldots, \hat{x}_t)$:
  - If (sorted) equals $\{x_i\}_{i \in S^*}$, output uniform random $r^* \xleftarrow{\$} \mathbb{Z}_p$
  - Otherwise, behave exactly like original PKE

$\mathcal{C}$ obfuscates PKE' via iO to get $iO(\mathsf{PKE}')$, replacing $iO(\mathsf{PKE})$ in pp.

Indistinguishability: PKE and PKE' are functionally equivalent. By iO security:

$$|\Pr[\mathsf{Hyb}_3 = 1] - \Pr[\mathsf{Hyb}_2 = 1]| \leq \mathsf{Adv}^{\mathsf{IO}}_{\mathcal{D}_1}(\lambda)$$

where $\mathcal{D}_1$ is a PPT distinguisher constructed from $\mathcal{A}$.

Game Hyb_4: Replace CPRF Outputs with Randomness (CPRF Security)

The scheme uses CPRF to generate auxiliary values $f_i(j)$ for $i, j \in S$.

For guessed S^*, $\mathcal{C}$ replaces CPRF-generated $f_i(j)$ (for $i, j \in S^*$) with uniform random $\tilde{f}_i(j) \xleftarrow{\$} \mathbb{Z}_p$. For non-$S^*$ sets, CPRF is used normally.

Indistinguishability: In Hyb_3, PKE' outputs random r^* for S^*, decoupling CPRF outputs. By CPRF security:

$$|\Pr[\mathsf{Hyb}_4 = 1] - \Pr[\mathsf{Hyb}_3 = 1]| \leq \mathsf{Adv}^{\mathsf{CPRF}}_{\mathcal{D}_2}(\lambda)$$

Game Hyb_5: Embed co-CDH Challenge

$\mathcal{C}$ receives co-CDH challenge $(g_1, g_2, u_1 = g_1^\alpha, u_2 = g_2^\alpha, v_1 = g_1^\beta)$ and sets:

- System master public key $\mathsf{PK} = u_1 = g_1^\alpha$ (master secret α unknown)
- For target message m^*, set $H_{\mathsf{msg}}(m^*) = v_1 = g_1^\beta$
- For key shares: generate $\{\mathsf{sk}_i\}_{i \notin S^*}$ normally; for $i \in S^*$, generate sk_i such that $\sum_{i \in S^*} \lambda_i^{S^*} \mathsf{sk}_i = \alpha$

Indistinguishability: $\mathcal{A}$'s view in Hyb_4 and Hyb_5 is identical:

$$\Pr[\mathsf{Hyb}_5 = 1] = \Pr[\mathsf{Hyb}_4 = 1]$$

Correctness: Key share simulation preserves threshold property; combining t shares from S^* yields α.

Game Hyb_6: Simulate Signing Oracle (ZK Proof Security)

For SIGN queries where $m \neq m^*$, $\mathcal{C}$ simulates:

1. Choose random $r \xleftarrow{\$} \mathbb{Z}_p$

2. Compute simulated signature $\sigma = H_{\mathsf{msg}}(m)^r$ (instead of $H_{\mathsf{msg}}(m)^\alpha$)
3. Simulate CP ZK proof π using ZK simulator

Indistinguishability:

- Signature distribution: $H_{\mathsf{msg}}(m)^r$ is uniform over $\mathbb{G}_1$, matching real distribution
- Proof indistinguishability: By ZK property of CP proof

$$|\Pr[\mathsf{Hyb}_6 = 1] - \Pr[\mathsf{Hyb}_5 = 1]| \leq Q_S \cdot \mathsf{Adv}^{\mathsf{ZK}}_{\mathcal{D}_3}(\lambda)$$

where Q_S is number of signing queries.

We construct a PPT co-CDH solver $\mathcal{B}$ that uses $\mathcal{A}$ to solve the co-CDH challenge:

1. **Receive co-CDH Challenge:** $\mathcal{B}$ gets $(g_1, g_2, u_1 = g_1^\alpha, u_2 = g_2^\alpha, v_1 = g_1^\beta)$
2. **Simulate Hybrid Game** Hyb_6: $\mathcal{B}$ acts as challenger in Hyb_6, embedding co-CDH challenge into PK and $H_{\mathsf{msg}}(m^*)$
3. **Receive Forgery:** If $\mathcal{A}$ outputs valid forgery (m^*, σ^*, S^*) in Hyb_6, $\mathcal{B}$ extracts co-CDH solution

Why σ^* Solves co-CDH: By BLS signature correctness, valid forgery σ^* must satisfy:

$$e(\sigma^*, g_2) = e(H_{\mathsf{msg}}(m^*), \mathsf{PK})$$

Substituting $\mathsf{PK} = g_1^\alpha$ and $H_{\mathsf{msg}}(m^*) = g_1^\beta$:

$$e(\sigma^*, g_2) = e(g_1^\beta, g_1^\alpha) = e(g_1, g_1)^{\alpha\beta}$$

Since $\sigma^* \in \mathbb{G}_1$, let $\sigma^* = g_1^\gamma$. Then:

$$e(g_1^\gamma, g_2) = e(g_1, g_2)^\gamma = e(g_1, g_1)^{\alpha\beta}$$

By bilinearity and non-degeneracy of e, we have $\gamma = \alpha\beta$, thus:

$$\sigma^* = g_1^{\alpha\beta}$$

which is exactly the solution to the co-CDH challenge.

We now combine the indistinguishability results to bound $\mathcal{B}$'s co-CDH advantage. From the hybrid games:

$$\begin{aligned}\Pr[\mathsf{Hyb}_6 = 1] &\geq \Pr[\mathsf{Hyb}_2 = 1] - \left(\mathsf{Adv}^{\mathsf{IO}}_{\mathcal{D}_1}(\lambda) + \mathsf{Adv}^{\mathsf{CPRF}}_{\mathcal{D}_2}(\lambda) + Q_S \cdot \mathsf{Adv}^{\mathsf{ZK}}_{\mathcal{D}_3}(\lambda)\right) \\ &= \frac{\epsilon}{Q_H \cdot \binom{n}{t}} - \left(\mathsf{Adv}^{\mathsf{IO}}_{\mathcal{D}_1}(\lambda) + \mathsf{Adv}^{\mathsf{CPRF}}_{\mathcal{D}_2}(\lambda) + Q_S \cdot \mathsf{Adv}^{\mathsf{ZK}}_{\mathcal{D}_3}(\lambda)\right)\end{aligned}$$

Since $\mathcal{B}$'s success probability equals $\Pr[\mathsf{Hyb}_6 = 1]$:

$$\mathsf{Adv}^{\mathsf{co-CDH}}_{\mathcal{B}}(\lambda) = \Pr[\mathcal{B} \text{ solves co-CDH}] \geq \frac{\epsilon}{Q_H \cdot \binom{n}{t}} - \left(\mathsf{Adv}^{\mathsf{IO}}_{\mathcal{D}_1}(\lambda) + \mathsf{Adv}^{\mathsf{CPRF}}_{\mathcal{D}_2}(\lambda) + Q_S \cdot \mathsf{Adv}^{\mathsf{ZK}}_{\mathcal{D}_3}(\lambda)\right)$$

By the co-CDH assumption, $\mathsf{Adv}^{\mathsf{co-CDH}}_{\mathcal{B}}(\lambda) \leq \mathsf{negl}(\lambda)$ (no PPT solver can solve co-CDH with non-negligible advantage). Additionally:

- $Q_H, Q_S, \binom{n}{t}$ are polynomially bounded (since $\mathcal{A}$ is PPT)
- $\mathsf{Adv}^{\mathsf{IO}}_{\mathcal{D}_1}(\lambda), \mathsf{Adv}^{\mathsf{CPRF}}_{\mathcal{D}_2}(\lambda), Q_S \cdot \mathsf{Adv}^{\mathsf{ZK}}_{\mathcal{D}_3}(\lambda)$ are all negligible (by security of iO, CPRF, and ZK)

Thus, the only way the inequality holds is if $\epsilon \leq \mathsf{negl}(\lambda)$ (otherwise $\mathsf{Adv}^{\mathsf{co-CDH}}_{\mathcal{B}}(\lambda)$ would be non-negligible, contradicting the co-CDH assumption).

Theorem 1 (Main Security Theorem). Under the assumptions of secure iO, CPRF, PRG, CP ZK proof, and the co-CDH assumption in the random oracle model, the proposed threshold BLS signature scheme is existentially unforgeable under chosen message attacks (EUF-CMA secure).

Proof. The proof follows directly from the hybrid argument and reduction to co-CDH. The advantage of any PPT adversary $\mathcal{A}$ is bounded by:

$$\mathsf{Adv}^{\mathsf{EUF-CMA}}_{\mathcal{TS},\mathcal{A}}(\lambda) \leq Q_H \cdot \binom{n}{t} \cdot \left(\mathsf{Adv}^{\mathsf{IO}}_{\mathcal{D}_1}(\lambda) + \mathsf{Adv}^{\mathsf{CPRF}}_{\mathcal{D}_2}(\lambda) + Q_S \cdot \mathsf{Adv}^{\mathsf{ZK}}_{\mathcal{D}_3}(\lambda) + \mathsf{negl}(\lambda)\right)$$

which is negligible under the stated assumptions.

7 Performance Evaluation

7.1 Theoretical Evaluation

We analyze the performance of this scheme by comparison. Table 1 shows the comparison of the computation comlexity of the standard threshold BLS signature and our scheme (CPABLS-T).

Table 1. Computational complexity of different protocols

	Treshold BLS	CPABLS-T
Key Generation	$O(t)$	$O(1)$
Signing	$O(1)$	$O(1)$
Verification	$2P + 1C_T$	$1P + 2A_1 + 2M_1$

P denotes the pairing operation. C_T denotes $\mathbb{G}_T$ comparison. A_1 denotes $\mathbb{G}_1$ addition. M_1 denotes $\mathbb{G}_1$ scalar multiplication.

Based on the Table 1, it can be observed that our scheme holds advantages over the standard threshold BLS signature scheme in both signature generation and verification. By eliminating multi-round communication overhead and interaction delays, and replacing costly $\mathbb{G}_2$ operations as well as complex share verification processes with computationally efficient $\mathbb{G}_1$ group operations, our approach significantly enhances the overall system efficiency. Although fixed additional overhead is introduced during the signature generation and aggregation phases, this is offset by a substantial performance improvement in the verification stage, representing a typical and beneficial trade-off.

7.2 Experimental Evaluation

An efficiency evaluation of our proposed scheme, designated as CPABLS-T, was conducted via an implementation in the C programming language utilizing the Pairing-Based Cryptography (PBC) library, followed by systematic performance measurements. We will conduct a comprehensive efficiency comparison analysis between our proposed scheme and the standard threshold BLS signature scheme in Table 2.

Table 2. Performance summery

Operation	Threshold BLS	CPABLS-T
Key Generation	1.965 (ms)	3.991 (ms)
Signing	2.984 (ms)	0.846 (ms)
Final Verification	8.835 (ms)	4.429 (ms)

8 Conclusion

This research designs and implements a fast-verifiable aggregatable threshold BLS signature scheme that achieves exceptional efficiency, strong security, and remarkable scalability. By incorporating program indistinguishability obfuscation and constrained pseudorandom functions, the proposed scheme establishes a non-interactive distributed key generation protocol that significantly simplifies deployment procedures and enhances system agility. Furthermore, through a randomized verification equation, the scheme effectively circumvents computationally expensive bilinear pairing operations, substantially reducing the computational overhead of the verification process. This work represents a significant step toward realizing efficient and secure next-generation distributed cryptographic systems.

Acknowledgment. The work is supported by the National Key R&D Program of China (No. 2023YFB2703700), the National Natural Science Foundation of China (Nos. 62302457, 62402444, 62402448, 62441228), the Fundamental Research Funds of Zhejiang Sci-Tech University under Grants No. 22222266-Y, the Program for Leading Innovative Research Team of Zhejiang Province (No. 2023R01001), the Zhejiang Provincial Natural Science Foundation of China (Nos. LQ24F020008, LQ24F020009, LQ24F020012), the "Pioneer" and "Leading Goose" R&D Program of Zhejiang (Nos. 2025C02033, 2023C01119).

References

1. Boneh, D., Lynn, B., Shacham, H.: Short signatures from the weil pairing. J. Cryptol. **17**, 297–319 (2004)
2. Boldyreva, A.: Threshold signatures, multisignatures and blind signatures based on the gap-diffie-hellman-group signature scheme. In: Public Key Cryptography–PKC 2003: 6th International Workshop on Practice and Theory in Public Key Cryptography, Miami, FL, USA, 6–8 January 2003. Proceedings 6, pp. 31–46. Springer, Heidelberg (2003). https://doi.org/10.1007/3-540-36288-6_3
3. Pedersen, T.P.: A threshold cryptosystem without a trusted party. In: Workshop on the Theory and Application of of Cryptographic Techniques, pp. 522–526. Springer, Heidelberg (1991). https://doi.org/10.1007/3-540-46416-6_47
4. Gennaro, R., Goldfeder, S., Narayanan, A.: Threshold-optimal dsa/ecdsa signatures and an application to bitcoin wallet security. In: International Conference on Applied Cryptography and Network Security, pp. 156–174. Springer, Heidelberg (2016). https://doi.org/10.1007/978-3-319-39555-5_9
5. Kuchta, V., Sharma, G., Sahu, R., Ruj, S.: Secure and efficient threshold bls signature scheme and its applications. Comput. Secur. **97**, 101936 (2020)
6. Boneh, D., Drijvers, M., Neven, G.: Compact multi-signatures for smaller blockchains. In: International Conference on the Theory and Application of Cryptology and Information Security, pp. 435–464. Springer, Heidelberg (2018). https://doi.org/10.1007/978-3-030-03329-3_15
7. Boneh, D., Lynn, B., Shacham, H.: Batch verification of short signatures. In: Advances in Cryptology—EUROCRYPT 2007, pp. 276–292. Springer, Heidelberg (2007). https://doi.org/10.1007/978-3-540-72540-4_14
8. Zhang, L., Qian, W., Domingo-Ferrer, J., Qin, B., Cheng, H.: A lightweight certificateless aggregate signature scheme without pairing for vanets. IEEE Trans. Intell. Transp. Syst. **24**(5), 5312–5325 (2023)
9. Gennaro, R., Jarecki, S., Krawczyk, H., Rabin, T.: Secure distributed key generation for discrete-log based cryptosystems. In: International Conference on the Theory and Applications of Cryptographic Techniques, pp. 295–310. Springer, Heidelberg (1999). https://doi.org/10.1007/3-540-48910-x_21
10. Kate, A., Goldberg, I.: Distributed key generation for the internet. In: 2010 IEEE International Conference on Distributed Computing Systems, pp. 119–128. IEEE (2010)
11. Garg, S., Gentry, C., Halevi, S., Raykova, M., Sahai, A., Waters, B.: Candidate indistinguishability obfuscation and functional encryption for all circuits. In: 2013 IEEE 54th Annual Symposium on Foundations of Computer Science, pp. 40–49. IEEE (2013)
12. Boneh, D., Waters, B.: Constrained pseudorandom functions and their applications. In: Advances in Cryptology–ASIACRYPT 2013: 19th International Conference on the Theory and Application of Cryptology and Information Security, Bengaluru, India, 1–5 December 2013, Proceedings, Part II 19, pp. 280–300. Springer, Heidelberg (2013). https://doi.org/10.1007/978-3-642-42045-0_15
13. Garg, S., Gentry, C., Halevi, S., Zhandry, M.: Functional encryption without obfuscation. In: Theory of Cryptography: 13th International Conference, TCC 2016-A, Tel Aviv, Israel, 10–13 January 2016, Proceedings, Part II 13, pp. 480–511. Springer, Heidelberg (2016). https://doi.org/10.1007/978-3-662-49099-0_18
14. Ablon, J., Bogdanov, D., Lauter, K., Schneider, T.: Toward practical privacy for genomic computation. In: 2014 IEEE Symposium on Security and Privacy, pp. 216–233. IEEE (2014)

15. Chaum, D., Pedersen, T.P.: Wallet databases with observers. In: Advances in Cryptology—CRYPTO'92: 12th Annual International Cryptology Conference Santa Barbara, California, USA, 16–20 August 1992, Proceedings 12, pp. 89–105. Springer, Heidelberg (1993). https://doi.org/10.1007/3-540-48071-4_7
16. Maxwell, G., Poelstra, A., Seurin, Y., Wuille, P.: Simple schnorr multi-signatures with applications to bitcoin. In: International Conference on Applied Cryptography and Network Security, pp. 125–142. Springer, Heidelberg (2016). https://doi.org/10.1007/s10623-019-00608-x
17. Yang, K., Yang, B., Wang, T., Zhou, Y.: Zero-cerd: a self-blindable anonymous authentication system based on blockchain. Chin. J. Electron. **32**(3), 587–596 (2023)

Cracking Passwords with LLMs by Exploiting Linguistic Features

Tianyu Zuo, Wenying Zhang(✉), and Dewen Ding

School of Information Science and Engineering, Shandong Normal University, Jinan 250014, China

2023317152@stu.sdnu.edu.cn, zhangwenying@sdnu.edu.cn

Abstract. Passwords remain the primary authentication method in computer systems and are expected to prevail for the foreseeable future. Previous works on password security have mainly focused on the passwords created by English-speaking users. As a result, the proposed password guessing methods are confined to the password composed by English speakers. However, language structure plays a significant role in password creation, analysis that overlooks the language-specific inherent features may yield biased results. To address this limitation, we perform a large-scale empirical study using 64.5 million passwords from seven real-world webs. By using the cosine similarity measure, we find significant differences in character distribution between Chinese and English websites. In addition, we explore the use of Chinese Pinyin chunks and English words in both Chinese and English passwords, analyzing their impact on cracking rates. Finally, we propose a large language model (LLM) based password-guessing method to analyze the vulnerability of Chinese web passwords. Our experimental results demonstrate that incorporating linguistic features into the model improves the cracking rate by 3.97%–12.34% compared to traditional non-language-based models. Additionally, to validate the effectiveness of our method, we compare its performance to that reported by Wang et al. At 10^7 guesses, our approach achieves a cracking rate of 37.21%, which is 7.15% higher than that of the leading state-of-the-art method.

Keywords: Password security · Linguistic feature · Large Language Models · Password cracking

1 Introduction

Passwords are expected to remain a dominant access control mechanism in the foreseeable future due to their practical usability [1]. Researchers have long been studying how to attack or protect users passwords [2,3]. However, existing studies predominantly focus on passwords created by English-speaking users, with limited attention given to passwords generated by speakers of other native languages [4,5].

In [1], the authors studied password strength based on languages by performing an empirical study on Yahoo users and concluded that Chinese passwords are

Y. Xiang and J. Shen (Eds.): ML4CS 2025, LNCS 16456, pp. 52–68, 2026.
https://doi.org/10.1007/978-981-95-7820-7_4

among the hardest ones to guess. China had over 1.09 billion Internet users by the end of 2024. Yet, there has been limited research on passwords that utilize the structural principles of Chinese Pinyin. Overlooking this area can expose significant vulnerabilities in Chinese passwords, posing high risks to associated accounts.

Language plays a critical role in password formation. English users often employ common words, phrases, or keyboard patterns [6], while Chinese users tend to create passwords based on Pinyin or cultural expressions such as idioms and ancient poems [7]. These Pinyin-based passwords, however, follow predictable phonetic and structural regularities, making them more susceptible to guessing attacks. To better evaluate and mitigate such vulnerabilities, recent works have applied deep learning to password modeling. RNN- and transformer-based large language models (LLMs) have shown strong potential for learning conditional character dependencies [8,9]. For instance, PassGPT [9] and PagPassGPT [10] demonstrate that incorporating structural patterns can enhance guessing efficiency and reduce redundancy.

Given these considerations, we specifically focus on Chinese web passwords, using large language models to analyze their vulnerability. Unlike previous studies, our approach also considers the unique structural characteristics of Chinese Pinyin and cultural phrases such as idioms and ancient poems to assess the security of these passwords. To fill the existing research gap, we conduct a large-scale empirical study on seven real-world webs. This study evaluates the vulnerability and security of 64.5 million passwords by utilizing patterns from Chinese Pinyins and ancient poems. The contribution of our work lies on the combination of linguistic features and LLMs. Compared to password-guessing models that rely solely on LLMs, our model reduces the generation of meaningless substrings and achieves a higher coverage rate of Chinese passwords with the same number of guesses. The primary contributions of our paper are summarized as follows:

1. **Creating a password-guessing model via LLMs.** We propose a password-guessing model for Chinese web passwords, considering that users prefer using the phonetic spellings of Chinese Pinyins. Experimental results on five real-world datasets show that incorporating these linguistic features improves the cracking rate by 3.97%–13.24% versus a baseline LLM without linguistic features. Moreover, our language-enhanced model yields an improvement of 7.94% over state-of-the-art guessing methods in [7].
2. **Exploring the distribution difference between Chinese and English.** We quantify these differences in character usage with 2-gram cosine similarity, finding that password similarity scores across cultural contexts are markedly lower than those within the same culture. Building on these insights, we design a Chinese-specific password-guessing model that leverages Pinyin-based patterns and semantic information. Our approach substantially improves cracking performance compared to state-of-the-art methods, highlighting the necessity of semantic information modeling in password security research.
3. **Extensive evaluation.** We perform an empirical analysis leveraging 49.3 million passwords from five real-world Chinese websites and 15.1 million passwords from two English websites. We conduct a comprehensive analysis on

the use of language-related patterns in seven datasets. Our findings reveal that both Chinese and English users exhibit a preference for language-based patterns when creating passwords. Specifically, Chinese users often rely on Chinese Pinyins and frequently incorporate culturally significant elements. Additionally, many Chinese users create passwords in the form of acronyms.

The rest of the paper is organized as follows: Sect. 2 provides some preliminaries. We illustrate our observations on the characters of Chinese letter-only passwords in Sect. 3. Section 4 presents our password-cracking method. Section 5 describes the experimental results of our method. Finally, conclusions are drawn in Sect. 6.

2 Preliminaries

Let us start by pre-processing the datasets employed in our experiments, and analyze of their characteristics. Next, we detail our methods for characterizing Personally Identifiable Information (PII) in passwords. Finally, we present the architecture of large language model and the improved Probabilistic Context-Free Grammar (PCFG) model used in our study.

2.1 Data Cleaning

To ensure the consistency and accuracy of the data, only passwords composed of the 52 printable English letters (case-sensitive) are considered, and all samples containing other characters are removed. In addition, in the 12306 dataset, we exclude samples with ID numbers that are not 18-digit integers. This is because these users may have registered accounts using alternative documents such as passports. Consequently, we retain only accounts registered with Chinese ID numbers. We divide the dataset into training, validation and test sets in the ratio of 8:1:1. Table 1 lists the seven cleaned real password sets used in this study. Our analysis leverages five large-scale real-world password datasets, encompassing over 52 million passwords in total.

Though ever publicly available and widely used in password studies [11,12], these datasets contain private data. We promise to use the relevant datasets only for the research in our paper, undertaking not to disclose any private information about the users or engage in any commercial activities.

2.2 Improved PCFG-Based Model

In recent years, various data-driven password guessing methods have been proposed, including the Probabilistic Context-Free Grammar (PCFG) [13] and Markov models [14]. These methods rely heavily on representative training data, and their performance improves as the dataset grows. Wang *et al.* [7] evaluated Chinese password security using such techniques and enhanced PCFG by incorporating Pinyin dictionaries derived from user names, thereby improving

Table 1. Basic Information Of The Five Datasets

Dataset	Language	Type	Original PWs	Valid PWs	Percentage (%)
12306	Chinese	Train Ticketing	131653	6999	5.31
7k7k	Chinese	Gaming	19138452	2007202	10.49
rrw	Chinese	Campus Social	4768600	925888	19.41
Dodonew	Chinese	Commercial	16283143	1616451	9.93
178	Chinese	Gaming	9072966	831746	9.17
rockyou	English	Social Networking	14344391	4116060	28.69
000webhost	English	Web Hosting	720303	2174	3.02

the cracking rate for Chinese passwords. Inspired by this idea, we develop an improved PCFG model as a preprocessing module to describe password structures and generate base strings for LLM training. This design allows the model to capture both structural regularities and linguistic features. In our improved framework, each password is segmented into substrings of similar types, which are then used to infer base structures and their probabilities. Unlike the traditional PCFG that uses three tags L (letters), D (digits), and S (special characters) our model refines the L tag into three distinct categories: C for Chinese Pinyin strings, U for English words, and L for unmatched alphabetic substrings. This refinement enables more accurate modeling of Chinese letter-based passwords. During training, we estimate the probability of each component by counting its occurrence within the same structural category:

$$\mathrm{P}(W \rightarrow w) = \frac{\mathrm{count}(w)}{\mathrm{count}(W)}. \tag{1}$$

where W represents structure, and w represents a specific pinyin string, and

$$\sum_{w} P(W \rightarrow w) = 1. \tag{2}$$

For example, the password "zhanglovelz" is divided into the C segment "zhang", the U segment "love" and the L segment "lz", resulting in a base structure $C_5U_4L_2$. The probability of "zhang" is calculated as $\frac{\#\text{of `zhang'}}{\#\text{of Pinyin structures}}$. Such information is used to generate the probabilistic context-free grammar. The probability of each guess is the product of the probabilities of the productions used in its derivation. For instance, the probability of "lovezhang" is computed as $\mathrm{P}(\text{lovezhang}) = \mathrm{P}(U_4C_5) \cdot \mathrm{P}(U_4 \rightarrow \text{love}) \cdot \mathrm{P}(C_5 \rightarrow \text{zhang})$. Additionally, the probability for L segments is handled by learning from the LLMs.

2.3 Model Architecture

Large Language Models (LLMs), a family of machine learning models, have shown remarkable effectiveness in natural language processing and natural lan-

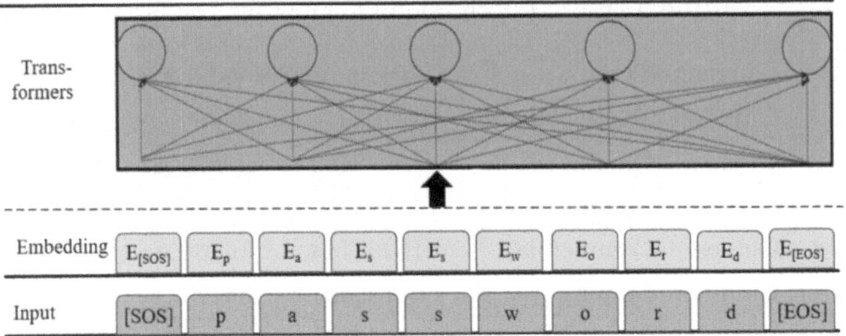

Fig. 1. Model architecture.

guage understanding. Unlike traditional models, which rely on sequential processing, LLMs utilize self-attention mechanisms to capture long-range dependencies and contextual information more effectively. The architecture of our model in this study is depicted in Fig. 1. In this work, passwords are preprocessed and tokenized before being input into the LLM. Each password is divided into tokens, where each character is mapped to an integer within the vocabulary Σ, consisting of 98 UTF-8 symbols. A one-hot encoding is applied to represent each token σ as a vector of dimension $|\Sigma|$, with only the corresponding index set to 1. These vectorized tokens are then fed into the model to learn password generation patterns. During training, the model predicts the next token given the preceding ones, effectively modeling the conditional probability of a character sequence. Formally, for a sequence $x = (x_0, x_1, \cdots, x_i)$, the joint probability is factorized as:

$$p(x) = \prod_{i=0}^{n} p(x_i | x_{<i}; \theta), \tag{3}$$

where x_i denotes the i-th token, $x_{<i}$ represents all preceding tokens, and θ is the set of learnable parameters.

The model employs the decoder component of the transformer architecture with 8 layers, 12 attention heads, and GeLU activation. Training is performed for one epoch using the AdamW optimizer, an initial learning rate of 1×10^{-5}, and linear decay scheduling. The resulting model generates a password guess set by learning structural dependencies and semantic regularities from the training corpus.

3 The Characters of Letter-Only Passwords on Various Websites

3.1 The Letter Distribution in Passwords

To understand the frequency of the 26 case-insensitive letters, we calculate the distribution of each letter across Chinese and English passwords. These results are depicted in Fig. 2.

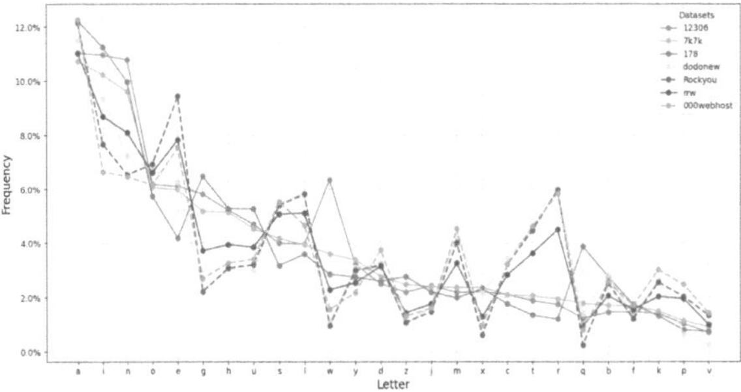

Fig. 2. Letter Distributions in Passwords.

Figure 2 illustrates that passwords from different datasets exhibit significantly varied letter distributions. Surprisingly, even though they are used across diversified web services, passwords from the same language group display similar letter distributions. For Chinese websites, the descending order of letter frequency is *ainoeghlwuysz xqcdjmbtfrkpv*, whereas for English websites it is *aeionrlstmucdhykbgpjvfzwxq*.

Although several letters such as '*a*', '*e*', and '*i*' appear frequently in both groups, others exhibit language-specific biases. For example, the letter "q" occurs more frequently in Chinese passwords due to its common use in Pinyin (e.g., *qi*, *qian*, *qing*), while "r" is more frequent in English passwords. To quantify such distinctions, we employ the 2-gram cosine similarity metric described below.

3.2 The Similarity of Passwords Between Different Websites

To measure the similarity of the letter distribution sequences (sorted in descending order), we introduce the 2-gram cosine similarity [15] as a metric. The similarity between the sequences str_1 and str_2 is defined as:

$$\frac{\sum_{\mathrm{g} \in \mathrm{G}} (\mathrm{count}(str_1, \mathrm{g}) \cdot \mathrm{count}(str_2, \mathrm{g}))}{\sqrt{\sum_{\mathrm{g} \in \mathrm{G}} (\mathrm{count}(str_1, \mathrm{g}))^2} \cdot \sqrt{\sum_{\mathrm{g} \in \mathrm{G}} (\mathrm{count}(str_2, \mathrm{g}))^2}}. \tag{4}$$

where, G denotes the set of all 2-gram substrings in str_1 and str_2, and $\mathrm{count}(str_1, \mathrm{g})$ represents the number of occurrences of substring g in str_1. The similarity ranges from 0 to 1, with higher values indicating greater resemblance. The computed similarities among different datasets are listed in Table 2.

Table 2 shows that the cosine similarity between Chinese and English password datasets is generally lower than between Chinese datasets. The 12306 and 7k7k datasets share the highest similarity (48%), indicating that user-generated passwords are significantly influenced by their native language and cultural background. Notably, the rrw dataset shows minimal differences in similarity with

Table 2. The Cosine Similarity Between Datasets

	12306	7k7k	178	Dodonew	rrw	RockYou	000webhost
12306	1	0.48	0.24	0.28	0.16	0	0.08
7k7k	0.48	1	0.24	0.24	0.16	0	0.12
178	0.24	0.24	1	0.32	0.16	0.08	0.04
Dodonew	0.28	0.24	0.32	1	0.24	0.2	0.16
rrw	0.16	0.16	0.16	0.24	1	0.18	0.16
RockYou	0	0	0.08	0.2	0.18	1	0.28
000webhost	0.08	0.12	0.04	0.16	0.16	0.28	1

both Chinese and English datasets. This is due to Renren.com's initial registration restrictions, which required users to have specific university IP addresses or email addresses. This ensured that the majority of registered users were college students, who typically have high level education and proficiency in English. In subsequent sections, We will analyze word patterns from both Chinese and English perspectives.

3.3 Comparing of Password Composed by Chinese Pinyin and English Word

Since websites do not support passwords composed of **Hanzi**, it is unsurprising that Chinese Pinyin, similar to English words, are widely used in the passwords of Chinese users. We count passwords containing Chinese Pinyin with at least two characters and apply the principle of the longest prefix. However, users may combine multiple Pinyin chunks in their passwords, such as the popular password "woaini", which is composed of three parts: "wo", "ai" and "ni". Additionally, we select the Wiktionary for English words and extract more than 20,000 common English words.

Table 3. The Percentage Of Chinese Pinyin And English Words In Passwords

	Password	
	Chinese Pinyings(%)	English Words(%)
12306	41.61	15.59
7k7k	44.70	10.04
rrw	40.63	10.39
Dodonew	33.25	15.35
178	57.31	2.20
RockYou	6.94	25.47
000webhost	1.37	16.34

A password is classified as containing Pinyin or English words if it includes any substring found in the corresponding dictionary. Table 3 shows that Pinyin usage dominates in passwords created by Chinese users, while English words are predominant in English-speaking datasets. These findings highlight the linguistic influence on password composition and suggest that incorporating language-specific dictionaries could enhance the effectiveness of password strength evaluation and cracking models.

4 Password Guessing Model via LLMs

In this section, we employ large language models (LLMs) to generate guessing passwords. The model is divided into three phases: preprocessing, model training, and password guessing. In the preprocessing phase, the password data is tokenized and formatted to ensure compatibility with the language model, enabling it to learn the intricate patterns and structures of password construction. Finally, in the password generation phase, the trained model is used to produce guessing passwords to evaluate the security of passwords. Each of these phases is discussed in detail in the following sections.

4.1 Preprocessing

During this stage, all passwords in a training set are parsed into segments of similar character sequences: Pinyin structure C, common characters U and basic character string L. Ignoring the tones, Chinese Pinyins usually consist of 23 initials and 24 finals. These two combine to form about 420 different basic Pinyin elements. We count passwords containing Chinese Pinyin with at least two characters. Single-character pinyin are considered ordinary letters (a, e, m and o). A Chinese Pinyin can be a prefix of others, such as "ni", "nin" and "ning". To avoid splitting each Chinese Pinyin during the training process, we use tags to differentiate them and further divide C into six subsets $C_1, C_2, C_3, \ldots, C_6$ according to their length. There are three inputs in this process: the training set, the Pinyin list CS (where all Pinyins in CS consist of at least two characters) and the common characters list US (which includes English words and compositions with special phrases). The output consists of a password structure base table and password structure dictionaries with corresponding probabilities.

The Pinyin Structure Parsing Algorithm is developed to identify and extract Pinyin structures from a collection of passwords using a predefined Pinyin table. Each password is parsed to locate the longest valid prefixes that match entries in the Pinyin table. The frequency of each identified Pinyin is then computed to construct a frequency-sorted Pinyin dictionary. Subsequently, the probability of each dictionary word is determined based on its frequency, defined as the ratio of the number of occurrences of a given word in the training set (N_{word}) to the total number of words within the same structural category (N_{total}), i.e., P

$= N_{word}/N_{total}$. After completing the matching of all Chinese Pinyin segments (CSs) and English word segments (USs), all successfully matched substrings and their corresponding probabilities are stored in their respective dictionaries. Unmatched substrings are retained in the basic string table to serve as input for subsequent model training.

4.2 Model Training

During the data preprocessing stage, passwords are classified into structured passwords based on established segmentation rules. For example, the password "zhanglovelz" will be segmented into $C_5U_4L_2$ according to these rules. Each token σ is then mapped to a unique index defined by the tokenizer (see Sect. 2.3). Considering that the majority of passwords have lengths less than 16 characters, we only encode segments with lengths less than or equal to 16. Moreover, special start and end segments are added to facilitate the generation of structured password and to normalize probability calculations.

The model employs the decoder component of the Transformer architecture and is trained to autoregressively predict the next token in a sequence. During the training process, the model not only learns the structural patterns of passwords, but also learns the specific character strings corresponding to each structure. Given the preceding tokens $x_{<i}$, the model estimates the conditional probability $p(x_i|x_{<i};\theta)$, which is optimized using the cross-entropy loss:

$$\boldsymbol{L} = -\sum_{i=1}^{\mathrm{n}} x_i \log(\hat{x}_i). \tag{5}$$

where n represents the number of possible next segments in the model's predicted output and i denotes the tag index. Our aim is to minimize the loss function, thereby improving the model's accuracy in predicting the correct output.

Since the final guessed passwords are output in descending order of probability, the probabilities of structured passwords must be used to assess those of the guessed passwords. Therefore, during the generation stage of structured passwords, we output not only the structured passwords but also the probabilities of the corresponding structures. Additionally, for the basic string table, we convert the segment sequence into a character sequence, encode it, and subsequently input it into our model for training.

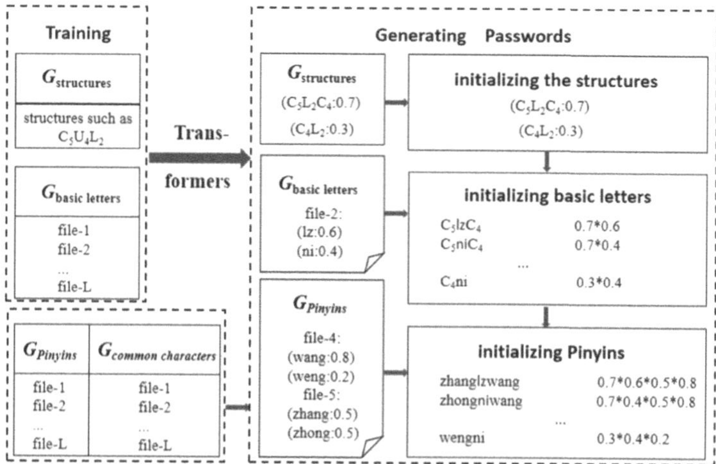

Fig. 3. Model Architecture.

As shown in Fig. 3, the proposed framework consists of two main phases: *training* and *password generation*. During training, the preprocessed structured segments ($G_{structures}$), basic letters ($G_{basic\_letters}$), and Pinyin components ($G_{Pinyins}$) are tokenized and fed into the model. The decoder learns the conditional distributions of tokens, capturing both structural and linguistic dependencies. In the generation phase, password sequences are produced autoregressively, beginning with the start token (<s>) and continuing until the end token (</s>) is reached.

4.3 Password Guessing

After generating structured passwords and computing their probability distribution, the next step is to fill segments with appropriate dictionary words to generate the final guessed passwords. In this model, the dictionary words, Pinyin_dict and U_dict for structures C and U, are derived from statistical data obtained from the training set, as shown in Sect. 4.1. The structure L is instantiated with alphabetic strings generated by our model, where a string of length n is used to fill the structural segment L_n.

Algorithm 1. Password Guessing Algorithm

Input: probability *threshold*
Output: guess set *guess_list*
1: *segs_list* ← StructureGenerate()
2: *dictionarys_words* ← DictGenerate(*TS*)
3: priority_queue.pop(*segs_list*)
4: **while** priority_queue **not** empty **do**
5: *segs* ← heappop(priority_queue)
6: segment ← *segs.nextseg()*
7: **if** segment == EndSegment **then**
8: *guess_list.append(segs)*
9: **else**
10: *values* ← *dictionaries_words*[*segment*]
11: **for each** value **in** *values* **do**
12: *current_p* ← *segs.p* × *value.p*
13: **if** *current_p* > *threshold* **then**
14: *new_segs* ← *segs.copy()*
15: *new_segs.p* ← *current_p*
16: heappush(priority_queue, *new_segs*)
17: **end if**
18: **end for**
19: **end if**
20: **end while**
21: **return** *guess_list*

After obtaining the structural templates and their associated probabilities, we perform a filling process analogous to the substitution step in PCFG-based password models, in which the basic structures are instantiated with concrete tokens such as Pinyin words, user-specific PII segments, and alphabetic strings. Our main idea is shown in the following password-guessing algorithm (Algorithm 1). The Password Guessing Algorithm is designed to generate a set of passwords based on a probability threshold. The algorithm requires a probability threshold, *threshold*, to determine which password segments are considered for further expansion. It initializes an empty *segs_list* to store the final set of password guesses. In steps 1–10, *segs_list* is inserted into a standard priority queue, sorted in descending order based on the segment probabilities. In each iteration, the segment with the highest priority (i.e., highest probability) is popped from the priority queue and stored in *segs*. The next segment from *segs* is retrieved using the *nextseg()* method. If this segment is identified as the EndSegment, indicating the end of a potential password, the complete segment sequence (*segs*) is appended to the *guess_list*. In steps 11–12, for each value, the algorithm calculates the probability of the new segment sequence as the product of the current segment's probability, *segs.p* and the value's probability, *value.p*. From steps 13–16, if the calculated probability, *current_p*, exceeds the predefined threshold, the current segment's probability is updated and it is pushed back into the priority queue for further filling.

This process continues until a termination segment is encountered, signifying that all segments of the sequence have been filled. The algorithm continues until the desired number of guessed passwords has been generated. Throughout this process, a probability threshold of 1×10^{-9} is maintained. This algorithm guarantees that the generated passwords are sorted by decreasing probability, thus prioritizing the most likely guesses.

Based on the dictionary and the trained large language model, the probability of generating any given password can be computed. For instance, for the password "zhanglovelz":

$$
\begin{aligned}
P(zhanglovelz) = & P(\boldsymbol{S} \longrightarrow \mathbf{C}_5\mathbf{U}_4\mathbf{L}_2) \times P(\mathbf{C}_5 \longrightarrow \text{zhang}) \\
& \times P(\mathbf{U}_4 \longrightarrow \text{love}) \times P(\mathbf{L}_2 \longrightarrow \text{lz}).
\end{aligned} \tag{6}
$$

4.4 Mixing Popular Passwords

Inspired by the approach used in TarGuess-II [16], we incorporate a popular password mixing strategy to enhance the effectiveness of our guessing model (see Fig. 4). This method combines model-generated guesses with globally popular passwords, ensuring that high-frequency real-world passwords are adequately represented in the final guessing list. Specifically, as shown in Fig. 4, the guessing set on the left contains the passwords generated by our model along with their output probabilities. Since these probabilities are obtained in logarithmic form (i.e., log probabilities), they are represented as negative exponential values. To better reflect the influence of popular passwords, we first scale each model-generated probability by a factor γ, which denotes the proportion of users who do not typically use popular passwords. Meanwhile, the popular-password set (right) consists of the top 1,000 most frequent passwords observed in the training corpus. The probability of each entry in this set is estimated based on its empirical frequency in the data. These probabilities are then normalized to ensure consistency with the model-generated probabilities. Finally, we merge the scaled model-generated list and the popular-password list. The merged passwords are sorted in descending order of probability to form the final guess list. This mixing process effectively balances data-driven model predictions and real-world popularity patterns, resulting in significantly improved guessing coverage.

5 Evaluations

In this section, we employ our password-attacking algorithm to assess the strength of Chinese web passwords. To evaluate the efficacy of our transformer-based model in password guessing, we conduct extensive experiments using multiple training datasets. By leveraging our model's ability to capture linguistic patterns, we delve into how these patterns impact on password guessing. Our experiments are structured to use our model to evaluate the strength of Chinese web passwords. We evaluate its cracking rate in guessing passwords compared to state-of-the-art password-attacking algorithms, specifically contrasting our approach with that of Han et al. [17].

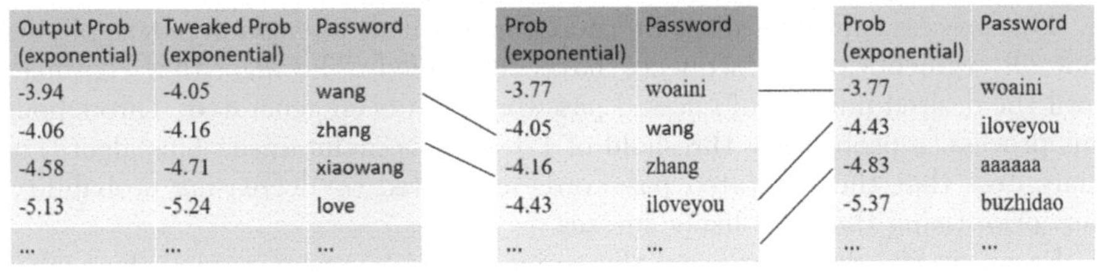

Fig. 4. Mixing Popular Passwords.

5.1 Cracking Effectiveness

To investigate the significance of language patterns in password guessing, we conduct experiments on five Chinese datasets. In this phase of the experiment, since we aim to better understand the impact of linguistic patterns on password security, we sieve the datasets to get letter-only passwords. For each dataset, we generate approximately 10^6 guessing passwords. We then compare the cracking rates of our enhanced model, which includes common Chinese character patterns, with those of a conventional LLM lacking these language-specific features. This comparison allows us to evaluate how much language patterns improve the model s password-cracking rate. The cracking rate (CR) is calculated as the ratio of successfully matched passwords (N_{match}) from the guessing set to the total number of passwords in the test set (N_{test}). Mathematically, CR is expressed as $\text{CR} = N_{match} / N_{test}$, where N_{test} represents the total number of passwords in the test sets.

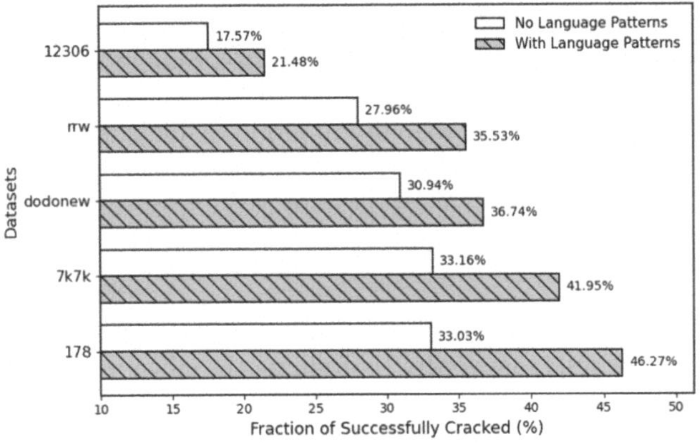

Fig. 5. The Evaluation Results of LLM.

Figure 5 presents the comparison of cracking rates across the five datasets, using models both with and without language pattern integration. For example, in row 178, the pink cell indicates the results of the model with language pattern integration. The test set contains 81,122 passwords, among which 35,912 are successfully matched, yielding a cracking rate of $35,912/81,122 = 46.27\%$. This corresponds to an improvement of 13.24% over the baseline model. The results demonstrate that incorporating linguistic patterns significantly increases the cracking rate, thus highlighting the key role of Pinyin structures in predicting Chinese passwords. It is worth noting that the 12306 dataset shows a relatively low success rate. This is primarily due to its smaller size, which limits the model s ability to capture comprehensive features during training. This observation further confirms that the size of the training set has a substantial impact on the effectiveness of password guessing models.

Overall, the large language model proves strong adaptability in learning from the distinctive features of passwords, and our language-integrated approach achieves markedly higher cracking rates than models relying solely on simple character distribution. This result underscores the substantial impact of incorporating language patterns in enhancing the predictive power of large language models in password guessing.

5.2 Comparison with State-of-the-Art

In this section, to further evaluate the effectiveness of our model in password cracking, we compare our results with those of [7]. In [7], the authors employed PCFG-based and Markov-based password-cracking algorithms on 73.1 million real-life Chinese passwords and proposed a practical heuristic to reduce structural redundancy: long sequences composed of alternating short segments (e.g., $(D_2L_2)_3$) are consolidated into a single, more compact structure (e.g., D_6L_6). Such consolidation permits more efficient probability computation for strings like "1q2w3e4r" via Bayes' Theorem: $P(\text{"1q2w3e4r}) = P((D_1L_1)_4) \cdot \mathrm{P}((D_1L_1)_4 \rightarrow (D_4L_4)) \cdot \mathrm{P}(D_4 \rightarrow 1234) \cdot \mathrm{P}(L_4 \rightarrow \text{qwer})$. To better capture the characteristics of Chinese passwords, Wang et al. enhanced the PCFG model by incorporating a "Pinyin name" dictionary into the L-segment and a date dictionary into the D-segment, thereby improving the model s accuracy in guessing Chinese passwords. However, their approach primarily focuses on augmenting the L and D tags with external dictionaries, while still relying on the original independence assumption of PCFG segments. In contrast, our model integrates Pinyin and English words as structural tags (C and U), leveraging the native grammatical constructs of each language. This structural refinement allows us to capture linguistic patterns more directly and systematically. For a more rigorous comparison, we use the Dodonew dataset, a representative set of Chinese passwords, as the training set. This training set contains passwords randomly chosen from Dodonew, representing a scenario in which attackers have obtained Chinese password sets. From this dataset, we generate six sets of passwords with varying size. We compare our model with the method used in [7], and the results are shown in Fig. 6. When the number of allowed guesses is low (e.g., 10^3), our model demonstrates only a modest improvement in the cracking success rate. However, as the number of guesses increases, the advantage of our model becomes increasingly evident. our model successfully cracks 37.21% of passwords in the Chinese dataset, achieving a 7.15% improvement over the method proposed by Wang et al. This improvement highlights the effectiveness of our approach in leveraging language-specific patterns and incorporating additional password structure knowledge, particularly for Chinese passwords.

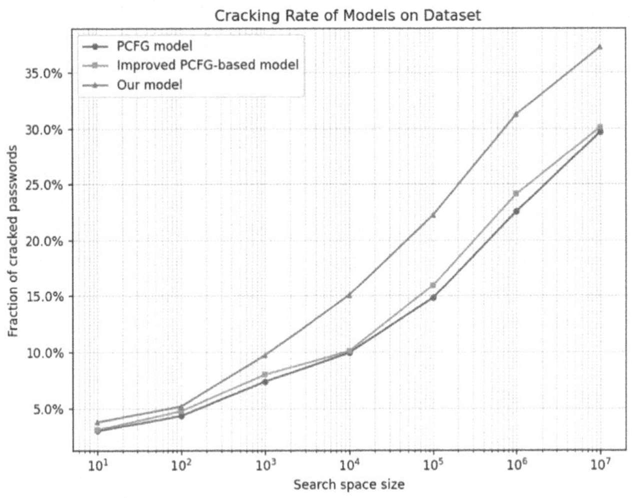

Fig. 6. Cracking rate of dodonew dataset.

6 Conclusion

This paper provides a new technical route to guess users' passwords through chunks in their native language. We perform an empirical analysis of 49.3 million passwords extracted from leaked datasets of Chinese websites in comparison with 15.1 million English counterparts. We reveal the different character distribution between the Chinese and English datasets. Our analysis confirms that users tend to compose passwords by using chunks in their native language. Based on these observations, we perform a series of experiments using large language model for the password-guessing model. Our experiments show that incorporating Chinese Pinyin chunks into password guessing can effectively improve the Chinese password cracking rate. Additionally, we demonstrate that using linguistic features can effectively improve the password cracking rate.

The effectiveness of our findings illuminates the impact of language patterns on password composition, it also demonstrates how these patterns can be integrated into password-guessing algorithms. Given the vast scale of China's internet population (1.092 billion netizens), understanding their password practices is of significant importance. Therefore, the patterns and vulnerabilities identified in this study offer insights that are both broadly applicable and valuable for enhancing cybersecurity measures.

References

1. Bonneau, J., Herley, C., Van Oorschot, P.C., Stajano, F.: Passwords and the evolution of imperfect authentication. Commun. ACM **58**(7), 78–87 (2015)
2. Han, W., Xu, M., Zhang, J., Wang, C., Zhang, K., Wang, X.S.: Transpcfg: transferring the grammars from short passwords to guess long passwords effectively. IEEE Trans. Inf. Forensics Secur. **16**, 451–465 (2021)
3. Wang, D., Shan, X., Dong, Q., Shen, Y., Jia, C.: No single silver bullet: measuring the accuracy of password strength meters. In: 32nd USENIX Security Symposium (USENIX Security 23), pp. 947–964 (2023)
4. Hanamsagar, A., Woo, S.S., Kanich, C., Mirkovic, J.: Leveraging semantic transformation to investigate password habits and their causes. In: Proceedings of the 2018 CHI Conference on Human Factors in Computing Systems, pp. 1–12 (2018)
5. Mori, K., Watanabe, T., Zhou, Y., Hasegawa, A.A., Akiyama, M., Mori, T.: Comparative analysis of three language spheres: are linguistic and cultural differences reflected in password selection habits? IEICE Trans. Inf. Syst. **103**(7), 1541–1555 (2020)
6. Yang, K., Xuexian, H., Zhang, Q., Wei, J., Liu, W.: Studies of keyboard patterns in passwords: Recognition, characteristics and strength evolution. In: Information and Communications Security: ICICS 2021, pp. 19–21 (2021)
7. Wang, D., Wang, P., He, D., Tian, Y.: Birthday, name and bifacial-security: understanding passwords of Chinese web users. In: 28th USENIX Security Symposium (USENIX Security 19), pp. 1537–1555 (2019)
8. Bond-Taylor, S., Leach, A., Long, Y., Willcocks, C.G.: Deep generative modelling: a comparative review of vaes, gans, normalizing flows, energy-based and autoregressive models. IEEE Trans. Pattern Anal. Mach. Intell. **44**(11), 7327–7347 (2021)
9. Rando, J., Perez-Cruz, F., Hitaj, B.: Passgpt: password modeling and (guided) generation with large language models. arXiv preprint arXiv:2306.01545 (2023)
10. Su, X., Zhu, X., Li, Y., Li, Y., Chen, C., Esteves-Veríssimo, P.: Pagpassgpt: pattern guided password guessing via generative pretrained transformer. In: 54th Annual IEEE/IFIP International Conference on Dependable Systems and Networks (DSN), pp. 429–442 (2024)
11. Wang, D., Zou, Y., Dong, Q., Song, Y., Huang, X.: How to attack and generate honeywords. In: 2022 IEEE Symposium on Security and Privacy (SP), pp. 966–983. IEEE (2022)
12. Xu, M., Wang, C., Yu, J., Zhang, J., Zhang, K., Han, W.: Chunk-level password guessing: towards modeling refined password composition representations. In: Proceedings of the 2021 ACM SIGSAC Conference on Computer and Communications Security, pp. 5–20 (2021)
13. Weir, M., Aggarwal, S., De Medeiros, B., Glodek, B.: Password cracking using probabilistic context-free grammars. In: 2009 30th IEEE symposium on security and privacy, pp. 391–405. IEEE (2009)
14. Ma, J., Yang, W., Luo, M., Li, N.: A study of probabilistic password models. In: 2014 IEEE Symposium on Security and Privacy, pp. 689–704. IEEE (2014)
15. Wang, D., Zou, Y., Xiao, Y-A., Ma, S., Chen, X.: {Pass2Edit}: A {Multi-Step} generative model for guessing edited passwords. In: 32nd USENIX Security Symposium (USENIX Security 23), pp. 983–1000 (2023)

16. Wang, D., Zhang, Z., Wang, P., Yan, J., Huang, X.: Targeted online password guessing: an underestimated threat. In: Proceedings of the 2016 ACM SIGSAC Conference on Computer and Communications Security, pp. 1242–1254 (2016)
17. Han, W., Li, Z., Yuan, L., Wenyuan, X.: Regional patterns and vulnerability analysis of Chinese web passwords. EEE Trans. Inf. Forensics Secur. **11**(2), 258–272 (2015)

AgentGuard: An Active Threat Discovery System for Package Confusion Using Multi-agent Collaboration

Wei Ma[1], Yu Li[2], Zhi Chen[1], Ye Liu[1], Lingxiao Jiang[1], Qiang Hu[2](✉), and Junyi Tao[3]

[1] Singapore Management University, Singapore, Singapore
{weima,yeliu,lxjiang}@smu.edu.sg, zhi.chen.2023@phdcs.smu.edu.sg
[2] Tianjin University, Tianjin, China
{liyu2025,qianghu}@tju.edu.cn
[3] Amazon Web Services, Seattle, USA

Abstract. The proliferation of open-source software (OSS) has made software supply chains prime targets for attacks like Package Confusion, where adversaries publish malicious packages with names deceptively similar to legitimate ones. Existing detection methods often rely on simple lexical similarity or passive analysis of known package pairs, struggle with high false positive rates (FPR), fail to proactively identify emerging threats, and are vulnerable to adversarial evasion. To overcome these limitations, we introduce AgentGuard, a novel framework for proactive, single-input package confusion detection. AgentGuard employs a multi-agent architecture that autonomously discovers potential confusion targets using fine-tuned word embedding model to hybird semantic search and subsequently evaluates the risk via a machine learning model incorporating multi-dimensional feature groups to enhance robustness. This design enables scalable, real-time monitoring across diverse software ecosystems. We evaluate AgentGuard on the challenging ConfuDB and NeupaneDB datasets. Our results demonstrate that AgentGuard significantly outperforms state-of-the-art baselines, improving accuracy by 10%–24% while simultaneously reducing the false positive rate by 9%–31%.

Keywords: package confusion detection · LLM agent · Cybersecurity

1 Introduction

Modern software development relies heavily on open-source package ecosystems, with registries like NPM and PyPI hosting millions of packages and serving billions of weekly downloads [11,12,15,17,19,23]. This scale and openness create significant attack surfaces for software supply chain threats [5,16]. Among these, package confusion attacks pose a particularly insidious risk: adversaries publish malicious packages with names designed to closely resemble legitimate

Y. Xiang and J. Shen (Eds.): ML4CS 2025, LNCS 16456, pp. 69–83, 2026.
https://doi.org/10.1007/978-981-95-7820-7_5

ones, deceiving developers into installing them and achieving arbitrary code execution. These attacks exploit diverse confusion mechanisms spanning lexical (typosquatting), syntactic (delimiter modifications, reordering), and semantic (synonym substitution) levels [7,10].

Prior work on package confusion detection has evolved from simple lexical matching [20,21] to semantic analysis [10] and metadata-based filtering [6,13,25]. However, existing approaches face three key limitations: high false positive rates due to benign naming similarities, susceptibility to adversarial metadata manipulation, and reliance on pre-defined package pairs that hinder proactive detection of newly published threats. First, *high false-positive rates* arise because the inherent naming similarity among benign packages makes distinguishing innocuous resemblance from deliberate impersonation difficult, leading to excessive alerts and alert fatigue [2]. Second, *susceptibility to adversarial evasion* remains problematic as defenses relying on static rules or easily manipulable metadata features remain fragile against attackers who can forge or obfuscate these signals. Third, *retrospective and pair-dependent analysis* limits prior work, as most existing approaches operate reactively on known package pairs, misaligning with the *proactive* need to assess newly published packages of unknown intent against the entire ecosystem.

To address these challenges, we introduce AgentGuard, a proactive multi-agent framework for package confusion detection. Given only a single package name, AgentGuard autonomously discovers potential legitimate targets using similarity search and evaluates confusion risk using a machine learning model fortified with multi-dimensional features. The main contributions are:

1. A robust detection model incorporating multi-dimensional feature groups, achieving significantly improved resilience compared to easily-forgeable feature-based approaches.
2. A proactive, single-input detection framework that autonomously discovers confusion targets across diverse package ecosystems without requiring pre-defined pairs.
3. Empirical evaluation on NeupaneDB and ConfuDB showing AgentGuard outperforms state-of-the-art baselines by 10%–24% in accuracy and 9%–31% in false positive reduction. The source code of AgentGuard is publicly available at: https://sites.google.com/view/agentguard/home.

Roadmap. The rest of this paper is organized as follows. We first introduce the relevant background and related work in Sect. 2, followed by the design of AgentGuard in Sect. 3. We then present our experimental setup and the results in Sect. 4. After that, we discuss the limitations in Sect. 5. Finally, Sect. 6 concludes this paper.

2 Background and Related Work

Package confusion attacks exploit naming similarities to deceive developers into installing malicious packages that impersonate legitimate ones. These attacks employ diverse confusion techniques [7,10]: lexical typosquatting, syntactic delimiter manipulation, and semantic synonym substitution. Once installed, malicious packages can execute arbitrary code, steal credentials, or inject backdoors into the software supply chain.

Name-Based Detection. Early approaches focused on detecting lexical similarities using edit distance metrics. Taylor et al. [20] and Vu et al. [21] applied Levenshtein distance to identify typosquatting. Neupane et al. [10] extended this by using FastText embeddings [3] to capture semantic similarities, categorizing 13 distinct confusion mechanisms. While effective for identifying name-level resemblance, these methods suffer from high false positives when legitimate packages share similar names, and struggle to distinguish malicious intent from benign similarity.

Metadata-Based Detection. To reduce false positives, subsequent work incorporated package metadata as additional signals. Zimmermann et al. [25] correlated maintainer count with security risk. Ohm et al. [13] employed machine learning with package metadata and dependency information. Sejfia et al. [18] verified code reproducibility as a trust signal. ConfuGuard [6] combined deep metadata analysis with heuristic rules in a "Benignity Filter", achieving significant false positive reduction. However, these approaches either require pre-identified candidate pairs [6] or rely on metadata that sophisticated adversaries can forge [13,25], limiting their effectiveness against adaptive attackers.

Adversarial Robustness. MeMPtec [4] introduced the Easy-to-Manipulate (ETM)/Difficult-to-Manipulate(DTM) framework, distinguishing between ETM (e.g., descriptions, homepages) and DTM features (e.g., package age, release history). This framework provides a principled approach to building evasion-resistant detectors. However, prior work has not systematically integrated DTM features into a comprehensive detection pipeline that addresses both target discovery and classification, nor empirically quantified robustness under adversarial manipulation.

3 Design of AgentGuard

We begin by formalizing the problem and establishing our threat model, then articulate our design goals, followed by a system overview, and finally detail each agent's design.

3.1 Problem Formulation, Threat Model and Design Goals

Problem Statement. Given a newly published package p with name n_p in ecosystem $\mathcal{E}$, our goal is to determine whether p is a confusion attack impersonating a legitimate package. Unlike prior pair-based approaches that assume knowledge of both the suspicious package and its target, we address the *single-input detection problem*: given only p, the system must autonomously (1) discover potential legitimate targets $\mathcal{T} = \{t_1, t_2, \ldots, t_k\}$ that p may impersonate, and (2) classify whether p constitutes a malicious confusion attack.

Threat Model. We consider an adversary aiming to deceive developers into installing malicious packages by exploiting naming similarities with legitimate ones. The adversary's primary weapon is the package name itself, which can be crafted using diverse confusion techniques spanning Lexical (typosquatting), Syntactic (delimiter changes, reordering), and Semantic (synonym substitution).

To maximize the deception's effectiveness and evade automated detectors, this primary name-based attack is often accompanied by adversarial metadata manipulation. The adversary may attempt to forge signals related to what our model defines as Metadata Quality (MQ) featuresy (e.g., repository url).

However, we assume the adversary cannot trivially forge the signals central to our model's robustness, particularly those we categorize as DTM features. These include immutable temporal signals like package age and release history. We assume package registries maintain basic integrity (e.g., immutable publication time) and are not fully compromised.

Design Goals. To address the challenges identified in Sect. 1 and operate effectively under our threat model, AgentGuard is designed to satisfy the following objectives:

G1 **Proactive Single-Input Detection.** Operate with only a package name as input, autonomously discovering confusion targets without pre-defined pairs, enabling real-time monitoring of newly published packages.

G2 **Robust Multi-Dimensional Model.** Effectively distinguish malicious confusion from benign similarities while resisting adversarial metadata forgery through four-dimensional feature groups, achieving high precision and recall with resilience against evasion.

G3 **Multi-Ecosystem Generalization.** Generalize across diverse package ecosystems (NPM, PyPI, RubyGems, etc.) without ecosystem-specific hard-coding.

G4 **Practical Deployment Readiness.** Provide interpretable results with actionable context for human decision-making, while supporting concurrent analysis with reasonable latency for large-scale monitoring.

3.2 System Overview

AgentGuard is a proactive multi-agent framework that integrates LLM-based reasoning, lightweight machine learning, and tool-augmented analysis for automated package confusion detection. As illustrated in Fig. 1, AgentGuard comprises three agents: the *Orchestrator Agent* coordinates task scheduling and data flow; the *Threat Analyst Agent* performs semantic search to discover potential legitimate targets (**G1**); the *Confusion Checker Agent* conducts ML-based risk

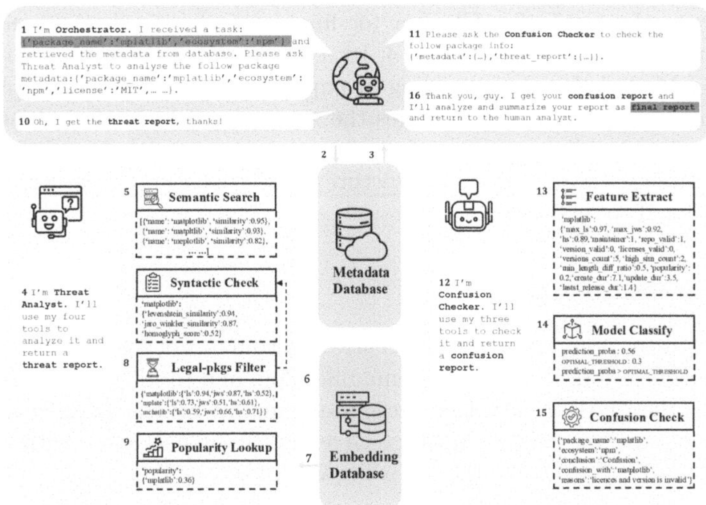

Fig. 1. The overall architecture and workflow of the AgentGuard system. The Orchestrator Agent coordinates three specialized agents through a discovery-evaluation pipeline, processing packages from detection request to final threat assessment.

classification using multi-dimensional features (**G2**); we use multiple ecosystems as our datasets (**G3**); and the real-world *Human Analyst* receives aggregated final reports for final decision-making (**G4**).

Why Multi-Agent Architecture? The multi-agent design is necessitated by three key characteristics: *(1) Task Heterogeneity*: Target discovery (hybrid similarity search) and classification prediction require fundamentally different computational paradigms, which independent agents handle optimally without architectural compromises. *(2) Independent Evolution*: The agent-based architecture enables updating individual components (e.g., retraining word embedding model for new ecosystems or incorporating new confusion patterns) without modifying downstream agents, reducing deployment risk (**G2**). *(3) Graceful Degradation*: When external services fail (e.g., `Libraries.io` [1] API unavailable), agents can fall back to cached data and continue operation, ensuring continuous availability for large-scale monitoring (**G4**). This design maintains independent state, explicit failure handling, and asynchronous communication, distinguishing it from simple modular pipelines.

Overview. The Orchestrator receives a target package and retrieves its metadata from the metadata database (steps 1–3), then assigns it to the Threat Analyst for rapid analysis (steps 4). The Threat Analyst queries an embedding database to perform hybrid semantic–syntactic retrieval of the K most similar popular packages (steps 5–7), computes Levenshtein, Jaro–Winkler, and homoglyph similarities, applies legitimate-package filtering and popularity lookup (steps 8–9), and returns a structured threat report (step 10). The Orchestrator then forwards the results to the Confusion Checker for final confusion prediction and report generation (steps 11–16). At steps 1, 4, 10, 11, 12, and 16, AgentGuard interacts with the LLM, and the corresponding prompts are provided in our public code.

In summary, AgentGuard leverages the strengths of LLMs for adaptive reasoning, small embedding model, and machine learning models for reliable classification, forming a cooperative architecture that achieves both analytical depth and operational robustness.

3.3 Orchestrator Agent

The Orchestrator Agent serves as the central coordinator of AgentGuard, managing task initialization, inter-agent communication, and result aggregation (**G4**). Powered by the LLM for adaptive decision-making, it bridges high-level reasoning with tool-assisted data operations. Given an input package p with name n_p and ecosystem $\mathcal{E}$, it executes the following workflow:

Step 1: Resilient Data Acquisition. The Orchestrator first retrieves package metadata from the local database. If local data is unavailable or incomplete, it automatically falls back to the API service provided by `Libraries.io`, ensuring robustness in data retrieval.

Step 2: Task Dispatch and Conditional Scheduling. The Orchestrator constructs a detection request $\langle n_p, \mathcal{E} \rangle$ and dispatches it to the Threat Analyst Agent for target discovery. Upon receiving the threat report (containing identified targets $\mathcal{T}$), it validates metadata completeness. If sufficient, it forwards the enriched task (including p, $\mathcal{T}$, and all metadata) to the Confusion Checker Agent for classification; otherwise, it flags the case for manual review.

Step 3: Result Aggregation and Reporting. The Orchestrator consolidates the threat report and confusion report (if available) into a comprehensive assessment, annotating the confidence level and forwarding it to the human analyst for final decision-making.

3.4 Threat Analyst Agent

The Threat Analyst Agent addresses autonomous target discovery (**G1**), transforming single-input detection into a comparison problem by identifying potential legitimate targets $\mathcal{T}$ that a suspicious package may impersonate. Guided by the LLM, it coordinates semantic embedding queries and syntactic similarity analyses, balancing semantic breadth (capturing synonym-based confusion) with syntactic precision (detecting typosquatting).

Step 1: Semantic Embedding and Hybrid Search. The agent encodes the input package name n_p using a fine-tuned word embedding model, whose subword-based mechanism captures morphological variations critical for handling diverse naming patterns across 34 ecosystems. The agent queries a pre-built embedding database [14] using a hybrid strategy combining *Cosine Similarity* (semantic relatedness between embeddings) and *Trigram Similarity* (syntactic overlap of character trigrams). After retrieving, merging, and deduplicating candidates ranked by both metrics, this yields up to 30 packages balancing semantic breadth with lexical precision.

Step 2: Legitimate-Package Filtering and Ranking. Since attackers typically mimic popular packages to maximize impact, the agent filters candidates by download counts and repository verification. For each retained candidate c_i, it computes three syntactic similarity scores: Levenshtein distance [8], Jaro–Winkler similarity [22], and Homoglyph score [24]. Candidates are ranked by $\max\{\text{Lev}, \text{Jaro}, \text{Homo}\}$, and the top three form the final target set $\mathcal{T} = \{t_1, t_2, t_3\}$.

Step 3: Popularity Assessment and Report Generation. For each target $t_i \in \mathcal{T}$, the agent computes a normalized popularity score (0 to 1) by aggregating download counts, stars, forks, and dependencies. It generates a *threat report* containing the target set $\mathcal{T}$, similarity scores, and popularity scores, which is returned to the Orchestrator for further classification. This LLM-guided and tool-augmented process enables interpretable and high-precision target discovery under minimal prior knowledge.

3.5 Confusion Checker Agent

The Confusion Checker Agent performs the final stage of analysis (**G2**), integrating metadata and similarity results to assess the likelihood of a confusion attack. This agent complements the LLM-driven reasoning of upstream components with a lightweight machine learning classifier to ensure reliability and interpretability.

Step 1: Multi-Dimensional Feature Extraction. Given the input package p, the target set $\mathcal{T}$, and metadata for both, the agent extracts a 14-dimensional feature vector $X \in \mathbb{R}^{14}$ organized into four categories (Table 1). The features span *Syntactic Similarity (SS)* (name-level resemblance), *Metadata Quality (MQ)* (maintenance and validity signals), *Contextual and Differential (CD)* (comparative ecosystem context), and critically, *Difficult-to-Manipulate (DTM)* [4] (temporal signals like package age that resist forgery), thereby enhancing robustness (**G3**).

Step 2: Random Forest Classification. The feature vector $X \in \mathbb{R}^{14}$ is input into a pre-trained Random Forest (RF) classifier with decision trees (tuned via cross-validation). The RF aggregates individual tree predictions via majority voting, outputting a confusion probability $\hat{P}(p \text{ is confusion} \mid X) \in [0, 1]$ that provides both a classification decision and confidence estimate for human review prioritization (Table 1).

Step 3: Threshold-Based Decision and Report Generation. The agent compares $\hat{P}$ with an empirically optimized threshold (0.29, determined via F1-maximization in Sect. 4). If $\hat{P} > 0.29$, the package is classified as *Confusion*; otherwise, as *Benign*. The agent generates a *confusion report* with the classification decision, confidence score, and low-confidence flag for manual review (**G4**), which is returned to the Orchestrator.

Table 1. Extracted features and their corresponding categories.

Feature Name	Feature Category
Maximum Levenshtein Similarity	Syntactic Similarity (SS)
Maximum Jaro–Winkler Similarity	
Maximum Homoglyph Score	
Maintainer Adequacy	Metadata Quality (MQ)
Repository URL Validity	
Version Format Validity	
License Validity	
Version Count	
High-Similarity Count	Contextual and Differential (CD)
Minimum Length Difference Ratio	
Target Popularity	
Package Age	Difficult-to-Manipulate (DTM)
Time Since Last Release	
Time Since Last Update	

Through this modular multi-agent design, AgentGuard achieves a balance between scalability, analytical precision, and robustness against adversarial behavior. The empirical validation is presented in Sect. 4.

4 Experiments

4.1 Experimental Setups

Baselines. We compared AgentGuard against two established baselines: *Typomind* [10], which utilizes semantic embeddings alongside lexical analysis to detect confusion primarily on package pairs, and *ConfuGuard* [6] that employs deep metadata analysis.

Datasets. Two datasets were used for evaluation. *ConfuDB* [6] contains 2,361 packages analyzed by security experts during tool development and deployment, representing complex real-world cases with confirmed attacks, stealthy threats, and benign samples. *NeupaneDB* [10] comprises 1,840 packages from prior research, featuring a higher proportion of confirmed and publicly documented confusion attacks.

Fine-Tuned Word Embedding Model. While advanced Transformer embedding models (like Qwen3) excel at general semantic tasks, we selected FastText(cc.en.300.bin) because its architecture, which is based on subword (n-gram) information, makes it inherently adept at generating robust vector representations for misspellings and Out-of-Vocabulary words. To further enhance its domain adaptation, we fine-tuned the cc.en.300.bin model using a comprehensive corpus of 10,015,794 package names spanning 34 distinct ecosystems.

Classification Model. AgentGuard's Confusion Checker Agent utilizes a Random Forest classifier. We employed 5-fold stratified cross-validation on subsets from ConfuDB and NeupaneDB to robustly evaluate performance using the 14 defined features and select optimal settings. A single, final model was then trained using these settings on the entire combined dataset (all 5 folds) for deployment.

4.2 Research Questions

To comprehensively evaluate AgentGuard, we designed experiments addressing three research questions:

- **RQ1 (Model Capability):** How does AgentGuard select its classification threshold, and what is its overall classification capability?
- **RQ2 (Baseline Comparison):** How does AgentGuard compare to state-of-the-art tools (Typomind, ConfuGuard) in detecting real-world confusion attacks?
- **RQ3 (Feature Robustness):** What is the contribution of each feature category (SS, MQ, CD, DTM), and how robust is the model against adversarial metadata manipulation?

4.3 RQ1 - Threshold Selection and Overall Capability

Methodology. Rather than using an arbitrary threshold (e.g., 0.5), we employ a principled approach by conducting a grid search over the range [0.01, 0.99] with step size 0.01 on a validation set, selecting the threshold that maximizes the F1 score (a harmonic mean that balances precision and recall). This data-driven strategy ensures the threshold is optimized for the specific characteristics of package confusion detection.

Results. As shown in Fig. 2a, the F1 score peaks at threshold $= 0.29$, significantly lower than the conventional 0.5. This deviation reflects an important characteristic of confusion detection: the severe consequences of false negatives (missing malicious packages) often outweigh those of false positives (flagging benign packages for human review). The threshold of 0.29 favors recall while maintaining acceptable precision, aligning with the practical requirement of minimizing security risks in supply chain monitoring (**G2**).

The ROC curve in Fig. 2b demonstrates robust classification capability with AUC ≈ 0.8. This indicates that our model assigns higher confidence scores to malicious confusion packages than to benign ones in approximately 80% of all possible pairwise comparisons, which represents strong discriminative performance considering the subtle differences between sophisticated confusion attacks and legitimate similarly-named packages.

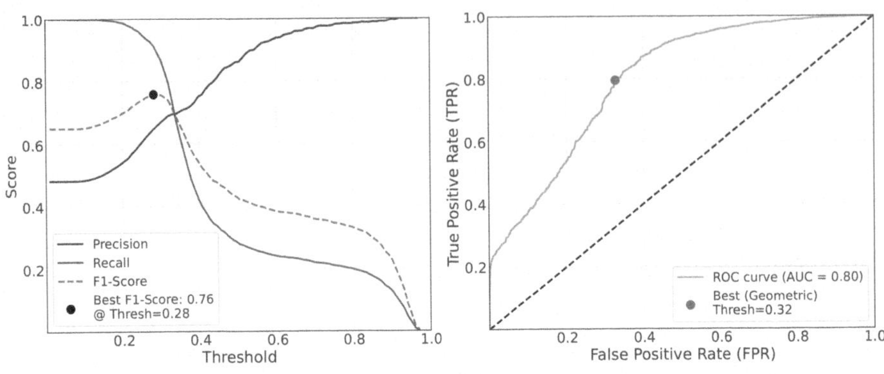

(a) Relationship of precision, recall and F1 with threshold

(b) ROC curve showing FPR vs TPR trade-off

Fig. 2. Performance evaluation: (a) Threshold selection analysis showing F1 score optimization at 0.29, and (b) ROC curve demonstrating model classification capability with AUC $\approx$ 0.8.

Takeaway. The optimized threshold of 0.29 and strong AUC validate that AgentGuard's hybrid feature-based classifier possesses solid foundational classification capability. The threshold's deviation from 0.5 appropriately reflects the asymmetric costs in security-critical applications.

4.4 RQ2 - Performance Comparison with Baselines

Overall Performance. We evaluated AgentGuard against two state-of-the-art baselines (Typomind and ConfuGuard) on both ConfuDB (2,361 packages, analyst-triaged real-world cases) and NeupaneDB (1,841 packages, publicly documented attacks). Table 2 presents the comprehensive results. AgentGuard consistently outperforms both baselines across all metrics on both datasets, achieving improvements of 6%–43% in precision, 10%–24% in recall/accuracy, and 16%–42% in F1-score.

Dataset-Specific Analysis. On *ConfuDB*, the most challenging real-world dataset, AgentGuard achieves weighted F1 of 0.78 versus 0.46 (ConfuGuard) and 0.36 (Typomind), representing a 70% and 117% relative improvement, respectively. Notably, AgentGuard's recall for the *Confusion* class (0.76) substantially exceeds both baselines (0.53 and 0.31), demonstrating superior capability in identifying actual attacks (**G2**). This is critical in security contexts where false negatives carry severe consequences.

On *NeupaneDB*, which contains more clear-cut, publicly documented attacks, all methods perform better, but AgentGuard maintains its advantage with weighted F1 of 0.92 versus 0.76 (ConfuGuard) and 0.69 (Typomind). The smaller performance gap on this dataset suggests that AgentGuard's advantages are

Table 2. Experiments result for AgentGuard with Typomind and ConfuGuard on the ConfuDB and NeupaneDB datasets

Class	Metric	ConfuDB			NeupaneDB		
		AgentGuard	ConfuGuard	Typomind	AgentGuard	ConfuGuard	Typomind
Benign	Precision	0.93	0.40	0.31	0.89	0.91	0.38
	Recall	0.76	0.51	0.69	0.93	0.62	0.84
	F1-score	0.84	0.45	0.30	0.91	0.67	0.81
Confusion	Precision	0.53	0.55	0.31	0.87	0.79	0.74
	Recall	0.76	0.53	0.31	0.85	0.82	0.68
	F1-score	0.62	0.49	0.52	0.93	0.79	0.65
Weighted	Precision	**0.82**	0.44	0.31	**0.88**	0.82	0.65
	Recall	**0.76**	0.52	0.61	**0.87**	0.77	0.72
	F1-score	**0.78**	0.46	0.36	**0.92**	0.76	0.69
	Accuracy	**0.76**	0.52	0.61	**0.87**	0.77	0.72
Total Support		2361	2361	2361	1840	1840	1840

most pronounced when handling subtle, analyst-triaged real-world cases, precisely the challenging scenarios where automated detection provides the most value.

Understanding the Performance Gains. AgentGuard's superior performance stems from three key design choices that address fundamental limitations of prior work:

(1) Proactive Target Discovery. Unlike baselines that require pre-identified package pairs, AgentGuard's Threat Analyst Agent autonomously discovers confusion targets using fine-tuned word embedding model to semantic search (**G1**). This enables detection of sophisticated semantic confusion attacks that purely lexical approaches (like aspects of Typomind) may miss, while avoiding the coverage limitations of pair-based methods.

(2) Multi-Dimensional Feature Engineering. Rather than relying primarily on name similarity or simple heuristics, AgentGuard employs 14 features spanning four categories (SS, MQ, CD, DTM, as shown in Table 1). This holistic feature space captures signals beyond superficial naming patterns, including metadata quality, contextual relationships, and temporal characteristics, enabling more nuanced discrimination between malicious packages and benign similarly-named ones.

(3) ML-Based Classification. The Random Forest classifier adaptively learns the complex, non-linear relationships between features and maliciousness from labeled data, providing more flexible decision boundaries than rule-based systems. This explains AgentGuard's higher precision compared to systems relying on fixed heuristic thresholds.

Takeaway. The consistent and substantial performance improvements across both datasets validate AgentGuard's core hypothesis: combining proactive semantic discovery with multi-dimensional ML-based evaluation effectively addresses the limitations of prior confusion detection approaches. The particularly strong performance on ConfuDB's challenging real-world cases demonstrates practical deployment readiness.

4.5 RQ3 - Feature Contribution and Robustness

To understand which feature categories drive AgentGuard's performance and assess its resilience against adversarial manipulation, we conducted controlled ablation experiments comparing four model configurations: *Baseline* (SS only), *Vulnerable* (SS + MQ), *Robust* (SS + CD + DTM, excluding MQ), and *AgentGuard* (all features). Each model was evaluated on two test conditions:

Clean: Original, unmodified test data from ConfuDB and NeupaneDB.

Adversarial (Adv.): Simulated attack where all MQ feature values in *Confusion* samples are flipped (0→1, 1→0), mimicking an adversary's attempt to forge legitimate-appearing metadata, while *Benign* samples remain unchanged.

Table 3. The ablation experiment results using four model configurations

Model	Dataset	Clean			Adv.	ΔRecall$_{(c.)}$
		AUC	F1	Recall$_{(c.)}$	Recall$_{(c.)}$	
Baseline	ConfuDB	0.54	0.65	0.28	0.28	0.00
	NeupaneDB	0.78	0.73	0.73	0.73	0.00
Vulnerable	ConfuDB	0.77	0.76	0.41	0.08	0.33
	NeupaneDB	0.95	0.90	0.88	0.30	0.58
Robust	ConfuDB	0.75	0.74	0.36	0.36	0.00
	NeupaneDB	0.94	0.90	0.88	0.88	0.00
AgentGuard	ConfuDB	**0.81**	**0.78**	**0.68**	0.22	0.46
	NeupaneDB	**0.96**	**0.92**	**0.89**	0.74	0.15

The key metric is the recall drop, $\Delta\text{Recall} = Recall_{\text{Clean}} - Recall_{\text{Adv.}}$ for the *Confusion* class, quantifying performance degradation under attack. Table 3 presents the complete results.

Feature Contribution (Clean Data). On unmodified data, each feature group demonstrates clear value. The Baseline (SS only) achieves modest performance (F1: 0.65 on ConfuDB, 0.73 on NeupaneDB), confirming that syntactic similarity alone is insufficient (**G2**). Adding MQ features (Vulnerable) substantially improves performance (F1: 0.76 and 0.90), indicating that metadata quality signals are highly informative for identifying poorly-maintained malicious packages. The Robust configuration (SS + CD + DTM) also achieves strong performance (F1: 0.74 and 0.90) through different signals, specifically contextual relationships and temporal patterns. Finally, AgentGuard with all features achieves the best performance (F1: 0.78 and 0.92, AUC: 0.81 and 0.96), demonstrating that combining complementary feature types captures the most comprehensive view of package maliciousness.

Robustness Against Adversarial Manipulation. The adversarial evaluation reveals stark differences in resilience. The Vulnerable model, relying on SS and easily-forged MQ features, suffers catastrophic performance collapse under attack, with Recall Drop of 0.33 (ConfuDB) and 0.58 (NeupaneDB). This represents up to 66% of its detection capability lost, rendering it vulnerable when adversaries manipulate metadata.

In sharp contrast, the Robust model exhibits *perfect resilience*: $\Delta Recall = 0.00$ on both datasets. Since it excludes MQ features entirely, flipping MQ values has no effect whatsoever. This validates the fundamental premise behind DTM features [4]: temporal characteristics like package age and release history are inherently difficult for adversaries to manipulate without waiting extended periods, providing attack-resistant signals (**G2**).

The complete AgentGuard model strikes a crucial balance. While it includes MQ features (and thus is affected by their manipulation), the presence of robust DTM and CD features provides substantial protection. Its $\Delta Recall$ (0.15–0.46) is dramatically lower than the vulnerable model's (0.33–0.58), demonstrating that DTM features act as a *defensive hedge*. Even when some features are compromised, the model retains significant detection capability through manipulation-resistant signals.

Takeaway. All feature categories contribute to detection performance, but they differ fundamentally in robustness. MQ features provide strong signals on clean data but are trivially manipulable. DTM features, while individually less powerful, are inherently attack-resistant and essential for maintaining performance against adversarial evasion (**G2**). AgentGuard's multi-dimensional feature design achieves both high baseline accuracy and substantial resilience, a necessary combination for practical security applications.

5 Discussion

Cross-Ecosystem Generalization. AgentGuard's design explicitly targets multi-ecosystem applicability (**G3**). Our evaluation validates this: both datasets contain packages from diverse ecosystems, yet our experiments make *no ecosystem-specific adaptations*. This generalization stems from (1) FastText fine-tuning on 10M package names across 34 ecosystems, and (2) universal feature signals that transcend individual package managers. Current results demonstrate practical multi-ecosystem deployment feasibility.

Limitations and Future Work. AgentGuard has several limitations that suggest future research directions. The semantic search (**G1**) may struggle with very short names, acronyms, or domain-specific terms, suggesting exploration of hybrid approaches with character-level models. While DTM features resist basic metadata forgery (**G2**), sophisticated adversaries might employ long-term strategies such as account nurturing or Sybil attacks [9], requiring complementary approaches like behavioral anomaly detection. Additionally, continuous model retraining and feedback loops are essential for adapting to evolving attacks, and full-scale deployment requires further optimization (**G4**), including incremental index updates, caching strategies, and distributed processing.

6 Conclusion

This paper proposed AgentGuard, an innovative multi-agent system that fundamentally transforms package confusion detection from traditional passive, pair-based analysis to an active, single-input detection model. By integrating a word embedding model for autonomous target discovery with a machine learning classifier that fuses a multi-dimensional feature groups, AgentGuard achieves superior performance: evaluation on the ConfuDB and NeupaneDB datasets shows its accuracy is 10%–24% higher than state-of-the-art baselines, while reducing the false positive rate by 9%–31%, and it also significantly enhances robustness against adversarial metadata forgery. Agent Guard provides a practical, scalable, and adversarially robust automated defense tool, which is crucial for protecting the modern software supply chain from complex and evasive threats.

References

1. libraries.io (2025). https://libraries.io/api
2. Agency for Healthcare Research and Quality: Alert fatigue (2019). https://psnet.ahrq.gov/primer/alert-fatigue
3. ojanowski, P., Grave, E., Joulin, A., Mikolov, T.: Enriching word vectors with subword information (2017). https://arxiv.org/abs/1607.04606
4. Halder, S., et al.: Malicious package detection using metadata information. In: Proceedings of the ACM Web Conference 2024. WWW 202424, pp. 1779–1789. Association for Computing Machinery, New York (2024). https://doi.org/10.1145/3589334.3645543
5. Herr, T.: Breaking trust – shades of crisis across an insecure software supply chain. USENIX Association (2021)
6. Jiang, W., Çakar, B., Lysenko, M., Davis, J.C.: ConfuGuard: using metadata to detect active and stealthy package confusion attacks accurately and at scale. arXiv e-prints arXiv:2502.20528 (2025). https://doi.org/10.48550/arXiv.2502.20528
7. Kaplan, B., Qian, J.: A survey on common threats in npm and pypi registries (2021). https://arxiv.org/abs/2108.09576
8. Levenshtein, V.I.: Binary codes capable of correcting deletions, insertions, and reversals. Soviet Phys. Doklady **10**, 707–710 (1965). https://api.semanticscholar.org/CorpusID:60827152
9. Lynn Neary: Real 'Sybil' Admits Multiple Personalities Were Fake. NPR. (2011)
10. Neupane, S., Holmes, G., Wyss, E., Davidson, D., De Carli, L.: Beyond typosquatting: an in-depth look at package confusion. In: Proceedings of the 32nd USENIX Conference on Security Symposium. SEC 2023, USENIX Association, USA (2023)
11. npm: (2024). https://www.npmjs.com/

12. NPM Contributors: Npm package json: name (2024). https://docs.npmjs.com/cli/v9/configuring-npm/package-json#name
13. Ohm, M., Stuke, C.: Sok: Practical detection of software supply chain attacks. In: Proceedings of the 18th International Conference on Availability, Reliability and Security. ARES 2023. Association for Computing Machinery, New York (2023). https://doi.org/10.1145/3600160.3600162
14. pgvector Contributors: pgvector: A vector extension for postgresql (2023). https://github.com/pgvector/pgvector
15. Python Software Foundation: Acceptable use policy (2024). https://policies.python.org/pypi.org/Acceptable-Use-Policy/
16. Scalco, S., Paramitha, R., Vu, D.L., Massacci, F.: On the feasibility of detecting injections in malicious npm packages. In: Proceedings of the 17th International Conference on Availability, Reliability and Security. ARES '22, Association for Computing Machinery, New York, NY, USA (2022). https://doi.org/10.1145/3538969.3543815
17. Schorlemmer, T.R., et al.: Signing in four public software package registries: Quantity, quality, and influencing factors (2024). https://arxiv.org/abs/2401.14635
18. Sejfia, A., Schäfer, M.: Practical automated detection of malicious npm packages. In: Proceedings of the 44th International Conference on Software Engineering, pp. 1681–1692. ACM (2022). https://doi.org/10.1145/3510003.3510104,
19. Soto-Valero, C., Benelallam, A., Harrand, N., Barais, O., Baudry, B.: The emergence of software diversity in maven central. In: Proceedings of the 16th International Conference on Mining Software Repositories, MSR 2019, pp. 333–343. IEEE Press (2019). https://doi.org/10.1109/MSR.2019.00059
20. Taylor, M., Vaidya, R., Davidson, D., De Carli, L., Rastogi, V.: Defending against package typosquatting. In: Network and System Security: 14th International Conference, NSS 2020, Melbourne, VIC, Australia, November 25–27, 2020, Proceedings, pp. 112–131. Springer, Heidelberg (2020). https://doi.org/10.1007/978-3-030-65745-1_7
21. Vu, D.L., Pashchenko, I., Massacci, F., Plate, H., Sabetta, A.: Typosquatting and combosquatting attacks on the python ecosystem. 2020 IEEE European Symposium on Security and Privacy Workshops (EuroS&PW), pp. 509–514 (2020). https://api.semanticscholar.org/CorpusID:220792403
22. Winkler, W.E.: String comparator metrics and enhanced decision rules in the fellegi-sunter model of record linkage (1990). https://api.semanticscholar.org/CorpusID:54580585
23. Wyss, E., De Carli, L., Davidson, D.: What the fork? finding hidden code clones in npm. In: Proceedings of the 44th International Conference on Software Engineering, ICSE 2022, pp. 2415–2426. Association for Computing Machinery, New York (2022). https://doi.org/10.1145/3510003.3510168
24. Yazdani, R., van der Toorn, O., Sperotto, A.: A case of identity: Detection of suspicious idn homograph domains using active dns measurements. In: 2020 IEEE European Symposium on Security and Privacy Workshops (EuroS&PW), pp. 559–564 (2020). https://doi.org/10.1109/EuroSPW51379.2020.00082
25. Zimmermann, M., Staicu, C.A., Tenny, C., Pradel, M.: Smallworld with high risks: a study of security threats in the npm ecosystem. In: Proceedings of the 28th USENIX Conference on Security Symposium, SEC 2019, pp. 995–1010. USENIX Association, USA (2019)

Parallelizable Oblivious Non-equi-Joins in Trusted Execution Environments

Xingquan Li[1,3,4], Sen Zhao[1], Guohua Tian[1], and Meixia Miao[2,3,4](✉)

[1] State Key Laboratory of Integrated Service Networks (ISN), Xidian University, Xi'an 710126, China
{xingquanli,senzhao}@stu.xidian.edu.cn, ghtian@xidian.edu.cn

[2] School of Cyberspace Security, Xi'an University of Posts and Telecommunications, Xi'an 710121, China
miaofeng415@163.com

[3] Key Laboratory of Cyberspace Security, Ministry of Education of China, Zhengzhou 450001, China

[4] Henan Key Laboratory of Cyberspace Situation Awareness, Zhengzhou 450001, China

Abstract. A common approach to protecting data confidentiality against potential adversaries is to encrypt the databases. Nevertheless, it is infeasible to perform meaningful computations on a ciphertext. Trusted Execution Environments (TEEs) offer a promising alternative by enabling computations on plaintext within a secure enclave, thereby supporting rich and complex queries. However, existing works either fall short in providing strong oblivious guarantees, fail to support queries such as non-equi joins, or suffer from significant efficiency bottlenecks. In this paper, we first address the oblivious order counting and encoding problem in a parallelized manner, enabling the counting and encoding of elements that satisfy a given order within an unordered sequence. Building on this, we propose parallelizable non-equi join algorithms for both single condition and multiple conditions. The experimental results show that our scheme completes a non-equi-join with a single condition, producing 16,000,000 output records in 26.4 s, and a multiple conditions non-equi-join producing 26,366,724 output records in 19.4 s, achieving up to 4.7× and 2.04× speedups over the state-of-the-art scheme, respectively.

Keywords: Oblivious · Non-Equi-Joins · Trusted Execution Environments · Single Condition · Multiple Conditions

1 Introduction

With the rapid growth of cloud computing, users generate massive amounts of data continuously. Since users are typically limited in storage and computational resources, they tend to outsource their databases to cloud servers for more efficient data management [20,21]. However, outsourcing sensitive data inevitably

Y. Xiang and J. Shen (Eds.): ML4CS 2025, LNCS 16456, pp. 84–104, 2026.
https://doi.org/10.1007/978-981-95-7820-7_6

raises security concerns and challenges, including confidentiality, integrity, and authenticity. A common approach to protecting data confidentiality against potentially semi-honest cloud servers is to encrypt the databases before outsourcing them [21]. Nevertheless, Goldwasser et al. [10] pointed out that performing meaningful computations on a ciphertext is computationally infeasible.

To mitigate this issue, plenty of research has been conducted in the past decades. One line of research focuses on developing encrypted primitives to enable search functionality in databases. However, such approaches incur significant computational overhead due to extensive use of cryptographic primitives, which limits their practicality. Another line of research leverages trusted execution environments (TEEs) to provide isolated environments where data can be decrypted and queried securely [2]. Owing to their efficiency, flexibility, and robustness, this line has become a mainstream research direction. Nevertheless, TEEs remain vulnerable to side-channel attacks. In particular, side-channel attackers can recover sensitive information from leaked memory access patterns [6,14].

The notion of obliviousness was proposed to formally capture privacy guarantees on the memory access patterns of algorithms. To achieve this property while enhancing the search functionality of TEE-based encrypted databases, various oblivious schemes have been developed [9,16]. Krastnikov et al. [12] proposed an oblivious equi-join scheme that guarantees data-independent memory access and provides strong protection against leakage of memory access patterns. Building on this line of work, Qiu et al. [18] and Qin et al. [17] independently developed equi-join schemes leveraging differential privacy, designed to satisfy differential obliviousness. After that, Mavrogiannakis et al. [14] introduced the concept of parallelizable obliviousness, pioneering high-performance oblivious queries and laying the foundation for future designs that aim to combine oblivious guarantees with parallel execution. However, these schemes all focus on the oblivious equi-join problem and do not provide solutions for oblivious non-equi joins. Compared with oblivious equi-joins, oblivious non-equi joins face greater challenges. Their matching conditions are often based on inequalities. As a result, each record may correspond to a variable number of matches, making the access patterns highly dependent on the underlying data and difficult to predict. To achieve oblivious non-equi-join, Chang et al. [8] first proposed a scheme and further emphasized that non-equi joins of this kind are of considerable practical importance, and the typical application scenarios are summarized below.

Scenario 1 (Flight Connection). In a flight connection scenario, let T_1 denote the arrival flight table containing the flight identifier $T_1.id$ and arrival time $T_1.t$. Let T_2 denote the departure flight table, which contains the flight identifier $T_2.id$ and its departure time $T_2.t$. By performing a join on the condition $T_1.t \leq T_2.t$, it can identify all feasible transfer pairs $(T_1.id, T_2.id)$, where passengers arriving on T_1 may transfer to T_2.

Scenario 2 (Housing Recommendation). In a housing recommendation scenario, let T_1 denote the tenant table, which contains identifier $T_1.id$, desired rental period $T_1.p$, and maximum budget $T_1.b$. Let T_2 denote the housing information table, which contains the identifier $T_2.id$, available rental period $T_2.t$, and the monthly rent $T_2.r$. By performing a join on the condition $T_1.p \leq T_2.t \wedge T_1.b \geq T_2.r$, it identifies all feasible tenant-house pairs $(T_1.id, T_2.id)$ that satisfy both the rental period and budget constraints.

However, the scheme proposed by Chang et al. [8] cannot be parallelized due to its iterative nature, where each iteration depends on the previous one. Consequently, its efficiency is inherently limited. In addition, the scheme exhibits limited scalability, making it difficult to support and optimize various types of non-equi joins. Therefore, all of these naturally bring us to a question:

Is it possible to design an efficient, parallelizable, and scalable oblivious non-equi-join algorithm ?

In this paper, we design efficient and parallelizable oblivious non-equi-join algorithms, including oblivious non-equi-join for single condition $(T_1.t \leq T_2.t)$ and oblivious non-equi-join for multiple conditions $(T_1.p\ (\leq or \geq)\ T_2.t \wedge T_1.b\ (\leq or \geq)\ T_2.r)$. Our main contributions are summarized as follows.

1.1 Our Contributions

- We propose a parallelizable oblivious non-equi-join algorithm (SCNonEJoin) that efficiently supports single condition of the form $T_1.t \leq T_2.t$, overcoming the sequential dependencies in existing methods, achieving parallel execution, and ensuring data-independent access patterns.
- We propose a parallelizable oblivious non-equi-join algorithm for multiple conditions (MCNonEJoin), which addresses non-equi-join of the form $T_1.p \leq T_2.t$ and $T_1.b \geq T_2.r$. It can be naturally generalized to support other combinations of conditions, such as $T_1.p \geq T_2.t \wedge T_1.b \leq T_2.r$, thus solving the problem of parallel oblivious execution for various non-equi-join scenarios.
- We conduct extensive experiments on the TPC-C benchmark. Our proposed SCNonEJoin outperforms the implementation in [8] by up to 4.74×, while MCNonEJoin achieves up to 2.36× improvement. Both schemes demonstrate strong parallel scalability: SCNonEJoin achieves about 2.0× speedup and MCNonEJoin 2.1× when scaling from 1 to 16 threads.

2 Related Work

In this section, we review existing research on oblivious query processing, with particular emphasis on both equi-join and non-equi-join operations.

Oblivious equi-Join. Agrawal et al. [1] first introduced an oblivious join algorithm leveraging secure coprocessors to mitigate access-pattern leakage, establishing one of the secure computation frameworks for relational databases. Later, Li et al. [13] identified security weaknesses in this model and proposed an improved protocol that enhanced data confidentiality but yielded limited performance gains. Subsequently, Arasu and Kaushik [3] extended oblivious query processing to handle more complex relational operators, though their work remained primarily theoretical without implementation. The SMCQL system developed by Bater et al. [5] took a more practical approach, enabling secure SQL query execution over federated databases using garbled circuits. However, its join evaluation still required $O(n_1 \times n_2)$ oblivious comparisons, leading to substantial computational overhead. With the emergence of trusted execution environments (TEEs), subsequent systems such as Opaque [23] and ObliDB [9] integrated oblivious join primitives into large-scale analytical frameworks, bridging the gap between theoretical protocols and practical deployment. To further improve efficiency, Krastnikov et al. [12] proposed two new oblivious primitives to supports oblivious equi-joins. Then, Chang et al. [7] employed ORAM-based optimizations to design scalable multi-way oblivious equi-join algorithms. More recently, Mavrogiannakis et al. [14] introduced a parallel framework to supports parallelizable equi-joins, marking a step forward toward practical oblivious query processing.

Oblivious Non-equi-Join. Non-equi-join are inherently challenging due to complex comparison semantics and data-dependent access patterns. Li et al. [13] first proposed an oblivious algorithm for non-equi-join, which enhanced privacy but offered only modest performance improvements over Cartesian product-based approaches. Building on the primitives of Krastnikov et al. [12], Chang et al. [8] proposed an oblivious framework for non-equi-join that prevents access-pattern leakage through oblivious primitives. However, their method is limited to single-condition joins and does not support parallel execution. Wei et al. [22] later introduced an oblivious Yannakakis-based algorithm supporting acyclic multi-way band joins.

3 Problem Formulation and Preliminaries

In this section, we define the problem, outline the threat model, and provide relevant preliminaries.

3.1 Problem Definition

Non-equi-joins. Given two tables T_1 and T_2, a non-equi-join returns the set of tuple pairs (t_1, t_2) that satisfy a predicate ϕ:

$$\text{Result}(T_1, T_2, \phi) = \{(t_1, t_2) \mid t_1 \in T_1,\ t_2 \in T_2,\ \phi(t_1, t_2) = \text{true}\},$$

where ϕ can be a single relational condition (e.g., $t_1.a \leq t_2.b$) or a combination of multiple conditions (e.g., $t_1.p \leq t_2.t \wedge t_1.b \geq t_2.r$).

Oblivious Non-equi-join Algorithms. Let D be a relational database and Q be a non-equi-join query over relations $T_1, T_2 \subseteq D$ with predicate ϕ. Let Π be an algorithm that evaluates a non-equi-join query $Q(T_1, T_2, \phi)$ over a database $D = (T_1, T_2)$ and produces the result $\text{Result}(T_1, T_2, \phi)$. We say that Π is an oblivious non-equi-join algorithm if and only if, for any two databases $D_1 = (T_1^{(1)}, T_2^{(1)})$ and $D_2 = (T_1^{(2)}, T_2^{(2)})$ satisfying

$$|T_1^{(1)}| = |T_1^{(2)}|, \quad |T_2^{(1)}| = |T_2^{(2)}|, \quad |\text{Result}(T_1^{(1)}, T_2^{(1)}, \phi)| = |\text{Result}(T_1^{(2)}, T_2^{(2)}, \phi)|$$

the execution traces of Π on D_1 and D_2 are computationally indistinguishable. Formally, $\mathsf{Trace}_\Pi(D_1) \equiv \mathsf{Trace}_\Pi(D_2)$

where $\mathsf{Trace}_\Pi(D)$ denotes the sequence of memory accesses and control flows observable to an adversary during the execution of Π on D. $\equiv$ denotes the computational indistinguishability of two distributions. Intuitively, this means that an adversary, given access to the execution trace of Π, cannot infer any information about the contents of D beyond the sizes of the input relations and the output result.

3.2 System Model and Threat Model

System Model. The system consists of a client and a server. The client owns data and issues non-equi-join queries, while the server stores the database D and executes queries on behalf of the client within a TEE, which provides a hardware-isolated and secure environment to run the oblivious non-equi-join algorithm Π, protecting data and computation from the semi-honest server.

Threat Model. We assume a powerful adversary who controls the server outside the TEE, and is capable of observing memory access patterns, control flow, and I/O operations, but cannot access the contents of the TEE or tamper with its computation. The security goal is to ensure that such an adversary learns nothing about the database beyond the sizes of the input and outputs. In this work, we focus on protecting information leaked through memory access patterns, and we do not consider other types of side-channel attacks (e.g., cache-timing).

3.3 Preliminaries

Oblivious Sort. Given an input array of N elements, the oblivious sort algorithm outputs an array in a desired order while ensuring that the sequence of memory accesses is independent of the input values. The classical bitonic sort [4] is one of the earliest oblivious sorting networks with a time complexity of $O(N \log^2 N)$. Later studies proposed more efficient $O(N \log N)$ oblivious sorting algorithms [11,15,19], among which [11] and [15] incorporate parallel processing to achieve $O(N \log N/p)$ with p processing units. We adopt the algorithm from [11] in our implementation.

Oblivious Expand. Given an input array of N elements and a count array assigning a non-negative integer count to each element, the oblivious expand algorithm computes the starting position of each element in the output sequence based on its count and places the element at its designated position, while ensuring that the sequence of memory accesses is independent of the input values.

Krastnikov et al. [12] proposed an inherently sequential oblivious expand algorithm with a time complexity of $O(M \log M)$, where M denotes the output length. Mavrogiannakis et al. [14] later presented a parallel version that employs a fixed, data-independent access pattern, achieving $O(M \log M/p)$ with p processing units. We adopt the algorithm from [14] in our implementation.

Oblivious Aggregation Tree. Given an input array of length N and a tag array that already encodes the partitioning of the array, the oblivious aggregation tree algorithm computes prefix sums, suffix sums, full sums, or duplication for each partition based on this tag array, while ensuring that memory access patterns remain independent of the actual data values. Mavrogiannakis et al. [14] proposed the oblivious aggregation tree, an oblivious two-phase framework with $O(N)$ time complexity, reduced to $O(N/p)$ using p processing units. We extend it to a *Display* mode, which records the preceding elements for each array position through an *upstream* aggregation and a *downstream* propagation process.

4 Oblivious Order Counting and Encoding

In this section, we present our algorithm for oblivious order counting and encoding (OCCE), and analyze its efficiency and obliviousness properties.

4.1 Construction

Our algorithm supports two modes (*Unmark* and *Mark*) and two operations (*Smaller* and *Greater*). In the *Unmark* mode, OCCE counts, for each element, the number of preceding or succeeding elements depending on the operation, and records the resulting count as Cnt, while outputting the corresponding polynomial encoding of these elements, denoted as Trc. In the *Mark* mode, OCCE performs the same operations but only with respect to marked elements, computing the number and the polynomial encoding of preceding or succeeding marked elements for each element. In the implementation, we distinguish operations using superscript markers: no marker for *Unmark* mode, † for *Smaller* operation, and * for *Greater* operation. The overall workflow of OCCE, which computes, for each element, the number of preceding elements with smaller values, is illustrated in Fig. 1. The proposed algorithm is presented in Algorithm 1, whose construction is detailed as follows.

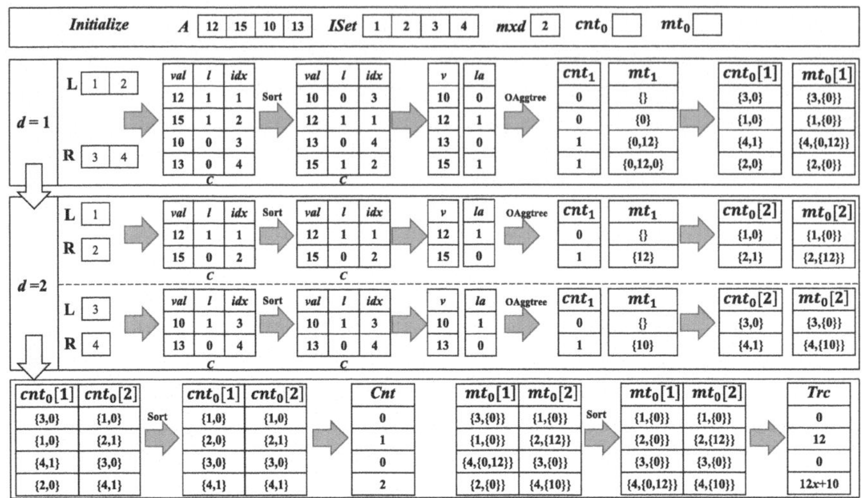

Fig. 1. Example of Oblivious Order Counting and Encoding (OCCE).

Detailed Implementation. We consider an array of length n with the *Unmark* type and the *Smaller* operation, based on which we provide a detailed description of the following construction.

Lines 1–9: The algorithm first initializes the index set $ISet = [1, n]$ and two empty sets cnt_0 and mt, which are combined into $Res = (cnt_0, mt)$ (lines 2–3). Then, it computes the maximum partition depth $mxd = \lceil \log_2 n \rceil$ and packs the parameters into $Args = (A, mxd, M, f)$ (lines 4–5). Next, `SubOCCE` recursively partitions the input and updates Res with intermediate statistics (line 6). Afterward, `AggCount` aggregates the results to obtain, for each element, the count of preceding smaller ones (Cnt) (line 7). Finally, `EPoly` encodes these counts into non-zero constant-coefficient polynomials to generate the encoded trace Trc (line 8), and the algorithm outputs (Cnt, Trc) (line 9).

Lines 10–47: In `SubOCCE`, the algorithm first initializes the parameters from $Args$, computes the size m of the index set I, its midpoint mid, and initializes an empty set P (lines 10–13). The index set I is then partitioned into two halves: $L = I[1, \ldots, mid]$ with label $l = 1$ and $R = I[mid + 1, \ldots, m]$ with label $l = 0$ (lines 14–19). For each index, the corresponding value in A is retrieved, and triples (val, l, idx) are stored in array C (lines 20–23). An oblivious sort is applied to C by val, and its components $C.val$ and $C.l$ are extracted as v and la (lines 24–30). `OAggtree` is invoked in *Prefix* mode to compute the prefix sum of la using B as the tag array, yielding cnt_1 (line 31), and in *Display* mode to process v with the same tags (line 33). The results are consolidated by la: for $la = 1$, t is set to 0 and trc to the initialized value vis; for $la = 0$, t and trc retain cnt_1 and trc, respectively. These are appended as (idx, t) to $Res.cnt_0[s + i - 1]$ and (idx, trc) to $Res.mt_0[s + i - 1]$ (lines 34–43). Finally, if the current depth d is smaller than the maximum depth, `SubOCCE` is recursively applied to the left and right subarrays, updating $Res.cnt_0$ and $Res.mt_0$ with results from subsequent splits (lines 44–47).

Lines 48–57: After computing $Res.cnt_0$ for each partition, the results are merged to obtain the final output $Result_1$. Specifically, $cnt_2[i]$ is retrieved and denoted as Ly_1 (line 51), which is then sorted by idx to align indices across partitions (line 52). Finally, the t-values are merged by idx to obtain the total count of preceding smaller elements for each index (lines 53–56).

Lines 58–74: After computing $Res.mt$ for each partition, the results are merged to obtain the final output $Result_2$. Specifically, $mt[i]$ is retrieved as Ly_2 (line 61) and sorted by idx to align indices (line 62). Then, the trc values are merged by idx, taking the union of corresponding sets across partitions (lines 65–66). For each index, the union is polynomially encoded: the $(p+1)$-th nonzero element is multiplied by $x^{cnt_3-(p+1)}$ and added to P_j, yielding the encoded polynomial (lines 67–72). For example, the union $\{0, 3, 0, 2, 0\}$ is encoded as $3x + 2$.

Lines 75–84: To decode a polynomial, it is evaluated at $x = 1$ to obtain $b = P(1)$ (line 76), and then $P(b + 1)$ is evaluated and interpreted in base $b + 1$ (line 77). Each digit in this base representation corresponds to an encoded element (lines 78–83). For instance, for $P(x) = 3x + 2$, we have $P(1) = 5$ and $P(6) = 20$, whose base-6 form $20 = 3 \cdot 6^1 + 2 \cdot 6^0$ reveals the elements 3 and 2.

4.2 Efficiency and Obliviosness

Efficiency. The algorithm consists of several subroutines. In `SubOCCE`, constructing the array C and subsequent `OAggtree` operations each require $O(n)$ time, while the oblivious sort on C costs $O(n \log n)$. Since `SubOCCE` is recursively invoked $\log n$ times, its total complexity is $O(n \log^2 n)$. Other procedures, including `AggCount` and `EPoly`, mainly involve $\log n$ rounds of oblivious sorting, leading to $O(n \log^2 n)$ complexity, while `DPoly` performs linear-time decoding with $O(n)$ complexity. Thus, the overall complexity is $O(n \log^2 n)$, which can be reduced to $O\big((n \log^2 n)/p\big)$ with p processors.

Obliviousness. Regarding obliviousness, the algorithm adopts a fixed partitioning and recursive strategy inspired by bitonic sorting. At each partitioning stage, all memory accesses follow a pre-defined manner with no data-dependent branches or loop conditions, ensuring that for any two inputs with the same length and operation type, the execution proceeds through exactly the same sequence of control-flow steps and memory accesses. In the final `AggCount`, `EPoly`, and `DPoly` operations, the entire sequences are scanned systematically, ensuring access patterns remain independent of the data values. Collectively, these designs guarantee full obliviousness.

Algorithm 1: Oblivious Order Counting and Encoding (OCCE)

Input: An array A with length n; A marked array M and marked flag f;

Output: Cnt: number of previous(next) elements smaller(greater) than A_i;
Trc: polynomial encoding of those smaller(greater) elements.

```
1  function OOCE⟨TYPE,OP⟩(A, M, f):
2      ISet ← [1,n], cnt0 ← ∅, mt0 ← ∅;
3      Res ← (cnt0, mt0);
4      mxd ← ⌈log2 n⌉;
5      Args ← (A, mxd, M, f);
6      SubOOCE(ISet, 1, 1, Args, Res);
7      Cnt ← AggCount(cnt0, mxd);
8      Trc ← EPoly(mt0, Cnt, mxd, n);
9      return Cnt, Trc;
10 function SubOOCE(I, d, s, Args, Res):
11     A ← Args.A, mxd ← Args.mxd;
12     M ← Args.M, f ← Args.f;
13     m ← |I|, mid ← ⌊m/2⌋, P ← ∅;
14     L ← I[1...mid];
15     R ← I[mid+1...m];
16     foreach x ∈ L ∪ R do in parallel
17         l† ← (x ∈ L) ? 1 : 0;
18         r* ← (x ∈ R) ? 1 : 0;
19         P ← P ∪ (x, l†, r*);
20     for (x, l†, r*) ∈ P do in parallel
21         idx ← x, val ← A[x];
22         src ← M[x];
23         C ← C ∪ (val, l†, r*, src, idx);
24     C ← OSort(C, val ↑);
25     B ← 0||1^(|C|−1), v ← C.val * l† * r*;
26     for i ← 1 to m do in parallel
27         val ← C[i].val;
28         v[i] ← (C[i].src ≠ f) ? val : 0;
29     la† ← C.l† * (C.src ≠ f);
30     ra* ← C.r* * (C.src ≠ f);
31     cnt1† ← OAggtree<Prefix,+>(la, B);
32     cnt1* ← OAggtree<Suffix,+>(ra, B);
33     vis ← OAggtree<Display,+>(v, B);
34     for i ← 1 to m do in parallel
35         bit† ← 1 − la[i], bit* ← 1 − ra[i];
36         t ← cnt1[i] * bit;
37         trc ← vis[i] * bit;
38         idx ← C[i].idx;
39         src ← C[i].src;
40         t ← (src ≠ f) * cnt1[i] * bit;
41         trc ← (src ≠ f) * vis[i] * bit;
42         Res.cnt0[d][s+i−1] ← {idx, t};
43         Res.mt0[d][s+i−1] ← {idx, trc};
44     if d < mxd then
45         s1 ← s, s2 ← s + mid;
46         SubOOCE(L, d+1, s1, Args, Res);
47         SubOOCE(R, d+1, s2, Args, Res);
48 function AggCount(cnt2, d):
49     Result1 ← ∅;
50     for i ← 1 to d do in parallel
51         Ly1 ← cnt2[i];
52         Ly1 ← OSort(Ly1.idx ↑);
53         for j ← 1 to |Ly1| do
54             idx ← Ly1[j].idx;
55             t ← Ly1[j].cnt;
56             Result1[idx] += t;
57     return Result1;
58 function EPoly(mt1, cnt3, d, n):
59     Result2 ← ∅;
60     for i ← 1 to d do in parallel
61         Ly2 ← mt1[i];
62         Ly2 ← OSort(Ly2.idx ↑);
63         mt1[i] ← Ly2;
64     for j ← 1 to n do in parallel
65         trace ← ∅;
66         trace ← ⋃_{k=1}^{d} mt1[k][j].trc;
67         exp ← cnt3[j] − 1;
68         Pj ← 0, p ← 0;
69         for t ← 1 to |trace| do
70             val ← trace[t];
71             Pj ← Pj + v * x^(exp−p);
72             p ← p + (val ≠ 0);
73         Result2[j] ← Pj;
74     return Result2;
75 function DPoly(Poly):
76     P(x) ← Poly, b ← P(1);
77     sum ← P(b+1);
78     dgts ← ∅;
79     Result3 ← ∅;
80     while sum > 0 do
81         dgts ← sum%(b+1);
82         sum ← ⌊sum/(b+1)⌋;
83         Result3 ← Result ∪ dgts;
84     return Result3;
```

5 Oblivious Non-equi-Join for Single Condition

5.1 Overview

In this section, we introduce an oblivious non-equi-join algorithm for single condition, e.g., $T_1.j \leq T_2.j$. While the scheme by Chang et al. [8] can be adapted to support such a join, it inherently operates in an iterative manner, where each iteration depends on the previous result. This sequential dependency prevents parallelization and thus significantly limits its scalability on large datasets. To address this limitation, we use multiple parallelizable oblivious primitives and eliminate inter-iteration dependencies. As a result, we develop the first parallelizable oblivious non-equi-join algorithm for single condition (SCNonEJoin).

5.2 Construction

The proposed construction is presented for the condition $T_1.j \leq T_2.j$ as an illustrative example. The procedure is given in Algorithm 2, and an example is illustrated in Fig. 2. The key steps are outlined below.
Lines 1–3: In the initialization phase, it assigns source labels to T_1 and T_2. Specifically, tuples in T_1 are labeled with 1 and tuples in T_2 are labeled with 2. The two labeled tables are then vertically concatenated to form table S. Finally, S is sorted in ascending order by $S.j$ and $S.tid$.
Lines 4–12: In the degree computation phase, the algorithm initializes f, B_1, and B_2 of length $|S|$, where $f[1] = 0$ and $f[i] = 1$ for $i = 2, \ldots, |S|$. The array f is set such that $f[1] = 0$ and $f[i] = 1$ for all $i = 2, \ldots, |S|$. The arrays B_1 and B_2 indicate the origin of each tuple in S: $B_1[i] = 1$ if $S[i].tid = 1$ and $B_2[i] = 1$ if $S[i].tid = 2$. Next, using f as the tag array, the `OAggtree` is applied to B_1 and B_2 under both *Prefix* and *Suffix* modes, producing the arrays g_1 and g_2, which represent the degree of each tuple in T_1 and T_2. Finally, it invokes oblivious sort and outputs T_1' and T_2', where each tuple is augmented with the corresponding degree information M_1 (for T_1) or M_2 (for T_2).

Algorithm 2: Oblivious Non-Equi-Join for Single Condition

Input: $T_1(j, d)$, $T_2(j, d)$;
Output: $Result(T_1.j, T_1.d, T_2.j, T_2.d)$

1 **function** $\texttt{SCNonEJoin}(T_1,\ T_2)$:
2 $\quad S \leftarrow T_1(j, d, 1) \cup T_2(j, d, 2)$;
3 $\quad S \leftarrow \texttt{OSort}(S,\ S.j \uparrow,\ S.tid \uparrow)$;
4 $\quad f \leftarrow 0 \mid\mid 1^{|S|-1}$;
5 $\quad$ **for** $i \leftarrow 1$ **to** $|S|$ **do in parallel**
6 $\quad\quad B_1[i] \leftarrow (S[i].tid == 1)$;
7 $\quad\quad B_2[i] \leftarrow (S[i].tid == 2)$;
8 $\quad g_1 \leftarrow \texttt{OAggtree}_{(\text{Prefix},+)}(B_1,\ f)$;
9 $\quad g_2 \leftarrow \texttt{OAggtree}_{(\text{Suffix},+)}(B_2,\ f)$;
10 $\quad S \leftarrow \texttt{OSort}(S||g_1||g_2,\ S.tid \uparrow)$;
11 $\quad T_1',\ M_1 \leftarrow \pi_{(j,d),g_2}(S[1...|T_1|])$;
12 $\quad T_2',\ M_2 \leftarrow \pi_{(j,d),g_1}(S[|T_1|+1...|S|])$;
13 $\quad T_1'' \leftarrow \texttt{OExpand}(T_1', M_1)$;
14 $\quad T_2'' \leftarrow \texttt{OExpand}(T_2', M_2)$;
15 $\quad C' \leftarrow \emptyset,\ C'' \leftarrow \emptyset$;
16 $\quad$ **for** $i \leftarrow 1$ **to** $|T_1''|$ **do in parallel**
17 $\quad\quad C' \leftarrow (T_1''[i] == T_1''[i-1])$;
18 $\quad\quad C'' \leftarrow (T_2''[i] == T_2''[i-1])$;
19 $\quad T_1'' \leftarrow \texttt{OAggtree}_{(\text{Prefix},\text{dup})}(T_1', C')$;
20 $\quad T_2'' \leftarrow \texttt{OAggtree}_{(\text{Prefix},\text{dup})}(T_2', C'')$;
21 $\quad S_1 \leftarrow \texttt{OSort}(T_1''.j \uparrow)$;
22 $\quad C \leftarrow 0^{|T_2''|}$;
23 $\quad$ **for** $i \leftarrow 1$ **to** $|T_2''|$ **do in parallel**
24 $\quad\quad e \leftarrow (T_2''[i].j == T_2''[j-1].j)$;
25 $\quad\quad f \leftarrow (T_2''[i].d == T_2''[j-1].d)$;
26 $\quad\quad C[i] \leftarrow e \wedge f$;
27 $\quad C \leftarrow \texttt{OAggtree}_{(\text{Prefix},+)}(C, C)$;
28 $\quad S_2 \leftarrow \texttt{OSort}(T_2'',\ C \uparrow)$;
29 $\quad Result \leftarrow (S_1.j, S_1.d, S_2.j, S_2.d)$;
30 $\quad$ **return** $Result$;

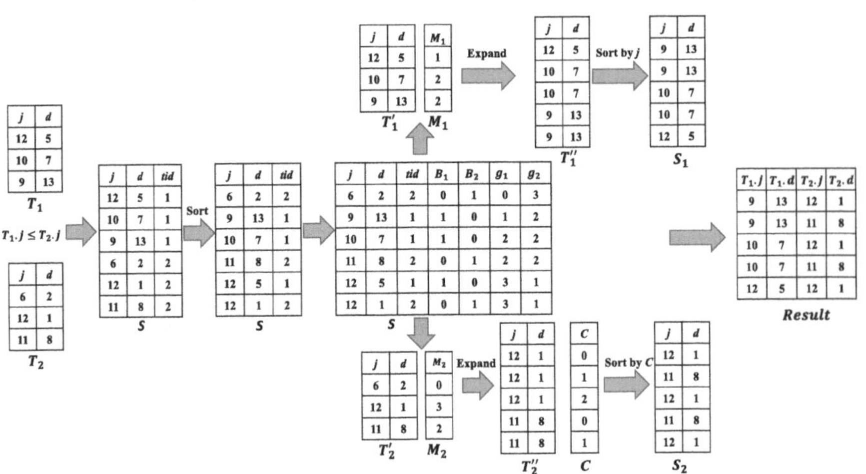

Fig. 2. Example of the SCNonEJoin algorithm for a single join condition.

Lines 13–20: In the expand phase, T_1' is expanded obliviously under the guidance of M_1, yielding T_1''. Similarly, T_2' is expanded obliviously according to the M_2, resulting in T_2''. Then, the expanded tuples T_1' and T_2' are marked using C' and C'', respectively, to indicate the positions of tuples within the same partition. Subsequently, it invokes `OAggtree` under *Prefix* mode and *Dup* operation, ensuring that the first element of each partition is replicated to all other positions within the corresponding partition.

Lines 21–28: In the align phase, T_1'' is sorted by the attribute j to generate S_1. Next, for T_2'', an array C is used to distinguish different partitions. Meanwhile, using C as the tag array, `OAggtree` is applied in the *Prefix* mode to compute the prefix sums over C. This operation not only differentiates the partitions but also assigns sequential labels within each partition. Consequently, sorting T_2'' according to C establishes a one-to-one correspondence between S_1 and S_2.
Lines 29–30: In the output phase, it outputs $(S_1.j, S_1.d, S_2.j, S_2.d)$ row by row and returns the final result.

5.3 Extended Methods

The proposed approach can naturally extend to other conditions. For example, for $T_1.j \geq T_2.j$, the tuples are first sorted in descending order of $T.j$. Next, the tuples from T_1 are then marked with 1, and computing the prefix sums yields the degrees for tuples in T_2. Subsequently, the tuples from T_2 are marked with 1 (and those from T_1 with 0), and computing the suffix sums yields the degrees for tuples in T_1. Finally, it expands and aligns using the respective degree values produce the resulting join output under this non-equi-join condition.

5.4 Efficiency

Let $n = |T_1| + |T_2|$ denote the total input size, and m denote the output size. The `OSort` operation is performed to compute degree, extract tuples from S and align S_1 and S_2, each with a complexity of $O(n \log n)$. The `OAggtree` executes prefix and suffix aggregation with a complexity of $O(n)$. The `OExpand` duplicates tuples in T_1' and T_2', with a complexity of $O(m \log m)$ $(m \geq n)$. Consequently, the overall complexity of the protocol is $O(m \log m)$. Since the protocol can be fully parallelized, its parallel complexity reduces to $O((m \log m)/p)$, where p is the number of processing units.

5.5 Obliviousness

Theorem 1. Let Π denote the proposed oblivious non-equi-join scheme for evaluating $Q(T_1, T_2, \phi)$ under the predicate $T_1.j \leq T_2.j$. Assume the availability of the `OSort`, `OAggtree`, and `OExpand` as defined in our construction. Then, for any two databases $D_1 = (T_1^{(1)}, T_2^{(1)})$ and $D_2 = (T_1^{(2)}, T_2^{(2)})$ satisfying

$$|T_1^{(1)}| = |T_1^{(2)}|, \quad |T_2^{(1)}| = |T_2^{(2)}|, \quad |\mathrm{Result}(T_1^{(1)}, T_2^{(1)}, \phi)| = |\mathrm{Result}(T_1^{(2)}, T_2^{(2)}, \phi)|,$$

the execution traces $\mathrm{Trace}_\Pi(D_1)$ and $\mathrm{Trace}_\Pi(D_2)$ are computationally indistinguishable.

Proof. The scheme Π executes the algorithm through a sequence of oblivious steps with fixed, data-independent memory access patterns. Tagging, concatenation, and array construction reveal only input sizes, while oblivious sorts and `OAggtree` access memory deterministically based on public parameters, and `OExpand` depends only on output cardinality. Thus, no step leaks information beyond input and output sizes, and the execution traces $\text{Trace}_{\Pi}(D_1)$ and $\text{Trace}_{\Pi}(D_2)$ are computationally indistinguishable, formally establishing obliviousness.

6 Oblivious Non-equi-Join for Multiple Conditions

6.1 Overview

In this section, we introduce an oblivious non-equi-join algorithm for multiple conditions, e.g., $T_1.j \leq T_2.j \wedge T_1.t \geq T_2.t$. Compared with the single-condition case, the presence of multiple conditions introduces two major challenges. First, computing degrees become substantially more complex. It can compute the degree for each condition independently and take the minimum. However, it can fail because some tuples satisfy only a subset of the conditions, resulting in inconsistent counts. Second, achieving correct alignment for all predicates simultaneously poses a significant challenge. This is mainly because tuples must maintain consistent correspondence across all predicate dimensions, while differing alignment boundaries among conditions are difficult. Third, it is possible to apply SCNonEJoin twice to filter the results of $T_1.j \leq T_2.j$ and $T_1.t \geq T_2.t$ separately, and then perform an equi-join on the two intermediate results. However, this approach leaks intermediate results and cannot ensure obliviousness. Padding the intermediate results to prevent leakage would incur an unacceptably high overhead. To address these issues, we propose the first parallelizable oblivious non-equi-join algorithm for multiple conditions (MCNonEJoin).

6.2 Construction

The proposed construction is presented for the condition $T_1.j \leq T_2.j \wedge T_1.t \geq T_2.t$ as an illustrative example. The procedure is given in Algorithm 3, and an example is illustrated in Fig. 3. The key steps are outlined below:

Lines 1–3: In the initialization phase, it assigns source labels to T_1 and T_2. Specifically, tuples in T_1 are labeled with 1 and tuples in T_2 are labeled with 2. The two labeled tables are then vertically concatenated to form table S. Finally, S is sorted in ascending order by $S.j$ and $S.tid$.

Lines 4–15: In the degree computation phase, the algorithm initializes f and C of length $|S|$, where $f[1] = 0$ and $f[i] = 1$ for $i = 2, \ldots, |S|$. The array C is set such that $C[i] = 1$ for all $i = 1, \ldots, |S|$. Next, `OAggtree` is invoked in *Prefix* mode, using f as the tag array to compute the prefix sums over C, which yields the indices of table S assigned to S.idx. The tuple identifiers S.tid are then copied to M. Subsequently, `OCCE` is invoked in *Prefix* mode, the *Greater* and *Smaller* operations are applied to $(A, M, 1)$ and $(A, M, 2)$, respectively, resulting in (g_1, trc_1) and (g_2, trc_2). Here, g_1 denotes, for each tuple t in T_1, the number of tuples in T_2 that are larger than t, and trc_1 represents their corresponding polynomial encodings; similarly, g_2 denotes, for each tuple j in T_2, the number of tuples in T_1 that are smaller than j, with trc_2 encoding these tuples. The arrays g_1, g_2, and trc_2 are then merged into S, which is subsequently re-sorted by ascending S_1.tid and descending $S.t$. Finally, oblivious sorting is applied to obtain the tuples (T_1', M_1) and $(T_2', M_2, \text{trc}_3)$.

Algorithm 3: Oblivious Non-Equi-Join for Multiple Conditions

Input: $T_1(j,t,d)$, $T_2(j,t,d)$;
Output: $Result(T_1.j, T_1.t, T_1.d, T_2.j, T_2.t, T_2.d)$

1 **function** MCNonEJoin(T_1, T_2):
2 $\quad S \leftarrow T_1(j,t,d,1) \cup T_2(j,t,d,2)$;
3 $\quad S \leftarrow$ OSort$(S, S.t \downarrow, S.tid \uparrow)$;
4 $\quad f \leftarrow 0 \,||\, 1^{|S|-1},\ C \leftarrow 1^{|S|}$;
5 $\quad S.idx \leftarrow$ OAggtree$_{(\text{Prefix},+)}(C,\ f)$;
6 $\quad S \leftarrow$ OSort$(S, S.j \uparrow, S.tid \uparrow)$;
7 $\quad A \leftarrow S.idx,\ M \leftarrow S.tid$;
8 $\quad g_1, trc_1 \leftarrow$ OOCE$_{(Mark,\geq)}(A, M, 2)$;
9 $\quad g_2, trc_2 \leftarrow$ OOCE$_{(Mark,\leq)}(A, M, 1)$;
10 $\quad S_1 \leftarrow S||g_1||g_2||trc_2$;
11 $\quad S_2 \leftarrow$ OSort$(S_1, S_1.tid \uparrow, S_1.t \downarrow)$;
12 $\quad T_1', M_1 \leftarrow \pi_{(j,t,d),g_1}(S_2[1...|T_1|])$;
13 $\quad T_2' \leftarrow \pi_{(j,t,d)}(S_2[|T_1|+1...|S|])$;
14 $\quad M_2 \leftarrow \pi_{g_2}(S_2[|T_1|+1...|S|])$;
15 $\quad trc_3 \leftarrow \pi_{trc_2}(S_2[|T_1|+1...|S|])$;
16 $\quad T_1'' \leftarrow$ OExpand(T_1', M_1);
17 $\quad T_2'' \leftarrow$ OExpand(T_2', M_2);
18 $\quad C' \leftarrow \emptyset,\ C'' \leftarrow \emptyset$;
19 $\quad$ **for** $i \leftarrow 1$ **to** $|T_1''|$ **do in parallel**
20 $\quad\quad C' \leftarrow (T_1''[i] == T_1''[i-1])$;
21 $\quad\quad C'' \leftarrow (T_2''[i] == T_2''[i-1])$;
22 $\quad T_1'' \leftarrow$ OAggtree$_{(\text{Prefix},\text{dup})}(T_1', C')$;
23 $\quad T_2'' \leftarrow$ OAggtree$_{(\text{Prefix},\text{dup})}(T_2', C'')$;
24 $\quad Loc \leftarrow \emptyset$;
25 $\quad$ **for** $i \leftarrow 1$ **to** $|trc_3|$ **do**
26 $\quad\quad Loc \leftarrow Loc \cup$ DPoly$(trc_3[i])$;
27 $\quad S_3 \leftarrow$ OSort$(T_2'', Loc \uparrow)$;
28 $\quad Result \leftarrow (T_1''.(j,t,d), S_3.(j,t,d))$;
29 $\quad$ **return** $Result$;

Lines 16–23: In the expand phase, T_1' is expanded obliviously under the guidance of M_1, yielding T_1''. Similarly, T_2' is expanded obliviously according to the M_2, resulting in T_2''. Then, the expanded tuples T_1' and T_2' are marked using C' and C'', respectively, to indicate the positions of tuples within the same partition. Subsequently, it invokes OAggtree under *Prefix* mode and *Dup* operation, ensuring that the first element of each partition is replicated to all other positions within the corresponding partition to construct T_1'' and T_2''.
Lines 21–28: In the align phase, the polynomial decoding of trc_3 for T_2'' is performed, which effectively inserts the tuples sequentially into the expanded partitions to obtain the corresponding locations, denoted by T_2''.Loc. Consequently, sorting T_2'' according to T_2''.Loc establishes a one-to-one correspondence between S_1 and S_2.
Lines 29–30: In the output phase, it outputs $(T_1''.j, T_1''.t, T_1''.d, S_3.j, S_3.t, S_3.d)$ row by row and returns the final result.

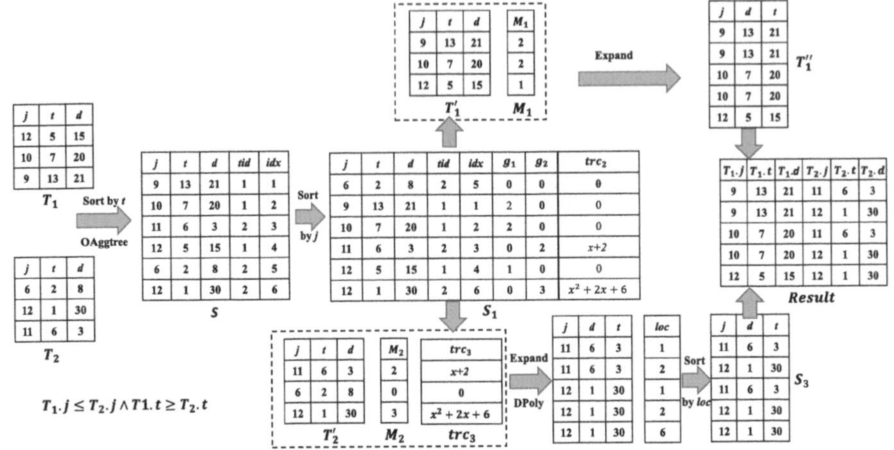

Fig. 3. Example of the MCNonEJoin algorithm for multiple join conditions.

6.3 Extended Methods

The proposed approach naturally generalizes to any condition of the form $T_1.j$ ($\leq$ *or* $\geq$) $T_2.j \wedge T_1.t$ ($\leq$ *or* $\geq$) $T_2.t$. Specifically, we first sort all tuples according to $T.t$: in ascending order for $\leq$, and descending order for $\geq$, while ensuring that for tuples with equal $T.t$ values, T_1 always precedes T_2. After that, a secondary sort is applied on $T.j$ following the same ascending/descending rule. Once the tuples are sorted in a fixed order, the OCCE routine is invoked. In this step, T_1 finds all matching later larger T_2 tuples, while T_2 finds all matching earlier smaller T_1 tuples. By keeping this order, the scheme finds all matching pairs correctly and works for all conditions.

6.4 Efficiency

Let $n = |T_1| + |T_2|$ denote the total input size and m denote the output size. The OSort is invoked to compute degree, extract tuples from S, align S_1 and S_2, and reorder the final result, each incurring a complexity of $O(n \log n)$. The OAggtree performs aggregation and duplication with linear complexity $O(n)$. The OCCE in invoked to get preceding elements that are either smaller than it, and outputs the corresponding sets of these elements, with a complexity of $O(n \log^2 n)$. The OExpand duplicates tuples in T_1' and T_2' with complexity $O(m \log m)$. Summing all components, the protocol achieves an overall complexity of $O(n \log^2 n)$. Since all primitives, including sorting, aggregation, and conditional expansion, are fully parallelizable, the parallel complexity reduces to $O((n \log^2 n)/p)$, where p denotes the number of processing units.

6.5 Obliviousness

Theorem 2. Let Π_1 denote the proposed oblivious non-equi-join scheme for evaluating $Q(T_1, T_2, \phi)$ under the predicate $T_1.j \leq T_2.j \wedge T_1.t \geq T_2.t$. Assume the availability of the `OSort`, `OAggtree`, `OCCE`, and `OExpand` as defined in our construction. Then, for any two databases $D_1 = (T_1^{(1)}, T_2^{(1)})$ and $D_2 = (T_1^{(2)}, T_2^{(2)})$ satisfying

$$|T_1^{(1)}| = |T_1^{(2)}|, \quad |T_2^{(1)}| = |T_2^{(2)}|, \quad |\text{Result}(T_1^{(1)}, T_2^{(1)}, \phi)| = |\text{Result}(T_1^{(2)}, T_2^{(2)}, \phi)|,$$

the execution traces $\text{Trace}_{\Pi_1}(D_1)$ and $\text{Trace}_{\Pi_1}(D_2)$ are computationally indistinguishable.

Proof. The obliviousness proof of Π_1 follows the same reasoning as in Theorem **1**, where all operations exhibit deterministic, data-independent access patterns. The difference lies in the introduction of additional primitives, such as `OCCE` and `DPoly`, whose behaviors depend only on public parameters and output sizes. Therefore, Π_1 preserves the same obliviousness guarantee, and $\text{Trace}_{\Pi_1}(D_1)$ and $\text{Trace}_{\Pi_1}(D_2)$ remain computationally indistinguishable.

7 Experiments

In this section, we perform a series of comprehensive experiments to evaluate the effectiveness and efficiency of our proposed schemes. We present the experimental setup, datasets, and results in detail to provide a clear and reproducible validation of our method.

7.1 Experiments Setup and Datasets

All experiments are conducted on a server equipped with an Intel Xeon Scalable 8369B processor featuring 16 physical cores and 128 GB of RAM. The system runs Ubuntu 22.04 and supports Intel SGX for secure computation, with 64 GB of trusted memory allocated for enclave execution.

To ensure a comprehensive comparison, we implement several baseline schemes based on the work of Chang [8]. The first baseline, CXWLS, is a band-join approach that we extend to support the oblivious non-equi-join for a single condition. Since the original CXWLS lacks parallelism, we further optimize it by introducing parallel execution, resulting in an improved version denoted as CXWLS1+. For multi-condition joins, we extend CXWLS1+ to form CXWLS2+, where it is executed twice—once for each predicate—to produce the intermediate results R_1 and R_2. These results are then combined using the OBLIVIATOR join framework [14] to obtain the final output. However, CXWLS2+ does not conceal the sizes of intermediate join results, potentially leaking information about the data distribution. To prevent this, we pad all intermediate results to their maximum possible size before applying the OBLIVIATOR join, thereby eliminating size leakage and producing a secure variant referred to as CXWLS3+.

For performance evaluation, we evaluate our schemes on the TPC-C dataset, whose scale is determined by the number of entries in the `warehouse` table, denoted as the scale factor c. As shown in Fig. 4, we design six SQL queries in total: SQL_1–SQL_3 correspond to single-condition joins, while SQL_4–SQL_6 correspond to multi-condition joins.

SQL_1: SELECT o_id, d_next_o_id FROM
orders o JOIN district d ON o.o_id ≤ d.d_next_o_id;

SQL_2: SELECT no_o_id, d_next_o_id FROM
new_order n JOIN district d ON n.no_o_id ≤ d.d_next_o_id;

SQL_3: SELECT s_quantity, d_next_o_id FROM
stock s JOIN district d ON s.s_quantity ≤ d.d_next_o_id;

SQL4: SELECT o.o_id, o.o_d_id, d.d_id, d.d_next_o_id FROM
orders o, district d WHERE o.o_id ≤ d.d_next_o_id AND o.o_d_id ≥ d.d_id;

SQL5: SELECT d.d_id, d.d_next_o_id, s.s_w_id, s.s_i_id FROM
district d, stock s WHERE s.s_i_id ≤ d.d_next_o_id AND s.s_w_id ≥ d.d_w_id;

SQL6: SELECT ol.ol_number, ol.ol_d_id, d.d_id, d.d_next_o_id FROM
order_line ol, district d WHERE ol.ol_number ≤ d.d_next_o_id AND ol.ol_d_id ≥ d.d_id;

Fig. 4. SQL Query.

7.2 Performance of SCNonEJoin Scheme

We evaluate the proposed SCNonEJoin scheme against baseline methods CXWLS and CXWLS1+ on three single-condition queries (SQL_1–SQL_3) under the TPC-C benchmark. The experiments analyze runtime performance and scalability with varying scale factors and thread counts.

Different Scale Factors. As shown in Fig. 5a –Fig. 5c, SCNonEJoin consistently outperforms CXWLS1+ and CXWLS under varying scale factors. For SQL_1, when c increases from 2 to 4, SCNonEJoin's runtime grows from 2,254 ms to 8,862 ms, compared to 2,784–10,490 ms for CXWLS1+ and 9,207–40,834 ms for CXWLS, yielding 1.18–1.24× and 4.08–4.61× speedups, respectively. For SQL_2, SCNonEJoin completes in 695–2,532 ms, versus 849–3,011 ms for CXWLS1+ and 2,409–10,433 ms for CXWLS, achieving 1.19–1.22× and 3.47–4.12× improvements. A similar trend holds for SQL_3, where runtimes increase from 6,798 ms to 26,370 ms for SCNonEJoin, 8,503–31,732 ms for CXWLS1+, and 29,228–123,542 ms for CXWLS, leading to 1.19–1.25× and 4.30–4.74× gains. Overall, SCNonEJoin consistently outperforms both baselines and scales efficiently with increasing data size.

Different Threads. We evaluate the parallel scalability of SCNonEJoin under varying thread counts, as shown in Fig. 5d. For SQL_1, when the number of threads increases from 1 to 16, the runtime decreases from 26,117 ms to 12,373 ms at $c = 5$, achieving a 2.1× speedup; from 107,814 ms to 49,907 ms at $c = 10$, achieving a 2.2× improvement; and from 337,970 ms to 169,686 ms at $c = 15$, achieving a 2.0× acceleration. These results demonstrate that SCNonEJoin can be efficiently parallelized, achieving runtime reduction with increasing threads.

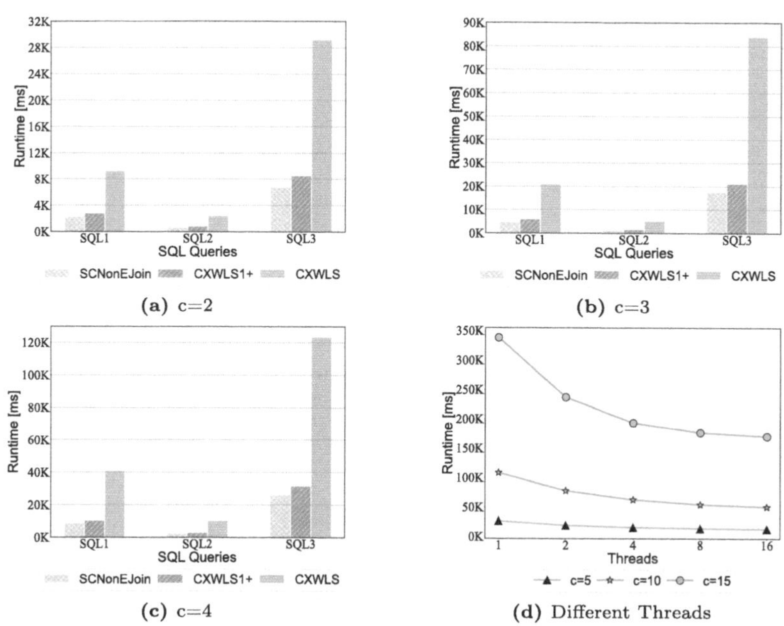

Fig. 5. Performance of SCNonEJoin scheme under various settings.

7.3 Performance of MCNonEJoin Scheme

We conduct extensive experiments on multi-condition queries (SQL_4-SQL_6) to evaluate the proposed MCNonEJoin scheme against baseline methods CXWLS2+ and CXWLS3+. The evaluation focuses on runtime efficiency and scalability under different data scales and thread counts.

Different Scale Factor. As shown in Fig. 6a –Fig. 6c, MCNonEJoin consistently outperforms CXWLS2+ and CXWLS3+ across all scale factors. For SQL_4, when c increases from 2 to 4, the runtime of MCNonEJoin grows from 6,028 ms to 17,517 ms, compared with 9,917–36,958 ms for CXWLS2+ and 10,877–41,256 ms for CXWLS3+, achieving 1.65–2.11× and 1.80–2.36× speedups. For SQL_5, MCNonEJoin runs in 14,151–33,084 ms versus 14,788–49,541 ms for

CXWLS2+ and 19,437–66,476 ms for CXWLS3+, yielding 1.02–1.50× and 1.37–2.01× improvements. For SQL_6, MCNonEJoin completes in 72,446–193,944 ms as c increases from 2 to 4, while CXWLS2+ and CXWLS3+ require 98,256–393,566 ms and 106,949–421,917 ms, respectively, yielding 1.36–2.04× and 1.48–2.18× performance improvements. Overall, MCNonEJoin achieves substantial runtime reductions and scales more efficiently than both baselines.

Different Threads. We evaluate the parallel efficiency of MCNonEJoin under scale factors c = 5, 10, and 15, varying the number of threads from 1 to 16. As shown in Fig. 6d, the runtime of SQL_4 decreases steadily with increasing threads—from 32,299 ms to 22,439 ms at $c = 5$, from 111,848 ms to 69,075 ms at $c = 10$, and from 347,966 ms to 168,879 ms at $c = 15$. These results confirm that MCNonEJoin scales efficiently with parallelism, achieving consistent runtime reductions as both data size and thread count increase.

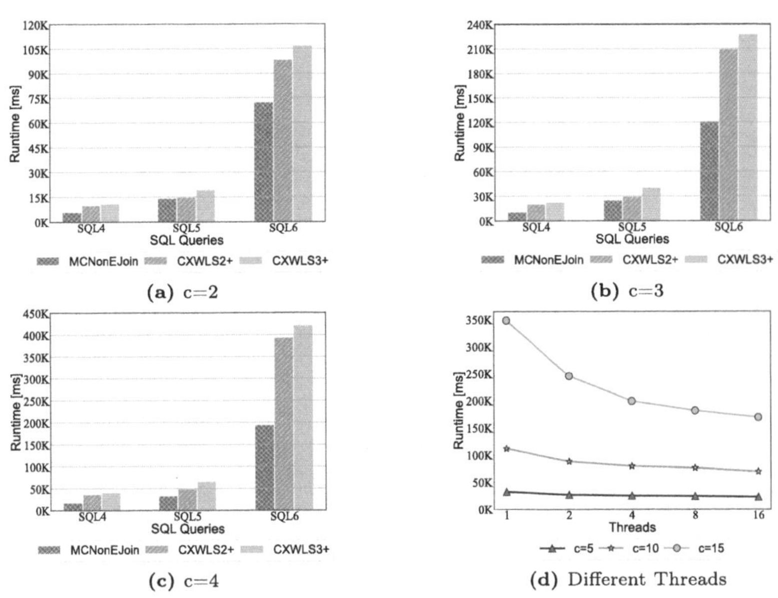

Fig. 6. Performance of MCNonEJoin scheme under various settings.

8 Conclusion

In this paper, we propose parallelizable oblivious non-equi-join algorithms for both single condition and multiple conditions, which enable secure execution in TEEs with strong privacy protection and practical efficiency. In future work, we will explore various parallel oblivious query operators to further advance practical privacy-preserving database systems.

Acknowledgments. This work is funded by the Open Foundation of Key Laboratory of Cyberspace Security, Ministry of Education of China and Henan Key Laboratory of Cyberspace Situation Awareness (No.KLCS20240103), the National Nature Science Foundation of China under Grants (No. 62402360), the China National Postdoctoral Program for Innovative Talents (No. BX20240274), the Shaanxi Province Postdoctoral Program for Innovative Talents (No. 2024SQBC008), and the Fundamental Research Funds for the Central Universities, China (No. XJSJ24065).

References

1. Agrawal, R., Asonov, D., Kantarcioglu, M., Li, Y.: Sovereign joins. In: 22nd International Conference on Data Engineering, p. 26 (2006)
2. Antonopoulos, P., et al.: Azure SQL database always encrypted. In: Proceedings of the 2020 International Conference on Management of Data, pp. 1511–1525 (2020)
3. Arasu, A., Kaushik, R.: Oblivious query processing. arXiv preprint arXiv:1312.4012 (2013)
4. Batcher, K.E.: Sorting networks and their applications. In: Proceedings of the April 30–May 2, 1968, Spring Joint Computer Conference, pp. 307–314 (1968)
5. Bater, J., Elliott, G., Eggen, C., Goel, S., Kho, A., Rogers, J.: smcql: secure querying for federated databases. Proc. VLDB Endowment, 673–68 (2017)
6. Brasser, F., Müller, U., Dmitrienko, A., Kostiainen, K., Capkun, S., Sadeghi, A.R.: Software grand exposure:{SGX} cache attacks are practical. In: 11th USENIX Workshop on Offensive Technologies (2017)
7. Chang, Z., Xie, D., Wang, S., Li, F.: Towards practical oblivious join. In: Proceedings of the 2022 International Conference on Management of Data, pp. 803–817 (2022)
8. Chang, Z., Xie, D., Wang, S., Li, F., Shen, Y.: Towards practical oblivious join processing. IEEE Trans. Knowl. Data Eng. 1829–1842 (2023)
9. Eskandarian, S., Zaharia, M.: Oblidb: Oblivious query processing for secure databases. Proc. VLDB Endowment, 169–183 (2019)
10. GoLDwAssER, S., Micali, S.: Probabilistic encryption (1984)
11. Gu, T., Wang, Y., Chen, B., Tinoco, A., Shi, E., Yi, K.: Efficient oblivious sorting and shuffling for hardware enclaves. Cryptology ePrint Archive (2023)
12. Krastnikov, S., Kerschbaum, F., Stebila, D.: Efficient oblivious database joins. Proc. VLDB Endowment, 2132–2145 (2020)
13. Li, Y., Chen, M.: Privacy preserving joins. In: 2008 IEEE 24th International Conference on Data Engineering, pp. 1352–1354 (2008)
14. Mavrogiannakis, A., Wang, X., Demertzis, I., Papadopoulos, D., Garofalakis, M.: Obliviator: oblivious parallel joins and other operators in shared memory environments. In 34th USENIX Security Symposium, pp. 8521–8540 (2025)
15. Ngai, N., Demertzis, I., Chamani, J.G., Papadopoulos, D.: Distributed & scalable oblivious sorting and shuffling. In: 2024 IEEE Symposium on Security and Privacy, pp. 4277–4295 (2024)
16. Priebe, C., Vaswani, K., Costa, M.: Enclavedb: a secure database using sgx. In: 2018 IEEE Symposium on Security and Privacy, pp. 264–278 (2018)
17. Qin, L., Jayaram, R., Shi, E., Song, Z., Zhuo, D., Chu, S.: Adore: Differentially oblivious relational database operators. Proc. VLDB Endowment, 842–855 (2022)

18. Qiu, L., Kellaris, G., Mamoulis, N., Nissim, K., Kollios, G.: Doquet: differentially oblivious range and join queries with private data structures. Proc. VLDB Endowment, 4160–4173 (2023)
19. Shi, E.: Path oblivious heap: Optimal and practical oblivious priority queue. In: 2020 IEEE Symposium on Security and Privacy, pp. 842–858 (2020)
20. Wang, J., Chen, X., Huang, X., You, I., Xiang, Y.: Verifiable auditing for outsourced database in cloud computing. IEEE Trans. Comput. 3293–3303 (2015)
21. Wang, S., et al.: Operon: an encrypted database for ownership-preserving data management. Proc. VLDB Endowment, 3332–3345 (2022)
22. Wei, R.: Oblivious multi-way band joins: an efficient algorithm for secure range queries (2025)
23. Zheng, W., Dave, A., Beekman, J.G., Popa, R.A., Gonzalez, J.E., Stoica, I.: Opaque: an oblivious and encrypted distributed analytics platform. In: 14th USENIX Symposium on Networked Systems Design and Implementation, pp. 283–298 (2017)

Blockchain-Based Anonymous Aggregate Signature Scheme for Medical Internet of Things

Lifeng Zhou[1(✉)], Xinchun Yin[2,3], Su Jia[1], and Hongbin Zhou[1]

[1] School of Digitization and Microelectronics, Shazhou Professional Institute of Technology, Suzhou 215600, China
lfengzhou@outlook.com

[2] College of Guangling, Yangzhou University, Yangzhou 225000, China
xcyin@yzu.edu.cn

[3] Party Committee Department, Jiangxi University of Science and Technology, Nanchang 330200, China

Abstract. Medical Internet of Things (MIoT), also known as smart healthcare or Medical 4.0, typically refers to intelligent devices such as medical equipment, wearable sensors, and remote monitoring instruments connected to healthcare applications. These devices are used to collect, transmit, exchange, and analyze health data, thereby improving the quality, efficiency, and safety of medical services. However, these medical data are often vulnerable to security threats during transmission. To safeguard secure communication and privacy preservation in MIoT, several certificateless aggregate signature (CLAS) schemes have been introduced. Nevertheless, most of these schemes depend on a centralized key generation center (KGC) and remain susceptible to coalition attacks, KGC compromise attacks, and distributed denial-of-service (DDoS) attacks. In this paper, we design a blockchain-based certificateless anonymous aggregate signature (CLAAS) scheme for MIOT and demonstrate that it can achieve complete decentralization of entities, thereby resisting KGC compromised attacks. This blockchain-based CLAAS scheme has strong robustness, which can resist DDoS attacks and coalition attacks launched by several medical sensor nodes. The proposed scheme can safeguard provable security in the random oracle model and no longer rely on secure channels to obtain the partial private key. Furthermore, performance evaluation reveals that the decentralized CLAAS scheme outperforms existing schemes in terms of both communication and computational overhead, highlighting its strong practical applicability in MIoT systems.

L. Zhou—Led the project, designed the scheme, and developed the theoretical framework.

X. Yin—Performed the experiments and analyzed the data.

S. Jia—Conducted the collection and organization of extensive literature.

H. Zhou—Did numerous tests and provided a lot of suggestions.

Y. Xiang and J. Shen (Eds.): ML4CS 2025, LNCS 16456, pp. 105–123, 2026.
https://doi.org/10.1007/978-981-95-7820-7_7

Keywords: Medical Internet of Things (MIoT) · Certificateless anonymous aggregate signature (CLAAS) · Blockchain · Coalition attacks · KGC compromise attacks

1 Introduction

With the maturity and popularization of the Internet of Things and sensor technology, the Medical Internet of Things (MIoT) has brought tremendous help to human health. Medical sensor nodes in the MIoT environment can monitor patients' heart rate, blood oxygen, blood pressure, emotions, and other parameters in real-time [1–4]. However, medical data in MIoT is transmitted through public channels, and adversaries can easily eavesdrop, tamper with, and forge medical data [5,6]. Hence, how to safeguard secure communication and privacy protection has become an significant topic for MIoT.

The aggregate signature (AS) is considered as one of the most effective technologies to solve the above hot topic. It can provide identity authentication, data integrity, and non-repudiation. In recent years, several AS schemes [7–9] have been proposed by scholars and the AS technology was widely employed in various fields. In 2007, Gong *et al.* [10] applied AS technology to certificateless public key cryptography and put forward the first certificateless AS (CLAS) scheme. Shortly after, Zhang *et al.* [11] improved Gong *et al.*'s scheme. Unfortunately, Shim *et al.* [12] defined "coalition attacks" and asserted that Zhang *et al.*'s improved scheme lacks ability to resist this type of attacks. As the CLAS technology matures, it has been expanded to MIoT environments to address security and privacy issues. In 2018, Kumar *et al.* [13] formulated a CLAS scheme to safeguard the security of medical data during transmission for MIoT. Unfortunately, Wu *et al.* [14] asserted that Kumar *et al.*'s scheme is vulnerable to malicious medical server attacks. To cater for the requirements of high efficiency and security, the claim by Liu *et al.* [15] that their certificateless batch verification scheme ensures secure medical data authentication was later challenged by Zhang *et al.* [16], who pointed out its vulnerabilities to malicious participants and data centers.

Before long, several pairing-free CLAS schemes [17–19] were put forward in MIoT. However, almost all of the CLAS schemes used in MIoT cannot resist coalition attacks. Since an aggregate signature is formed by combining multiple individual signatures, the aggregation process itself does not inherently verify the validity of each component [20]. Malicious medical sensor nodes can exploit the aggregation process to generate a valid aggregate signature from invalid individual signatures. Hence, doctors may receive incorrect data and make erroneous diagnoses, thereby posing a significant threat to patient safety. Furthermore, most CLAS schemes depend on a single key generation center (KGC), which represents a systemic vulnerability. Once the only KGC suffers invasion, adversaries can steal the system master key and forge a signature to deceive the verifier, which may destroy the security of the entire medical system. Distributed denial of service (DDoS) attack is one of the most harmful attacking methods in MIoT environments. This type of attack can initiate a large number of requests to the medical server simultaneously and consume its resources on a large scale, ultimately paralyzing the medical server. Furthermore, the susceptibility of existing CLAS schemes [15–19] to KGC compromise and DDoS attacks poses a significant challenge, ultimately hindering their real-world deployment in MIoT. In addition, if the patient suffers from a specific disease and wants his medical data to be obtained by the attending doctor, these schemes [13–19] would no longer be suitable for MIoT environments.

Deng et al. [21] recently introduced a certificateless designated verifier anonymous aggregate signature (CLAAS) scheme for the MIoT, designed to restrict medical data access to designated doctors. In their scheme, the authors asserted its resilience against forgery attacks on any message. However, Deng *et al.*'s [21] scheme cannot resist coalition attacks, as attackers can deceive validators by generating invalid aggregate signatures through the cancellation of forged individual signature elements. Consequently, we devise a blockchain-based CLAAS scheme to solve this type of security flaw. Our contributions are as follows.

- We invent a CLAAS scheme that can protect the privacy of patients by using pseudonyms as identity symbols during communication. This approach ensures that even if attackers eavesdrop on the transmitted data, they cannot use pseudonyms to trace their real identity.
- We utilize the smart contract to take place of the centralized KGC and devise a decentralized CLAAS scheme that can resist coalition attacks, KGC compromised attacks, and DDoS attacks. In addition, we demonstrate that our scheme does not require secure channels to obtain the partial private key, which greatly improves the robustness of our CLAAS scheme.
- On the basis of Type I and Type II adversaries, the third type of adversary is put forward which can launch coalition attacks in MIoT. Moreover, we prove that the blockchain-based CLAAS scheme is secure against attacks from these three types of adversaries.
- The included performance evaluation indicates that our CLAAS scheme has higher efficiency than other schemes discussed in the literatures [13,15,21–23]. Furthermore, we illustrate that the proposed scheme achieves unforgeability, anonymity, identity authentication, and traceability, which satisfies all security requirements of MIoT.

2 Preliminaries

2.1 Intractable Problems

Elliptic Curve Discrete Logarithm Problem (ECDLP): G is a group with prime q and P is a generator of G. Given $P, Q \in G$, $Q = aP$, it is difficult to figure out $a \in Z_q^*$.

Computational Diffie-Hellman Problem (CDHP): G is a group with prime q and P is a generator of G. Given $aP, bP \in G$, it is difficult to figure out $abP \in G$, where $a, b \in Z_q^*$.

2.2 Blockchain Technology

Blockchain technology maintains a tamper-resistant record through a chain of blocks, where each block is composed of a header and a body. The header, containing a previous block hash, a Merkle tree (which cryptographically secures the transactions), a timestamp, and a nonce, establishes the chain's integrity. The transaction data within the block body is individually signed to ensure its validity. This structure, combined with a distributed consensus protocol for data updates and robust cryptography, ensures the security of all data operations.

The smart contract is a computer protocol designed to automate agreement execution. Its lifecycle comprises three phases: generation, release, and execution [24]. The concrete structure is shown in Fig. 1. The smart contract not only processes information efficiently but also ensures that both parties to the contract can enforce the contract without a third-party authority, avoiding the appearance of the breach of contract. The smart contract is characterized by their high formulation efficiency, low maintenance costs, and execution accuracy, which collectively contribute to their widespread adoption in various industries.

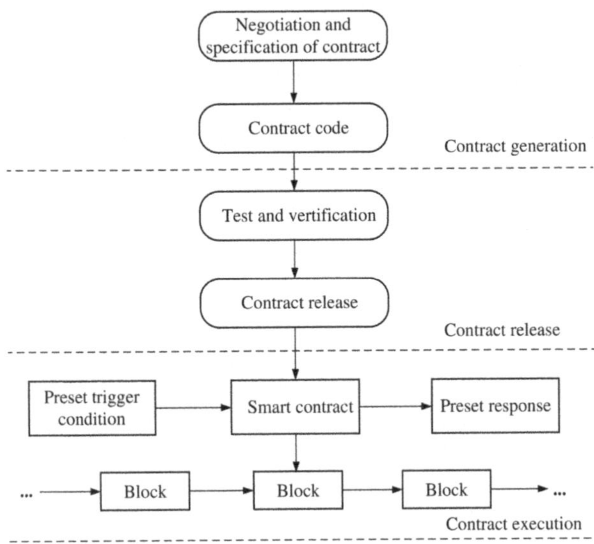

Fig. 1. The whole life cycle of the smart contract.

2.3 System Model of Our CLAAS Scheme

As illustrated in Fig. 2, the proposed system model features five interacting entities: Sensor Nodes (SN_i), Smart Contract (SC), Signature Aggregator (SA), Designated Doctor (DD), and Blockchain.

- SN_i: SN_i is employed to collect medical data of patients. SN_i calculates cryptographic parameters to generate a signature and transmits it to SA.

- SC: SC is responsible for generating both the system parameters and the partial private key of SN_i. Then, SC transmits them to SN_i.
- SA: SA polymerizes single signatures to the aggregate signature(AS) and transmits the AS to DD.
- DD: DD receives AS from SA. Subsequently, DD verifies the legality of AS by its private key.
- Blockchain: Blockchain is responsible for storing valid medical data.

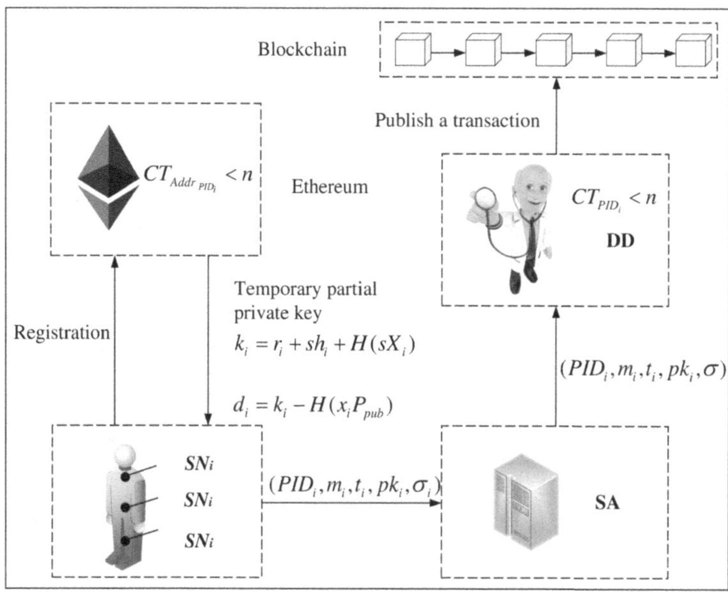

Fig. 2. The system model of our CLAAS scheme.

2.4 Security Model of Our CLAAS Scheme

In the traditional cryptographic models, two types of adversaries are typically considered [25]. To demonstrate the resilience of our CLAAS scheme against coalition attacks, we devise a third type of adversary A_3 in our model. A_1: This adversary is assumed to be capable of replacing the public key of SN_i, but it lacks the capability to retrieve the master key s. A_2: This adversary is assumed to have access to the master key s but is restricted from replacing public keys. A_3: This adversary is assumed to have access to forge invalid AS and pass verification by exchanging signature information.

3 Our Blockchain-Based CLAAS Scheme

In this section, we use the smart contract to devise a blockchain-based CLAAS scheme. The symbols of blockchain-based CLAAS scheme are shown in Table 1.

For ease of reading, the details of the smart contract are described in Algorithm 1. To resist coalition attacks, we employ a collision-resistant hash function in the *Generate-AS* algorithm. This ensures that if any malicious SN_i alters the composition of single signatures, the resulting hash value will change, thus causing the aggregate signature verification to fail. Besides, we demonstrate that our scheme is able to withstand KGC compromised attacks and DDoS attacks. Detailed algorithms are displayed in Fig. 3 and described as follows:

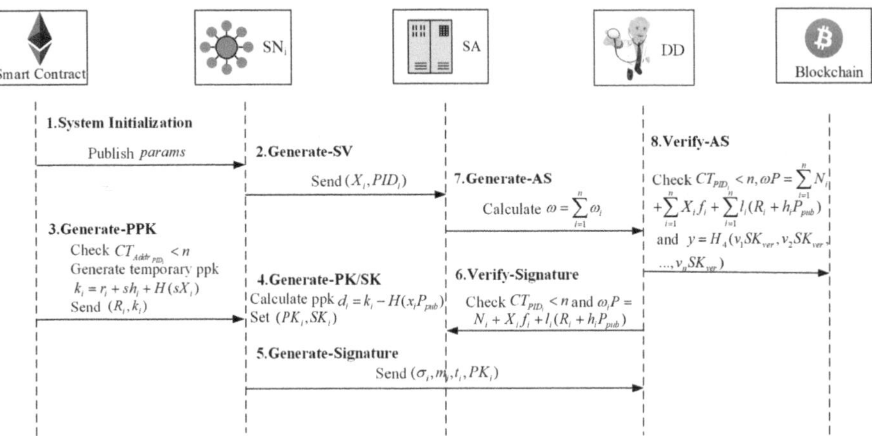

Fig. 3. The algorithm procedure.

Table 1. Symbols Used in blockchain-based CLAAS scheme.

Symbol	Description
v	Security parameter
(s, P_{pub})	Master secret key and public key
RID_i	Real identity of SN_i
PID_i	Pseudo identity of SN_i
k_i	Temporary partial private key of SN_i
d_i	Partial private key of SN_i
x_i	Secret value of SN_i
σ_i	Single signature
σ	Aggregate signature
(PK_i, SK_i)	Public key and Private key of SN_i
(PK_{ver}, SK_{ver})	Public and private key pair of DD
$CT_{Addr_{PID_i}}$	Counter controlled by SC
$Addr_{PID_i}$	Address of SN_i on the ethereum
CT_{PID_i}	Counter controlled by DD
n	Preset threshold
H_1, H_2, H_3, H_4	Four hash functions

Algorithm 1: SC related algorithm

Input: Security parameter v
Output: Temporary partial private key k_i
1 G is a group with prime q and generator $P \leftarrow v$;
2 $s \leftarrow Random(Z_q^*)$;
3 $P_{pub} \leftarrow sP$;
4 $H_i \leftarrow Random(Z_q^*)$;
5 Public $\leftarrow params = \{P, G, q, H, H_i, P_{pub}\}$;
6 $Generate\text{-}PPK(params, s, X_i, PID_i)$;
7 **if** $CT_{Addr_{PID_i}} < n$ **then**
8 $\quad r_i \leftarrow Random(Z_q^*)$;
9 $\quad R_i \leftarrow r_i P$;
10 $\quad h_i \leftarrow H_1(R_i, PID_i, P_{pub})$;
11 $\quad k_i \leftarrow [r_i + sh_i + H(sX_i)]$;
12 $\quad$ return k_i;
13 **else**
14 $\quad$ Terminate;
15 end if

- *System Initialization* $(1^v) \rightarrow params$: The administrator inputs the security parameter $v \in Z_q^*$ to initialize and invoke SC. And the algorithm outputs system parameter $params$. Concrete steps are as follows:
  a) The administrator selects a group G whose order is q and P is a generator of G.
  b) SC computes $P_{pub} = sP$ as system master key, where $s \in Z_q^*$ is selected as system secret key at random.
  c) SC selects hash functions: $H : G \rightarrow Z_q^*$, $H_1 : G \times \{0,1\}^* \times G \rightarrow Z_q^*$, $H_2, H_3 : \{0,1\}^* \times \{0,1\}^* \times \{0,1\}^* \times G \times \{0,1\}^* \rightarrow Z_q^*$ and $H_4 : \{0,1\}^* \rightarrow Z_q^*$.
  d) SC publishes $params = \{P, G, q, H, H_i, P_{pub}\}$ as the system parameters and saves s secretly, where $1 \leq i \leq 4$.
- *Generate-SV*$(RID_i, params) \rightarrow (PID_i, X_i)$: SN_i performs *Generate-SV* algorithm. The algorithm employs $params$, RID_i as inputs and outputs PID_i, X_i. Concrete steps are as follows:
  a) Selects $x_i \in Z_q^*$ randomly and figures out $X_i = x_i P$.
  b) Computes $PID_i = RID_i \oplus H(x_i P_{pub})$.
  c) delivers (PID_i, X_i) to SC through public channels.
- *Generate-PPK*$(PID_i, s, params, X_i) \rightarrow k_i$: SC performs *Generate-PPK* algorithm. The algorithm inputs s, PID_i, X_i and $params$. It outputs the temporary partial private key k_i.
  a) Checks whether $CT_{Addr_{PID_i}} < n$, where $CT_{Addr_{PID_i}}$ is a counter controlled by SC, $Addr_{PID_i}$ is the address of SN_i on the ethereum platform, n is a preset threshold. If the access time is less than n, the algorithm will continue to execute. Otherwise, SC rejects to generate the partial private key.

b) Selects $r_i \in Z_q^*$ stochastically and figures out $R_i = r_i P$.
c) Computes $h_i = H_1(R_i, PID_i, P_{pub})$ and the temporary partial private key $k_i = [r_i + sh_i + H(sX_i)] \bmod q$.
d) delivers (R_i, k_i) to SN_i through public channels.

- *Generate-PK/SK*$(PID_i, R_i, k_i, X_i, params, x_i) \rightarrow (PK_i, SK_i)$: SN_i performs *Generate-PK/SK* algorithm. The algorithm inputs $params$, x_i, PID_i, k_i, X_i, and R_i. It employs PK_i, and SK_i as outputs.
  a) Computes $d_i = k_i - H(x_i P_{pub})$ and sets d_i as the partial private key.
  b) Checks whether the formula $d_i P = R_i + h_i P_{pub}$ holds, if it is valid, SN_i accepts d_i. Otherwise, it must reapply to SC for a new partial private key.
  c) Employs $PK_i = (R_i, X_i)$ as its own public key and employs $SK_i = (d_i, x_i)$ as its own private key.

  What we need to emphasize is that the goal of using the idea of key agreement is to ensure that the partial private key is secure during the transmission from SC to SN_i [26].
- *Generate-Signature*$(PID_i, params, m_i, PK_i, t_i) \rightarrow \sigma_i$: SN_i performs *Generate-Signature* algorithm. The algorithm inputs $params$, PID_i, PK_i, m_i and t_i. It employs σ_i as output.
  a) Selects $n_i \in Z_q^*$ randomly and computes $N_i = n_i P$.
  b) Computes $f_i = H_2(PID_i, m_i, t_i, N_i, PK_i)$ and $l_i = H_3(PID_i, m_i, t_i, N_i, P_{pub})$.
  c) Computes $\omega_i = (f_i x_i + l_i d_i + n_i) \bmod q$.
  d) Outputs $\sigma_i = (N_i, \omega_i)$ on $m_i || t_i$ and delivers $(m_i, \sigma_i, t_i, PK_i)$ to DD via public and open channels.
- *Verify-Signature*$(params, PK_i, m_i, t_i) \rightarrow$ (0 or 1): DD performs *Verify-Signature* algorithm. The algorithm will employ 1 as output if σ_i is a valid signature. Otherwise, the algorithm will employ 0 as output.
  a) Checks whether $CT_{PID_i} < n$, where CT_{PID_i} is a counter controlled by DD. If it holds, DD continues to validate whether t_i is fresh. If it is, the algorithm will continue to execute. Otherwise, DD rejects the signature.
  b) Figures out $f_i = H_2(PID_i, m_i, t_i, N_i, PK_i)$, $h_i = H_1(R_i, P_{pub}, PID_i)$, and $l_i = H_3(PID_i, N_i, P_{pub}, m_i, t_i)$.
  c) Validates whether the formula $\omega_i P = N_i + X_i f_i + l_i(R_i + h_i P_{pub})$ holds. If it holds, DD accepts σ_i, outputs 1 and delivers $(m_i, \sigma_i, t_i, PK_i)$ to SA through public channels. Otherwise, DD rejects σ_i and outputs 0.
- *Generate-AS*$(params, PK_i, \{m_i, t_i, \sigma_i\}) \rightarrow \sigma$: SA performs *Generate-AS* algorithm. The algorithm inputs $params$, PK_i, PK_{ver}, $\{m_i, t_i\}$ and σ_i. It employs σ as output, where the public key of DD is $PK_{ver} = zP$, $z \in Z_q^*$.
  a) Figures out $y = H_4(\omega_1 PK_{ver}, \omega_2 PK_{ver}, ..., \omega_n PK_{ver})$.
  b) Figures out $\omega = \sum_{i=1}^{n} \omega_i$.
  c) Employs an aggregate signature $\sigma = (a, N_1, N_2 ..., N_n, \omega)$ as output and delivers σ to DD via public and open channels.
- *Verify-AS*$(params, \{m_i, t_i\}_{1 \le i \le n}, \sigma) \rightarrow$ (0 or 1): DD performs *Verify-AS* algorithm. The algorithm inputs $params$, $\{m_i, t_i\}$, SK_{ver} and σ, where the private key of DD is $SK_{ver} = z$, $z \in Z_q^*$. The algorithm will employ 1 as output if σ is valid. Otherwise, the algorithm will employ 1 as output.

a) Verifies whether $CT_{PID_i} < n$, where CT_{PID_i} is a counter controlled by DD. If it holds, DD continues to check whether t_i is fresh. If t_i is valid, the algorithm will continue to execute. Otherwise, DD rejects σ.
b) Computes $h_i = H_1(R_i, PID_i, P_{pub})$, $f_i = H_2(PID_i, m_i, t_i, N_i, PK_i)$ and $l_i = H_3(PID_i, m_i, t_i, N_i, P_{pub})$, where $1 \leq i \leq n$.
c) Sets $v_i = N_i + X_i f_i + l_i(R_i + h_i P_{pub})$.
d) Validates whether formula $\omega P = \sum_{i=1}^{n} N_i + \sum_{i=1}^{n} X_i f_i + \sum_{i=1}^{n} l_i(R_i + h_i P_{pub})$ and equation $y = H_4(v_1 SK_{ver}, v_2 SK_{ver}, ..., v_n SK_{ver})$ hold. If they hold, DD outputs 1 and accepts σ. Simultaneously, DD will post a transaction to the blockchain. Finally, these medical data will be stored on the blockchain after miners verify that the transaction is valid. Otherwise, DD outputs 0 and rejects the aggregate signature σ.

3.1 Correctness of Our Blockchain-Based CLAAS Scheme

1) The following formula can ensure the correctness of the verification:

$$\begin{aligned} \omega P &= \sum_{i=1}^{n} (n_i + f_i x_i + l_i d_i) P \\ &= \sum_{i=1}^{n} n_i P + \sum_{i=1}^{n} f_i x_i P + \sum_{i=1}^{n} l_i d_i P \\ &= \sum_{i=1}^{n} N_i + \sum_{i=1}^{n} f_i X_i + \sum_{i=1}^{n} l_i (r_i + h_i s) P \\ &= \sum_{i=1}^{n} N_i + \sum_{i=1}^{n} f_i X_i + \sum_{i=1}^{n} l_i (R_i + h_i P_{pub}). \end{aligned}$$

2) The following formula can ensure the correctness of the verification:

$$\begin{aligned} y &= H_4(\omega_1 PK_{ver}, \omega_2 PK_{ver}, ..., \omega_n PK_{ver}) \\ &= H_4(\omega_1 SK_{ver} P, \omega_2 SK_{ver} P, ..., \omega_n SK_{ver} P) \\ &= H_4(\omega_1 PSK_{ver}, \omega_2 PSK_{ver}, ..., \omega_n PSK_{ver}) \\ &= H_4(v_1 SK_{ver}, v_2 SK_{ver}, ..., v_n SK_{ver}). \end{aligned}$$

3.2 Security Analysis

Theorem 1: If A_1 succeeds in generating a forged signature in polynomial time with the non-negligible probability ε_1 after querying H_i, the challenger δ_1 is capable of cracking the ECDLP problem with the probability $(1 - \frac{q_{ppk}}{q})(1 - \frac{q_{h_i}}{q})(\frac{q_s}{1+q_s})$ (A_1 can perform at most times q_{h_i} *Hash Queries*, q_s *Signature Queries* and q_{ppk} *PPK Queries*).

Proof: The challenger δ_1 is capable of cracking the ECDLP problem. Assuming that δ_1 is given $(P, P_{pub} = sP)$, the aim of δ_1 is to calculate $s \in Z_q^*$, where $P \in G, P_{pub} \in G$.

Setup: δ_1 conducts *System Initialization* algorithm to generate *params* and s. δ_1 delivers *params* to A_1 and keeps s secretly.

Query Phase: A_1 is capable of consulting hash function H_i, where $1 \leq i \leq 4$. In the meantime, A_1 creates eight empty *list* L_i, where $1 \leq i \leq 8$.

- H_1 *Queries:* When A_1 consults $H_1(R_i, PID_i, P_{pub})$, δ_1 checks the *list* L_1. If the tuple $(R_i, PID_i, P_{pub}, h_i)$ exists in the *list* L_1, δ_1 will return existing h_i to A_1; Otherwise, δ_1 will select $h_i \in Z_q^*$ stochastically and stores the tuple $(R_i, PID_i, P_{pub}, h_i)$ into *list* L_1. Finally, δ_1 returns h_i to A_1.
- H_2 *Queries:* When A_1 consults $H_2(m_i, PID_i, t_i, PK_i, N_i)$, δ_1 checks the *list* L_2. If the tuple $(m_i, PID_i, t_i, PK_i, N_i, f_i)$ exists in the *list* L_2, δ_1 will return existing f_i to A_1; Otherwise, δ_1 will select $f_i \in Z_q^*$ stochastically and stores the tuple $(m_i, PID_i, t_i, PK_i, N_i, f_i)$ into *list* L_2. Finally, δ_1 returns f_i to A_1.
- H_3 *Queries:* When A_1 consults $H_3(m_i, PID_i, t_i, P_{pub}, N_i)$, δ_1 checks the *list* L_3. If the tuple $(m_i, PID_i, t_i, P_{pub}, N_i, l_i)$ exists in the *list* L_3, δ_1 will return existing l_i to A_1; Otherwise, δ_1 will select $l_i \in Z_q^*$ stochastically and stores the tuple $(m_i, PID_i, t_i, P_{pub}, N_i, l_i)$ into *list* L_2. Finally, δ_1 returns l_i to A_1.
- H_4 *Queries:* When A_1 consults $H_4(\omega_1 PK_{ver}, \omega_2 PK_{ver}, ..., \omega_n PK_{ver})$, δ_1 checks the *list* L_4. If the tuple $(\omega_1 PK_{ver}, \omega_2 PK_{ver}, ..., \omega_n PK_{ver}, y)$ exists in the *list* L_4, δ_1 will return existing y to A_1; Otherwise, δ_1 will choose $y \in Z_q^*$ randomly and stores the tuple $(\omega_1 PK_{ver}, \omega_2 PK_{ver}, ..., \omega_n PK_{ver})$ into *list* L_4. Finally, δ_1 returns y to A_1.
- *SV Queries:* When A_1 consults the secret value of SN_i with PID_i, δ_1 checks the *list* L_5. If the tuple (x_i, PID_i) exists in the *list* L_5, δ_1 will give x_i to A_1; Otherwise, δ_1 will choose $x_i \in Z_q^*$ stochastically and stores the tuple (x_i, PID_i) into $list_5$. Finally, δ_1 returns x_i to A_1.
- *PPK Queries:* When A_1 consults the partial private key of SN_i with PID_i, δ_1 checks the *list* L_6. If the tuple (R_i, PID_i, d_i) exists in the *list* L_6, δ_1 will give (R_i, d_i) to A_1; Otherwise, δ_1 will query the tuple $(R_i, PID_i, P_{pub}, h_i)$ of SN_i in *list* L_1, choose $d_i \in Z_q^*$ stochastically, calculate $R_i = d_i P - h_i P_{pub}$ and store the tuple (R_i, PID_i, d_i) into *list* L_6. Finally, δ_1 returns (R_i, d_i) to A_1.
- *PK Queries:* When A_1 consults the public key of SN_i with PID_i, δ_1 checks the *list* L_7. If the tuple (PID_i, X_i, R_i) exists in the *list* L_7, δ_1 will return existing (R_i, X_i) to A_1; Otherwise, δ_1 will perform following steps. 1) If the formula $PID_i \neq PID_i^*$ holds, δ_1 will select $x_i, d_i, h_i \in Z_q^*$ randomly, compute $X_i = x_i P$ and $R_i = d_i P - h_i P_{pub}$. Then, δ_1 stores the tuple (R_i, PID_i, X_i) into *list* L_7 and returns (R_i, X_i) to A_1.2) If the formula $PID_i = PID_i^*$ holds, δ_1 will select $x_i, r_i \in Z_q^*$ randomly, calculate $X_i = x_i P$ and $R_i = r_i P$. Then, δ_1 sets d_i as $\perp$ and stores the tuple (R_i, PID_i, X_i) into *list* L_7. Finally, it returns (R_i, X_i) to A_1.

- *PK Replacement Queries:* When A_1 selects another public key $PK_i^* = (X_i^*, R_i^*)$ and provides (PID_i, PK_i^*) to δ_1. When A_1 consults the public key replacement of SN_i with PID_i, δ_1 update $list_7$ and records this replacement.
- *Signature Queries:* When A_1 consults the signature of SN_i with PID_i, δ_1 checks the *list* L_8. If the tuple $(m_i, PID_i, \omega_i, x_i)$ exists in the *list* L_8, δ_1 chooses $n_i \in Z_q^*$ randomly, calculates $N_i = n_i P$, $f_i = H_2(PID_i, N_i, PK_i, m_i, t_i)$, $l_i = H_3(PID_i, N_i, m_i, t_i, P_{pub})$ and $\omega_i = (f_i x_i + l_i d_i + n_i) \bmod q$. Then δ_1 returns (N_i, ω_i) to A_1; Otherwise, δ_1 chooses $\omega_i \in Z_q^*$ randomly, calculates $N_i = \omega P - f_i X_i - l_i(R_i + h_i P_{pub})$ and stores the tuple (N_i, ω_i) into *list* L_8. Finally, δ_1 returns (N_i, ω_i) to A_1.

Forgery: A_1 employs forged signature $\sigma_i^* = (N_i^*, \omega_i^*)$ as outputs under (PID_i^*, m_i^*, PK_i^*). The forking lemma [27] allows A_1 to produce another forged signature $\sigma_i^{*(2)} = (N_i^{*(2)}, \omega_i^{*(2)})$. Consequently, according to the equation $\omega_i^* P = N_i^* + X_i^* f_i^* + l_i^*(R_i^* + h_i^* P_{pub})$ and the equation $\omega_i^{*(2)} P = N_i^{*(2)} + X_i^{*(2)} f_i^{*(2)} + l_i^{*(2)}(R_i^{*(2)} + h_i^{*(2)} P_{pub})$, s constitutes a solution of the ECDLP. Otherwise, δ_1 cannot handle the ECDLP.

To succeed in generating a forged signature, the outputs of δ_1 must fulfill the following requirements:

1) T_1: δ_1 continuously attempts to forge the signature;
2) T_2: σ_i^* is an efficacious signature;
3) T_3: σ_i^* meets the requirement of $PID_i = PID_i^*$.

From the above we can see that $P_r[T_1] \geq (1 - \frac{q_{ppk}}{q})$, $P_r[T_1 \mid T_2] \geq (1 - \frac{q_{h_i}}{q})$ and $P_r[T_1 \mid T_2 \wedge T_3] \geq (\frac{q_s}{1+q_s})$. Hence, the probability that δ_1 can compute the ECDLP is $(1 - \frac{q_{ppk}}{q})(1 - \frac{q_{h_i}}{q})(\frac{q_s}{1+q_s})$.

Theorem 2: If A_2 succeeds in generating a forged signature in polynomial time with the non-negligible probability ε_2 after querying H_i, there is a challenger δ_2 that is capable of cracking the ECDLP with the probability $(1 - \frac{q_{ppk}}{q})(1 - \frac{q_{h_i}}{q})(\frac{q_s}{1+q_s})$ (A_2 can perform at most times q_{h_i} *Hash Queries*, q_s *Signature Queries* and q_{pk} *PK Queries*).

Proof: The challenger δ_2 is capable of cracking the ECDLP. Assuming that δ_2 is given the tuple $(P, X_i = x_i P)$, the aim of δ_2 is to compute $x_i \in Z_q^*$, where $P \in G, X_i \in G$.

Setup: δ_2 conducts *System Initialization* algorithm to generate *params* and s. δ_2 delivers *params* and s to A_2.

Query Phase: The available queries of A_2 is identical to A_1, which are H_i *Queries*, *SV Queries*, *PK Queries*, *PPK Queries* and *Signature Queries*.

Forgery: A_2 employs forged signature $\sigma_i^* = (N_i^*, \omega_i^*)$ as outputs under (PID_i^*, m_i^*, R_i^*). The forking lemma [27] allows A_2 to produce another forged signature $\sigma_i^{*(2)} = (N_i^{*(2)}, \omega_i^{*(2)})$. Consequently, according to the equation $\omega_i^* P = N_i^* + X_i f_i^* + l_i^*(R_i^* + h_i^* P_{pub})$ and the equation $\omega_i^{*(2)} P = N_i^{*(2)} + X_i f_i^{*(2)} +$

$l_i^{*(2)}(R_i^{*(2)} + h_i^{*(2)} P_{pub})$, x_i constitutes a solution of the ECDLP. Otherwise, δ_2 cannot handle the ECDLP.

To succeed in generating a forged signature, the outputs of δ_2 must fulfill the following requirements:

1) T_1: δ_2 continuously attempts to forge the signature;
2) T_2: σ_i^* is an efficacious signature;
3) T_3: σ_i^* meets the requirement of $PID_i = PID_i^*$.

From the above we can see that $P_r[T_1] \geq (1 - \frac{q_{pk}}{q})$, $P_r[T_1 \mid T_2] \geq (1 - \frac{q_{h_i}}{q})$ and $P_r[T_1 \mid T_2 \wedge T_3] \geq (\frac{q_s}{1+q_s})$. Hence, the probability that δ_2 can compute the ECDLP is $(1 - \frac{q_{pk}}{q})(1 - \frac{q_{h_i}}{q})(\frac{q_s}{1+q_s})$.

Theorem 3: Assume that the hash function H_4 is collision-resistant. If A_3 is able to generate the forged signature in polynomial time with the non-negligible probability ε_3, there is a challenger δ_3 that is capable of destroying the collision resistance of hash function H_4.

Proof: The challenger δ_3 aims to crack the collision resistant of H_4. Its objective is to find a pair of distinct inputs that produce the same hash value.

Setup: δ_3 performs *System Initialization* algorithm to generate *params* and *s*. δ_3 delivers *params* to A_3.

Query Phase: The possible queries of A_3 are the same as those of A_1. Besides, A_3 has occasion to perform *Verify-AS Queries.*

- *Verify-AS Queries:* In response to A_3's query to verify the AS of SN_i under (m_i, PID_i, PK_i), δ_3 executes *Verify-AS* algorithm with the private key SK_{ver} and delivers the outcome to A_3.

Forgery: A_3 employs forged signature $\sigma_i^* = (N_i^*, \omega_i^*)$ as outputs under (PID_i^*, m_i^*, PK_i^*) for DD.

To succeed in generating a forged signature, the outputs of δ_3 must fulfill the following requirements:

1) σ_i^* is an efficacious signature. Consequently, $y^* = H_4(v_1 SK_{ver}, v_2 SK_{ver}, ..., v_n SK_{ver})$, where $v_i = N_i + X_i f_i + l_i(R_i + h_i P_{pub})$;
2) σ^* is formed from the $(\sigma_1, \sigma_2, ..., \sigma_n)$, which includes at least one invalid signature among an otherwise valid set. Consequently, $y^* = H_4(\omega_1 PK_{ver}, \omega_2 PK_{ver}, ..., \omega_n PK_{ver})$.

Assume that σ_1^* is an invalid signature. It is obvious that $\omega_1^* P \neq N_1^* + X_1^* f_1^* + l_1^*(R_1^* + h_1^* P_{pub})$. Hence, $\omega_1^* PK_{ver} \neq SK_{ver}[N_1^* + X_1^* f_1^* + l_1^*(R_1^* + h_1^* P_{pub})]$. Furthermore, accroding to the above equation, we can konw that $H_4(\omega_1 PK_{ver}, \omega_2 PK_{ver}, ..., \omega_n PK_{ver}) = H_4(v_1 SK_{ver}, v_2 SK_{ver}, ..., v_n SK_{ver}) = H_4([N_1 + X_1 f_1 + l_1(R_1 + h_1 P_{pub})]SK_{ver}, ..., [N_n + X_n f_n + l_n(R_n + h_n P_{pub})]SK_{ver})$ when entering two different values. Finding a collision in H_4 by δ_3 implies that A_3 can forge a signature with non-negligible advantage ε_3.

3.3 Other Security Analysis

1) *Message authentication and integrity:* Based on **Theorem 1** and **Theorem 2**, if the adversary lacks the ability to crack the ECDLP problem, it means that no adversary can generate an efficacious signature.
2) *Anonymity:* The pseudo identity of SN_i is $PID_i = RID_i \oplus H(x_i P_{pub})$. Consequently, it is difficult for adversaries to utilize the pseudonyms to identify the real identity of SN_i.
3) *Traceability:* SC can use s to extract real identity of SN_i by computing $RID_i = PID_i \oplus H(sX_i)$, where $sX_i = sx_i P = sPx_i = x_i P_{pub}$.
4) *Resistance to many types of attacks:* Our scheme is able to withstand the following attacks.
   a) *Coalition attack:* The mechanism outlined in **Theorem 3** prevents coalition attacks by linking the integrity of the signature elements to the hash function H_4. Any attempt to exchange elements alters the hash value, thereby allowing the DD to check and reject the resulting AS.
   b) *KGC compromised attack:* We utilize SC to replace KGC, which can ensure that our scheme can withstand KGC compromised attacks. If adversaries try to control the ethereum system and forge a valid signature, they must launch the 51% attack on the ethereum platform. However, since the current hashrate on the ethereum is very high, the probability of adversaries cracking the system is quite low. Besides, no one can modify the SC which has been deployed. Consequently, even if adversaries obtain the master key s, they are unable to alter the logic of deployed SC to forge the signature.
   c) *DDoS attack:* We adopt two counters $CT_{Addr_{PID_i}}$ and CT_{PID_i} to resist this type of attack, where $CT_{Addr_{PID_i}}$ is used to verify the frequency of SN_i. If SN_i's frequency is higher than or equal to a preset threshold n, the current SN_i will be blocked for a period of time. Besides, CT_{PID_i} has the same role in the verification algorithm.

4 Performance Evaluation

In this section, we compare with other related articles [13,15,21–23] in terms of computational overhead, communication costs, and security features. The experiment was performed on a desktop computer running the Win 11 operating system with an Intel i9-12900@5.10 GHz processor and 32 GB RAM, and the MIRACL library [28] was called for time calculation of related cryptographic operations. The runtime of cryptography-related operations is shown in Table 2. We refer to the length of parameters of bilinear pairing and elliptic curve cryptography in the literature [17]. ($| G_1 |$: 1024 bits, $| G |$: 320 bits, $| Z_q^* |$: 160 bits).

Table 2. Runtime of cryptographic operations.

Operations	Symbols	Runtime (ms)
A pairing-based scalar multiplication	T_{pm}	2.0439
A pairing-based point addition	T_{pa}	0.0090
A bilinear pairing computation	T_p	4.4320
A map-to-point hash	T_h	4.8760
A scalar multiplication on elliptic curve	T_m	0.5438
A point addition on elliptic curve	T_a	0.0020

4.1 Computational Overhead

As is shwon in Table 3, our scheme is compared with related schemes in [13,15, 21–23]. Since schemes in [13,15,22,23] entails bilinear pairing and map-to-point hash operations, it suffers from low computational efficiency during signature and verification.. While the total runtime of our scheme is $T_m + 4T_m + 3T_a = 2.7250$ ms. Our scheme delivers a superior level of security while maintaining computational efficiency comparable to that of Deng *et al.*'s scheme [21]. We can see from Fig. 4 that our CLAAS scheme respectively saves 92.46%, 86.3%, 92.01%, 91.06% of the computational time than Kumar *et al.*'s scheme [13], Liu *et al.*'s scheme [15], Shen *et al.*'s scheme [22], Wu *et al.*'s scheme [23]. Hence, our CLAAS scheme demonstrates superior computational efficiency compared to the aforementioned schemes.

Table 3. Comparison of computational cost.

Schemes	Signature	Verification	Total cost
[13]	$3T_{pm} + 2T_{pa} + T_h$	$3T_p + T_{pm} + T_{pa} + 2T_h$	36.1266 ms
[15]	$2T_{pm} + T_{pa}$	$2T_p + T_{pm} + T_{pa} + T_h$	19.8897 ms
[21]	T_m	$4T_m + 3T_a$	2.7250 ms
[22]	$3T_{pm} + T_{pa} + T_h$	$3T_p + 2T_h$	34.0647 ms
[23]	$4T_{pm}+3T_{pa}$	$3T_p+2T_{pm}+2T_{pa} + T_h$	30.4804 ms
Our scheme	T_m	$4T_m + 3T_a$	2.7250 ms

4.2 Communication Overhead

As described in Table 4, the communication overhead comparison of different schemes is compared as follows: in Kumar *et al.*'s scheme [13], the single-signature format is (R_i, V_i), the communication cost is $2|G_1| = 2048$ bits during sending a single signature, where $R_i, V_i \in G_1$. In Liu *et al.*'s scheme [15], because the single-signature format is (V_i, U_i), the communication cost is

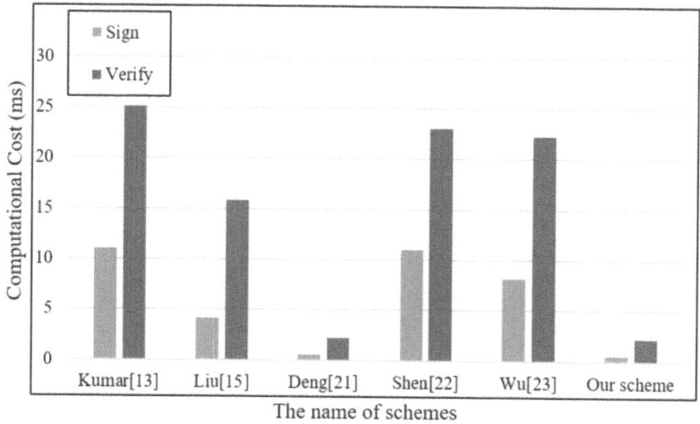

Fig. 4. Computational cost of the signature and verification phase.

$2|G_1| = 2048$ bits during sending a single signature, where $V_i, U_i \in G_1$. Deng *et al.*'s scheme [21]employs the signature format (s_i, U_i, T_i), the communication cost is $|G| + 2|Z_q^*| = 640$ bits during sending a single signature, where $U_i \in G, (s_i, T_i) \in Z_q^*$. Wu *et al.*'s scheme [23] employs signature format (U, V), the communication cost is $2|G_1| = 2048$ bits during sending a single signature, where $U, V \in G_1$. In our scheme, the single signature takes the forms of σ_i is (N_i, ω_i), where $N_i \in G$, $\omega_i \in Z_q^*$, the communication cost in our CLAAS scheme is 480 bits during sending a single signature. Our scheme yields a substantially lower communication cost per single signature than the schemes in [13,15,21–23], with reductions of 76.57%, 76.57%, 25%, 76.57%, 76.57% (in the same order as the cited schemes). The comparison in Fig. 5 confirms the advantage of our scheme in terms of a lower single-signature communication cost. As the number of medical sensor nodes increases, the communication overhead of n signatures in our scheme grows at a substantially slower rate than that of the schemes in [13,21–23], as evidenced by Fig. 6. Although the communication overhead of n signatures in Liu *et al*'s scheme [15] is slightly lower than our CLAAS scheme, their scheme is insecure. In general, our scheme offers superior performance in communication overhead, making it particularly suitable for bandwidth-constrained MIoT environments.

Table 4. Comparison of communication cost and security features.

Schemes	Single signature	n signatures	Type I	Type II	Anonymity	Traceability
[13]	$2\|G_1\| = 2048$	$(n+1)\|G_1\| = 1024(n+1)$	✓	×	×	×
[15]	$2\|G_1\| = 2048$	$3\|G_1\| = 3072$	×	×	✓	×
[21]	$\|G\| + 2\|Z_q^*\| = 640$	$(n+1)\|G\| + n\|Z_q^*\| = 160(3n+2)$	✓	✓	✓	✓
[22]	$2\|G_1\| = 2048$	$(n+1)\|G_1\| = 1024(n+1)$	✓	✓	×	×
[23]	$2\|G_1\| = 2048$	$(n+1)\|G_1\| = 1024(n+1)$	✓	✓	×	×
Our scheme	$\|G\| + \|Z_q^*\| = 480$	$n\|G\| + 2\|Z_q^*\| = 320(n+1)$	✓	✓	✓	✓

4.3 Security Features

As demonstrated in Table 5, Kumar *et al.*'s scheme [13] is susceptible to Type II attacks. The scheme [15] has been shown to be vulnerable to Type I attacks and Type II attacks in [16]. In the meantime, the scheme [21] has been demonstrated that is susceptible to coalition attacks launched by several malicious medical sensor nodes. Although the schemes in [22,23] can resist Type I and Type II attacks, it cannot realize anonymity, traceability, resistance to KGC compromised attacks, and DDoS attacks. Compared with existing schemes, our blockchain-based CLAAS scheme demonstrates significant improvements in computational efficiency, communication overhead, and security. These combined advantages collectively ensure that our blockchain-based CLAAS scheme meets all security requirements for the MIoT while maintaining high operational efficiency.

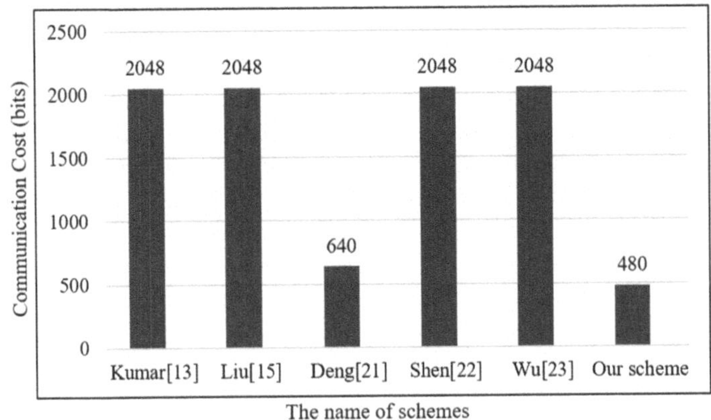

Fig. 5. Communication cost of the single signature.

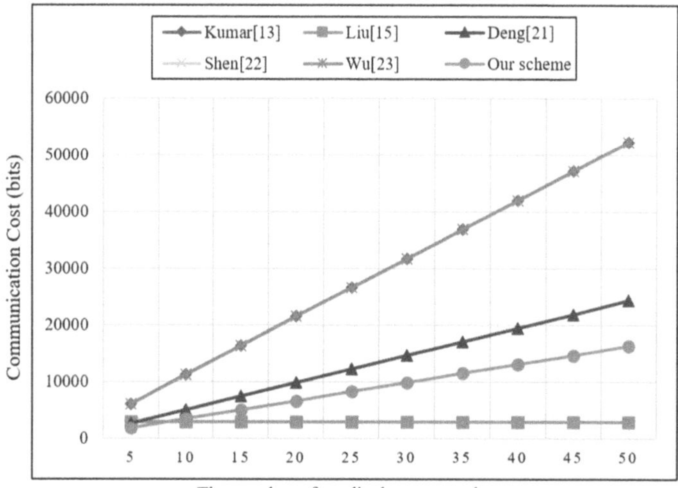

Fig. 6. Communication cost of n signatures.

Table 5. Comparison of resistance to various attacks.

Schemes	Coalition attacks	KGC compromised attacks	DDoS attacks
[13]	×	×	×
[15]	×	×	×
[21]	×	×	×
[22]	✓	×	×
[23]	✓	×	×
Our scheme	✓	✓	✓

5 Conclusion

In this paper, we first designed blockchain-based CLAAS scheme that can protect the privacy of patients by using pseudonyms as identity symbols during communication. Then we used smart contract technology to devise a blockchain-based CLAAS scheme which can withstand coalition attacks, DDoS attacks and KGC compromised attacks. Simultaneously, we put forward the third type of adversary on the basis of Type I and Type II adversaries. The security analysis demonstrated that our CLAAS scheme is secure against three types of adversaries. Besides, our CLAAS scheme did not need to rely on secure channels to transmit the partial private key. The comparative analysis demonstrates the superior efficiency of our CLAAS scheme over existing approaches.

Acknowledgements. This work is supported by the Teacher Enterprise Practice Project of Shazhou Professional Institute of Technology in 2025 (No. QYSJ25025); the Research Fund Project for Young Teachers of Shazhou Vocational and Technical College in 2024 (No. JJ202401).

References

1. Wang, L., Xu, J., Qin, B., Wen, M., Chen, K.: An efficient fuzzy certificateless signature-based authentication scheme using anonymous biometric identities for vanets. IEEE Trans. Dependable Secure Comput. **22**(1), 292–307 (2025). https://doi.org/10.1109/TDSC.2024.3392470
2. Huang, H., Wang, X., Au, M.H., Cao, S., Zhao, Q., Yu, J.: An enhanced linearly homomorphic network coding signature scheme for secure data delivery in IoT networks. IEEE Trans. Inf. Forensics Secur. **20**, 5534–5548 (2025). https://doi.org/10.1109/TIFS.2025.3563074
3. Zhou, M., Lin, C., Xu, S., Wu, W.: Sphinx: certificateless conditional privacy-preserving authentication with secure transmission for vanets. IEEE Trans. Dependable Secure Comput. 1–14 (2025). https://doi.org/10.1109/TDSC.2025.3595141
4. Yao, H., Chen, J., Bibo, T.: An efficient authentication scheme with key leakage-resistance. IEEE Trans. Industr. Inf. **21**(8), 6081–6089 (2025). https://doi.org/10.1109/TII.2025.3558330
5. Ming, Y., Zhang, X., Liu, H., Wang, C., Wang, S.: Communication-efficient conditional privacy-preserving authentication based on ring signature in vanets. IEEE Trans. Veh. Technol. 1–11 (2025). https://doi.org/10.1109/TVT.2025.3610447
6. Li, Y., Zhang, F., Sun, Y.: Lightweight certificateless linearly homomorphic network coding signature scheme for electronic health system. IET Inf. Secur. (2021). https://doi.org/10.1049/ise2.12011
7. Boneh, D., Gentry, C., Lynn, B., Shacham, H.: Aggregate and verifiably encrypted signatures from bilinear maps. In: International Conference on the Theory and Applications of Cryptographic Techniques, pp. 416–432. Springer (2003)
8. Lysyanskaya, A., Micali, S., Reyzin, L., Shacham, H.: Sequential aggregate signatures from trapdoor permutations. In: International Conference on the Theory and Applications of Cryptographic Techniques, pp. 74–90. Springer (2004). https://doi.org/10.1007/978-3-540-24676-3_5
9. Castro, R., Dahab, R.: Efficient certificateless signatures suitable for aggregation. Cryptology ePrint Archive (2007)
10. Gong, Z., Long, Y., Hong, X., Chen, K.: Two certificateless aggregate signatures from bilinear maps. In: Proceedings of SNPD, pp. 188–193. IEEE (2007). https://doi.org/10.1109/SNPD.2007.132
11. Zhang, L., Zhang, F.: A new certificateless aggregate signature scheme. Comput. Commun. **32**(6), 1079–1085 (2009). https://doi.org/10.1016/j.comcom.2008.12.042
12. Shim, K.-A.: On the security of a certificateless aggregate signature scheme. IEEE Commun. Lett. **15**(10), 1136–1138 (2011). https://doi.org/10.1109/LCOMM.2011.081011.111214
13. Kumar, P., Kumari, S., Sharma, V., Sangaiah, A.K., Wei, J., Li, X.: A certificateless aggregate signature scheme for healthcare wireless sensor network. Sustain. Comput. Inform. Syst. **18**, 80–89 (2018). https://doi.org/10.1016/j.suscom.2017.09.002
14. Wu, L., Xu, Z., He, D., Wang, X.: New certificateless aggregate signature scheme for healthcare multimedia social network on cloud environment. Secur. Commun. Netw. **2018**, 2595273:1–2595273:13 (2018). https://doi.org/10.1155/2018/2595273
15. Liu, J., Cao, H., Li, Q., Cai, F., Du, X., Guizani, M.: A large-scale concurrent data anonymous batch verification scheme for mobile healthcare crowd sensing. IEEE Internet Things J. **6**(2), 1321–1330 (2019). https://doi.org/10.1109/JIOT.2018.2828463

16. Zhang, Y., Shu, J., Liu, X., Li, J., Zheng, D.: Comments on "a large-scale concurrent data anonymous batch verification scheme for mobile healthcare crowd sensing". IEEE Internet Things J. **6**(1), 1287–1290 (2019). https://doi.org/10.1109/JIOT.2018.2862381
17. Gayathri, N.B., Thumbur, G., Rajesh Kumar, P., Rahman, M.Z.U., Reddy, P.V., Lay-Ekuakille, A.: Efficient and secure pairing-free certificateless aggregate signature scheme for healthcare wireless medical sensor networks. IEEE Internet Things J. **6**(5), 9064–9075 (2019). https://doi.org/10.1109/JIOT.2019.2927089
18. Liu, J., Wang, L., Yu, Y.: Improved security of a pairing-free certificateless aggregate signature in healthcare wireless medical sensor networks. IEEE Internet Things J. **7**(6), 5256–5266 (2020). https://doi.org/10.1109/JIOT.2020.2979613
19. Zhan, Y., Wang, B., Lu, R.: Cryptanalysis and improvement of a pairing-free certificateless aggregate signature in healthcare wireless medical sensor networks. IEEE Internet Things J. **8**(7), 5973–5984 (2021). https://doi.org/10.1109/JIOT.2020.3033337
20. Yingzhe Hou, H., Xiong, X.H., Kumari, S.: Certificate-based parallel key-insulated aggregate signature against fully chosen key attacks for industrial internet of things. IEEE Internet Things J. **8**(11), 8935–8948 (2021). https://doi.org/10.1109/JIOT.2021.3056477
21. Deng, L., Yang, Y., Gao, R.: Certificateless designated verifier anonymous aggregate signature scheme for healthcare wireless sensor networks. IEEE Internet Things J. **8**(11), 8897–8909 (2021). https://doi.org/10.1109/JIOT.2021.3056097
22. Shen, L., Ma, J., Liu, X., Wei, F., Miao, M.: A secure and efficient id-based aggregate signature scheme for wireless sensor networks. IEEE Internet Things J. **4**(2), 546–554 (2017). https://doi.org/10.1109/JIOT.2016.2557487
23. Ge, W., Zhang, F., Shen, L., Guo, F., Susilo, W.: Certificateless aggregate signature scheme secure against fully chosen-key attacks. Inf. Sci. **514**, 288–301 (2020). https://doi.org/10.1016/j.ins.2019.11.037
24. Li, T., Wang, H., He, D., Jia, Yu.: Permissioned blockchain-based anonymous and traceable aggregate signature scheme for industrial internet of things. IEEE Internet Things J. **8**(10), 8387–8398 (2021). https://doi.org/10.1109/JIOT.2020.3045451
25. Wanqing, W., Ye, F.: A secure and efficient certificateless aggregate signature authentication scheme with pseudonyms for vanets. IEEE Internet Things J. **12**(1), 124–139 (2025). https://doi.org/10.1109/JIOT.2024.3459033
26. Abbasinezhad-Mood, D., Mazinani, S.M., Nikooghadam, M., Ostad-Sharif, A.: Efficient provably-secure dynamic ID-based authenticated key agreement scheme with enhanced security provision. IEEE Trans. Dependable Secure Comput. **19**(2), 1227–1238 (2020). https://doi.org/10.1109/TDSC.2020.3024654
27. Pointcheval, D., Stern, J.: Security proofs for signature schemes. In: International Conference on the Theory and Applications of Cryptographic Techniques, pp. 387–398. Springer (1996). https://doi.org/10.1007/3-540-68339-9_33
28. Shamus Software Ltd., Miracl library. http://www.shamus.ie/index.php?page=home

A Structured Chinese Encoding Framework for Multi-field Encrypted Fuzzy Query with Non-bootstrapping CKKS

Shutong Liu, Liping Zhuang, Jin Peng, Yuying Lin, and Zheng Gong(✉)

School of Computer Science, South China Normal University, Guangzhou 510631, China
{2025010261,linyy}@m.scnu.edu.cn, cis.gong@gmail.com

Abstract. The CKKS scheme enables approximate arithmetic over encrypted vectors, supporting SIMD computation and controlled ciphertext rotations without revealing plaintexts. Prior encrypted fuzzy-query systems for English text typically map each character to a small, contiguous code and evaluate equality or similarity with low-degree polynomials. This design does not transfer to Chinese: the Unicode space is large and discontinuous, and after normalization for CKKS distinct characters can become numerically proximate, leading to collisions under approximation noise and undermining both equality tests and fuzzy comparisons. We address these limitations with two encoding strategies Digit Decomposition Embedding (DDE) and Bit Slicing (BS) that represent each Chinese character by several low-magnitude integer components, preserving inter-character separability at low multiplicative depth and remaining compatible with non-bootstrapping CKKS. We further introduce a slot-masking and sliding-window mechanism that leverages structured slot alignment and bounded rotations to realize fuzzy matching and substring retrieval. Together, these components provide a structured Chinese encoding framework for multi-field encrypted fuzzy query that maintains numeric distinguishability, controls depth growth, and exploits CKKS batch parallelism for efficient end-to-end execution.

Keywords: Homomorphic Encryption · CKKS · Chinese Fuzzy Query · Digit Decomposition · Bit Slicing

1 Introduction

In financial compliance and anti-fraud systems, sensitive fields such as personal names, national identification numbers, phone numbers, and addresses constitute the core information for user identity verification. Financial institutions need to perform strict blacklist screening and fraud detection across multiple stages of account creation and transaction monitoring [12]. Accordingly, there is an urgent

Y. Xiang and J. Shen (Eds.): ML4CS 2025, LNCS 16456, pp. 124–138, 2026.
https://doi.org/10.1007/978-981-95-7820-7_8

need for a privacy-preserving solution to enable fuzzy search and retrieval with encrypted Chinese databases.

FHE provides a cryptographic foundation for performing arbitrary computations directly over encrypted data. For the encrypted string matching and fuzzy search, related studies can be divided into two methodological paradigms [11]: the *Boolean approach*, which performs bit-level comparison through logic gates on ciphertexts, and the *Arithmetic approach*, which constructs similarity metrics via homomorphic multiplication–addition or squared-distance computation. Both rely on FHE as the computational backend, aiming to achieve high-accuracy matching and retrieval without plaintext exposure.

Boolean Approach. The Boolean approach works primarily relied on Boolean circuits to perform bitwise comparison or string matching operations over ciphertexts. A representative example is the secure approximate string-matching scheme proposed by Essex et al. [1], which introduces a novel public-key construction that enables secure bidirectional evaluation of threshold functions within a constrained domain. The scheme embeds messages in the plaintext space of an additive homomorphic encryption system and builds an efficient two-party protocol for privately computing the threshold Dice coefficient.

Arithmetic Approach. Exploiting the arithmetic structure of FHE by mapping strings or feature vectors into numerical space and constructing distance or similarity functions via homomorphic addition and multiplication. Boddeti [2] first introduced an FHE-based privacy-preserving facial recognition framework in biometric authentication, computing Euclidean distances directly in the encrypted domain for secure matching. The DeepPrint system by Engelsma et al. [3] extended this approach to fingerprint recognition, achieving 1:N encrypted search. Wen et al. [4] proposed the LEAF algorithm, which theoretically reduced multiplicative complexity through a three-step procedure—Localization, Extraction, and Reconstruction—lowering the circuit complexity from $O(n \log n)$ to $O(n)$ while maintaining constant multiplicative depth.

Extended and Optimized Approaches. To further reduce computational overhead, Ibarrondo et al. [9] proposed the *Grote* algorithm, which reformulates large-scale homomorphic matching into a group-testing paradigm over subgroup spaces, executing multiple homomorphic cosine-similarity operations within each subgroup to minimize the number of matching rounds. Choi et al. proposed the *Blind-Match* system [10] represents one of the most recent optimizations along the arithmetic path. It partitions high-dimensional biometric feature vectors into sub-blocks for partial homomorphic similarity computation, which are then aggregated into a global matching score. This design significantly reduces multiplicative depth and ciphertext size, achieving plaintext-equivalent accuracy on the LFW and PolyU datasets while reducing per-query matching latency to sub-second levels.

Encrypted Databases and System-Level Implementations. In general-purpose encrypted data retrieval, CipherMatch [11] introduced a system framework for exact string matching, featuring memory-efficient plaintext packing and implementation optimization. Kasyap et al. [12] proposed the *Fuzzy Name Matching* framework, which represents names using MinHash signature vectors and employs CKKS-based homomorphic cosine-similarity computation for encrypted comparison. Their system further integrates pre-clustering to reduce the number of pairwise comparisons. In cross-institutional anti–money-laundering (AML) blacklist screening, this framework achieved 99% matching accuracy with substantial acceleration compared to prior solutions.

Among existing FHE schemes, CKKS [8] supports approximate arithmetic on encrypted real numbers, which has been widely adopted for encrypted vector operations and privacy-preserving machine learning inference. However, when applied to high-code-point and nonuniform Chinese character encodings, CKKS encounters severe challenges: Normalizing Chinese Unicode code, the numerical gaps become extremely small. The differences will be obscured by the intrinsic noise when mapping the normalized values into CKKS slots. Consequently, ciphertext-based equality comparison becomes infeasible; equality-evaluating functions typically require high-degree polynomial approximations, which are impractical in non-bootstrapping CKKS settings where the computation depth is tightly limited.

Chinese sensitive fields often exhibit heterogeneous structures for address, name, identification, and phone numbers. For privacy-preserving scenarios, ciphertext matching functions are required for fuzzy tolerance, substring recognition, and independent field-level comparison. However, existing FHE-based query mechanisms lack dedicated support for structured, multi-field fuzzy matching.

Our Contribution. Motivated by the above challenges, this work aims to achieve a Structured Chinese Encoding Framework for Multi-Field Encrypted Fuzzy Query. Our primary contributions are as follows: we construct a structured encoding scheme for Chinese characters, enabling efficient mapping of character sequences into CKKS ciphertext slots while preserving both order information and representation compactness; we design a slot-based sliding-window matching mechanism that performs cyclic shifts and parallel comparisons over ciphertext slots, allowing encrypted evaluation of continuous substrings within strings.

Organization. Section 2 presents the background; Sect. 3 describes the proposed framework; Sect. 4 reports the experimental results; finally, we conclude the paper in Sect. 5.

2 Background

2.1 The CKKS Scheme

The CKKS scheme [8] is an RLWE-based FHE scheme with five algorithms (KeyGen, Enc, Dec, Add, Mult). The plaintext space is a cyclotomic polynomial ring $\mathcal{R} = \mathbb{Z}[X]/(X^N + 1)$. It supports approximate arithmetic over real or complex numbers $\mathbb{C}^{N/2}$. Consequently, CKKS requires an encoding and decoding process for the domain transformation.

Encoding and Decoding. Since $\mathbb{R}[X]/(X^N+1)$ is isomorphic with $\mathbb{C}^{N/2}$, the encoding process is $\mathbb{C}^{N/2} \to \mathbb{R}[X]/(X^N+1) \to \mathcal{R}$. The projects are illustrated as follows:

- canonical embedding $\sigma : \mathbb{C}[X]/(X^N+1) \to \mathbb{C}^N$. It satisfies

$$\forall m \in \mathbb{C}[X]/(X^N+1), \sigma(m) = (m(\xi), m(\xi^3), \cdots, m(\xi^{2N-1})) \in \mathbb{C}^N,$$

  where ξ^{2i-1} is the root of X^N+1.
- natural projection $\pi : \mathbb{H} = \{z \in \mathbb{C}_N : z_j = \bar{z_{N-j}}\} \to \mathbb{C}^{N/2}$. It satisfies:

$$\forall t \in \mathbb{H}, \pi(t) = (t_0, t_1, \cdots, t_{N/2}) \in \mathbb{C}^{N/2}.$$

Since σ and π are surjection, the inverse project σ^{-1} and π^{-1} exist. Therefore, for a plaintext $\boldsymbol{m} \in \mathbb{C}^{N/2}$, before encryption, the encoding process is $m(X) = \lfloor \sigma^{-1}(\Delta \cdot \pi^{-1}(\boldsymbol{m})) \rceil \in \mathcal{R}$, while after decryption, the decoding process is $\boldsymbol{m} = \pi(\sigma(\Delta^{-1} \cdot m(X))) \in \mathbb{C}^{N/2}$.

Key Algorithms. CKKS scheme is a leveled HE scheme with a pre-defined maximum length L. The modulus of ℓ layer is defined by $q_\ell = p^\ell \cdot q_0$, where q_0 is the initial modulus and $p > 0$ is a fixed base. For a security parameter λ, the parameter $M = M(\lambda, q_L)$ is for M-th cyclotomic polynomial $\Phi_M(X) = X^N + 1, M = 2N$. The ciphertext of level ℓ is a vector in the polynomial space $\mathcal{R}_{q_\ell}^k$, where k is fixed.

- KeyGen(1^λ). Given the security parameter λ, **KeyGen** algorithm generates a secret key sk, a public key pk, and an evaluation key evk.
- Enc$_{pk}(m)$. Given a polynomial $m \in \mathcal{R}$, **Enc** algorithm outputs a ciphertext $\boldsymbol{c} \in \mathcal{R}_{q_L}^k$, which satisfies $\langle \boldsymbol{c}, sk \rangle = m + e \mod q_L$ for some small e.
- Dec$_{sk}(\boldsymbol{c})$. Given a ciphertext $\boldsymbol{c}$ at level ℓ, **Dec** algorithm outputs a polynomial $m' \leftarrow \langle \boldsymbol{c}, sk \rangle \mod q_\ell$.
- Add($\boldsymbol{c_1}, \boldsymbol{c_2}$). Given ciphertexts of m_1 and m_2, **Add** algorithm outputs a ciphertext of $m_1 + m_2$.
- Mult$_{evk}(\boldsymbol{c_1}, \boldsymbol{c_2})$. Given ciphertexts of m_1 and m_2, **Mult** algorithm outputs a ciphertext $\boldsymbol{c}_{\text{mult}} \in \mathcal{R}_{q_\ell}^k$, satisfying $\langle \boldsymbol{c}_{\text{mult}}, sk \rangle = \langle \boldsymbol{c_1}, sk \rangle \cdot \langle \boldsymbol{c_2}, sk \rangle + e_{\text{mult}} \mod q_L$ for some small polynomial $e_{\text{mult}} \in \mathcal{R}$.

2.2 Decomposition and Bit-Slicing

Decomposition is a fundamental technique in homomorphic encryption that expresses an integer or polynomial under a radix B as a vector of low-magnitude digits. Formally, for $x \in \mathbb{Z}$ (or a coefficient of a polynomial in $\mathcal{R}$), the radix-B decomposition is

$$x = \sum_{i=0}^{\ell-1} x_i B^i, \qquad 0 \le x_i < B,$$

where ℓ is the decomposition level determined by the dynamic range of x. In HE systems, such decomposition bounds intermediate values, reduces rescaling pressure (for approximate schemes), and enables structured, component-wise evaluation with low multiplicative depth.

Bit-Slicing (radix $B = 2$). When the radix is fixed to $B = 2$, decomposition specializes to *bit-slicing*: an integer x is represented by its bit vector

$$\mathrm{BS}(x) = [b_0, b_1, \ldots, b_{d-1}], \qquad b_i \in \{0, 1\}, \; x = \sum_{i=0}^{d-1} b_i 2^i,$$

where d is the bit-width. In the homomorphic setting, each b_i is embedded as a plaintext/ciphertext slot value in $\{0, 1\}$.

3 A Structured Chinese Encoding Framework for Multi-field Encrypted Fuzzy Query

3.1 Application Scenario

The proposed framework is intended for practical environments where sensitive data must be processed under strict privacy requirements.

It targets organizations such as financial institutions and law enforcement agencies that need to perform fuzzy record screening without revealing plaintext information. During account registration, banks must verify that the birth date and regional code in a customer national identification number are consistent with the personal information submitted by the user.

In payment and risk-control systems, the proposed framework assists in detecting high-risk addresses that are frequently linked to fraudulent activity. For law enforcement agencies, when tracing criminal behavior or investigating financial crimes, it enables encrypted searches within blacklist databases to locate names or address fragments that approximately correspond to a given query. This form of fuzzy retrieval extends the scope of record recall while maintaining full data confidentiality.

These scenarios share several defining characteristics: they involve diverse query fields, tolerate approximate or partial matches, demand high responsiveness at scale, and operate under strict privacy and regulatory requirements. Together, these properties define a class of applications that require multi-field fuzzy query in FHE.

3.2 Overall Framework Design

Based on the above scenarios, this work proposes a structured Chinese encrypted fuzzy query framework under a non-bootstrapping CKKS setting. The framework is designed to achieve efficient multi-field encrypted comparison through deterministic slot allocation, structured field encoding, and ciphertext-level fuzzy matching. It integrates three functional layers: Encoding Layer, Query Layer, and Computation Layer as illustrated conceptually in Fig. 1.

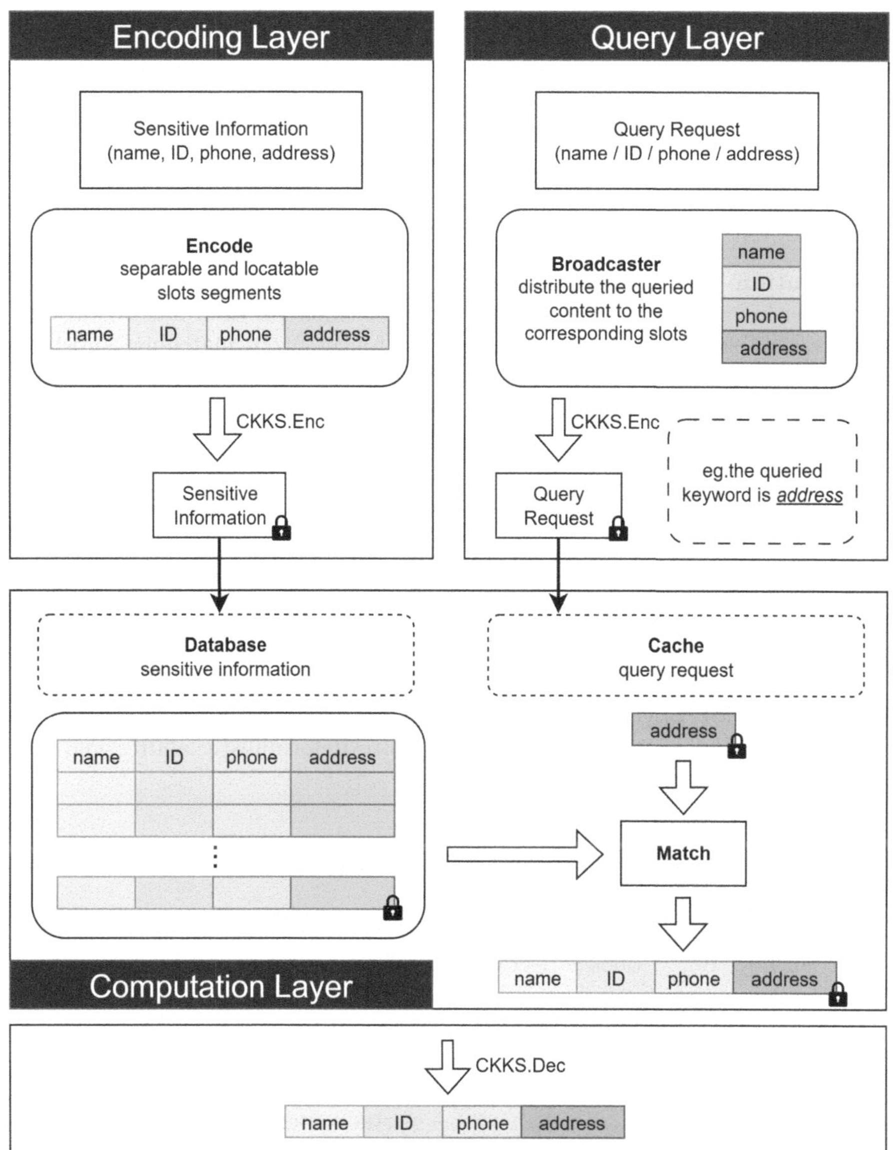

Fig. 1. Conceptual architecture of the proposed structured encrypted fuzzy query framework under CKKS.

Encoding Layer. Each record is transformed into a fixed-length CKKS slot vector where heterogeneous attributes (name, identity, phone, and address) are independently encoded and spatially separated. The address field is further divided into subfields (*province, city, district, landmark, detailed address*) to preserve logical hierarchy. This deterministic slot allocation allows the ciphertext to remain index-addressable and enables efficient field-wise rotations and comparisons.

Query Layer. A query is encoded using the same structured layout and broadcast across all ciphertext slots using Galois rotations. This layer supports both global and field-specific broadcasting, allowing the same query template to interact simultaneously with multiple encrypted records through CKKS SIMD parallelism.

Computation Layer. All homomorphic matching operations are performed entirely within the encrypted domain. Pre-generated rotation and relinearization keys enable the system to conduct field-level fuzzy matching, substring localization through controlled slot rotations and element-wise ciphertext multiplications. Each field applies its own matching logic executed independently to preserve modularity and maintain a low multiplicative depth throughout the computation process.

3.3 Structured Encoding Mechanism

The framework establishes a structured encoding mechanism to support encrypted fuzzy query over multi-field Chinese, unifying heterogeneous data fields within a CKKS slot vector under fixed positional boundaries.

Field-Level Slot Layout. Each encrypted record occupies 128 slots in total, with statically defined field intervals to ensure deterministic addressing. The configuration is summarized in Table 1.

Table 1. CKKS Slot Layout per Record (128 slots)

Field	Start	Length	Encoding	Description
Name	[0, 15]	16	Boolean 1-gram hash	Boolean $\{0, 1\}$ slot vectors for encrypted substring matching.
Identity	[16, 31]	16	Numeric	Decomposed by region code, birth date, and sequence number.
Phone	[32, 47]	16	Numeric slicing	Prefix/middle/suffix segmentation for partial matching.
Address	[48, 127]	80	DDE/BS	Five subfields: province, city, district, landmark, detailed address.
Total	128 slots in total			

Each field listed in Table 1 is encoded according to its structural characteristics and matching requirements. For the Name field, each Chinese character is represented by a Boolean slot vector $\{0, 1\}$ generated through 1-gram hashing. The ID field is numerically encoded, where each component such as the administrative region code, date of birth, and check digit is mapped to a fixed slot segment to preserve positional determinism during equality comparison. The Phone number field adopts a fixed-length numeric representation that partitions the number into prefix, middle, and suffix segments, allowing independent encrypted matching for partial digit queries. Finally, the Address field leverages the hybrid Digit Decomposition Embedding/bit-sliced encoding strategy: higher-level components (province, city, district, landmark) are expressed using Digit Decomposition Embedding to maintain numeric stability, while lower-level details are represented with bit-sliced binary vectors to support fine-grained structural matching. Collectively, these field-specific designs enable heterogeneous attributes to be represented in a unified slot structure, ensuring consistent aligned encrypted comparisons across all record fields.

Character Encoding of the Address Field. The address field exhibits the highest complexity among all attributes due to its variable length and multi-character composition. To preserve both numerical stability and representational accuracy, we propose two encoding strategies: Digit Decomposition Embedding (DDE) and Bit Slicing (BS).

Digit Decomposition Embedding (DDE). DDE transforms the UTF encoded integer value x of each Chinese character after remapping from the Unicode code space to a compact index range into a four-dimensional low radix vector

$$\mathrm{DDE}(x) = [d_0, d_1, d_2, d_3], \qquad d_i = \left\lfloor \frac{x}{b^i} \right\rfloor \bmod b, \quad b = 16. \tag{1}$$

where b is a configurable radix (e.g., $b = 16$ used in our implementation).

For example, the characters "Lin" ("林", U+6797), "Sen" ("森", U+68EE), and "Shu" ("树", U+6811) have UTF integer values $x_{林} = 26519$, , $x_{森} = 26862$, , and $x_{树} = 26641$. . Their corresponding four-dimensional DDE vectors are:

$$\mathrm{DDE}(林) = [7, 3, 10, 6], \quad \mathrm{DDE}(森) = [14, 3, 10, 6], \quad \mathrm{DDE}(树) = [1, 4, 10, 6].$$

Direct use of Unicode code points in CKKS leads to large magnitude variance and unstable precision. In CKKS, plaintexts are encoded as scaled real numbers with factor Δ (e.g., $\Delta = 2^{40}$), and the scale interacts multiplicatively during ciphertext operations. When Unicode differences reach several hundred units (e.g., $|x - y| = 343$), the quadratic kernel

$$K(x, y) = 1 - \alpha(x - y)^2$$

requires an extremely small $\alpha \approx 8.5 \times 10^{-6}$ to keep $K \in [0, 1]$. Such a small constant reduces ciphertext scale from $\Delta \approx 2^{40}$ to $\Delta' \approx 2^{23}$, making it incompatible with the constant term 1 and forcing extra rescaling and alignment operations. Each rescale step consumes modulus levels and amplifies relative noise, degrading precision and shrinking the distinguishable margin between characters.

To avoid this issue, DDE decomposes each character into a fixed number of digits under a low radix b. The choice of b influences the numerical range of each digit as well as the spatial layout of encoded characters in the CKKS slot structure. A smaller radix produces more digits, increasing slot consumption and reducing the number of records that can be packed into a ciphertext; a larger radix compresses slot usage but enlarges the per-digit dynamic range, making the kernel more sensitive to scaling and rescaling. In practice, choosing a radix such as $b = 16$ provides a balanced trade-off: it keeps each digit within a predictable and compact range, preserves stable precision across homomorphic computations, and aligns well with the fixed slot layout used for multi-field Chinese records.

Bit-Slicing (BS). For fine-grained components within addresses, such as building or room numbers in Chinese expressions ("113号", "255房"), BS encodes the entire mixed-format into a binary vector suitable for homomorphic equality evaluation. Each character is first mapped to an integer index (e.g., using UTF-8), and the concatenated integer sequence is expanded into a fixed-width binary vector of dimension d. Formally,

$$\mathrm{BS}(x) = [b_{d-1}, b_{d-2}, \ldots, b_0], \qquad b_i = \left\lfloor \frac{x}{2^i} \right\rfloor \bmod 2, \quad b_i \in \{0, 1\}. \tag{2}$$

Here b_{d-1} denotes the most significant bit (MSB) and b_0 the least significant bit (LSB). The bit width d is determined by the combined encoding range of all characters, and zero-padding is applied when necessary to maintain fixed length.

For example, the address fragment "113号" is first represented as a concatenated integer sequence

$$[49, 49, 51, 21495],$$

where digits "1", "3" and the Chinese character "Hao" ("号", U+53F7) are mapped to their respective code points. This sequence is then concatenated into a single binary representation and expanded (for $d = 24$) as

$$\mathbf{BS_{24}(\texttt{"113号"}) = [0,0,1,1,0,0,1,1,\ 0,0,1,1,0,0,1,1,\ 0,1,0,1,1,1,0,1],}$$

which is directly embedded into contiguous ciphertext slots. Such representation preserves bit-level fidelity for each character, allowing encrypted equality checks and prefix matching at the binary granularity while maintaining deterministic slot alignment under the CKKS framework. For addresses, we combine *DDE* and *BS* in one deterministic layout: hierarchical tokens such as "广东省广州市天河区" are encoded per character with low-radix DDE to keep values numerically stable in CKKS, while the free-form tail like "石牌东路125号" is bit-sliced (BS) to support precise Chinese and digit/prefix matching. These segments are placed in fixed positions within the Address field, so the encoder, query broadcaster, and matcher can align them consistently without extra depth or control flow. In short, DDE handles the structured (省/市/区) part, BS handles the numeric/detail suffix, and the two encodings coexist in a single, orderly slot layout.

3.4 Encrypted Matching and Sliding-Mask Mechanism

The matching phase operates entirely on ciphertexts. Query ciphertexts and encrypted records share an identical slot structure, enabling local alignment via homomorphic rotations and Sliding Masking.

Sliding Masking for Field Alignment. Let the encrypted slot vector be $\mathbf{x} \in \mathbb{C}^n$ (a CKKS ciphertext with n complex slots), and let the query embedding be $\mathbf{q} \in \mathbb{C}^k$ with $k \leq n$. For a window starting at index $i \in \{0, \ldots, n-k\}$, define a binary mask $\mathbf{m}^{(i)} \in \{0,1\}^n$ by

$$m_j^{(i)} = \begin{cases} 1, & i \leq j < i+k, \\ 0, & \text{otherwise}, \end{cases} \qquad j \in \{0, \ldots, n-1\}. \tag{3}$$

The Hadamard (element-wise) product

$$\tilde{\mathbf{x}}^{(i)} = \mathbf{x} \odot \mathbf{m}^{(i)} = [0, \ldots, 0, x_i, x_{i+1}, \ldots, x_{i+k-1}, 0, \ldots, 0], \tag{4}$$

isolates the length-k substring of $\mathbf{x}$ located at indices $[i, i+k]$. By applying controlled CKKS rotations to $\mathbf{x}$ (or equivalently, padding or rotating $\mathbf{q}$ into an n-slot vector $\mathbf{q}^{(i)}$) and sweeping $i = 0, \ldots, n-k$, the system aligns each encrypted substring with the query template. All masks are pre-encoded as plaintext vectors and applied via ciphertext–plaintext Hadamard products, while rotations use CKKS automorphisms enabled by the corresponding Galois keys, enabling parallel field alignment across large batches of encrypted records.

Matching and Quadratic Evaluation. Each query is compared exclusively with the ciphertext slots corresponding to the fields within the encrypted database. A match signifies that the values encoded in the identical slot positions of the query and the database record are approximately equal. Upon match detection, the system returns the complete record, thus achieving global fuzzy retrieval through local exact evaluation.

To achieve slot-wise equality determination, the system employs a quadratic evaluation kernel (Eq. 5), which serves to quantify the degree of similarity between encoded values.

$$k_{i,j} = 1 - \alpha(x_{i,j} - q_{i,j})^2, \qquad e_i = \prod_{j=1}^{J} k_{i,j}, \tag{5}$$

where $x_{i,j}$ and $q_{i,j}$ denote the j-th encoded component of the i-th slot for a database record and the query, respectively. Here, J represents the total number of components per slot.

The kernel value, $k_{i,j}$, functions as a component similarity metric between the two ciphertext elements. This value approaches 1 when the components are identical and smoothly decreases toward 0 as the magnitude of their difference increases. Consequently, the overall slot score $e_i \in [0,1]$ is derived by aggregating the component similarities via multiplication and represents the total approximate equality degree for the i-th slot. The coefficient $\alpha > 0$ is designed to constrain the magnitude of the quadratic term $(x_{i,j} - q_{i,j})^2$ so that its contribution to the kernel remains below 1. In practice, α is selected to regulate the magnitude of the quadratic penalty term $\alpha(x_{i,j} - q_{i,j})^2$, ensuring that the kernel yields a meaningful and interpretable similarity response for both matching and non-matching components. The DDE digit range provides a natural upper bound on the deviation. Using this range as a reference, choosing

$$\alpha \leq \frac{1}{b^2}$$

guarantees that $\alpha(x_{i,j} - q_{i,j})^2 < 1$ for all valid components, thereby keeping the kernel output $k_{i,j}$ within a numerically stable scale under CKKS evaluation. It should be emphasized that b does not determine the value of α; rather, it provides a convenient bound.

The coefficient α fundamentally governs the kernel's ability to differentiate equality. When $x_{i,j} = q_{i,j}$, the kernel remains fixed at $k_{i,j} = 1$ independent of α. When the components differ, the value of α dictates the degree to which the similarity measure decreases. An α that is too small results in only negligible reductions in $k_{i,j}$ for mismatching components, making it difficult to distinguish mismatches from true matches after aggregation across digits and slots. A moderate choice of α therefore achieves a controlled and discriminative decay in the kernel, enhancing the robustness of the final encrypted match decision.

3.5 Security Analysis

The security of the proposed framework directly derives from the underlying CKKS scheme, which is proven IND-CPA secure under the *Ring Learning With Errors (RLWE)* assumption. All homomorphic operations—additions, multiplications, and rotations are performed on semantically secure ciphertexts without access to plaintexts or keys. Neither intermediate results nor query parameters leak any information beyond ciphertext size and operation count. Hence, the proposed structured fuzzy query mechanism inherits CKKS semantic security while introducing no additional leakage.

4 Experimental Results

Existing encrypted fuzzy-search baselines cannot be meaningfully applied to Chinese text due to the lack of character-level separability under CKKS, so we omit direct baseline comparison and directly report the experimental results of our proposed framework. The implementation adopts cryptographic parameters consistent with current security standards. The lattice dimension is set to $D = 2^{17}$, yielding a ciphertext slot count of $N = D/2 = 2^{16}$ and a maximum ciphertext modulus of $Q_L = 3{,}516$ bits. The secret key is sampled from a ternary distribution, following the parameterization recommended by Cheon *et al.* [14]. According to the analyses of Albrecht *et al.* [13] and Bossuat *et al.* [15], this configuration provides approximately 128-bit security strength, meeting the recommended level for practical fully homomorphic encryption implementations.

All experiments were conducted on Ubuntu 20.04.4 LTS with an Intel Core i9-14900K processor. The homomorphic encryption scheme was implemented using Open-FHE v1.3.0, compiled with `g++`/`clang++`. All rotation (Galois automorphism) and relinearization keys were pre-generated once during the system initialization stage. The complete parameter configuration and data layout are summarized in Table 2.

Table 2. Parameter configuration and data layout (single thread, CKKS, non-bootstrapped)

Category	Item	Symbol	Value
Security and Parameter Settings	Lattice dimension (ring dimension)	D	131072
	Slot count ($N = D/2$)	N	65536
	Maximum ciphertext modulus (bits)	Q_L	3516
	Security level (bits)		128
	Secret key distribution		Ternary distribution
Data Layout	Slots per record		128
	Slot partition (Name/ID/Phone/Address)		16/16/16/80
	Parallel records per ciphertext		512

Module-Level Latency. We evaluate each module on a single ciphertext that packs four records (128 slots per record) at ringDim $= 2^{17}$, repeating the test 10 times; the resulting per-batch latency ranges are 16.2–22.8 ms (Name), 9.9–13.7 ms (ID), 10.1–13.9 ms (Phone), and for Address sub-fields 14.6–20.4 ms (Province), 15.3–20.8 ms (City), 14.2–19.6 ms (District), 16.0–21.2 ms (LName), with a 14.8–20.5 ms Combine step; the results are shown in Fig. 2.

End-to-End Throughput (B2). Under the parameter and environment settings listed in Table 2, the system achieved a mean evaluation time of **8.5–9.5 s per ciphertext** (processing 512 records concurrently), corresponding to an **average matching time of 0.016–0.019 s per record**. For a dataset of **10,000 encrypted records**, the overall matching phase required approximately **3.0–3.3 min**. The encrypted kernel outputs remained stable across evaluations: similarity scores for matched samples approached unity, while non-matched samples remained well below the decision threshold, and no misclassifications were observed due to approximation noise (Table 3).

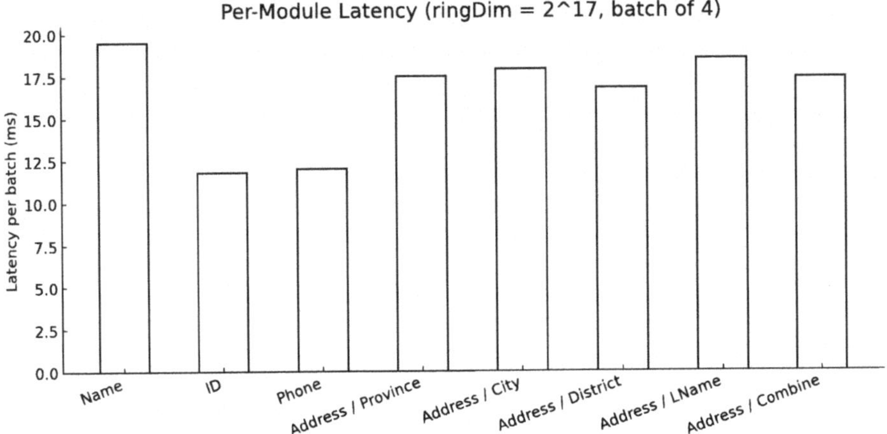

Fig. 2. Per-module latency at ringDim $= 2^{17}$ (batch of four records).

Table 3. Summary of End-to-End Throughput and Scalability (B2).

Metric	Value
Batch Size	512
Evaluation Time (per Ciphertext)	8.5–9.5 s
Average Matching Time (per Record)	0.016–0.019 s
Total Dataset Size (Records)	10,000
Total Matching Time	3.0–3.3 min
Classification Accuracy	No misclassifications observed

5 Conclusion

This work proposes an encrypted fuzzy query framework for multi-field Chinese data under a non-bootstrapping CKKS scheme. Through structured slot allocation and the integration of Digit Decomposition Embedding (DDE) and Bit-Slicing (BS) encodings, the framework supports parallel matching and substring retrieval for heterogeneous fields such as names, identity numbers, phone numbers, and addresses within a single ciphertext. It demonstrates the first complete realization of structure-aware, end-to-end fuzzy matching for Chinese text entirely in the homomorphic encryption domain.

The study resolves two key challenges: the indistinguishability of Chinese character encodings and the inefficiency of high-degree homomorphic evaluation. By decomposing high-codepoint characters into low-radix components, the proposed encoding enhances numerical separability and stability under CKKS arithmetic. Moreover, replacing high-order polynomial approximations with a quadratic evaluation kernel enables efficient and precise fuzzy comparison within limited multiplicative depth, avoiding excessive noise growth.

Future work will focus on adaptive field encoding to improve slot utilization and matching precision, hybrid encryption architectures that combine symmetric storage with homomorphic computation, and the extension of this framework toward expressive SQL-like encrypted query models. These developments aim to advance large-scale, privacy-preserving Chinese database systems built upon fully homomorphic encryption.

References

1. Essex, A.: Secure approximate string matching for privacy-preserving record linkage. IEEE Trans. Inf. Forensics Secur. **14**(10), 2623–2632 (2019)
2. Boddeti, V.N.: Secure face matching using fully homomorphic encryption. In: 2018 IEEE 9th International Conference on Biometrics Theory, Applications and Systems (BTAS), pp. 1–10. IEEE, California (2018). https://doi.org/10.1109/BTAS.2018.8698601
3. Engelsma, J.J., Jain, A.K.: Generalizing fingerprint spoof detector: Learning a one-class classifier. In: 2019 International Conference on Biometrics (ICB), pp. 1–8. IEEE, Crete (2019). https://doi.org/10.1109/ICB45273.2019.8987319
4. Wen, R., Yu, Y., Xie, X., Zhang, Y.: LEAF: a faster secure search algorithm via localization, extraction, and reconstruction. In: Proceedings of the 2020 ACM SIGSAC Conference on Computer and Communications Security, pp. 1219–1232. Association for Computing Machinery, New York (2020). https://doi.org/10.1145/3372297.3417237
5. Gentry, C.: Fully homomorphic encryption using ideal lattices. In: Proceedings of the Forty-First Annual ACM Symposium on Theory of Computing, pp. 169–178. Association for Computing Machinery, New York (2009). https://doi.org/10.1145/1536414.1536440
6. Brakerski, Z., Gentry, C., Vaikuntanathan, V.: (Leveled) fully homomorphic encryption without bootstrapping. In: Proceedings of the 3rd Innovations in Theoretical Computer Science Conference, pp. 309–325. Association for Computing Machinery, New York (2012). https://doi.org/10.1145/2090236.2090262
7. Fan, J., Vercauteren, F.: Somewhat practical fully homomorphic encryption. Cryptology ePrint Archive, Paper 2012/144 (2012). https://eprint.iacr.org/2012/144
8. Cheon, J. H., Kim, A., Kim, M., Song, Y.: Homomorphic encryption for arithmetic of approximate numbers. In: International Conference on the Theory and Application of Cryptology and Information Security, pp. 409–437. Springer (2017)
9. Ibarrondo, A., Chabanne, H., Despiegel, V., Önen, M.: Grote: group testing for privacy-preserving face identification. In: Proceedings of the Thirteenth ACM Conference on Data and Application Security and Privacy, pp. 117–128. Association for Computing Machinery, New York (2023). https://doi.org/10.1145/3577923.3583656
10. Choi, H., Kim, J., Song, C., Woo, S. S., Kim, H.: Blind-match: efficient homomorphic encryption-based 1: N matching for privacy-preserving biometric identification. In: Proceedings of the 2024 ACM Conference on Data and Application Security and Privacy, pp. 4423–4430. Association for Computing Machinery, New York (2024). https://doi.org/10.1145/3627673.3680017
11. Kabra, M., et al.: CIPHERMATCH: accelerating homomorphic encryption-based string matching via memory-efficient data packing and in-flash processing. In: Proceedings of the 30th ACM International Conference on Architectural Support for

Programming Languages and Operating Systems, Vol. 2, pp. 111–130. Association for Computing Machinery, New York (2025). https://doi.org/10.1145/3676641.3716251

12. Kasyap, H., Atmaca, U. I., Maple, C., Cormode, G., He, J.: Privacy-preserving fuzzy name matching for sharing financial intelligence. arXiv preprint arXiv:2407.19979 (2024)
13. Albrecht, M.R., Player, R., Scott, S.: On the concrete hardness of learning with errors. Cryptology ePrint Archive (2015)
14. Cheon, J.H., Son, Y., Yhee, D.: Practical FHE parameters against lattice attacks. Cryptology ePrint Archive (2021)
15. Bossuat, J.-P., et al.: Security guidelines for implementing homomorphic encryption. Cryptology ePrint Archive (2024)
16. Curtmola, R., Garay, J., Kamara, S., Ostrovsky, R.: Searchable symmetric encryption: improved definitions and efficient constructions. In: Editor, F., Editor, S. (eds.) Proceedings of the 13th ACM Conference on Computer and Communications Security, pp. 79–88. ACM (2006)
17. Hazay, C., Lindell, Y.: Efficient Secure Two-Party Protocols: Techniques and Constructions. Springer (2010)
18. Ohrimenko, O., et al.: Oblivious multi-party machine learning on trusted processors. In: 25th USENIX Security Symposium (USENIX Security 2016), pp. 619–636. USENIX Association (2016)

Evidential Deep Fusion for Multi-channel Analysis Against Public-Key Cryptosystems

Zeli Chen[1,2], Yuhan Qian[1], Jing Gao[3], Jing Yu[1], Yaoling Ding[1](✉), Xuexin Zheng[4](✉), and An Wang[1]

[1] Beijing Institute of Technology, Beijing 100081, China
{bitzel,qianyuhan,yujing93,dyl19,wangan1}@bit.edu.cn
[2] State Key Laboratory of Cryptography and Digital Economy Security, Shandong University, Qingdao 266200, China
[3] China Mobile Research Institute, Beijing 100032, China
gaojingyjy@chinamobile.com
[4] China Academy of Information and Communications Technology, Beijing 100142, China
zhengxuexin@caict.ac.cn

Abstract. Side-channel analysis evaluates cryptographic device security, but single channel methods can overlook combined leakage threats. Multi-channel fusion attacks exploit leakage more effectively. In this paper, we propose a decision-level fusion analysis method based on deep learning and Dempster-Shafer evidence theory, specifically tailored for side-channel analysis of public-key algorithms. To evaluate the reliability of sample classification probability distributions, we introduce a metric called the average separability index. Compared to data-level fusion and feature-level fusion, our method yields higher accuracy and confidence for cryptographic operations. In the side-channel analysis of ECC, RSA, and module-lattice-based key encapsulation mechanisms, key recovery accuracy is significantly improved, while the number of traces used is notably reduced. This approach achieves more than 98% cryptographic operation recovery accuracy, improving performance by 5.35%–43.93% over previous methods and boosting the average separability index. Whereas earlier techniques required 20 traces, this fusion method attains full key recovery with a single trace.

Keywords: Side-Channel Analysis · Multi-Channel Fusion Analysis · Public-Key Cryptosystems · Dempster-Shafer Evidence Theory

1 Introduction

Kocher introduced timing analysis in 1996 [7] and side-channel analysis has since become central to evaluating physical security of cryptographic devices.

Z. Chen and Y. Qian—The authors contributed equally to this work.

Y. Xiang and J. Shen (Eds.): ML4CS 2025, LNCS 16456, pp. 139–153, 2026.
https://doi.org/10.1007/978-981-95-7820-7_9

Public-key schemes such as RSA and Elliptic Curve Cryptography (ECC) produce distinctive leakages: modular exponentiation reveals square-multiply patterns, while ECC operations show power differences between point addition and point doubling. These characteristics make public-key algorithms prime targets for Side-Channel Analysis (SCA). Current mainstream analysis methods primarily rely on single-channel attacks, such as Simple Power Analysis (SPA) and Differential Power Analysis (DPA) [6]. SPA identifies key operations by directly observing computational patterns in power traces. However, detecting information leakage based solely on a single source of side-channel information not only fails to comprehensively reveal the potential leakage threats of cryptographic devices but may also lead to inaccurate analysis results due to the partial nature of the information.

Multi-Channel Fusion Analysis (MCFA) captures side-channel information from multiple channels in parallel, enhancing information complementarity and improving signal-to-noise ratio. These channels include timing [7,19], power [6,9], electromagnetic (EM) emission [1,24], fault [11,17], cache [10,23] and acoustic [4,21]. Yang et al. [22] divided MCFA into data-level [2], feature-level [16,22] and decision-level [12,15] categories. However, these methods fail to process long sequences efficiently and fail to adapt to implementation variations.

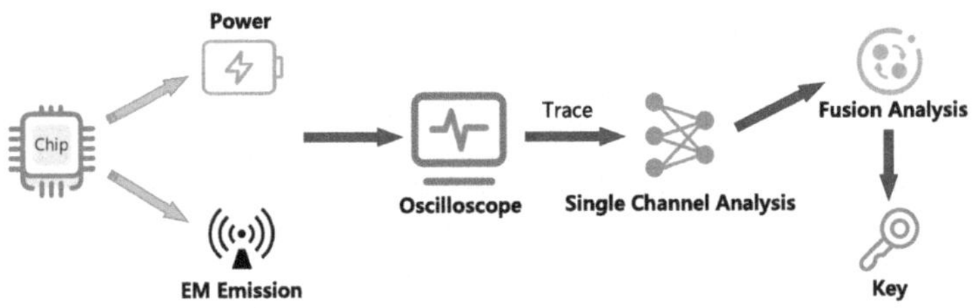

Fig. 1. CNN-DS Usage Scenario Diagram.

To address these issues, we propose a decision-level MCFA based on Dempster-Shafer (D-S) evidence theory [13,20]. Due to the powerful feature extraction ability of Convolutional Neural Networks (CNN) on side-channel traces [3,5,14], we derive propositions for D-S evidence theory from CNN output. Our method supports secret key recovery in public-key cryptosystems and Module-Lattice-Based Key Encapsulation Mechanisms (ML-KEM). As shown in Fig. 1, the diagram illustrates the process in which experimental personnel capture chip traces and utilize CNN with Dempster-Shafer fusion (CNN-DS) to extract the cryptographic key. Our contributions include:

- We propose a decision-level MCFA framework based on CNN-DS, which integrates D-S evidence theory into SCA of public-key cryptosystems. In this framework, CNNs extract and classify features from power and EM trace segments. D-S combination rules then merge these probability distributions to infer operation classes and enable secret key recovery.

- We collected power and EM traces from microcontrollers executing ML-KEM, ECC and RSA under real-world conditions. When trained on a single trace, CNN-DS recovers more than 98% of secret information. Compared with previous methods, average key recovery rates improve by 5.35%–43.93% and trace requirements fall by more than 95%.
- To evaluate the reliability of sample classification probability distributions, we introduce a metric called Average Separability Index (ASI). Comparative experiments show that CNN-DS can improve the confidence of traditional CNN classification, allowing the overall classification probability to deviate from uncertain values such as 50%, thus improving the classification precision.

2 Preliminaries

D-S evidence theory originated with Dempster in the late 1960s and was formalized by Shafer in 1976 [13,20]. It extends classical probability theory to handle incomplete or ambiguous information. The theory defines a frame of discernment encompassing all mutually exclusive hypotheses and assigns basic probability masses to subsets of that frame rather than to individual outcomes. It distinguishes belief from plausibility as measures of committed support and potential support, while any remaining mass represents explicit ignorance. When independent sources provide evidence, Dempster's rule of combination fuses their masses into a unified distribution that naturally manages conflict and uncertainty.

2.1 Frame of Discernment

The frame of discernment is a mutually exclusive and exhaustive set of hypotheses representing all possible answers or states.

In this paper, since we only utilize information from two channels, we introduce the D-S evidence theory using two parameters x and y as examples. The specific definition of Θ will be provided in Sect. 3.

$$\Theta = \{x, y\}, \tag{1}$$

which contains 2 mutually exclusive events. The power set $\mathcal{P}(\Theta)$ of the frame of discernment Θ contains 2^2 elements, and is represented as:

$$\mathcal{P}(\Theta) = \{\emptyset, \{x\}, \{y\}, \{x, y\}\}. \tag{2}$$

Properties:

- Mutual exclusivity: The elements in Θ do not overlap.
- Exhaustiveness: Θ must cover all possible scenarios.

2.2 Basic Probability Assignment Function

The Basic Probability Assignment (BPA) on the hypothesis space is a function $m : 2^{\Theta} \rightarrow [0,1]$, called the mass function. The basic probability assignment for each piece of evidence is implemented through the BPA function. Suppose there are n pieces of evidence $m_0, m_1, \ldots, m_n$, where each piece of evidence m_i is represented by a set of trust values $m_i(A_0), m_i(A_1), \ldots, m_i(A_l)$, where $m_i(A_q)$ denotes the degree of belief of evidence m_i that the proposition A_q is true. These values must satisfy the following three conditions:

1. First condition:

$$m_i(A_q) \in [0,1] \tag{3}$$

   This means that the basic probability value for each piece of evidence is within the range $[0,1]$.
2. Second condition:

$$\sum_{j=0}^{l} m_i(A_q) = 1 \tag{4}$$

   This means that the sum of all trust values equal to 1.
3. Third condition:

$$m_1(\emptyset) = 0 \tag{5}$$

   This means that the trust value for the empty set is 0.

2.3 Dempster's Combination Rule

The core of D-S evidence theory is the Dempster's combination rule. According to the rule of combination, any hypothesis assigned zero belief by one source remains unsupported in the fused result, even if other sources offer strong support. Let m_0 and m_1 denote the basic probability assignments from two evidence sources. Here, $m_0(x)$ represents the support for proposition x from the first source and $m_1(y)$ represents the support for proposition y from the second source.

The Dempster's combination rule is defined as follows:

$$M(A) = [m_0 \oplus m_1](A) \tag{6}$$

$$= \begin{cases} 0, & A = \emptyset \\ (1-K)^{-1} \sum_{x \cap y = A} m_0(x) m_1(y), & A \neq \emptyset, \end{cases} \tag{7}$$

where $M(A)$ represents the combined basic probability assignment, indicating the support for proposition A after integrating evidence from different sources.

The constant K is the conflict measure, which represents the degree of conflict between the two evidence sources. The equation for calculating the conflict measure is:

$$K = \sum_{x \cap y = \emptyset} m_0(x) m_1(y) \tag{8}$$

The normalization factor $(1 - K)^{-1}$ ensures that the combined basic probability assignment satisfies the condition that the sum of probabilities is equal to 1. If the conflict measure $K = 1$, it indicates a complete conflict and an effective fusion is not possible, making it impossible to derive a reasonable conclusion.

Through Eqs. (7) and (8), the two evidence sources m_0 and m_1 in D-S evidence theory can be fused to obtain the final predicted probability. In this way, the combined result not only reflects the support from each evidence source but also considers the conflict between the sources of evidence.

2.4 Scalar Multiplication and Modular Exponentiation

ECC is a modern public-key cryptosystem that relies on the algebraic structure of elliptic curves over finite fields and the computational complexity inherent in solving the elliptic curve discrete logarithm problem. The advantage of ECC lies in its ability to offer higher security, smaller key sizes, faster encryption speeds, and lower bandwidth requirements, making it especially suitable for resource-constrained environments. The main process of scalar multiplication involves point addition and point doubling operations. During this process, the key is identified bit by bit. When the key bit is 0, the point-doubling operation is performed; when the key bit is 1, both point-doubling and point-addition operations are performed. By analyzing the distinct characteristics produced by these operations in power or EM traces, one can identify each operation and ultimately recover the secret scalar.

RSA's security relies on the difficulty of factoring large composite numbers. Modular exponentiation is at the core of RSA, where exponentiation of private key bits is split into modular squaring and modular multiplication, each generating distinct side-channel leakage patterns. By analyzing the differences in these operations within power or EM traces, an attacker can infer the private key.

3 Methodology

CNN-DS focuses on fusion attacks combining two representative side-channel leakages, namely EM and power consumption, both measured simultaneously on a cryptographic device. Two trace datasets, denoted Ψ_{EM} and Ψ_{pow}, are collected. Since our trace acquisition is conducted separately, and the acquisition of the power trace and the EM trace does not interfere with each other, it satisfies the mutual exclusivity condition of the Dempster-Shafer theory. We use the automatic slicing algorithm proposed by Wang et al. in 2024 [18] to process the collected traces through a neural network, obtaining the trace features for each operation in both power traces and EM traces. Each trace comprises n cryptographic operation segments:

$$\psi_{e\alpha} = [\psi_{e\alpha,1}, \psi_{e\alpha,2}, \dots, \psi_{e\alpha,n}],$$

$$\psi_{p\beta} = [\psi_{p\beta,1}, \psi_{p\beta,2}, \dots, \psi_{p\beta,n}],$$

where $\psi_{e\alpha,k}$ denotes the k-th segment of the α-th EM trace, and $\psi_{p\beta,k}$ denotes the k-th segment of the β-th power trace.

3.1 Framework of CNN-DS Fusion Attack

To fully leverage complementary features of multi-channel traces for fusion analysis, CNN-DS, a fusion attack combining CNN with D-S evidence theory is proposed. First, CNNs extract features from cryptographic operation segments in each channel and produce category probability distributions for each segment. Next, D-S theory fuses these distributions to predict operation classes. Recovering all operation classes enables recovery of the secret key.

Algorithm 1 outlines the CNN-DS workflow. First, power trace segments ψ_{pow}, EM trace segments ψ_{EM} and operation labels L are split into training and testing sets. Two CNNs are trained independently, one on ψ_{pow} and one on ψ_{EM}. Each model predicts on the test set, yielding probability distributions P_{pow} and P_{EM}. Next, D-S theory fuses these distributions into a final probability mass function P_{fusion}. Finally, the most likely operation type l_{guess} is determined by taking the maximum value of the fused probability P_{fusion}. Integrating complementary information from both channels enhances key recovery accuracy. Section 3.3 describes the D-S theory application in detail.

Algorithm 1. The CNN-Based Fusion Attack Aided by D-S Evidence Theory

1: **Input:** ψ_{pow}, ψ_{EM}, L
2: **Output:** l_{guess}
3: Split datasets: $(\psi_{pow}, \psi_{EM}, L) \rightarrow (\psi_{pow}^{\text{train}}, \psi_{EM}^{\text{train}}, L^{\text{train}})$ and $(\psi_{pow}^{\text{test}}, \psi_{EM}^{\text{test}})$
4: train CNN model $\mathcal{M}_{pow}$ on $(\psi_{pow}^{\text{train}}, L^{\text{train}})$
5: train CNN model $\mathcal{M}_{EM}$ on $(\psi_{EM}^{\text{train}}, L^{\text{train}})$
6: $P_{pow} \leftarrow \mathcal{M}_{pow}(\psi_{pow}^{\text{test}})$
7: $P_{EM} \leftarrow \mathcal{M}_{EM}(\psi_{EM}^{\text{test}})$
8: $P_{fusion} \leftarrow$ D-S_fuse(P_{pow}, P_{EM})
9: $l_{guess} \leftarrow \arg\max \ P_{fusion}$
10: **return** l_{guess}

3.2 CNN Architecture Design for Single-Channel Traces

A CNN architecture processes one-dimensional time-series data from side-channel measurements, including power traces and EM traces. The model follows a compact architecture that balances representational capacity and computational efficiency, with a total of three convolutional blocks followed by a global feature aggregation and classification head. The complete model architecture is summarized in Table 1. The corresponding diagram of the architecture is presented in Fig. 2.

The neural network input consists of trace segments shaped as $(T, 1)$, where T is the number of sample points. The first convolutional layer uses 16 filters of size 3 with ReLU activation and same padding, followed by batch normalization and a pooling layer. Pooling type, either max or average, is chosen as a hyperparameter. The second convolutional block increases the filter count to 32 and repeats convolution, batch normalization and pooling. A third convolutional layer applies 64 filters and is followed by batch normalization. Instead of flattening or local pooling, a global average pooling layer aggregates temporal features into a compact representation. This design mitigates overfitting and enhances generalization in small-sample scenarios typical of SCA.

Classification head includes a dense layer with 64 units and ReLU activation and a dropout layer at rate 0.1 to reduce overfitting. A final dense layer with softmax activation produces a probability distribution over target classes. Training uses the Adam optimizer at a learning rate of 5×10^{-5} with sparse categorical cross-entropy loss. This architecture excels in limited-data scenarios and functions as an effective feature extractor for multi-channel fusion experiments.

Table 1. Network Architecture

Layer	Input Size	Output Size
Input	$(T, 1)$	$(T, 1)$
Conv1D	$(T, 1)$	$(T, 16)$
BatchNorm & ReLU	$(T, 16)$	$(T, 16)$
Pooling (avg or max)	$(T, 16)$	$(T', 16)$
Conv1D	$(T', 16)$	$(T', 32)$
BatchNorm & ReLU	$(T', 32)$	$(T', 32)$
Pooling (avg or max)	$(T', 32)$	$(T'', 32)$
Conv1D	$(T'', 32)$	$(T'', 64)$
BatchNorm & ReLU	$(T'', 64)$	$(T'', 64)$
GlobalAveragePooling1D	$(T'', 64)$	$(1, 64)$
Dense	$(1, 64)$	$(1, 64)$
Dropout	$(1, 64)$	$(1, 64)$
Dense	$(1, 64)$	$(1, num\_classes)$

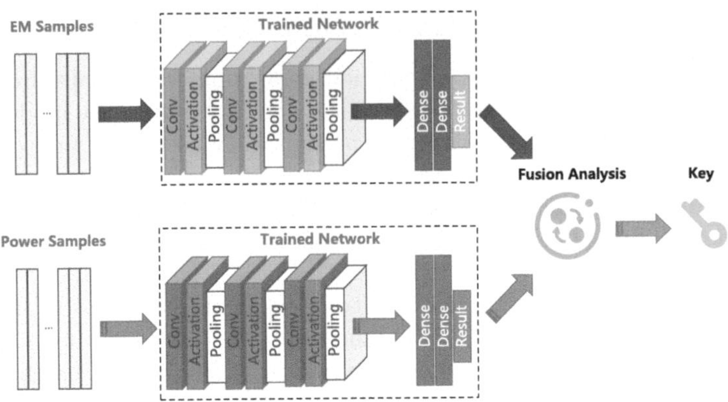

Fig. 2. Flowchart of CNN-DS Scheme.

3.3 Evidence Fusion via D-S Evidence Theory

Initially, a frame of discernment is defined to clarify the D-S evidence theory process. Two hypotheses are introduced: hypothesis A_0 when a trace segment $\psi_{e\alpha,k}$ or $\psi_{p\beta,k}$ corresponds to cryptographic operation 0, and hypothesis A_1 when $\psi_{e\alpha,k}$ or $\psi_{p\beta,k}$ corresponds to cryptographic operation 1. Accordingly, the frame of discernment Θ is defined as:

$$\Theta = \{A_0, A_1\}, \tag{9}$$

where A_0 and A_1 represent different cryptographic operations. For example, in ECC, A_0 corresponds to point addition on $\psi_{e\alpha,k}$ or $\psi_{p\beta,k}$ and A_1 to point multipe. Similar hypothesis can be defined for RSA and ML-KEM-512.

Based on the definition of m_i, we define two mass functions m_0 and m_1 corresponding to the power channel and the EM channel, respectively. The mass function m_0 represents the basic probability assignment in the hypothesis space for the power channel, while the mass function m_1 represents the basic probability assignment on the hypothesis space for the EM channel. Specifically, $m_0(A_q)$ denotes the degree of belief for the proposition A_q in the context of the power channel, and $m_1(A_q)$ denotes the degree of belief for the proposition A_q in the context of the EM channel. Both mass functions must satisfy the conditions outlined for a valid BPA, ensuring that the sum of all mass assignments equals 1 and the values are within the valid range of $[0, 1]$.

CNN classifiers output both a predicted label and its confidence probability. Probabilities serve directly as D-S evidence.

For each trace segment $\psi_{e\alpha,k}$ or $\psi_{p\beta,k}$, the CNN produces a confidence score:

$$p_1 = P\big(\text{operation} = 1 \mid \psi_{e\alpha,k} \text{ or } \psi_{p\beta,k}\big). \tag{10}$$

The basic probability assignments are then set to

$$m_i(A_q) = \begin{cases} p_1, & \text{if } q = 1, \\ 1 - p_1, & \text{if } q = 0. \end{cases} \tag{11}$$

In this manner, the classifier's output probabilities serve directly as evidence for the corresponding hypotheses.

Each CNN's output probability distribution is first interpreted as a Basic Belief Assignment (BBA) over the hypothesis set. These BBAs satisfy the requirement that all mass values sum to one, ensuring a legitimate probabilistic foundation. Fusion proceeds by applying Dempster's orthogonal sum rule across channels: when combining two BBAs, the mass assigned to each hypothesis is obtained by summing the products of channel-specific masses that support the same hypothesis, then normalizing by one minus the total conflict mass K. K measures the degree of contradiction between channels. When two basic belief assignments m_0 and m_1 are combined, K sums the products of masses that support mutually exclusive hypotheses. For example, one CNN strongly favoring operation 1 while another favors operation 0 for the same segment. In SCA, a large K indicates that different channels' CNNs disagree on the operation type. Dempster's rule then normalizes by $1 - K$, effectively down-weighting these conflicts and redistributing their mass across the remaining hypotheses. This fusion mechanism delivers more confident, robust decisions and significantly enhances key recovery performance.

4 Experimental Results

We collected power and EM traces from microcontroller implementations of ML-KEM-512, ECC and RSA. ML-KEM-512 was executed on an STM32F407 development board to process 256-bit messages. RSA was executed on an STM32F429 board with a 1024-bit key. The ECC implementation on SAKURA-G performs masked scalar multiplication by combining a 256-bit secret scalar with a 64-bit mask to yield a 320-bit masked scalar. Different analysis methods were then applied to each dataset to compare key recovery outcomes.

4.1 Evaluation Metrics

Accuracy and Number of Trace. To assess key recovery performance, we use classification accuracy of cryptographic operations. Let $S = [s_1, s_2, \ldots, s_T]$ be the true label sequence of T operations and let $\hat{S}$ denote the predicted sequence. Accuracy is defined as:

$$Accuracy = \frac{1}{T} \sum_{t=1}^{T} (s_t = \hat{s}_t). \tag{12}$$

Number of traces needed for key recovery measures attack difficulty, and fewer traces indicate lower demands on the adversary.

Average Separability Index. We introduce the ASI to quantify the trustworthiness of a model's predicted probability distribution. ASI computes the average absolute distance of each predicted probability from the chance level of 50%, thereby reflecting how confidently samples are classified. ASI captures overall separability of the distribution. It is defined as follows:

$$ASI = \frac{2}{T}\sum_{i=1}^{T}\left(\max(p_0^{(i)}, p_1^{(i)}) - 0.5\right). \tag{13}$$

Here, $p_0^{(i)}$ denotes the probability that sample i corresponds to operation 1, and $p_1^{(i)}$ denotes the probability that sample i corresponds to operation 2.

4.2 Comparison of Experimental Results

Experiments were conducted on three representative datasets: ML-KEM-512, ECC, and RSA. We evaluated four categories of methods, including the unsupervised non-fusion approach of Kulow et al. [8], Yang et al.'s SVD-based fusion method, the GSVD feature-level fusion technique [22], and our proposed CNN-DS framework. The comparison focused on classification accuracy, trace counts, and the reliability of cryptographic key recovery.

On ML-KEM-512 traces, Figs. 3(a) visualize Kulow et al.'s method [8] on EM traces. After PCA and K-Means, the predicted clusters diverge from the ground-truth operation classes, yielding only 54.69% accuracy. The scatter shows substantial overlap between the two operation types, which suggests that clustering is driven by variance along the principal components rather than the semantics of the operations. Figures 3(d) present the corresponding results on power traces. Accuracy rises to 89.45%, yet the cluster boundary still fails to align with the true labels, indicating that a single channel does not provide sufficiently separable structure for reliable recovery. Figures 3(b) visualize our method on EM traces. After CNN-DS, the predicted clusters are almost identical to the ground-truth operation classes, with only minor deviations, resulting in an accuracy of 99.61%. Figures 3(b) and 3(e) show the dimensionality reduction results obtained using PCA on the EM and power channels.

Table 2 shows that CNN-DS delivers significant improvements in both classification accuracy and trace efficiency. Averaging 100 power traces with PCA followed by K-Means attains 93.77%, which remains below the single trace performance of CNN-DS with the accuracy of 99.61%. SVD-based feature-level fusion improves to 95.31% [22], but it still falls short. In contrast, CNN-DS combines CNN-extracted evidence from EM and power and fuses the resulting probability distributions with D-S theory.

For ECC traces, a similar trend is observed. Dimensionality reduction followed by clustering achieves 97.16% accuracy only when at least 20 traces are averaged. With a single trace, accuracy decreases to 94.65%. The GSVD approach, although effective for symmetric algorithms, reaches only 55.84% in this case, which reveals its limitations for public-key ciphers. CNN-DS applied to individual channels alone does not outperform PCA-based clustering, but once

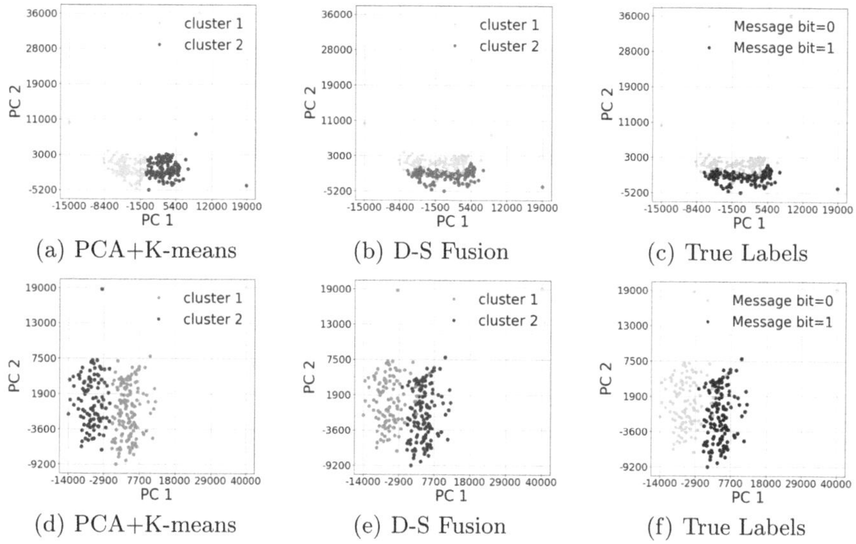

Fig. 3. Experimental results using the method of [8] on both the ML-KEM-512 EM and power traces. The first row shows the clustering results on the EM trace, and the second row shows the clustering results on the power trace.

D-S fusion is applied, the accuracy reaches 100%, enabling complete recovery of cryptographic operations with a single trace.

On RSA traces, traditional methods show limited effectiveness. PCA followed by K-Means produces 66.64% accuracy at best, and GSVD fusion further reduces accuracy to 54.24%. In contrast, CNN-DS maintains strong and consistent performance, achieving 98.17% accuracy. This confirms that CNN-DS generalizes effectively across different cryptographic algorithms, including lattice-based schemes, elliptic curve systems, and RSA.

In summary, conventional unsupervised clustering methods require averaging over multiple traces but still fail to reach the performance of CNN-DS with a single trace. Feature-level fusion methods such as GSVD can even reduce accuracy when applied to asymmetric cryptosystems. However CNN-DS, which combines CNN-based feature extraction with D-S-based decision fusion, consistently achieves superior accuracy and trace efficiency, enabling reliable secret key recovery under noisy and low-sample conditions.

4.3 Ablation Experiments

To demonstrate necessity of multi-channel fusion, classification probabilities before and after fusion were analyzed. Classification reliability across three datasets was then assessed using the ASI. ASI values closer to 1 indicate greater confidence in predicted probabilities and further enhances key recovery performance.

Table 2. Comparison of Experimental Results across Different Datasets

Dataset	Method	Trace Count	Accuracy		
			Power	EM	Fusion
ML-KEM-512	PCA & K-Means [8]	100	96.48%	55.08%	–
	PCA & K-Means [8]	1	89.45%	54.69%	–
	SVD [22]	1	–	–	95.31%
	CNN-DS	**1**	98.05%	96.48%	**99.61%**
ECC	PCA & K-Means [8]	20	97.16%	57.51%	–
	PCA & K-Means [8]	1	94.65%	53.50%	–
	GSVD [22]	1	–	–	55.84%
	CNN-DS	**1**	65.83%	79.54%	**100%**
RSA	PCA & K-Means [8]	1	66.64%	61.81%	–
	GSVD [22]	1	–	–	54.24%
	CNN-DS	**1**	97.78%	90.21%	**98.17%**

Figure 4 displays classification probability distributions on the RSA traces. Figure 4(a) and Fig. 4(b) show CNN outputs for the ϕ_{pow} and ϕ_{EM} segments, respectively, while Fig. 4(c) presents fused probabilities. Black markers represent correct classifications, red markers indicate errors, and the horizontal line denotes the 50% decision threshold. In Fig. 4(a), many predicted probabilities lie close to the threshold, producing frequent errors and yielding an ASI of 0.727, which reflects the weak separability of EM traces alone. Figure 4(b) shows that power traces provide stronger discrimination, with fewer red markers and an increased ASI of 0.934. After fusion, as illustrated in Fig. 4(c), probabilities concentrate near 1, errors are further reduced, and ASI rises to 0.958. This confirms that CNN-DS leverages complementary information from both channels to achieve higher confidence and accuracy.

Figure 5 of the same figure reports CNN-DS results on the ML-KEM-512 traces. In this case, both Fig. 5(a) and Fig. 5(b) already show strong separation, with probabilities mostly above 0.9 and ASI values of 0.967 and 0.983. Fusion in Fig. 5(c) further concentrates the predictions near 1.0, raising ASI to 0.998. The results demonstrate that multi-channel decision fusion not only corrects residual misclassifications but also improves confidence, thereby ensuring reliable cryptographic operation recovery from a single trace.

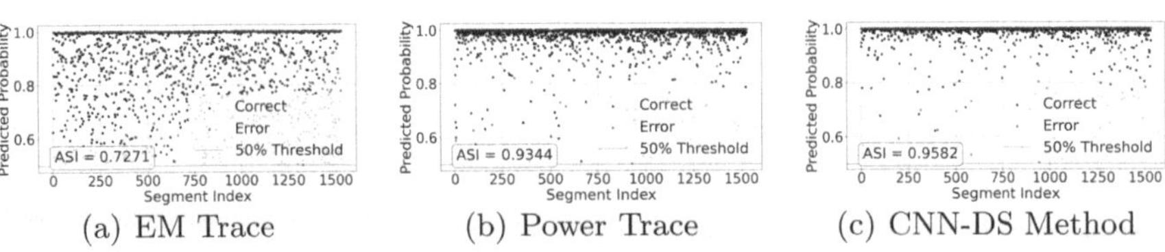

(a) EM Trace (b) Power Trace (c) CNN-DS Method

Fig. 4. Classification Probability Distribution of RSA.

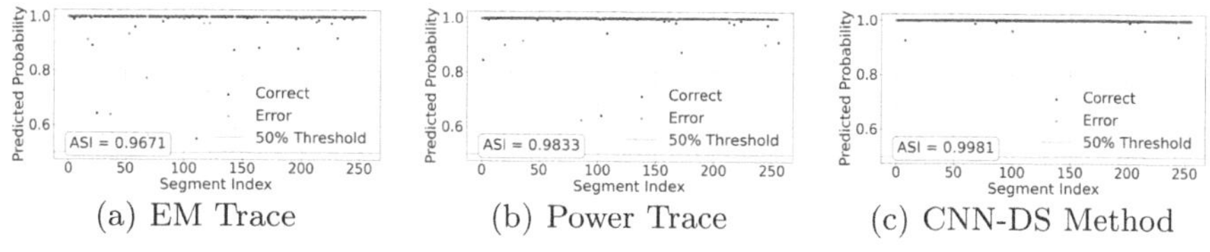

(a) EM Trace (b) Power Trace (c) CNN-DS Method

Fig. 5. Classification Probability Distribution of ML-KEM-512.

Table 3 reports ASI for power, EM, and fusion settings. On ML-KEM-512 and RSA, fusion pushes ASI close to 1, while the best single-channel result remains below this level. For ECC, both single channels yield low ASI about 0.26 for power and about 0.31 for EM. Fusion improves ASI to 0.439, which confirms that decision-level integration still provides a measurable gain even when individual channels are weak. Overall, CNN-DS consistently increases ASI across datasets and enhances reliability under single trace conditions.

Table 3. ASI Results for Fusion and Non-Fusion Methods

Dataset	Power Channel	EM Channel	Fusion Method
ML-KEM-512	0.983	0.967	**0.998**
ECC	0.261	0.306	**0.439**
RSA	0.934	0.727	**0.958**

5 Conclusion

To fully exploit the complementary features of multi-channel traces, we propose a fusion attack model, termed CNN-DS, which integrates CNN with D-S evidence theory. CNNs are employed to extract discriminative features from cryptographic operation segments in each channel and generate probability distributions, which are subsequently fused by D-S theory to predict operation classes.

Compared with traditional single-channel SCA methods, the proposed multi-source fusion approach CNN-DS achieves notable performance gains. By combining CNN-based feature extraction with D-S-based decision fusion, CNN-DS substantially advances public-key SCA. In particular, when applied to algorithms such as ML-KEM-512, ECC, and RSA, CNN-DS not only improves classification accuracy but also enhances robustness under high-noise conditions and with limited training samples. Experimental results demonstrate that CNN-DS attains over 98% accuracy in recovering cryptographic operations, outperforming prior approaches by 5.35%-43.93% and achieving a higher ASI. Moreover, while earlier methods typically required multiple traces for reliable key recovery, our fusion approach is able to succeed with a single trace.

In conclusion, the analysis method proposed in this paper maintains efficient performance and fully utilizes multi-channel information without significantly increasing computational burden, thereby enhancing the robustness and accuracy of side-channel attacks.

Acknowledgments. This work is supported by National Natural Science Foundation of China (Nos. 62272047, 62502035), Beijing Natural Science Foundation (Nos. QY25258, L244044, L251068), and State Key Laboratory of Cryptography and Digital Economy Security, Shandong University (No. KFZD2503).

References

1. Agrawal, D., Archambeault, B., Rao, J.R., Rohatgi, P.: The EM side—channel (s). In: International Workshop on Cryptographic Hardware and Embedded Systems, pp. 29–45. Springer (2002)
2. Agrawal, D., Rao, J.R., Rohatgi, P.: Multi-channel attacks. In: International Workshop on Cryptographic Hardware and Embedded Systems (2003)
3. Cagli, E., Dumas, C., Prouff, E.: Convolutional neural networks with data augmentation against jitter-based countermeasures. Lecture Notes in Computer Science, pp. 45–68 (2017)
4. Genkin, D., Shamir, A., Tromer, E.: RSA key extraction via low-bandwidth acoustic cryptanalysis. Lecture Notes in Computer Science, pp. 444–461 (2014)
5. Heuser, A., Picek, S., Guilley, S., Mentens, N.: Lightweight ciphers and their side-channel resilience. IEEE Trans. Comput. **69**(10), 1434–1448 (2020)
6. Kocher, P., Jaffe, J., Jun, B.: Differential power analysis. In: Wiener, M. (ed.) Advances in Cryptology – CRYPTO 1999, pp. 388–397. Springer, Heidelberg (1999)
7. Kocher, P.C.: Timing attacks on implementations of Diffie-Hellman, RSA, DSS, and other systems. In: Advances in Cryptology - CRYPTO '96, 16th Annual International Cryptology Conference, Santa Barbara, California, USA, August 18–22, 1996, Proceedings. Lecture Notes in Computer Science, vol. 1109, pp. 104–113. Springer (1996)
8. Kulow, A., Schamberger, T., Tebelmann, L., Sigl, G.: Finding the needle in the haystack: metrics for best trace selection in unsupervised side-channel attacks on blinded RSA. IEEE Trans. Inf. Forensics Secur. **16**, 3254–3268 (2021)
9. Lipp, M., et al.: Platypus: software-based power side-channel attacks on x86. In: 2021 IEEE Symposium on Security and Privacy (SP), pp. 355–371 (2021)
10. Osvik, D.A., Shamir, A., Tromer, E.: Cache attacks and countermeasures: the case of AES. Lecture Notes in Computer Science, pp. 1–20 (2006)
11. Paillier, P.: Evaluating differential fault analysis of unknown cryptosystems. Lecture Notes in Computer Science, pp. 235–244 (1999)
12. Schindler, W.: A combined timing and power attack. Lecture Notes in Computer Science, pp. 263–279 (2002)
13. Shafer, G.: A Mathematical Theory of Evidence. Princeton University Press, Princeton, N.J. (1976)
14. Shan, W., Zhang, S., He, Y.: Machine learning based side-channel-attack countermeasure with hamming-distance redistribution and its application on advanced encryption standard. Electron. Lett. **53**(14), 926–928 (2017)

15. Souissi, Y., Bhasin, S., Guilley, S., Nassar, M., Danger, J.L.: Towards different flavors of combined side channel attacks. In: Proceedings of CT-RSA, pp. 245–259. San Francisco, CA, USA (2012)
16. Specht, R., Heyszl, J., Kleinsteuber, M., Sigl, G.: Improving non-profiled attacks on exponentiations based on clustering and extracting leakage from multi-channel high-resolution EM measurements. Springer, New York (2015)
17. Vafaei, N., Bagheri, N., Saha, S., Mukhopadhyay, D.: Differential fault attack on skinny block cipher. Lecture Notes in Computer Science, pp. 177–197 (2018)
18. Wang, Z., et al.: SPA-GPT: general pulse tailor for simple power analysis based on reinforcement learning. IACR Transactions on Cryptographic Hardware and Embedded Systems, pp. 40–83 (2024)
19. Wei, C., et al.: Time is not enough: timing leakage analysis on cryptographic chips via plaintext-ciphertext correlation in non-timing channel. IEEE Trans. Inf. Forensics Secur. **19**, 8544–8558 (2024)
20. Yager, R.R.: On the dempster-shafer framework and new combination rules. Inf. Sci. **41**(2), 93–137 (1987)
21. Yang, L., et al.: Remote attacks on speech recognition systems using sound from power supply. In: Proceedings of the 32nd Usenix Security Symposium (2023)
22. Yang, W., Zhou, Y., Cao, Y., Zhang, H., Zhang, Q., Wang, H.: Multi-channel fusion attacks. IEEE Trans. Inf. Forensics Secur. (2017)
23. Zeng, C.S., Qingkai: survey of CPU cache-based side-channel attacks: systematic analysis, security models, and countermeasures. Secur. Commun. Netw. (2021)
24. Zhang, X., Zhu, Y., Hu, B., Cao, J., Lin, Z.: A novel power system side channel attack method based on machine learning CNN-transformer. J. Phys: Conf. Ser. **2615**(1), 12011 (2023)

Token-Efficient Binary Vulnerability Prioritization via Function Pre-filtering with LLMs

Zhuoyuan Niu[1], Chen Wang[1,2](✉), and Wei Wu[1]

[1] School of Information Science and Engineering (School of Cyber Science and Technology), Zhejiang Sci-Tech University, Hangzhou 310018, China
[2] Zhejiang Key Laboratory of Digital Fashion and Data Governance, Zhejiang Sci-Tech University, Hangzhou 310018, China
wangchen@zstu.edu.cn

Abstract. With the widespread use of the Internet of Things (IoT) and mobile devices, binary programs are widely used in human life. From smart homes and car systems to industrial control systems, underlying firmware and native executable files form the core of these critical infrastructures. In traditional vulnerability discovery, researchers need to manually analyze function relationships and function content. With the rapid development of Artificial Intelligence (AI), large language models (LLMs) are utilized for analysis, replacing manual analysis. However, sending fully decompiled functions to LLMs consumes a large number of tokens, resulting in high costs and slow responses, particularly for large binaries. Many existing methods treat all functions equally, without focusing on those more likely to be vulnerable. In this paper, we proposed a token-efficient binary vulnerability prioritization framework. Our framework allows the LLM to analyze function names to identify potentially risky functions, and then enables the LLM to examine only these selected functions in detail. What's more, we introduce a metric called token-detection efficiency (TDE) to better demonstrate the efficiency of our proposed framework. The experiment shows that our framework achieves higher vulnerability detection accuracy with fewer tokens.

Keywords: Vulnerability prioritization · LLMs · Function pre-filtering

1 Introduction

With the rapid advancement of the Internet of Things (IoT), an increasing number of terminal devices are running complex binary programs. These programs usually contain numerous third-party components and custom logic. They are developed within short cycles, and are not updated in a timely manner, making them highly susceptible to security vulnerabilities. These vulnerabilities could lead to serious privacy breaches or service disruptions. In addition, prior work

Y. Xiang and J. Shen (Eds.): ML4CS 2025, LNCS 16456, pp. 154–165, 2026.
https://doi.org/10.1007/978-981-95-7820-7_10

shows that embedded platforms such as Android require trusted computing architectures and secure data transmission mechanisms to mitigate increasing threats in real-world IoT ecosystems [1]. However, such system-level protections do not eliminate vulnerabilities inside the underlying binary programs, which remain a major attack surface lacking efficient automated analysis. Traditional firmware vulnerability analysis focuses primarily on analyzing individual executable files. However, in practical applications, vulnerabilities often do not appear within a single file but rather in the interaction logic between binary files [2], resulting in low efficiency of traditional analysis methods. Therefore, efficient vulnerability detection for binary programs has become one of the important research areas in cybersecurity.

Automated binary analysis techniques are mainly divided into two categories: static analysis and dynamic analysis. Static analysis locates potential vulnerabilities through data flow, control flow, or symbolic execution techniques without executing the program, but is often limited by false positives due to over-approximation [3]. Dynamic analysis, on the other hand, relies on runtime information and can more accurately capture the paths that trigger vulnerabilities. However, it is prone to missed detections due to limitations in input generation and code coverage.

In recent years, Large Language Models (LLMs) have demonstrated powerful capabilities in code understanding and semantic reasoning, bringing new possibilities to binary analysis [4]. Researchers have begun to explore using LLMs for semantic analysis of decompiled results and compiled assembly code to aid in vulnerability detection and program understanding. However, directly inputting complete decompiled functions or compiled assembly code into an LLM leads to severe token consumption and inference latency issues. This approach becomes extremely costly when analyzing large binary files that contain thousands of functions. Furthermore, most methods treat functions equally, failing to distinguish between high-risk and low-risk targets, which further reduces the efficiency of the analysis.

To address these challenges, we propose a novel framework that combines lightweight semantic feature extraction with the capabilities of LLMs to achieve scalable, interpretable, and low-cost identification of high-risk functions.

Our contributions in this paper are mainly as follows:

1) We propose a framework that improves the efficiency of LLM-based binary analysis by minimizing unnecessary token consumption through a lightweight pre-filtering mechanism.

2) We design a two-stage feedback pipeline, where a fast pre-filtering stage filters out low-risk functions, while a deep reasoning stage allocates the limited token budget to high-priority candidates for vulnerability detection.

3) We introduce a metric called token-detection efficiency (TDE) to quantify the efficiency improvement, and experimental results validate the effectiveness of our framework.

2 Background

2.1 Binary Program

Currently, most devices rely on Linux-based systems, with their core functions implemented by numerous user-space binary programs. These programs are responsible for providing critical services, such as network interfaces, device management, and data synchronization. However, limited by embedded development environments and vendor maintenance cycles, these binary programs often lack security hardening and are subject to delayed updates, leading to frequent vulnerabilities. Common vulnerabilities include stack overflows, command injection, format string errors, and use-after-free (UAF). Once exploited, attackers can remotely execute malicious commands or control the entire device, threatening personal privacy and critical infrastructure security.

Due to the large size and complex dependencies of binary files, manual auditing is virtually impossible, thus requiring automated and scalable vulnerability detection technologies. However, most firmware exists in closed-source binary form, making analysis using source code-level tools impossible. This "black box" characteristic poses a serious challenge to traditional detection methods. Meanwhile, due to the difference between kernel mode and user mode in the system, many programs running in kernel mode cannot be easily analyzed. Based on existing information, many researchers have proposed many new ideas, such as migrating individual processes in the firmware to run in the user space environment, in order to reduce the difficulty of emulating the kernel [5].

2.2 Existing Analytical Methods

Static Analysis and Dynamic Analysis. Static analysis examines binary code without executing it, enabling researchers to infer potential vulnerabilities through control flow graphs (CFG), data flow analysis, or symbolic reasoning. And researchers have proposed many detection approaches, such as Reaching Definition Analysis for binary files [3]. Static analysis is highly scalable and capable of uncovering deep logical flaws that may not manifest at runtime. However, static analysis often struggles with obfuscated code, indirect jumps, or simplified binaries that lack debugging information. Furthermore, the precision of static analysis is highly dependent on correct disassembly and intermediate representation (IR) transformations [6,7], steps that can introduce errors in complex instruction sets or firmware architectures.

In contrast, dynamic analysis observes program behavior during execution, enabling direct detection of vulnerabilities such as buffer overflows, format string manipulation, and use-after-free (UAF). Because it tracks actual runtime behavior and data flow, it offers high semantic accuracy. Despite these advantages, dynamic analysis faces significant challenges in terms of scalability: it requires a complete and accurate simulation environment, especially for firmware with hardware dependencies, drivers, or system calls. In that case, some researchers offer some new ideas in this field. For example, some researchers use binary instrumentation and a high-efficiency taint propagation engine to dynamically trace taint flows in firmware within a simulation environment [8]. The well-known Firmadyne uses dynamic simulation to run a complete firmware image and extracts behavior from its runtime state [9].

Researchers are increasingly combining static and dynamic techniques to fully leverage their respective strengths. Hybrid systems utilize static analysis for pre-filtering or guidance, thereby narrowing the search space for dynamic tests [2]. They also improve function naming recovery by leveraging execution context features and combining symbolic execution with semantic embedding [10].

Fuzz Testing. Fuzz testing is a branch of dynamic analysis that primarily uses automated large-scale inputs fed into a target program to trigger anomalous behavior or crashes, thus uncovering security vulnerabilities. Fuzz testing has become an important tool for software security detection due to its high degree of automation and ability to directly trigger exploitable runtime defects. Some researchers have also proposed μFUZZ, a parallel fuzzing system for microservice architectures, which improves fuzzing efficiency and has better coverage and vulnerability discovery rates than other tools in real-world programs [11]. However, while fuzz testing is widespread, evaluation methods still present challenges [12]. In recent years, with the development of AI, the combination of fuzz and AI has become a popular research area [13].

2.3 LLMs and MCP

In recent years, LLMs have achieved remarkable results in fields such as natural language understanding and task planning [14,15]. These models have demonstrated powerful capabilities in understanding code semantics [16,17]. However, traditional LLMs mainly rely on text interaction and lack the ability to directly interact with external systems or local environments. To address this issue, the industry has proposed various model extension frameworks that enable LLMs to invoke tools, access file systems, or execute programs. Among them, Model Context Protocol (MCP), as an emerging open standard, aims to achieve secure communication between models and local processes through a unified interface.

The design goal of MCP is to enable models to access external resources in a controlled environment, such as databases, command-line tools, system APIs, or private knowledge bases, thereby improving the executability and contextual understanding capabilities of LLM in practical tasks [18]. MCP also gives the LLM "operational agency", meaning that the LLM can actively select and execute external actions based on the results of semantic reasoning.

3 Our Design

Our framework is designed as a two-stage feedback pipeline:

1. A lightweight pre-filtering stage is used to quickly filter out a large number of low-risk functions with very few tokens.

2. The deep analysis stage concentrates the limited token budget on those high-priority candidate functions, thereby achieving a better trade-off between cost and detection coverage.

Our framework is shown in Fig. 1. We will analyze the implementation details of the framework in detail.

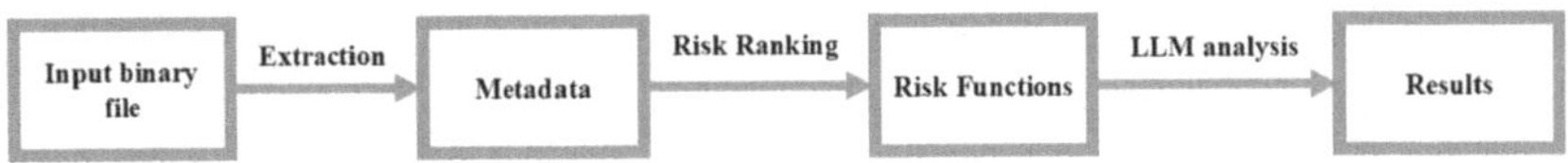

Fig. 1. This is a schematic diagram of the execution flow structure of our framework.

3.1 Function Metadata Extraction

First, we parse the binary file to extract the symbol table (such as .symtab in ELF), recording the function symbol names and addresses for later reference. Then, we recursively disassemble the code using a disassembler engine, constructing basic blocks and CFGs by identifying jump and return instructions. We then infer the function's local variables, parameters, and call relationships through register tracing and stack frame analysis. Finally, the analysis results are stored in a global function database, forming complete function metadata, including function name, starting address, size, type, and local variables.

Formally, the complete function set F extracted from the binary can be represented as:

$$meta(f_i) = \{name, size, nargs, nlocals, callrefs\} \tag{1}$$

$$F = \{meta(f_i) \mid i = 1, 2, \ldots, n\} \tag{2}$$

The features extracted by Algorithm 1 reflect the structural complexity of the function and are correlated with the vulnerability density. For example, functions with larger sizes or more local variables often involve complex memory operations and are more likely to contain out-of-bounds or memory management defects.

After extraction, the system categorizes the functions into two types: user-defined functions and imported library functions. User-defined functions may contain business logic and security risks, and imported library functions are typically system calls or standard library wrappers, so they have lower risk in security. The User-defined functions will be sent to the LLM in batches later.

Algorithm 1. Function Metadata Extraction Process

Require: Binary program P
Ensure: Function metadata list F
1: $symtab \leftarrow$ ParseSymbolTable(P)
2: **for all** $entry \in symtab$ **do**
3: Record function name and address
4: **end for**
5: $code \leftarrow$ LoadCodeSegment(P)
6: $funcs \leftarrow$ RecursiveDisassemble($code$)
7: **for all** $f \in funcs$ **do**
8: $BBs, CFG \leftarrow$ BuildBasicBlocksAndCFG(f)
9: $vars, params \leftarrow$ InferLocalsAndParams(f, via register & stack analysis)
10: $calls \leftarrow$ AnalyzeCallRelations(f)
11: $meta \leftarrow$ {name, size, nargs, nlocals, callrefs}
12: Add $meta$ to F
13: **end for**
14: Store F into Global Function Database
15: **return** F

3.2 LLM-Based Risk Ranking

To avoid costly, one-by-one analysis of all functions, the program uses LLM to perform fast inference sorting of function metadata. The function metadata extracted in the previous phase is first formatted into a prompt suitable for LLM input. This prompt includes contextual information such as function name, size of function, and call relationships to aid the model in security reasoning. Then, this prompt is input into the LLM model ϕ, which returns a JSON response containing risk assessment results for each function. The framework parses this JSON response, extracts functions marked as "high-risk," and adds these into a final high-risk function list F_{risk}.

Algorithm 2. LLM-based Risk Ranking Process

Require: Binary program P, LLM model ϕ
Ensure: High-risk function list F_{risk}
1: $query \leftarrow$ FormatPrompt(F)
2: $response \leftarrow \phi(query)$
3: $J \leftarrow$ ParseJSON($response$)
4: $F_{risk} \leftarrow$ ExtractHighRiskFunctions(J)
5: **return** F_{risk}

This process is similar to an "attention filter" mechanism, which allows the system to focus its limited token budget on the parts that are most worthy of in-depth analysis. Some researchers have also pointed out that more context (more tokens) does not necessarily help the model make more accurate inferences [19].

3.3 Analysis of High-Risk Functions

For each candidate function $f \in F_{risk}$, we extract the assembly code from the binary file. Then, the program submits the complete function code to the LLM and requests the model to perform vulnerability detection and exploitation analysis.

Algorithm 3. Submit High-Risk Functions to LLM for Vulnerability Analysis

Require: Binary P, high-risk function list F_{risk}, LLM ϕ
Ensure: Analysis report R
1: $R \leftarrow \varnothing$
2: **for** each function $f \in F_{risk}$ **do**
3: $asm \leftarrow \text{ExtractAssembly}(P, f.\text{address}, f.\text{size})$
4: $prompt \leftarrow \text{ComposePrompt}(f, asm)$
5: $response \leftarrow \phi(prompt)$
6: $result \leftarrow \text{ParseResponse}(response)$
7: Append $(f, result)$ to R
8: **end for**
9: **return** R

By using the above methods, we can combine the semantic reasoning capabilities of LLMs with the location of vulnerable program code, automatically evaluate the exploitability of candidate functions, and provide clear and actionable clues for subsequent vulnerability verification and exploitation.

3.4 Token Efficiency and Logging Mechanism

The system precisely records the token consumption at each stage during operation. Specifically, the program counts the number of tokens consumed in each session interacting with the LLM, thereby enabling a quantitative analysis of the overall inference cost. This refined statistical mechanism allows researchers to clearly understand the model's token usage at different stages (such as function selection, vulnerability analysis, and availability assessment), providing a reliable basis for subsequent cost optimization and performance evaluation.

The logging system provides unified monitoring of runtime status, outputting information such as function extraction progress, token consumption, and error messages, facilitating debugging and experimental reproduction. Through this precise resource monitoring and visual log mechanism, the entire system can achieve comprehensive control over LLM call costs while maintaining a high degree of automation, thus balancing efficiency, transparency, and reproducibility in large-scale binary analysis tasks.

3.5 Results Storage

The final analysis results are exported in structured JSON format. After analyzing each function, the system stores the results in a unified data structure in a 'result.json' file. These files contain the function name, the exploitability conclusions of the model analysis, and the corresponding token statistics. This design not only facilitates manual review and verification of the analysis's accuracy but also provides convenience for subsequent data analysis and visualization.

This structured storage mechanism gives the analysis results good scalability and reusability. Researchers can directly use these JSON files for batch statistics, aggregation analysis, or comparison with other static analysis results. Furthermore, because the results are formatted uniformly and contain rich contextual information (such as function name, offset address, vulnerability type, exploitability description, etc.), they can be easily converted into the data formats required for machine learning tasks, such as tables, labeled samples, or embedded representations.

4 Experiments

All experiments were conducted on a workstation equipped with an AMD Ryzen 5 6600H with Radeon Graphics CPU, 16GB RAM, and running Ubuntu 22.04. We run our program in Python 3.13 and used Radare2 6.0.5 for disassembly. The language model backend was based on qwen-max through the API, with our own token-efficient prompting pipeline.

We collected 24 CTF pwn binaries (binary files used in Capture The Flag hacking competitions) from competitions. Each challenge binary was manually verified and annotated based on official writeups and disassembly results. Table 1 gives a summary of all challenges.

Table 1. Summarizes the dataset composition.

Vulnerability	Number
buffer overflow	13
format string	5
heap exploitation	4
command injection	1
comprehensive exploitation	1

Among the 24 challenges tested, 22 were identified to have vulnerabilities. The detection rate is of 91.7%, demonstrating the effectiveness of our LLM-based analysis framework. The two challenges that were not detected corresponded to more complex exploitation scenarios or unusually large binaries, suggesting that extremely large or intricate functions may still pose difficulties for automated analysis.

The total token consumption for the 24 challenges was 206372 tokens, so we introduce the token-detection efficiency (TDE) metric, defined as follows:

$$\mathrm{TDE} = \frac{\text{Number of Vulnerabilities Detected}}{\text{Total Tokens Consumed}} \times 1000 \tag{3}$$

This metric measures the number of vulnerabilities discovered per thousand tokens, reflecting the cost-benefit ratio of the method. Experiments show that the TDE of our proposed method is 0.107, significantly higher than the baseline value of 0.031 for the full analysis. And the two challenges that failed to detect vulnerabilities had significantly higher token consumption (16101 and 14899, respectively), and overall, there was a significant negative correlation between token consumption and successful detection, indicating that more difficult or longer challenges were more likely to miss detections.

Figure 2 is the detailed data on the challenge names and the tokens consumed. Figure 3 is a scatter plot showing the relationship between the size of the challenges and the number of tokens consumed. Generally speaking, the size of the challenge is positively correlated with the number of tokens consumed. As expected, larger challenges generally required more tokens for thorough analysis, reflecting the model's increased workload when handling long or complex function decompilations.

In addition to raw detection performance, we also recorded detailed logs of function extraction progress, token usage at each stage, and any analysis errors encountered. This enabled reproducibility and provided insights into which types of functions or binaries lead to higher token consumption or potential analysis failures. Overall, these results validate the feasibility of applying LLM-based analysis for real-world binary vulnerability detection while providing guidance for future optimization and scaling.

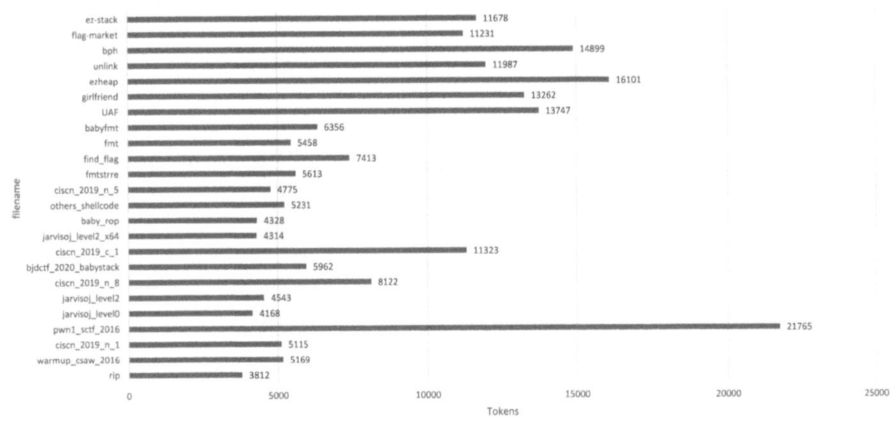

Fig. 2. The detailed data on the challenge name and the tokens consumed.

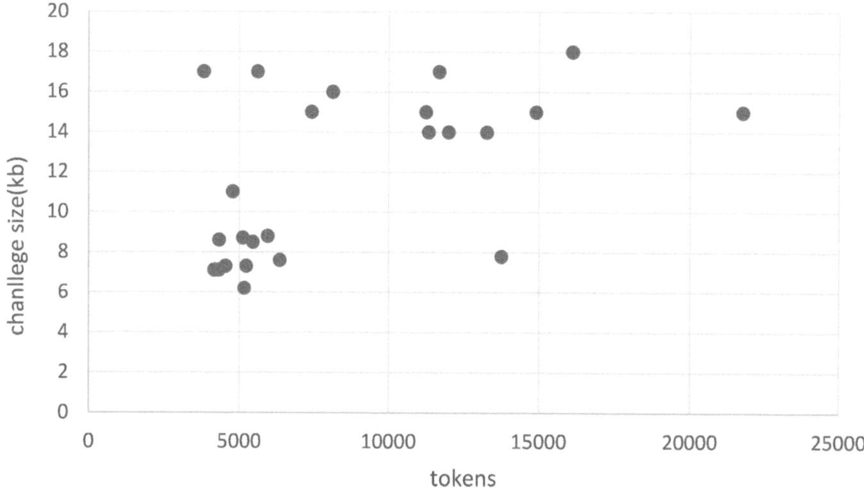

Fig. 3. The relationship between the size of the challenges and the number of tokens consumed.

5 Conclusion

This paper proposes a token-efficient binary vulnerability prioritization method based on LLMs. By combining function pre-screening with deep analysis, it achieves priority ranking and vulnerability detection of high-risk functions in binary programs. The program utilizes Radare2 to extract function metadata, performs feature representation of functions, and then uses LLMs to rank functions by vulnerability risk. Only functions most likely to contain vulnerabilities are analyzed in depth, thus significantly reducing token consumption while ensuring analysis accuracy.

Experimental results on 24 CTF pwn challenges show that this method successfully detected 22 challenges containing vulnerabilities, achieving a detection rate of 91.7%. The experiments revealed a positive correlation between token consumption and binary file size. Higher difficulty or longer functions were more prone to missed detections, further demonstrating the importance of efficient token analysis in practical applications. By recording token usage at each stage, we can accurately quantify system costs, and the structured output facilitates manual review and dataset construction.

Overall, this study demonstrates that LLMs can serve as an effective tool for automated binary vulnerability detection, especially in resource-constrained scenarios, where the efficient token strategy balances accuracy and efficiency. Future work can be expanded in the following directions: further optimizing token usage strategies, combining dynamic analysis methods to improve coverage and reliability, and extending to other vulnerability types beyond memory security to enhance the system's practicality and generalization capabilities. Additionally, a weakly supervised learning mechanism can be introduced to further analyze function names and optimize the model's output [20,21].

Acknowledgments. The work is supported by the National Natural Science Foundation of China (No. 6230245), the Fundamental Research Funds of Zhejiang Sci-Tech University (Nos. 22222266-Y), the Program for Leading Innovative Research Team of Zhejiang Province (No. 2023R01001), the Zhejiang Provincial Natural Science Foundation of China (Nos. LQ24F020008), the "Pioneer" and "Leading Goose" R&D Program of Zhejiang (Nos. 2025C02033, 2023C01119), and the College Students' Science and Technology Innovation Program of Zhejiang Province (Xinmiao Talent Program) (No. 2025R406A027).

References

1. Wang, Y., Gao, W., Hei, X., Du, Y.: Method and practice of trusted embedded computing and data transmission protection architecture based on android. Chin. J. Electron. **33**(3), 623–634 (2024)
2. Redini, N., et al.: Karonte: Detecting insecure multi-binary interactions in embedded firmware. In: 2020 IEEE Symposium on Security and Privacy (SP), pp. 1544–1561. IEEE (2020)
3. Gao, Z., et al.: Faster and better: Detecting vulnerabilities in linux-based iot firmware with optimized reaching definition analysis. In: Proceedings of the 2024 Network and Distributed System Security Symposium, San Diego, CA, USA. vol. 26 (2024)
4. Liu, P., et al.: Llm-powered static binary taint analysis. ACM Trans. Softw. Eng. Methodol. **34**(3), 1–36 (2025)
5. Tay, H.J., et al.: Greenhouse:Single-Service rehosting of Linux-Based firmware binaries in User-Space emulation. In: 32nd USENIX Security Symposium (USENIX Security 23), pp. 5791–5808 (2023)
6. Dasgupta, S., Dinesh, S., Venkatesh, D., Adve, V.S., Fletcher, C.W.: Scalable validation of binary lifters. In: Proceedings of the 41st ACM SIGPLAN Conference on Programming Language Design and Implementation, pp. 655–671 (2020)
7. Liu, Z., Yuan, Y., Wang, S., Bao, Y.: Sok: Demystifying binary lifters through the lens of downstream applications. In: 2022 IEEE Symposium on Security and Privacy (SP), pp. 1100–1119. IEEE (2022)
8. Gibbs, W., et al.: Operation mango: Scalable discovery of Taint-Style vulnerabilities in binary firmware services. In: 33rd USENIX Security Symposium (USENIX Security 24), pp. 7123–7139 (2024)
9. Chen, D.D., Woo, M., Brumley, D., Egele, M.: Towards automated dynamic analysis for linux-based embedded firmware. In: NDSS, vol. 1, pp. 1–1 (2016)
10. Jin, X., Pei, K., Won, J.Y., Lin, Z.: Symlm: Predicting function names in stripped binaries via context-sensitive execution-aware code embeddings. In: Proceedings of the 2022 ACM SIGSAC Conference on Computer and Communications Security, pp. 1631–1645 (2022)
11. Chen, Y., Zhong, R., Yang, Y., Hu, H., Wu, D., Lee, W.: μFUZZ: redesign of parallel fuzzing using microservice architecture. In: 32nd USENIX Security Symposium (USENIX Security 23), pp. 1325–1342 (2023)

12. Li, Y., et al.: UNIFUZZ: A holistic and pragmatic Metrics-Driven platform for evaluating fuzzers. In: 30th USENIX Security Symposium (USENIX Security 21), pp. 2777–2794 (2021)
13. Jiang, Y., et al.: When fuzzing meets llms: Challenges and opportunities. In: Companion Proceedings of the 32nd ACM International Conference on the Foundations of Software Engineering, pp. 492–496 (2024)
14. Fang, C., et al.: Large language models for code analysis: Do LLMs really do their job? In: 33rd USENIX Security Symposium (USENIX Security 24), pp. 829–846 (2024)
15. Artuso, F., Mormando, M., Di Luna, G.A., Querzoni, L.: Binbert: binary code understanding with a fine-tunable and execution-aware transformer. IEEE Trans. Dependable Secure Comput. **22**(1), 308–326 (2024)
16. Zhou, X., Cao, S., Sun, X., Lo, D.: Large language model for vulnerability detection and repair: literature review and the road ahead. ACM Trans. Softwa. Eng. Methodol. **34**(5), 1–31 (2025)
17. Guo, D., et al.: GraphcodeBERT: Pre-training code representations with data flow. In: International Conference on Learning Representations (ICLR 2021) (2021)
18. Hou, X., Zhao, Y., Wang, S., Wang, H.: Model context protocol (mcp): Landscape, security threats, and future research directions. arXiv preprint arXiv:2503.23278 (2025)
19. Levy, M., Jacoby, A., Goldberg, Y.: Same task, more tokens: the impact of input length on the reasoning performance of large language models. In: Proceedings of the 62nd Annual Meeting of the Association for Computational Linguistics (Volume 1: Long Papers), pp. 15339–15353 (2024)
20. Supervision, I.: Learning from incomplete and inaccurate supervision. IEEE Trans. Knowl. Data Eng. **34**(12), 5854–5868 (2022)
21. Ratner, A., Bach, S.H., Ehrenberg, H.R., Fries, J.A., Wu, S., Ré, C.: Snorkel: rapid training data creation with weak supervision. VLDB J. **29**(2–3), 709–730 (2020)

A Prefix-Based Homomorphic Encryption Protocol for Efficient Secure Comparison

Shutong Li[1], Baodong Qin[1,2(✉)], and Xiao Deng[1]

[1] School of Cyberspace Security, Xi'an University of Posts and Telecommunications, Xi'an 710121, China
qinbaodong@xupt.edu.cn

[2] National Engineering Research Center for Secured Wireless, Xi'an University of Posts and Telecommunications, Xi'an 710121, China

Abstract. Secure comparison protocols are a cornerstone of privacy-preserving computation, with critical applications in e-voting, federated learning, and financial analytics. However, the efficiency of classical protocols like DGK is often hampered by high computation and communication costs. This paper introduces an efficient two-party secure comparison protocol, termed the PSC (Prefix-based Secure Comparison) protocol, based on a variant of the ElGamal homomorphic cryptosystem. The core innovation of PSC is to process each prefix bit string of the input as a single encrypted unit, bypassing the need for costly bit-wise equality checks found in traditional approaches. The protocol determines the comparison result by constructing and analyzing an obfuscated comparison vector for zero-value occurrences. If we denote the bit string length by l, this method reduces the computational complexity by approximately $\mathcal{O}(l)$ and minimizes interaction rounds. Experimental evaluations confirm that PSC achieves a significantly lower average running time compared to the DGK protocol and its variants. The results demonstrate that reorganizing the encrypted data model enables substantial efficiency gains in secure comparison without sacrificing security, offering a practical solution for large-scale privacy-preserving tasks.

Keywords: Secure Comparison Protocol · Privacy Protection · Homomorphic Encryption · Cryptographic Protocol · Two-Party Computation

1 Introduction

1.1 Secure Comparison Protocol

The secure comparison protocol serves as a core foundational component in secure multi-party computation. Its objective is to enable two or more participating parties to jointly compare the magnitude relationship of their private inputs without disclosing these inputs to each other. The most famous illustration of this problem is Yao's Millionaires' Problem [15]: two millionaires wish

Y. Xiang and J. Shen (Eds.): ML4CS 2025, LNCS 16456, pp. 166–179, 2026.
https://doi.org/10.1007/978-981-95-7820-7_11

to know who is richer without revealing their actual wealth. This classic problem profoundly highlights the necessity and value of systematic research into two-party secure comparison.

To address such problems, numerous technical approaches and protocol solutions have been proposed in academia. Mainstream methods include garbled circuits [11], oblivious transfer [2], and homomorphic encryption [7]. Among these, a common and intuitive approach involves decomposing the integers to be compared into binary bit representations and then performing secure computations bit-by-bit within a Boolean circuit. Although theoretically universal, this method often faces challenges related to inefficient communication and computation in practical applications, typically requiring multiple interaction rounds. This becomes a performance bottleneck, particularly in large-scale data or high-latency network scenarios.

The value of secure comparison protocols is reflected in their broad application prospects. Beyond the basic "Millionaires' Problem," their general form supports more complex privacy-preserving computation tasks, such as multi-party sorting [9]. A typical application example is sealed-bid online auctions [5]. In auctions, it is necessary to securely determine the highest bidder (e.g., in English auctions) while ensuring the bid privacy of all participants throughout the process. With the rapid development of the Internet of Things, 5G communication, and e-commerce, the demand for efficient and secure online auction mechanisms is becoming increasingly urgent [8], further driving performance optimization research for the underlying secure comparison protocols.

However, as mentioned earlier, the efficiency of many existing protocols still falls short of meeting the demands of large-scale practical applications. Particularly in scenarios involving large-scale data or high real-time requirements, the computational and communication overhead of traditional bit-wise comparison protocols is especially significant. Therefore, designing a secure comparison protocol with fewer communication rounds and higher computational efficiency is crucial for promoting the real-world adoption of privacy-preserving computing technologies. It is within this context that this work focuses on optimizing the efficiency of secure comparison protocols, leading to the proposal of a prefix-based secure comparison protocol.

Our Contributions. In summary, we have the following contributions in this paper.

Firstly, we proposed an efficient prefix-based secure comparison protocol. Compared with the existing secure comparison protocol, our protocols have many strengths. It has a much lower computational complexity. In traditional comparison protocols (such as the DGK protocol), the processing of each bit requires multiple modulo operations, the total computational complexity is $\mathcal{O}(l(t+\log l))$ times modulo n multiplication. When the bit length $k = 1024$ for modulus n, the safety parameter is 160 and $l = 16$, the total computation is equivalent to 7 complete modulo integer operations. The total communication volume of the new protocol is $\mathcal{O}(lk)$, the protocol significantly reduces the communication complexity by utilizing the linear computational properties of homomorphic encryption and avoiding the multiple rounds of communication in traditional protocols.

2 Related Work

There are a variety of bit-based secure comparison protocols that implement comparisons on the same principle. For two encrypted t-bit inputs x and y, individual encrypted bits in $x = (x_1, x_2, \ldots, x_\ell)$ and $y = (y_1, y_2, \ldots, y_\ell)$ are computed and arithmetic computation is relied upon to determine whether the specified relationship holds. The DGK comparison protocol was first proposed in 2008 in a paper by Damgård, Geisler, and Krøigaard [7], and an efficient secure comparison computational circuit under the honest curiosity model is given in the literature. The protocol can compare the size of two integers, the main steps of its plaintext comparison is to first convert these two numbers into binary form, and then in accordance with the binary string from the high bit to start scanning by bit to compare, once found that a certain bit the two are inconsistent, then in the case of the high bit is equal to the size of the relationship between the two numbers depends on the result of the comparison of this bit.

Assuming that the binary bit strings of non-negative integers x and y are denoted as $(x_1, x_2, \ldots, x_\ell)$ and $(y_1, y_2, \ldots, y_\ell)$, and compare these two binary strings by bit position, calculated by the Eq. (1), in which $\oplus$ represents the XOR operator, it can be expressed as $x_i \oplus y_j = x_i + y_j - 2x_i y_j$.

$$Z_i = x_i - y_i + 1 + \sum_{j=1}^{i-1} (x_j \oplus y_j) \tag{1}$$

The result of the computation can be zero or non-zero integers encrypted. Therefore, it is necessary to check whether a z_i decrypts to zero in the encrypted integer vector, and if it exists, the result is true. Veugen [13] proposed an improvement to support both $x > y$ and $x < y$ comparison relations by adding a single-bit input. The improved DGK protocol performs the following computation:

$$z_i = x_i - y_i + s + 3 \sum_{j=1}^{i-1} (x_j \oplus y_j) \tag{2}$$

where $s = 1 - 2b_1$, $b_1 \in \{0, 1\}$, and the protocol checksums $x < y$ if $b_1 = 0$, otherwise $x > y$. The output bit is true if there is an encryption of zero in z_i.

In recent years, there has been a lot of work on comparative protocols for privacy protection. In 2015, Veugen et al. [14] proposed the scheme to optimize the bit decomposition process for homomorphic encryption based on the DGK protocol, which reduces the communication overhead by reducing the number of interaction rounds through precomputation and batch processing, the computational efficiency is improved by 40% compared to the original DGK protocol, but at the same time the security proof of the scheme requires stronger modeling assumptions. In 2016, Kolesnikov et al. [10] combined the homomorphic encryption properties of garbled circuits and DGK to propose a hybrid protocol that splits the comparison operation into an offline precomputation and an in-the-moment phase, which reduces the cost of real-time communication for large-scale data scenarios but has a high storage overhead in the offline phase. In 2018, Carlton et al. [6] proposed a new homomorphic encryption scheme based on prime power subgroups and utilized its unique threshold homomorphism property to construct an efficient secure integer comparison protocol. Specifically, this study revolutionizes the traditional bit-by-bit encryption comparison by comparing multiple input bits simultaneously in the ciphertext, but the scheme only supports one-side homomorphism, i.e., it can only hide the information when $m_1 \leq m_2$, and leaks the information in the case of $m_1 > m_2$. In 2019, a new protocol [1] for fast and secure comparison of medium-sized integers is proposed and applied to binarized neural networks. The protocol is based on Legendre notation, which allows Legendre notation to encode symbolic functions in a "noisy" way by reducing the requirement for prime modes, thus significantly improving the comparison range, and these methods are still limited by the theory of Legendre notation and prime modes. For example, for larger values of k, finding the right prime becomes more difficult and computationally expensive. In 2020, Bourse et al. [4] proposed an article about two new protocols for different scenarios. Both protocols avoid decomposition of integers into binary form and, based on the work of [3], propose a new homomorphic encryption scheme that utilizes fast bootstrapping techniques, is able to handle comparisons of large integers, introduces hash functions and random elements, and avoids the Plaintext Equivalence Test (PET), which is used in the protocol, thus reducing the number of interactions. However, the scheme relies on a specific choice of RSA parameters. In the same year, a privacy-preserving integer comparison scheme was proposed by the literature, which utilizes the nature of special cyclic subgroups, cleverly chooses parameters, avoids binary decomposition, and is resistant to malicious user attacks. However, the scheme has high requirements for RSA modulus and still has high communication and computational overheads, especially when the range of private inputs is large. Literature [12] proposes two Three-Party Integer Comparison (TPIC) protocols for semi-honest and malicious adversaries, allowing a referee with no private inputs to know the outcome of the comparison, while two competitors hold secret integers for privacy-preserving comparisons. The protocols can be utilized in areas such as blockchain, while the literature also proposes an online auction scheme that runs within a constant round. However, the scheme is not resistant to collusion attacks and is less secure.

3 Preliminaries

3.1 Variant ElGamal Homomorphic Cryptosystem

There are two types of Homomorphic Encryption: Partially Homomorphic Encryption (PHE) and Fully Homomorphic Encryption (FHE). In this paper we use the ElGamal algorithm with homomorphic properties as the encryption algorithm involved in the construction of the scheme.

Let $\mathcal{G}$ be a polynomial-time algorithm that takes as input 1^n and (except possibly with negligible probability) outputs a description of a cyclic group $\mathbb{G}$, its order q, and a generator g. The variant ElGamal homomorphic encryption scheme is described as follows.

1. **Key Generation (KeyGen)**: on input 1^n, run $\mathcal{G}(1^n)$ to obtain $(\mathbb{G}, q, g)$. Then choose a uniform $x \in \mathbb{Z}_q$ and compute $h = g^x$. The public key is $(\mathbb{G}, q, g, h)$ and the private key is $(\mathbb{G}, q, g, x)$. The message space is $\mathbb{G}$.
2. **Encryption (Enc)**: on input a public key $pk = (\mathbb{G}, q, g, h)$ and a message $m \in \mathbb{G}$, choose a uniform $y \in \mathbb{Z}_q$ and output the ciphertext

$$(c_1, c_2) = (g^y, h^y \cdot g^m). \tag{3}$$

3. **Decryption (Dec)**: on input a private key $sk = (\mathbb{G}, q, g, x)$ and a ciphertext (c_1, c_2), output

$$g^{\hat{m}} = c_2 / {c_1}^x. \tag{4}$$

To see that decryption succeeds, let $(c_1, c_2) = (g^y, h^y \cdot g^m)$ with $h = g^x$. Then

$$g^{\hat{m}} = \frac{c_2}{{c_1}^x} = \frac{h^y \cdot g^m}{(g^y)^x} = \frac{(g^x)^y \cdot g^m}{g^{xy}} = g^m. \tag{5}$$

4 Our Protocols

4.1 Prefix-Based Secure Comparison

This security comparison protocol is improved on the basis of the classic security comparison protocol mentioned above, which reduces the communication complexity and improves the operation efficiency of the algorithm, and the improved protocol on plaintext and the improved protocol on ciphertext are described in detail below, respectively.

For this protocol, it is assumed that Alice has generated a key pair $(\mathsf{sk}, \mathsf{pk})$ for the variant ElGamal homomorphic cryptosystem. Alice has a private unencrypted message x and Bob has a private unencrypted message y. The integers x and y have size ℓ. We denote their bits by x_i and y_i, for $1 \leq i \leq \ell$, where x_1 and y_1 are the highest significant bits. In our protocol, $[x]$ denotes the encryption of the data x, and the same applies to y. For an integer $x^l = \sum_{i=1}^{l} x_i 2^{\ell - i}$ where $1 \leq l \leq \ell$, this denotes the value of the first l bits of x, and similarly for y. Specifically, $x = x^\ell$ and $y = y^\ell$.

Alice splits the binary $x = x_1 x_2 \dots x_\ell$ to generate

$$(x^1, x^2, \dots, x^\ell) = (x_1, x_1 x_2, \dots, x_1 x_2 \dots x_\ell),$$

and then encrypts each x^i separately using pk to generate $X = \{[x^1], [x^2], \dots, [x^\ell]\}$.

Alice sends the ciphertext X generated by Algorithm 1 to Bob, which runs Algorithm 2.

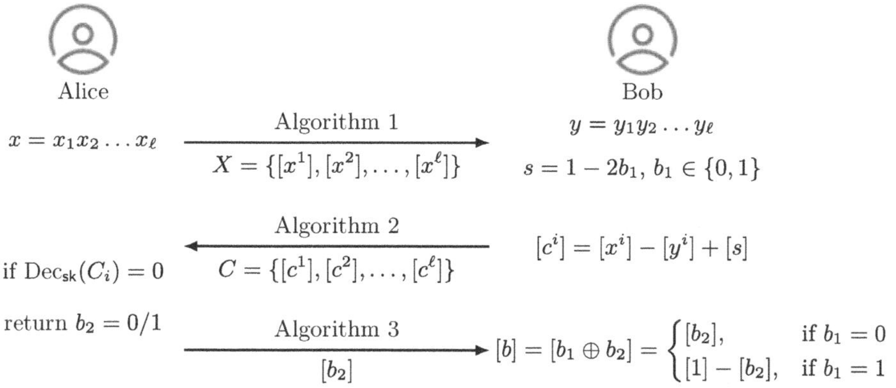

Alice

Bob

$x = x_1x_2 \ldots x_\ell$

Algorithm 1

$X = \{[x^1], [x^2], \ldots, [x^\ell]\}$

$y = y_1y_2 \ldots y_\ell$

$s = 1 - 2b_1,\ b_1 \in \{0, 1\}$

Algorithm 2

$C = \{[c^1], [c^2], \ldots, [c^\ell]\}$

$[c^i] = [x^i] - [y^i] + [s]$

if $\mathrm{Dec}_{\mathsf{sk}}(C_i) = 0$

return $b_2 = 0/1$

Algorithm 3

$[b_2]$

$[b] = [b_1 \oplus b_2] = \begin{cases} [b_2], & \text{if } b_1 = 0 \\ [1] - [b_2], & \text{if } b_1 = 1 \end{cases}$

Fig. 1. PSC protocol interaction diagram.

Algorithm 1. PSC-Encryption

Require: $x = x_1x_2 \ldots x_\ell$ and pk
Ensure: $X = \{[x^1], [x^2], \ldots, [x^\ell]\}$
1: generate $(x^1, x^2, \ldots, x^\ell) = (x_1, x_1x_2, \ldots, x_1x_2 \ldots x_\ell)$
2: **for** $i = 1$ to ℓ **do**
3: $\quad X_i = \mathrm{Enc}(x^i)$
4: **end for**
5: **return** $X = \{[x^1], [x^2], \ldots, [x^\ell]\}$

Bob splits the binary $y = y_1y_2 \ldots y_\ell$ to generate

$$(y^1, y^2, \ldots, y^\ell) = (y_1, y_1y_2, \ldots, y_1y_2 \ldots y_\ell),$$

and then encrypts each y^i separately using Alice's public key to generate $Y = \{[y^1], [y^2], \ldots, [y^\ell]\}$. The homomorphic operation with $X = \{[x^1], [x^2], \ldots, [x^\ell]\}$ sent by Alice generates $C = \{[c^1], [c^2], \ldots, [c^\ell]\}$, $[c^i] = [x^i] - [y^i] + [s]$, where $s = 1 - 2b_1$, $b_1 \in \{0, 1\}$, and its role obfuscates c^i.

Bob shuffles the ciphertext C generated by Algorithm ?? and sends it to Alice, which runs Algorithm 3.

Alice receives the ciphertext C sent by Bob and decrypts each $C_i = [c^i]$. If $c^i = 1$, then $b_2 = 0$; otherwise, $b_2 = 1$. Alice encrypts b_2, generated by Algorithm 3, and sends it to Bob.

Alice then performs a homomorphic operation on $[b_2]$ using b_1 to obtain $[b]$.

$$[b] = [b_1 \oplus b_2] = \begin{cases} [b_2], & \text{if } b_1 = 0 \\ [1] - [b_2], & \text{if } b_1 = 1 \end{cases} \tag{6}$$

Algorithm 2. PSC-Homomorphic Computation

Require: $y = y_1 y_2 \ldots y_\ell$, $X = \{[x^1], [x^2], \ldots, [x^\ell]\}$ and pk
Ensure: $C = \{[c^1], [c^2], \ldots, [c^\ell]\}$
1: using Algorithm 1 to generate $Y = \{[y^1], [y^2], \ldots, [y^\ell]\}$ from $y = y_1 y_2 \ldots y_\ell$
2: select a bit b_1, $b_1 \in \{0, 1\}$
3: $s = 1 - 2b_1$
4: **for** $i = 1$ to ℓ **do**
5: $\quad [c^i] = [x^i] - [y^i] + [s]$
6: **end for**
7: **return** $C = \{[c^1], [c^2], \ldots, [c^\ell]\}$

Algorithm 3. PSC-Decryption

Require: $C = \{[c^1], [c^2], \ldots, [c^\ell]\}$ and sk
Ensure: $b_2 \in \{0, 1\}$
1: **for** $i = 1$ to ℓ **do**
2: $\quad$ plaintext $\leftarrow \mathrm{Dec}_{\mathsf{sk}}([c^i])$
3: $\quad$ **if** plaintext $= 0$ **then**
4: $\quad\quad$ **return** $b_2 = 0$
5: $\quad\quad$ **break**
6: $\quad$ **end if**
7: **end for**
8: **return** $b_2 = 1$

The final comparison result is:

$$b = \begin{cases} 1, & x > y \\ 0, & x < y \end{cases} \tag{7}$$

Example: Let $x = 1011_{(2)}$, $y = 0110_{(2)}$, and the bit length $\ell = 4$. Alice generates the prefix sequence:

$$(x^1, x^2, x^3, x^4) = (1, 10, 101, 1011)_{(2)}$$

which corresponds to the decimal values $(1, 2, 5, 11)$, and encrypts them to obtain X. Bob similarly generates Y. In the comparison vector C, if $b_1 = 0$ (i.e., $s = 1$), then $[c^i] = [x^i] - [y^i] + [1]$ is computed. If, after decryption, any $c^i = 0$, it indicates equality at that prefix position, from which the comparison result can be inferred.

Figure 1 illustrates the specific protocol interaction process.

4.2 Correctness Analysis

Case 1: When $s = 1$ and $b_1 = 0$

(a) **When $x > y$:** Assume the binary strings start to differ at the j-th position, where $0 < j \leq \ell$, meaning the first $j - 1$ bits are identical. The differences from $(x_1)_B - (y_1)_B$ to $(x_1 x_2 \ldots x_{j-1})_B - (y_1 y_2 \ldots y_{j-1})_B$ are all 0, implying $c_1, c_2, \ldots, c_{j-1} \neq 0$. At position j, we have $x_j = 1$ and $y_j = 0$, so $(x_1x_2\ldots x_j)_B - (y_1y_2\ldots y_j)_B = (1)_D$, which means $c_j \neq 0$. For positions $j+1$ to ℓ, the differences are also non-zero. Therefore, when $x > y$, we have $c_i \neq 0$ for all i ($1 \leq i \leq \ell$). According to the protocol, $b_2 = 1$. From Eq. 7, $b = b_1 \oplus b_2 = 0 \oplus 1 = 1$, confirming that $x > y$ is correctly identified.

(b) **When $x < y$:** Similarly, assume the strings differ at the j-th position, with the first $j - 1$ bits identical. The differences up to position $j - 1$ are 0, so $c_1, c_2, \ldots, c_{j-1} \neq 0$. At position j, we have $x_j = 0$ and $y_j = 1$, giving $(x_1x_2\ldots x_j)_B - (y_1y_2\ldots y_j)_B = (-1)_D$, which implies $c_j = 0$. Thus, when $x < y$, there exists at least one i such that $c_i = 0$. According to the protocol, $b_2 = 0$. From Eq. 7, $b = b_1 \oplus b_2 = 0 \oplus 0 = 0$, confirming that $x < y$ is correctly identified.

Summarizing Case 1:

$$s = 1 \quad \Rightarrow \quad \begin{cases} x > y & c_i \neq 0 \text{ for all } i \\ x < y & \exists i : c_i = 0 \end{cases} \tag{8}$$

Case 2: When $s = -1$ and $b_1 = 1$

(a) **When $x > y$:** Again, assume the strings differ at the j-th position, with identical preceding bits. The differences up to $j - 1$ are 0, so $c_1, c_2, \ldots, c_{j-1} \neq 0$. At position j, with $x_j = 1$ and $y_j = 0$, we have $(x_1x_2\ldots x_j)_B - (y_1y_2\ldots y_j)_B = (1)_D$, but now, due to $s = -1$, we obtain $c_j = 0$. Hence, when $x > y$, there exists at least one i with $c_i = 0$. According to the protocol, $b_2 = 0$. From Eq. 7, $b = b_1 \oplus b_2 = 1 \oplus 0 = 1$, confirming that $x > y$ is correctly identified.

(b) **When $x < y$:** With the first $j-1$ bits identical, we have $c_1, c_2, \ldots, c_{j-1} \neq 0$. At position j, $x_j = 0$ and $y_j = 1$ yields $(x_1x_2\ldots x_j)_B - (y_1y_2\ldots y_j)_B = (-1)_D$, and because $s = -1$, we get $c_j \neq 0$. For the remaining positions, the differences are also non-zero. Therefore, when $x < y$, $c_i \neq 0$ for all i. According to the protocol, $b_2 = 1$. From Eq. 7, $b = b_1 \oplus b_2 = 1 \oplus 1 = 0$, confirming that $x < y$ is correctly identified.

Summarizing Case 2:

$$s = -1 \quad \Rightarrow \quad \begin{cases} x > y & \exists i : c_i = 0 \\ x < y & c_i \neq 0 \text{ for all } i \end{cases} \tag{9}$$

The analysis above demonstrates that for all combinations of s and b_1, the protocol correctly determines the relationship between x and y.

4.3 Security Analysis

We now present a formal security analysis of the PSC protocol. Our protocol is secure under the Decisional Diffie-Hellman (DDH) assumption in the random oracle model. We consider the semi-honest adversarial model, where both parties follow the protocol but may try to learn additional information. We also discuss extensions to the malicious model.

Theorem 1. Under the DDH assumption, the PSC protocol securely computes the comparison function in the semi-honest model.

Proof. We prove security by constructing simulators for Alice and Bob that generate views indistinguishable from the real protocol execution. The proof consists of the following steps.

Step 1: IND-CPA Security of the Variant ElGamal. We use an exponential variant of the ElGamal encryption scheme, where a message m (from a small message space) is encrypted as $\mathrm{Enc}(m) = (g^r, g^m h^r)$, with $h = g^a$ being the public key. This scheme is IND-CPA secure under the DDH assumption. Since we only encrypt small values (bits or small integers), decryption can be performed by brute-force searching the message space. The IND-CPA property ensures that no polynomial-time adversary can distinguish between encryptions of different messages.

Step 2: Indistinguishability of Comparison Ciphertexts. The core of the protocol is the homomorphic computation of $[c^i] = [x^i] - [y^i] + [s]$. We show that these ciphertexts do not leak any information about the inputs. For any adversary $\mathcal{A}$ against the protocol, we construct a simulator $\mathcal{S}$ that, without access to the private inputs, can generate a transcript indistinguishable from the real one.

The simulator $\mathcal{S}$ works as follows:

1. $\mathcal{S}$ chooses a random bit $b_1 \in \{0, 1\}$ and sets $s = 1 - 2b_1$.
2. For each i from 1 to ℓ, $\mathcal{S}$ generates $[c^i]$ as $\mathrm{Enc}(0)$ (i.e., encryption of zero).
3. When $\mathcal{A}$ makes a random oracle query, $\mathcal{S}$ returns a random value consistent with previous queries.

Due to the IND-CPA security of the encryption scheme, the adversary cannot distinguish between the simulated ciphertexts and the real ciphertexts (which are encryptions of either 0 or non-zero values). The random oracle queries are answered consistently, and thus the simulation is indistinguishable from the real protocol.

Step 3: Privacy of the Final Result. The final result $b = b_1 \oplus b_2$ is revealed to Bob. Note that Bob knows b_1 (chosen by himself) but not b_2. The value of b_2 is determined by the first zero in the decrypted vector C, which Alice computes. Since b_1 is random, b is random from Bob's perspective unless he knows b_2. However, the protocol ensures that Bob does not learn b_2 (only Alice does). Therefore, Bob cannot infer the exact relationship between x and y beyond the output b.

Step 4: Simulation for Alice and Bob. We now describe the full simulators for both parties.

- *Simulating Alice's view:* Alice's view consists of her private input x, the ciphertexts $[c^i]$ received from Bob, and the random coins used. The simulator

for Alice receives the output b and generates a view as follows: it encrypts random values for $[c^i]$ (using the public key) and uses the fact that these ciphertexts are indistinguishable from the real ones due to IND-CPA security. The random coins are chosen uniformly.
- *Simulating Bob's view:* Bob's view includes his private input y, the ciphertexts $[x^i]$ from Alice, and the final result b. The simulator for Bob, given b, chooses a random b_1 and sets $s = 1 - 2b_1$. It then generates encryptions of random values for $[x^i]$ and simulates the homomorphic operations to produce $[c^i]$ as encryptions of random values. Again, IND-CPA security ensures indistinguishability.

Since we can simulate the views of both parties, the protocol is secure in the semi-honest model.

Step 5: Security Against Malicious Adversaries. To defend against malicious adversaries, we can augment the protocol with zero-knowledge proofs. Specifically, we require each party to prove that they follow the protocol correctly. For example, Alice must prove that she correctly encrypted the prefix bits, and Bob must prove that he correctly computed the homomorphic operations. Using standard zero-knowledge proof techniques (e.g., Schnorr proofs for discrete logarithms), we can achieve security against malicious adversaries. The protocol then remains secure under the DDH assumption in the random oracle model.

Step 6: Composition Security. Our protocol is designed to be modular. The security of the overall protocol follows from the sequential composition theorem of secure multi-party computation. Since each sub-protocol (encryption, homomorphic operation, decryption) is secure, and they are composed sequentially, the entire protocol is secure.

5 Experiment

5.1 Setup

Our scheme is implemented with Python. Experiments are conducted on a laptop running Windows 10 with an Intel Core i7-9750H @ 2.60 GHz processor, 8.00 GB RAM, and an NVIDIA GeForce GTX 1650 GPU. The system uses a 477 GB KXG60ZNV512G KIOXIA SSD for storage. The security parameter k for all tests is uniformly set to 256 bits.

5.2 Efficiency Analysis

Prior to the comparative analysis of secure comparison protocols, an empirical evaluation of the underlying variant ElGamal cryptosystem was conducted to quantify the cost of its primitive operations. The efficiency of any cryptographic protocol is fundamentally constrained by the cost of its underlying operations. The results shown in Table 1 indicate the specific time required for a single encryption operation (L_E), a single decryption operation (L_D), and a single homomorphic operation (L_H). This profiling provides critical insight into the computational overhead intrinsic to protocols constructed upon this cryptographic foundation.

Table 1. Efficiency of variant ElGamal encryption algorithm

Operation	Time (s)
Encryption (L_E)	0.0095
Decryption (L_D)	0.0049
Homomorphic (L_H)	0.0004

Theoretical Complexity Analysis. As summarized in Table 2, the complexity of the DGK and Imp_DGK protocols is characterized by higher coefficients for the homomorphic operation L_H, specifically $(4\ell-1)$ and $(7\ell-1)$, respectively. In contrast, the PSC protocol requires only $3n$ homomorphic operations. This reduction stems from its prefix-based approach, which eliminates the need for the costly bit-wise equality verification loops inherent in the traditional protocols. Consequently, the PSC protocol is theoretically predicted to achieve lower computational overhead, a hypothesis that is validated by the subsequent experimental performance tests.

Table 2. Theoretical evaluation of computational efficiency in protocols

Protocol	Complexity
DGK	$2\ell L_E + (4\ell - 1)L_H + \ell L_D$
Imp_DGK	$2\ell L_E + (7\ell - 1)L_H + \ell L_D$
PSC	$2\ell L_E + 3\ell L_H + \ell L_D$

Since our work focuses on optimizing secure comparison protocols, we conduct experiments on different comparison protocols under identical network configurations using the same input sizes, and compare them with the most classical DGK protocol to demonstrate the superiority of our protocol. The main difference between the DGK protocol and our protocol lies in that our protocol does not require verifying whether the first $i-1$ bits are equal $\left(\sum_{j=1}^{i-1}(x_j \oplus y_j) = 0\right)$, which can reduce $\mathcal{O}(l)$ operations.

Empirical Performance Evaluation. To validate the theoretical analysis, we conducted experiments comparing the execution times of PSC and DGK for various input bit-lengths. The experimental setup consists of an Intel Core i7-10750H CPU @ 2.60 GHz, 16 GB RAM, and an NVIDIA GeForce GTX 1650 GPU. The system uses a 477GB KXC60ZXY512G KIOXIA SSD for storage. The security parameter k for all tests is uniformly set to 256 bits.

Table 3. Average execution time comparison (seconds)

Bit-length (ℓ)	DGK	imp_DGK	PSC
32	0.815	0.854	0.803
64	1.631	1.708	1.606
128	3.263	3.417	3.212
256	6.527	6.834	6.425

The experimental results in Table 3 and Fig. 2 demonstrate that PSC consistently outperforms DGK across all tested bit-lengths. As shown in Fig. 2, the execution time of DGK increases rapidly with increasing bit-length, growing from 0.815 s at $\ell = 32$ to 6.527 s at $\ell = 256$. In contrast, PSC shows much slower growth, from 0.803 s to only 6.425 s over the same range.

The key advantage of PSC lies in its ability to process prefix bit strings as single units and avoid iterative bit-wise equality checks, resulting in inherently lower computational complexity. Consequently, PSC not only achieves higher efficiency at a fixed data size but also scales more effectively, making it a robust solution for applications involving large integers.

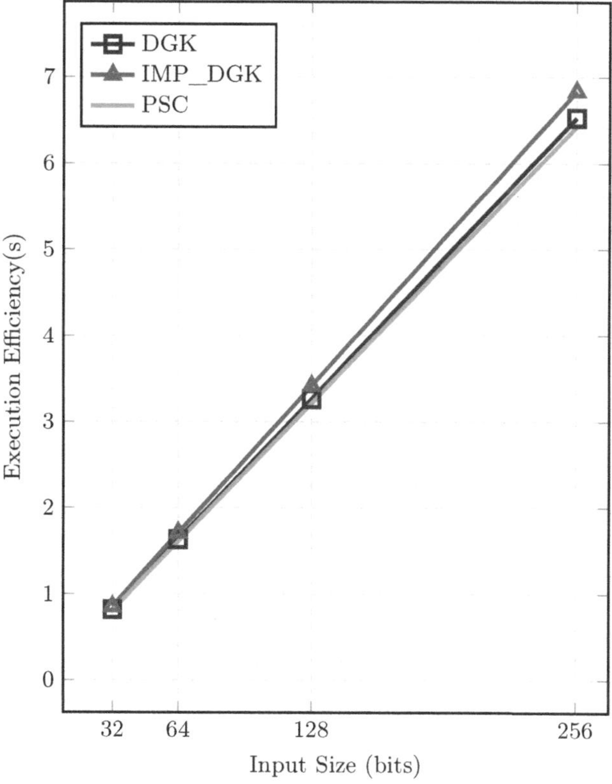

Fig. 2. Performance under different computational loads.

6 Conclusion

This paper addressed the critical challenge of high computational and communication overhead in existing secure comparison protocols, which limits their practicality in large-scale privacy-preserving applications. To tackle this issue, the PSC (Prefix-based Secure Comparison) protocol was introduced, leveraging a variant of the ElGamal homomorphic cryptosystem.

The core innovation of the PSC protocol lies in its departure from traditional bit-wise comparison methods. By processing each prefix bit string as a single encrypted unit and utilizing an obfuscated comparison vector, the protocol eliminates the need for computationally expensive bit-wise equality checks. This approach was analytically shown to reduce computational complexity by approximately $\mathcal{O}(l)$ and minimize the number of interaction rounds. The experimental results confirmed the theoretical advantages, demonstrating that the PSC protocol achieves a significantly lower average running time compared to the classical DGK protocol and its improved variant.

The primary theoretical contribution of this work is a novel protocol framework that shifts the computational paradigm from bit-level to prefix-level operations. In practice, the protocol offers a more efficient and scalable solution for secure comparison, enhancing its feasibility for real-world, large-scale data processing tasks in areas such as federated learning and confidential data analytics. In addition, the PSC protocol can be directly integrated into multi-party secure computing frameworks to support scenarios such as secure auctions, model update comparisons in federated learning, and privacy-preserving data queries. Its prefix batch processing mechanism is also compatible with existing homomorphic cryptographic libraries, which facilitates deployment in real systems. Furthermore, the performance evaluation was conducted on a specific hardware setup, and the impact of network latency on the reduced interaction rounds in a wide-area network setting warrants further investigation. Additionally, exploring its adaptation and optimization for more complex multi-party computation scenarios, as well as its integration into specific application frameworks like privacy-preserving machine learning and secure data auctions, presents a promising direction for further enhancing its utility and impact.

Acknowledgments. This paper is supported by the National Natural Science Foundation of China (grant number 62372370).

References

1. Abspoel, M., Bouman, N.J., Schoenmakers, B., de Vreede, N.: Fast secure comparison for medium-sized integers and its application in binarized neural networks. In: Cryptographers' Track at the RSA Conference. LNCS, vol. 11405, pp. 453–472. Springer, Cham (2019). https://doi.org/10.1007/978-3-030-12612-4_23
2. Applebaum, B., Ishai, Y., Kushilevitz, E., Waters, B.: Encoding functions with constant online rate, or how to compress garbled circuit keys. SIAM J. Comput. **44**(2), 433–466 (2015). https://doi.org/10.1137/130929643

3. Bourse, F., Minelli, M., Minihold, M., Paillier, P.: Fast homomorphic evaluation of deep discretized neural networks. In: Advances in Cryptology – CRYPTO 2018. LNCS, vol. 10993, pp. 483–512. Springer, Cham (2018). https://doi.org/10.1007/978-3-319-96878-0_17
4. Bourse, F., Sanders, O., Traoré, J.: Improved secure integer comparison via homomorphic encryption. In: Cryptographers' Track at the RSA Conference. LNCS, vol. 12006, pp. 391–416. Springer, Cham (2020). https://doi.org/10.1007/978-3-030-40186-3_17
5. Brandt, F.: Fully private auctions in a constant number of rounds. In: International Conference on Financial Cryptography. LNCS, vol. 2742, pp. 223–238. Springer, Cham (2003). https://doi.org/10.1007/978-3-540-45126-6_16
6. Carlton, R., Essex, A., Kapulkin, K.: Threshold properties of prime power subgroups with application to secure integer comparisons. In: CT-RSA, pp. 137–156 (2018)
7. Damgård, I., Geisler, M., Krøigaard, M.: Efficient and secure comparison for online auctions. In: Australasian Conference on Information Security and Privacy. LNCS, vol. 4586, pp. 416–430. Springer, Cham (2007). https://doi.org/10.1007/978-3-540-73458-1_30
8. Galal, H.S., Youssef, A.M.: Verifiable sealed-bid auction on the ethereum blockchain. In: International Conference on Financial Cryptography and Data Security. LNCS, vol. 10957, pp. 265–278. Springer, Cham (2018). https://doi.org/10.1007/978-3-662-58820-8_18
9. Goldreich, O., Micali, S., Wigderson, A.: How to play any mental game, or a completeness theorem for protocols with honest majority. In: Providing Sound Foundations for Cryptography: On the Work of Shafi Goldwasser and Silvio Micali, pp. 307–328. ACM (2019). https://doi.org/10.1145/3335741.3335755
10. Kennedy, W.S., Kolesnikov, V., Wilfong, G.: Overlaying circuit clauses for secure computation. In: Advances in Cryptology – EUROCRYPT 2016. LNCS, vol. 9666, pp. 499–528. Springer, Cham (2016). https://doi.org/10.1007/978-3-662-49896-5_18
11. Kolesnikov, V., Sadeghi, A.R., Schneider, T.: Improved garbled circuit building blocks and applications to auctions and computing minima. In: International Conference on Cryptology and Network Security. LNCS, vol. 5888, pp. 1–20. Springer, Cham (2009). https://doi.org/10.1007/978-3-642-10433-6_1
12. Ma, J., Qi, B., Lv, K.: Three-party integer comparison and applications. In: 2021 IEEE International Performance, Computing, and Communications Conference (IPCCC), pp. 1–8. IEEE (2021). https://doi.org/10.1109/IPCCC51483.2021.9679393
13. Veugen, T.: Improving the DGK comparison protocol. In: 2012 IEEE International Workshop on Information Forensics and Security (WIFS), pp. 49–54. IEEE (2012). https://doi.org/10.1109/WIFS.2012.6412624
14. Veugen, T., Blom, F., De Hoogh, S.J.A., Erkin, Z.: Secure comparison protocols in the semi-honest model. IEEE J. Sel. Topics Signal Process. **9**(7), 1217–1228 (2015). https://doi.org/10.1109/JSTSP.2015.2429117
15. Yao, A.C.C.: How to generate and exchange secrets. In: 27th Annual Symposium on Foundations of Computer Science, pp. 162–167. IEEE (1986). https://doi.org/10.1109/SFCS.1986.25

A Verifiable Data Possession Scheme for Distributed Computing

Wenying Zheng[1], Zelin Ni[1], Yahui Zhu[2], and Tianqi Zhou[2](✉)

[1] School of Computer Science and Technology (School of Artificial Intelligence), Zhejiang Sci-Tech University, Hangzhou 310018, Zhejiang, China
[2] School of Information Science and Engineering (School of Cyber Science and Technology), Zhejiang Sci-Tech University, Hangzhou 310018, Zhejiang, China
tq_zhou@126.com

Abstract. Distributed learning is widely regarded as an effective solution for edge computing in the current data-intensive era. By eliminating heavy data transfers inherent to centralized machine learning, it enables participants to train models locally without aggregating raw data on a cloud server. However, data at distributed clients is often missing or tampered with, which leads to inaccurate gradients during training and opens the door to falsified or manipulated updates. To address the issue that heterogeneous data quality among clients in distributed learning may degrade the performance of the global model, this paper proposes an admission and continuous verification mechanism for federated learning based on Proof of Data Possession (PDP). In this mechanism, the proof of data possession serves as a prerequisite for client participation. Each client must demonstrate the integrity and authenticity of its designated dataset, thereby filtering out clients with incorrect or unreliable data. Furthermore, a continuous random sampling verification strategy is innovatively introduced during the federated training process, where clients that repeatedly fail the proof are eliminated. In practical deployment, considering the differences in computational capabilities among devices, they are categorized into high-capacity and low-capacity devices. A hierarchical PDP mechanism is designed accordingly: high-capacity devices perform integrity verification using BLS signatures, while low-capacity devices adopt sampling-based verification. The scheme further integrates aggregated proofs to reduce time overhead and improve overall efficiency.

Keywords: Federated Learning · Proof of Data Possession · BLS Signature · Aggregated Proof

1 Introduction

With the advancement of artificial intelligence, an increasing volume of datasets requires training. To preserve data privacy, Federated Learning (FL) [1] is commonly adopted, owing to its strong capabilities in distributed data processing and user privacy protection [2,3]. FL mitigates the need to transfer massive

Y. Xiang and J. Shen (Eds.): ML4CS 2025, LNCS 16456, pp. 180–192, 2026.
https://doi.org/10.1007/978-981-95-7820-7_12

amounts of data to the cloud for training. Specifically, participating clients do not upload their local data; instead, they train models locally and transmit only the model parameters to the cloud server, which then aggregates the gradients into a global model. As a result, FL has been widely applied in domains such as medical imaging [4], smart cities [5] and autonomous driving [6].

Despite these advantages, model performance often degrades when client data is inaccurate or incomplete. Thus, it is essential to perform preliminary verification of client-side data before training. Moreover, when clients submit proofs of data possession to the server, issues such as forged or reused proofs may arise, necessitating further authentication of these proofs.

To address these challenges, techniques such as MAC [7] and digital signatures [8] are often employed. MAC-based schemes use a shared key between the sender and verifier to generate and validate message authentication codes. While efficient and tamper-resistant, MACs do not support public verifiability, limiting the ability of third-party auditors to assist the server efficiently. On the other hand, digital signatures allow the sender to sign with a private key, while anyone can verify with the corresponding public key. This public verifiability makes them widely applicable. However, RSA signatures suffer from long key sizes and slow verification, and although ECDSA [9] improves speed, it remains heavier than HMAC.

In this paper, we propose a Verifiable Data Possession Scheme for Distributed Computing to tackle the two issues mentioned above. Specifically, we introduce an admission mechanism for FL clients that requires them to perform a proof of data possession before participating in training. This ensures data authenticity and completeness. During training, we conduct continuous random sampling and verification of participating clients. Those failing multiple verification rounds are excluded. To prevent proof forgery by clients or tampering by third parties, we employ BLS [10] digital signatures to authenticate the submitted proofs. The contributions of this paper are as follows:

We incorporate Proof of Data Possession (PDP) as a precondition for federated learning. Clients must prove the integrity and authenticity of specified datasets before participation, thereby filtering out nodes with missing, tampered, or fraudulent data at the source. This reduces the impact of corrupted data on the global model while maintaining data privacy and compliance.

A lightweight random sampling mechanism is introduced during the training cycle, coupled with an elimination policy for clients that fail verification consecutively. This probabilistic detection framework ensures low-cost yet high-confidence online risk control, with manageable communication and computational overhead, preventing anomalous updates from being amplified over multiple aggregation rounds.

BLS aggregate signatures are applied to client-submitted proofs of data possession, enabling single-verification confirmation of signer identity, timestamp, and message binding. In large-scale concurrent scenarios, this reduces verification cost to a constant level, enhancing traceability and non-repudiation while remaining compatible with existing FL workflows.

2 Related Works

2.1 Data Quality Assurance in Federated Learning

To mitigate the negative impact of heterogeneous client data quality on the global model, existing studies have proposed NSPFL—a secure and privacy-preserving federated learning framework with data integrity auditing [11], which employs a scoring mechanism for client selection. Another study introduced a pairing-based certificateless signature (PCLS) scheme and, on this basis, proposed an anonymous authentication protocol for privacy-preserving deep learning [12]. In terms of privacy, secure aggregation, homomorphic encryption, and differential privacy are commonly adopted to reduce the risk of information leakage. While these methods can tolerate noisy or adversarial gradients to some extent, they share a common limitation: most perform filtering and weighting reduction only after the updates have been generated, failing to ensure from the outset that clients indeed possess untampered and designated datasets.

In contrast, the scheme proposed in this paper adopts Proof of Data Possession (PDP) as a precondition for participation: before submitting any updates, clients must prove the integrity and authenticity of the required dataset, thereby filtering out missing or tampered data at the source. Furthermore, continuous random sampling and verification are introduced during the training cycle, enabling low-overhead re-auditing and timely elimination of clients that repeatedly fail the proof. This shifts data quality assurance from post-hoc correction to a probabilistically guaranteed gating and continuous monitoring process.

2.2 Cryptographic Proof and Aggregation in Verifiable Federated Learning

Existing Verifiable Privacy-preserving Federated Learning (VPFL) schemes [13] focus on verifiability and have explored various cryptographic techniques, including per-update digital signatures, auditable logs, and zero-knowledge proofs to verify the correctness of protocol steps without exposing raw data. These methods enhance accountability and process auditability, yet achieving a balance between strong verification and communication costs remains challenging in large-scale client scenarios.

In this context, our scheme adopts BLS multi-signature aggregation to authenticate client-submitted PDP proofs: a single compact verification simultaneously confirms the signer's identity, timestamp, and message binding, offering greater scalability compared to individual verification [14]. Combined with PDP-based admission and continuous random sampling, the overall process achieves effective authentication of proof origin and content without exposing raw data. This maintains low verification overhead at scale and strengthens end-to-end integrity assurance.

3 Preliminaries

3.1 Federated Learning

Federated learning (FL) is a distributed training paradigm in which multiple participants and a coordinating server collaboratively build a single global model without centralizing raw data. At a high level, one FL round proceeds as follows:

- **Step 1:** The server initializes the global parameters $\mathbf{w}_0$ and selects hyper-parameters (e.g., learning rate η, total FL rounds). It then dispatches this information to a subset of clients chosen to engage in the current round.
- **Step 2:** After receiving the broadcasted global weights/gradients, each selected client i starts local training on its private dataset D_i. During round t, it produces a local gradient $\mathbf{g}_i^{(t)}$ and updates its local model $\mathbf{w}_i^{(t)}$. Upon finishing local computation, the client transmits $\mathbf{g}_i^{(t)}$ back to the server for aggregation.
- **Step 3:** Having collected the client updates, the server applies an aggregation rule to obtain the global update. A common choice is simple averaging:

$$\bar{\mathbf{g}}^{(t+1)} = \frac{1}{N}\sum_{i=1}^{N}\mathbf{g}_i^{(t)},$$

  where N is the number of participating clients in round t. The aggregated result is then sent to clients to initialize the next training round.

When a stopping condition is met (e.g., the maximum number of rounds is reached or the validation metric stabilizes), all parties terminate the procedure and output the final global model.

3.2 The Modified BLS Multi-signature Scheme

The modified BLS multi-signature scheme [10] works over a bilinear pairing $e : \mathbb{G}_0 \times \mathbb{G}_1 \rightarrow \mathbb{G}_T$ with generators $g_0 \in \mathbb{G}_0$, $g_1 \in \mathbb{G}_1$, and two hash functions treated as random oracles: $H_0 : \mathcal{M} \rightarrow \mathbb{G}_0$ and $H_1 : \mathbb{G}_1^n \rightarrow R^n$ where $R := \{1, 2, \dots, 2^{128}\}$ and $1 \leq n \leq \tilde{N}$. It consists of key generation, signing, aggregation, and verification as follows.

1. **Key generation**
   Choose a random $\alpha \overset{R}{\leftarrow} \mathbb{Z}_q$ as the secret key $sk := (\alpha)$ and set $h \leftarrow g_1^{\alpha} \in \mathbb{G}_1$. Output the public key $pk := (h)$.
2. **Signing**
   Given a message $m \in \mathcal{M}$, compute the group hash $H_0(m) \in \mathbb{G}_0$ and output the signature

$$\sigma \leftarrow H_0(m)^{\alpha} \in \mathbb{G}_0.$$

3. **Aggregate**
Given pairs $\big((pk_1, \sigma_1), \ldots, (pk_n, \sigma_n)\big)$ on the *same* message m, first compute coefficients $(t_1, \ldots, t_n) \leftarrow H_1(pk_1, \ldots, pk_n) \in R^n$. Output the multi-signature

$$\sigma \leftarrow \sigma_1^{t_1} \cdots \sigma_n^{t_n} \in \mathbb{G}_0.$$

4. **Verification**
To verify a multi-signature σ on m with public keys $pk_1, \ldots, pk_n$, recompute $(t_1, \ldots, t_n) \leftarrow H_1(pk_1, \ldots, pk_n)$ and the aggregated public key

$$apk \leftarrow pk_1^{t_1} \cdots pk_n^{t_n} \in \mathbb{G}_1.$$

Accept if

$$e(g_1, \sigma) \stackrel{?}{=} e\big(apk, H_0(m)\big).$$

3.3 Provable Data Possession (PDP)

PDP is a remote data auditing cryptographic mechanism. Without downloading the entire file, it has a high probability of confirming that the server still holds the undamaged file.The PDP is mainly divided into two parts:

- **Setup:** the client C first generates keys, obtaining the public key (N, g) and the secret key (e, d, v) (where $ed \equiv 1 \pmod{\varphi(N)}$), and fixes the system parameters (the security parameter κ, a hash function h, and optional seeds for a pseudorandom function f and a permutation π). The file F to be outsourced is then partitioned into n fixed-size blocks $m_1, \ldots, m_n$. For each index i, the client forms an auxiliary string bound to the secret key, $w_i = v \| i$, and generates a tag for block i as

$$T_{i,m_i} \;=\; \big(h(w_i) \cdot g^{m_i}\big)^d \bmod N,$$

optionally recording metadata such as block length, offset, and version number. The client assembles the tag set $\Sigma = (T_{1,m_1}, \ldots, T_{n,m_n})$ and uploads (pk, F, Σ) to the server S.
- **Challenge:** to sample c blocks $(1 \le c \le n)$, the client draws random seeds $k_1, k_2 \in \{0,1\}^\kappa$ and a random $s \in \mathbb{Z}_N^*$, calculates $g_s = g^{\,s} \bmod N$, and forms the challenge $\mathsf{chal} = (c, k_1, k_2, g_s, \mathsf{fid}, t)$ (optionally including a file identifier and round counter to prevent replay), which is sent to the server. The server uses the seeds to determine audited indices and coefficients via $i_j = \pi_{k_1}(j)$ and $a_j = f_{k_2}(j)$ for $j = 1, \ldots, c$, and homomorphically aggregates stored tags and blocks to produce the proof:

$$T = \prod_{j=1}^{c} T_{i_j, m_{i_j}}^{a_j} \bmod N,$$

$$\rho = H\big(g_s^{\sum_{j=1}^{c} a_j m_{i_j}} \bmod N\big).$$

It returns $\mathcal{V} = (T, \rho, \mathsf{fid}, t)$ to the client. Upon receipt, the client rewrites the challenge as $(c, k_1, k_2, s, \mathsf{fid}, t)$, verifies with the public exponent and removes hash factors by first computing $\tau = T^e \bmod N$, then reconstructing i_j, a_j and $w_{i_j} = v \| i_j$, and finally checking

$$\rho \stackrel{?}{=} H\Big((\tau \cdot \prod_{j=1}^{c} h(w_{i_j})^{-a_j})^s \bmod N\Big).$$

Equality indicates the server possesses the corresponding data in this round; otherwise the audit fails.

4 Protocol

4.1 System Model

The system model of the Verifiable Data Possession Scheme for Distributed Computing is shown in Fig. 1. First, the server preprocesses the data by partitioning it into multiple modified subsets and distributing them to different clients. Before participating in the training process, each client generates a Proof of Data Possession based on its locally stored data and submits it to the server for verification. Clients that fail this initial verification are excluded from the training. During the training process, the server continuously conducts random sampling-based Proof of Data Possession checks on participating clients. Those consistently failing the verification are progressively eliminated. For the proofs generated by clients, each signature is created by encrypting the hash value of the message using a private key. Multiple hash values are then aggregated, and the signatures are verified using a public key queue along with the aggregated value. The data auditing and proof verification processes can be delegated to a trusted third party, which ultimately generates an audit report submitted to the server. Based on this report, the server filters out and removes malicious clients.

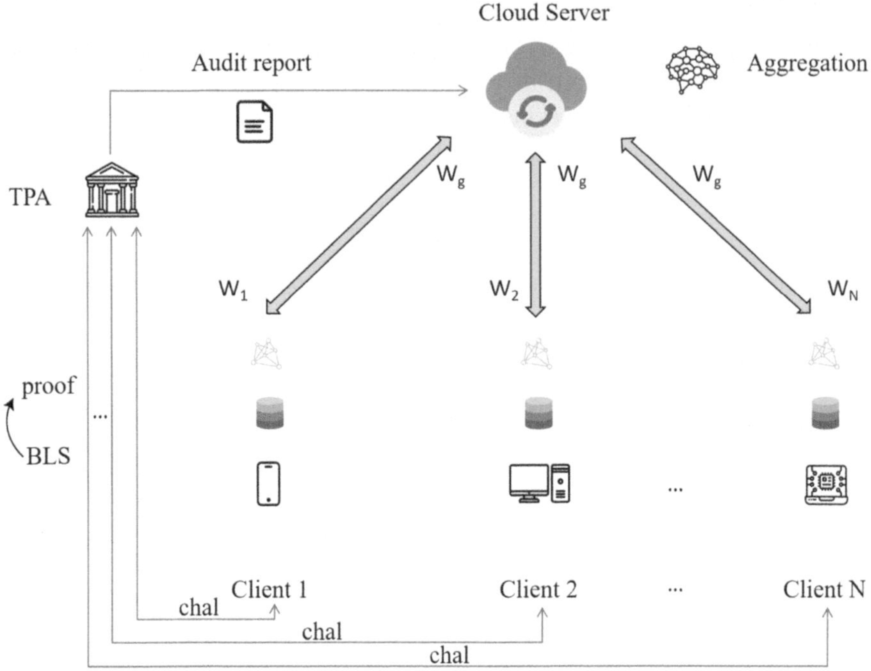

Fig. 1. The system model.

4.2 Detailed Procedures

1. Client Data Admission Mechanism

Before clients participate in federated learning training, they need to provide the server with proof of data integrity for the data they hold. The data first passes through the server, which generates metadata m and a modified dataset file F'. Storage occurs on the server and the client, respectively. The server generates a random challenge R, and the client computes a proof of possession P, which will be provided to the server. Cloud server verifies the validity of the proof to ensure the client's data is intact and unmodified.

2. Continuous Verification and Elimination Mechanism

age During the federated learning process, clients are require d to undergo periodic data verification. The server validates the authenticity of client data through random sampling-based PDP [15], the specific verification scheme is presented in Algorithm 1. If a client fails verification consecutively for multiple rounds, the server will eliminate it to prevent malicious nodes from affecting the training of the global model.

Algorithm 1. PDP Proof Generation

Require: Public key $pk = (N, g)$, secret key $sk = (e, d, v)$, message $m = (m_1, \dots, m_n)$, cryptographic hash function H
Ensure: Proof V
1: Let $(N, g) = pk$ and $(d, v) = sk$
2: Generate $w_i = v \parallel i$ for each block i
3: Compute $T_i, m = (h(w_i) \cdot g^m)^d \mod N$
4: **Output** $(T_1, m_1), (T_2, m_2), \dots, (T_n, m_n), \Sigma = (T_1, m_1, \dots, T_n, m_n)$
5: **Generate Proof:**
6: Let $(N, g) = pk$ and $(c_1, k_2, g_s) = chal$
7: **for** $j \leftarrow 1$ **to** c **do**
8: Calculate the indices of the blocks used to generate the proof: $i_j = \pi k_1(j)$
9: Calculate coefficients: $a_j = f_{k_2}(j)$
10: **end for**
11: Compute $T = T_{i_1,m_1}^{a_1} \cdot T_{i_2,m_2}^{a_2} \cdots T_{i_c,m_c}^{a_c} \mod N$
12: Compute $\rho = H(g_s^{a_1+\cdots+a_c})$
13: **Output** $V = (T, \rho)$
14: **Check Proof:**
15: Let $(N, g) = pk$ and $(e, v) = sk$, $(c_1, k_2, g_s) = chal$
16: Let $\tau = T^e$
17: **for** $j \leftarrow 1$ **to** c **do**
18: Calculate $i_j = \pi k_1(j)$, $w_j = v \parallel f_{k_2}(j)$
19: Calculate $\tau = \tau / h(w_j)^{a_j} \mod N$
20: **end for**
21: **if** $H(\tau \mod N) = \rho$ **then**
22: **Output** SUCCESS
23: **else**
24: **Output** FAILURE
25: **end if**

3. BLS Signature for Data Proof

Upon generating a proof in response to the server's challenge, each client in the federated learning process employs the BLS signature algorithm to digitally sign the proof, as detailed in Algorithm 2. Specifically, each client first generates its own private key and computes the corresponding public key. Subsequently, the client maps the proof message via a hash function, generates a corresponding signature share, and transmits this share along with the generated public key to the server.

Algorithm 2. BLS Multi-Signature

Require: Bilinear groups $(q, G_0, G_1, G_T, e, g_1)$; hashes $H_0 : \mathcal{M} \rightarrow G_0$, $H_1 : G_1^m \rightarrow R^m$ with $R = \{1, \ldots, 2^{128}\}$; number of signers m; a fixed public-key order $\mathcal{PK} = (pk_1, \ldots, pk_m)$
Ensure: Multi-signature $\sigma \in G_0$ and verification result $\{\textbf{ACCEPT}, \textbf{REJECT}\}$
Key Generation:
2: **for** each index $i = 1$ to m **do**
Sample secret key $\alpha_i \leftarrow \mathbb{Z}_q$
4: Set public key $pk_i \leftarrow g_1^{\alpha_i} \in G_1$
Publish pk_i
6: **end for**
Aggregation:
8: Compute weights $(t_1, \ldots, t_m) \leftarrow H_1(pk_1, \ldots, pk_m) \in R^m$
for each index $i = 1$ to m **do**
10: Let $apk_i \leftarrow pk_i^{t_i}$
end for
12: Compute the aggregate public key $apk \leftarrow \prod_{i=1}^{m} apk_i \in G_1$
Signature Generation:
14: **for** each index $i = 1$ to m **do**
Compute $h \leftarrow H_0(m) \in G_0$
16: Local signature $\sigma_i \leftarrow h^{\alpha_i} \in G_0$
end for
18: **Aggregated Signature:**
Using the weights, compute $\sigma \leftarrow \prod_{i=1}^{m} \sigma_i^{t_i} \in G_0$
20: Broadcast σ
Signature Verification (each verifier):
22: Recompute $(t_1, \ldots, t_m) \leftarrow H_1(pk_1, \ldots, pk_m)$
for each index $i = 1$ to m **do**
24: Recompute and multiply $apk_i \leftarrow pk_i^{t_i}$ to obtain $apk \leftarrow \prod_{i=1}^{m} apk_i$
end for
26: if $e(g_1, \sigma) = e(apk, H_0(m))$ **ACCEPT**; otherwise **REJECT**
Return σ and the verification result

4. BLS Signature Aggregation and Verification

After clients submit their respective public keys and signature shares, the server computes the corresponding coefficients based on the list of all submitted public keys using a hash function. It then proceeds to calculate the aggregated public key and the aggregated signature. Finally, the server utilizes these two aggregated values, along with the original proof message, to verify the aggregated signature. This process ensures the authenticity of the proof message's origin and the integrity of its content.

5 Security Analysis

5.1 Correctness Analysis

The correctness of the signature can be verified by following these steps:

$$\begin{aligned}
(t_1, \ldots, t_n) &= H_1(pk_1, \ldots, pk_n) \in R^n, \\
\sigma &= \prod_{i=1}^{n} \sigma_i^{t_i} \in \mathbb{G}_0, \\
apk &= \prod_{i=1}^{n} pk_i^{t_i} \in \mathbb{G}_1, \\
\sigma_i &= H_0(m)^{\alpha_i}, \\
pk_i &= g_2^{\alpha_i}.
\end{aligned}$$

We can get

$$\begin{aligned}
e(g_1, \sigma) &= e\left(g_1, \prod_{i=1}^{n} \sigma_i^{t_i}\right) = \prod_{i=1}^{n} e(g_1, \sigma_i)^{t_i} = \prod_{i=1}^{n} e(g_1, H_0(m)^{\alpha_i})^{t_i} \\
&= \prod_{i=1}^{n} e(g_1, H_0(m))^{\alpha_i t_i} = e(g_1, H_0(m))^{\sum_{i=1}^{n} \alpha_i t_i},
\end{aligned}$$

$$\begin{aligned}
e(apk, H_0(m)) &= e\left(\prod_{i=1}^{n} pk_i^{t_i}, H_0(m)\right) = \prod_{i=1}^{n} e(pk_i^{t_i}, H_0(m)) = \prod_{i=1}^{n} e(pk_i, H_0(m))^{t_i} \\
&= \prod_{i=1}^{n} e(g_2^{\alpha_i}, H_0(m))^{t_i} = e(g_2, H_0(m))^{\sum_{i=1}^{n} \alpha_i t_i} = e(g_1, H_0(m))^{\sum_{i=1}^{n} \alpha_i t_i}.
\end{aligned}$$

$$\boxed{e(g_1, \sigma) = e(apk, H_0(m))}$$

Our signing process proved to be correct.

5.2 Probabilistic Framework

The PDP scheme allows a server to prove possession of selected blocks of a file F. This *sampling* capability greatly reduces the server's workload while still achieving high probability of detecting server misbehavior.

Assume the server S deletes t blocks out of an n-block file F. Let c be the number of distinct blocks requested in a challenge by the client C. Let X be the discrete random variable that counts how many of the c queried blocks coincide with the blocks deleted by S. We compute P_X, the probability that at least one queried block matches a deleted block:

$$P_X = \Pr\{X \geq 1\} = 1 - \Pr\{X = 0\} = 1 - \frac{n-t}{n} \cdot \frac{n-1-t}{n-1} \cdots \frac{n-c+1-t}{n-c+1}.$$

Since, for all $i \in \{1, \ldots, c-1\}$,

$$\frac{n-i-t}{n-i} \geq \frac{n-1-t}{n-1},$$

it follows that

$$1 - \left(\frac{n-t}{n}\right)^c \leq P_X \leq 1 - \left(\frac{n-c+1-t}{n-c+1}\right)^c.$$

The quantity P_X is the probability that, if S deletes t blocks from the file, then after a challenge in which C asks for proofs of c blocks, the client detects server misbehavior. When t is a fixed fraction of the file, the PDP scheme can detect misbehavior with a prescribed probability using a *constant* number c of queried blocks, independent of the total number n of file blocks. For example, if $t = 1\% \cdot n$, then choosing $c \approx 460$ and $c \approx 300$ achieves detection probability at least 99% and 95%, respectively.

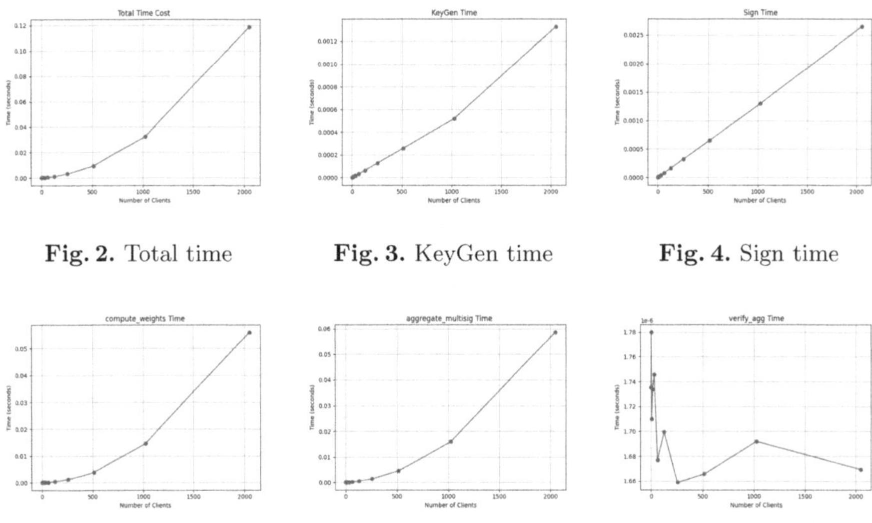

Fig. 2. Total time **Fig. 3.** KeyGen time **Fig. 4.** Sign time

Fig. 5. Weight time **Fig. 6.** Aggregate time **Fig. 7.** Verify time

6 Conclusion

Our experiments ran on a Windows 11 server equipped with an AMD Ryzen 7 H260 (3.80 GHz) and Radeon (TM) 780M Graphics, alongside 32 GB of RAM. The cryptographic components were implemented using the Pairing-Based Cryptography (PBC) library. We evaluated the overall time overhead of the BLS aggregate signature algorithm for generating client-side proofs for signature authentication, as well as the time overhead of each component, as detailed in Figs. 2, 3, 4, 5, 6 and 7. As the number of clients increases, the total time consumption exhibits a linear upward trend. The time overhead during the verification phase shows fluctuations, which are more pronounced when the number of clients is small. As the client count grows, the verification time gradually stabilizes.

Our proposed the Verifiable Data Possession Scheme for Distributed Computing effectively ensures the accuracy and security of the data set throughout the entire process of distributed computing. In this scheme, PDP-based proofs of data possession effectively detect data loss and malicious clients, enabling continuous sampling of participants throughout federated learning to efficiently identify adversarial behavior. The underlying probabilistic model ensures security while maintaining efficiency. For client-submitted proofs, BLS aggregate signatures allow the server to rapidly authenticate the provenance of signatures and the integrity of the evidence, providing stronger assurance for current FL computation. Looking ahead, fixed-rate sampling can be upgraded to adaptive, risk-aware sampling that allocates more queries to high-risk clients, thereby improving detection while reducing overall overhead.

Acknowledgments. This work is supported by the National Key R&D Program of China (No. 2023YFB2703700), the National Natural Science Foundation of China (Nos. U21A20465, 62402444, 62402448), the Fundamental Research Funds of Zhejiang Sci-Tech University under Grants No. 22222266-Y, the Program for Leading Innovative Research Team of Zhejiang Province (No. 2023R01001) and the Zhejiang Provincial Natural Science Foundation of China (Nos. LQ24F020009, LQ24F020012).

References

1. Konečný, J., McMahan, B., Ramage, D.: Federated optimization: distributed optimization beyond the datacenter. arXiv preprint arXiv:1511.03575 (2015)
2. McMahan, B., Moore, E., Ramage, D., Hampson, S., y Arcas, B.A.: Communication-efficient learning of deep networks from decentralized data. In: Artificial Intelligence and Statistics, pp. 1273–1282. PMLR (2017)
3. Yang, Q., Liu, Y., Chen, T., Tong, Y.: Federated machine learning: concept and applications. ACM Trans. Intell. Syst. Technol. (TIST) **10**(2), 1–19 (2019)
4. Ciupek, D., Malawski, M., Pieciak, T.: Federated learning: a new frontier in the exploration of multi-institutional medical imaging data. arXiv preprint arXiv:2503.20107 (2025)
5. Dritsas, E., Trigka, M.: Federated learning for IoT: a survey of techniques, challenges, and applications. J. Sens. Actuator Netw. **14**(1), 9 (2025)
6. Zhang, S., Tay, J., Baiz, P.: The effects of data imbalance under a federated learning approach for credit risk forecasting. arXiv preprint arXiv:2401.07234 (2024)
7. Bellare, M., Canetti, R., Krawczyk, H.: Keying hash functions for message authentication. In: CRYPTO 1996. LNCS, vol. 1109, pp. 1–15. Springer, Cham (1996)
8. FIPS PUB. Digital signature standard (DSS). Fips pub, pp. 186–192 (2000)
9. Johnson, D., Menezes, A., Vanstone, S.: The elliptic curve digital signature algorithm (ECDSA). Int. J. Inf. Secur. **1**(1), 36–63 (2001)
10. Boneh, D., Drijvers, M., Neven, G.: BLS multi-signatures with public-key aggregation (2018). https://crypto.stanford.edu/dabo/pubs/papers/BLSmultisig.html

11. Zhang, Z., Li, Y.: NSPFL: a novel secure and privacy-preserving federated learning with data integrity auditing. IEEE Trans. Inf. Forensics Secur. **19**, 4494–4506 (2024)
12. Yu, H., Xu, R., Zhang, H., Yang, Z., Liu, H.: Ev-fl: efficient verifiable federated learning with weighted aggregation for industrial IoT networks. IEEE/ACM Trans. Netw. **32**(2), 1723–1737 (2023)
13. Ma, J., Liu, H., Zhang, M., Liu, Z.: VPFL: enabling verifiability and privacy in federated learning with zero-knowledge proofs. Knowl.-Based Syst. **299**, 112115 (2024)
14. Tian, G., Miao, M., Wei, J., Liu, Z., Guo, L., Chen, X.: Verifiable and controllable data sharing with compliance checking in cloud computing. IEEE Trans. Dependable Secure Comput. 1–14 (2025)
15. Ateniese, G., et al.: Provable data possession at untrusted stores. In: Proceedings of the 14th ACM Conference on Computer and Communications Security, pp. 598–609 (2007)

Entropy-Aware Watermarking for Code Generation Models

Ying Shi[1], Siyuan Bao[1], Hanzhou Wu[1,2](✉), Jingyu Ye[3](✉), and Xinpeng Zhang[1]

[1] School of Communication and Information Engineering, Shanghai University, Shanghai 200444, China
{shiy,baosy,xzhang}@shu.edu.cn, h.wu.phd@ieee.org
[2] School of Big Data and Computer Science, Guizhou Normal University, Guiyang 550025, China
[3] Guangxi Investment Group Co., Ltd., Nanning 530000, China
newzolo@sina.com

Abstract. Watermark-based detection shows strong potential for identifying machine-generated content, but applying it to code generation is still hard due to low entropy and strict structure, which limit flexibility and cause a trade-off between quality and detectability. Existing methods like SWEET use fixed entropy thresholds. They cannot adjust to different levels of token uncertainty across coding contexts. To overcome this limitation, we propose **E**ntropy-**A**ware **W**atermarking (EAW), a framework that dynamically modulates watermark embedding strength based on local entropy signals. Specifically, EAW amplifies the greenlist bias in high-entropy regions, such as variable names or comments, while reducing interference in low-entropy, syntax-critical parts to maintain the functional correctness of the code. This adaptive mechanism enables EAW to maintain code naturalness without sacrificing detection robustness. Extensive experiments across multiple benchmarks demonstrate that EAW consistently outperforms prior baselines in both watermark detectability and code quality retention, establishing a better trade-off between transparency and reliability in code watermarking.

Keywords: Text Watermarking · Code Generation · Large Language Models · AI Security · Entropy-based Methods

1 Introduction

The rise of large language models (LLMs) has brought a major change to software engineering, making it possible to generate code snippets from natural language descriptions with impressive accuracy and skill [2–4,8,9,16,22]. These capabilities significantly accelerate development workflows and democratize programming for non-experts [6]. However, this powerful technology is a double-edged sword. The same models that boost productivity can be exploited to generate malicious software, such as ransomware and spyware, with alarming ease

Y. Xiang and J. Shen (Eds.): ML4CS 2025, LNCS 16456, pp. 193–206, 2026.
https://doi.org/10.1007/978-981-95-7820-7_13

and scale [13,17]. Furthermore, issues of code plagiarism, license violations, and the unattributed use of AI-generated code in academic or professional settings pose significant ethical and legal challenges [19,20]. As machine-generated code becomes harder to tell apart from human-written code, we urgently need reliable ways to trace its origin and ensure accountability.

Watermarking techniques have demonstrated effectiveness across multiple modalities, including text and images [1,21,23]. In recent years, similar approaches have been increasingly applied to code generation [5,10–12,24]. These methods embed subtle statistical signals during code generation, typically by biasing token selection toward a designated 'green list,' enabling subsequent verification of whether a piece of code was produced by a large language model. Among them, WLLM [11] introduced a simple but effective green-red list mechanism that has shown strong results in natural language generation. However, directly using such methods for code generation brings two main challenges. Even small changes in token probabilities can harm functional correctness. Also, only a small portion of tokens can safely hold watermarks without changing the meaning of the code.

To address these issues, SWEET [12] (Selective WatErmarking via Entropy Thresholding) introduces a selective watermarking approach. It targets only the tokens whose prediction entropy is higher than a fixed threshold. This method improves detectability while keeping the code correct, since it avoids syntax-critical tokens. However, SWEET still depends on fixed entropy thresholds and uniform bias scaling, which cannot fully adjust to the changing entropy patterns found in different coding contexts.

To overcome this rigidity, we propose EAW, a novel framework that dynamically adapts to the token-level entropy landscape. EAW introduces entropy-adaptive biasing, which adjusts the strength of watermark embedding based on token-level entropy. It applies stronger watermarking in high-uncertainty areas and reduces interference in deterministic regions to keep the code stable and correct.

This mechanism enables EAW to achieve higher watermark detectability without compromising code functionality or naturalness. Empirical results demonstrate that, under comparable code pass rates, EAW achieves an average AUROC improvement of 7.45% across different datasets without sacrificing code correctness.

Our contributions are summarized as follows:

- We identify the limitations of fixed-threshold watermarking in low-entropy code generation and analyze the role of entropy dynamics in watermark embedding.
- We propose EAW, a fully entropy-adaptive watermarking framework that integrates adaptive bias.
- We conduct extensive experiments on multi-language code datasets, and show that EAW achieves better correctness-detectability trade-offs and the highest overall evaluation among existing methods.

2 Preliminaries

2.1 Language Model Prediction

Large Language Models (LLMs) are trained by maximizing the likelihood of the next-token prediction given previous context, learning the conditional probability distribution

$$P(x_i \mid x_{<i}) = \mathrm{softmax}(s_i),$$

where s_i denotes the pre-softmax logits over the model vocabulary V at generation step i.

During inference, the model samples one token from this distribution and appends it to the output sequence. This process continues step by step to generate a complete text or code sequence:

$$x = (x_1, x_2, \ldots, x_n).$$

Through this iterative sampling, LLMs can produce coherent text or code that follows learned statistical and syntactic patterns. In watermarking, this probabilistic token generation process naturally allows the embedding of statistical signals without retraining the model.

2.2 LLM Watermarking

Watermarking aims to embed detectable patterns into model outputs while minimally affecting their quality. One well-established approach is WLLM [11], which partitions the vocabulary at each generation step into a green list G_i and a red list $R_i = V \setminus G_i$, with proportions γ and $1 - \gamma$, respectively. A fixed bias δ is added to green list logits, producing a modified probability distribution that favors green tokens while preserving overall softmax normalization.

Detection operates by counting the number of green tokens in the generated sequence and computing a z-score relative to the expected proportion. If a sequence exhibits a statistically significant overrepresentation of green tokens, it is classified as watermarked. This approach demonstrates that statistical signals can be embedded into model outputs during generation, enabling the attribution of AI-generated content.

2.3 Code Watermarking

Extending watermarking to code generation presents additional challenges due to the structured nature of programming languages. Tokens corresponding to control flow or syntax typically have low entropy, whereas identifiers, literals, and comments tend to have higher entropy. Token-level entropy therefore provides a useful signal for guiding watermark placement: high-entropy tokens can accommodate bias without affecting semantics, while low-entropy tokens should remain unchanged to preserve functionality.

Methods like SWEET [12] leverage this property by selectively applying watermark bias to high-entropy tokens. Let H_i denote the entropy at generation step i:

$$H_i = -\sum_{v \in V} p_i[v] \log p_i[v].$$

The bias is applied only if H_i exceeds a threshold τ, concentrating the watermark in flexible regions while avoiding deterministic, syntax-critical tokens. Although this selective strategy reduces functional interference, its reliance on a fixed threshold and constant bias limits adaptability. In regions with moderate entropy, the watermark may be too weak for reliable detection or too strong, potentially impairing code functionality. As a result, static methods may struggle to generalize across diverse coding contexts.

Prompt

Write a python function takes in an integer and check whether the frequency of each digit in the integer is less than or equal to the digit itself.
assert validate(1233) == True
assert validate(112) == False

(a) Unwatermarked Code

```
def validate(n):
    for i in str(n):
        if str(n).count(i) > int(i):
            return False
    return True
```

(b) SWEET(low threshold) Watermarked Code

```
def validate(num):
    num_str = str(num)
    freq_dict = {}
    for digit in num_str:
        if digit in freq_dict:
            freq_dict[digit] += 1
        else:
            freqDict[digit] = 1  # × undefined variable 'freqDict'
    for digit, freq in freq_dict.items():
        if int(digit) > freq:     # × logic flipped
            return False
    return True
```

Correctness: ×
Detection: √

(c) SWEET(high threshold) Watermarked Code

```
def validate(n):
    for char in str(n):
        if str(n).count(char) > int(char):
            return False
    return True
```

Correctness: √
Detection: ×

(d) EAW Watermarked Code

```
def validate(num):
    num_str = str(num)
    for char in num_str:
        if num_str.count(char) > int(char):
            return False
    return True
```

Correctness: √
Detection: √

Fig. 1. Demonstrative comparison between SWEET and EAW(ours). Code generated without watermarking (a) behaves normally. A low entropy threshold in SWEET (b) corrupts logic by modifying low-entropy tokens, while a high threshold (c) preserves correctness but yields almost no detectable watermark. Our EAW method (d) adapts watermark strength to token entropy, achieving both correctness and detectability.

2.4 Motivation

Existing watermarking frameworks demonstrate that structured token-level biases can enable post hoc detection of AI-generated content. However, static designs like SWEET, which use fixed thresholds and constant bias, cannot adapt to varying entropy landscapes. To address these limitations, we propose an entropy-aware watermarking framework that dynamically adjusts watermark strength based on local token entropy. This adaptive approach achieves a better balance between detection reliability and code fidelity.

3 Proposed Method

We introduce EAW (Entropy-Aware Watermarking), a watermarking framework designed for code-oriented large language models (LLMs). Unlike prior approaches that rely on fixed watermarking strength, EAW dynamically modulates greenlist bias according to token-level entropy. As shown in Fig. 1, this entropy-guided mechanism enables the model to adaptively balance between watermark detectability and code correctness under different coding contexts.

3.1 Overview

Given a token sequence $X = \{x_1, x_2, \ldots, x_n\}$, let s_i denote the pre-softmax logits of the model at generation step i, and $p_i = \text{softmax}(s_i)$ the corresponding token probability distribution. In standard autoregressive generation, the next token is sampled directly from p_i. In contrast, EAW introduces an entropy-aware modulation of the logits to embed a watermark selectively while preserving code quality. Specifically, at each step i, the model first computes the token-level entropy H_i, reflecting the uncertainty of the next token. Based on H_i, EAW modifies the original logits s_i to obtain entropy-aware logits s_i' as follows:

$$s_i'[v] = \begin{cases} s_i[v] + b_i, & v \in G_i, \\ s_i[v], & v \in R_i, \end{cases} \tag{1}$$

where G_i and R_i represent the greenlist and redlist of candidate tokens at step i, and b_i is the adaptive bias computed according to the local entropy H_i.

This adjustment effectively increases the probability of sampling tokens from the greenlist in high-entropy, flexible regions (e.g., identifiers or literals), while leaving low-entropy, syntax-critical tokens largely unaffected. After this logit modification, the model samples the next token from the adjusted distribution $\text{softmax}(s_i')$ following the standard autoregressive decoding procedure. By integrating entropy-adaptive biasing in this way, EAW embeds watermarks in a context-sensitive manner, improving detectability without reducing code correctness or naturalness.

3.2 Entropy-Adaptive Bias Mechanism

In standard watermarking approaches such as SWEET, the bias δ applied to greenlist tokens is fixed, which imposes a static and suboptimal trade-off between watermark strength and code quality. To achieve fine-grained adaptation to diverse coding contexts, EAW introduces an entropy-modulated adaptive bias b_i

that dynamically increases with the local uncertainty H_i, This approach allows stronger watermarking in high-entropy areas while keeping minimal interference in low-entropy regions.

The adaptive bias b_i is calculated as follows:

$$b_i = \min\Big(g \cdot \big(1 + \beta \cdot (1 - e^{-\alpha \cdot \max(0, H_i - H_0)})\big),\ m\Big), \tag{2}$$

where

- g is the base bias strength, defining the minimum bias around the reference entropy level H_0;
- α is the growth rate factor, controlling how rapidly the bias increases with entropy;
- β is the intensity factor, determining the maximum relative increase $g(1+\beta)$;
- H_0 is the entropy threshold for triggering the watermark; below this value, the model outputs normally without added bias;
- m is the upper bound for the adaptive bias b_i, ensuring that the applied bias does not grow too large and harm output quality.

The design of this function embodies several key properties: Smoothness is ensured by the exponential term, which makes b_i change continuously with H_i. Boundedness is guaranteed by the min operation, which keeps b_i within the range $[g, m]$. The adaptive bias b_i depends not only on the entropy of the current token but also indirectly captures local context uncertainty. This allows EAW to flexibly adjust watermark strength across different structural and functional parts of the code.

High-entropy tokens, such as variable names, literals, or optional expressions, are more flexible and less likely to affect code functionality. By applying stronger bias to these regions, EAW increases watermark detectability while keeping the code behavior unchanged. In contrast, low-entropy tokens, often related to syntax-critical elements like keywords and control-flow structures, receive minimal bias. This prevents EAW from introducing syntax or semantic errors.

This entropy-aware, context-sensitive adjustment enables EAW to achieve a better overall trade-off between watermark detectability and code quality than fixed-threshold methods like SWEET. Moreover, the continuous, bounded, and entropy-adaptive design of b_i allows EAW to generalize across various coding tasks and programming styles. It ensures that the watermark remains both reliable and non-intrusive. The parameters α and β are selected through grid search on a validation set to find the best balance between watermark detectability and code fidelity. The detailed tuning process and results are presented in the experimental section.

3.3 Entropy-Aware Generation and Detection

EAW builds upon the general generation—detection pipeline of SWEET, replacing its static components with entropy-adaptive counterparts.

Algorithm 1 Entropy-Adaptive Generation (EAW)

Require: Tokenized prompt $x = \{x_1, \dots, x_{M-1}\}$; parameters g, α, β, m
Ensure: Watermarked sequence $y = \{y_1, \dots, y_N\}$
1: **for** $t = 0, 1, 2, \dots$ **do**
2: Compute logits s_t and probabilities $p_t = \text{softmax}(s_t)$
3: Compute token-level entropy $H_t = -\sum_v p_t[v] \log p_t[v]$
4: Generate random green/red partitions (G_t, R_t) from the previous token hash
5: **if** $H_t > H_0$ **then**
6: Compute adaptive bias b_t using Eq. (2)
7: Adjust logits as in Eq. (1)
8: **end if**
9: Sample y_t from the adjusted distribution
10: **end for**

Algorithm 1 describes the generation process of EAW. Given a tokenized prompt and a set of hyperparameters (g, α, β, m), the algorithm iteratively generates each token in the output sequence while dynamically adjusting the watermark bias based on token-level entropy. At each generation step t, the model first computes the logits and corresponding probability distribution for the next token, followed by the calculation of the token's entropy H_t. Based on a hash of the previous token, a greenlist and redlist are generated to guide watermark embedding. If the entropy exceeds a threshold H_0, an adaptive bias b_t is computed according to Eq. (2) and applied to the greenlist tokens as in Eq. (1). Finally, the next token y_t is sampled from the adjusted probability distribution. This entropy-aware, step-wise modulation allows EAW to inject detectable watermarks in high-uncertainty regions while minimally disturbing low-entropy, syntax-critical tokens, achieving a balance between detectability and code correctness.

Algorithm 2 details the detection procedure of EAW for distinguishing watermarked and human-written code sequences. Given a prompt x, a test sequence y, and detection parameters $(\gamma, H_0, z_{\text{th}})$, the algorithm evaluates whether the sequence is watermarked. It initializes counters N^H and N_G^H to track the number of high-entropy tokens and the number of greenlist tokens within them, respectively. For each token y_t in the sequence, the model computes logits and the corresponding probability distribution, followed by the token-level entropy H_t. If the entropy exceeds the threshold H_0, green/red partitions are deterministically reconstructed using the hash of the previous token. The counters are updated according to whether y_t belongs to the greenlist. After processing the entire sequence, a z-score is calculated as $z = \frac{N_G^H - \gamma N^H}{\sqrt{\gamma(1-\gamma)N^H}}$. If the z-score exceeds the predefined threshold z_{th}, the sequence is classified as watermarked; otherwise, it is classified as human-written. This entropy-aware detection ensures that the method focuses on flexible, high-uncertainty regions while ignoring deterministic, syntax-critical tokens, maintaining robustness and minimizing false positives.

Algorithm 2 Entropy-Aware Detection (EAW)

Require: Prompt $x = \{x_1, \ldots, x_{M-1}\}$; test sequence $y = \{y_1, \ldots, y_N\}$; parameters $\gamma, H_0, z_{\text{th}}$
Ensure: True (watermarked) or False (human-written)

1: Initialize counters $N^H = 0$, $N_G^H = 0$
2: **for** $t = 0, 1, \ldots, N-1$ **do**
3: Compute logits s_t and probabilities $p_t = \text{softmax}(s_t)$
4: Compute token-level entropy $H_t = -\sum_v p_t[v] \log p_t[v]$
5: **if** $H_t > H_0$ **then**
6: Reconstruct green/red partitions (G_t, R_t) from the previous token hash
7: $N^H \leftarrow N^H + 1$
8: **if** $y_t \in G_t$ **then**
9: $N_G^H \leftarrow N_G^H + 1$
10: **end if**
11: **end if**
12: **end for**
13: Compute z-score $z = \dfrac{N_G^H - \gamma N^H}{\sqrt{\gamma(1-\gamma)N^H}}$
14: **if** $z > z_{\text{th}}$ **then**
15: **return** True (watermarked)
16: **else**
17: **return** False (human-written)
18: **end if**

3.4 Role of Entropy Adaptation

The central innovation of EAW lies in its entropy-aware modulation of watermarking strength. By dynamically adjusting the greenlist bias based on token-level entropy H_i, the framework adapts its behavior to the local uncertainty of code generation. Low-entropy regions, dominated by syntax or control tokens, receive only mild biasing to preserve execution correctness, while high-entropy regions allow stronger watermark embedding for enhanced detectability. This entropy-guided adaptivity enables EAW to outperform static watermarking methods such as SWEET, achieving a superior trade-off between watermark robustness and code quality across diverse programming tasks. In addition, EAW seamlessly integrates with standard autoregressive decoding without altering the underlying model architecture.

4 Experimental Results and Analysis

4.1 Experiment Settings

Datasets. We conduct experiments on the HumanEval+ and MBPP+ benchmarks [14], two widely adopted datasets for evaluating Python code completion and synthesis. To further examine the cross-language generalizability of our approach, we additionally employ HumanEvalPack [18], which extends HumanEval to multiple programming languages, including Python, C++, and Java.

Baselines. We compare EAW with three representative training-free watermarking approaches: KGW [11], which implants the watermark signal by partitioning the vocabulary into green and red lists during text generation and biasing the probabilities towards the green list; EWD [15], whose improvement lies on the detection side, where it enhances detection robustness in complex texts by assigning higher weights to high-entropy tokens; and SWEET [12], which addresses the key detection challenges posed by the low-entropy nature of code by selectively embedding watermarks in high-entropy tokens.

Base Model. We conduct all experiments using Qwen2.5-Coder [7], a state-of-the-art model for code generation. On the EvalPlus leaderboard, Qwen2.5-Coder achieves top-tier performance, ranking closely behind leading GPT-01 models. Due to its competitive results and reliability in generating high-quality code, we adopt Qwen2.5-Coder as the foundation LLM for all experiments in this work.

Evaluation Metrics. To comprehensively assess the performance of our watermarking framework, we consider both code correctness and watermark detectability.

Code Correctness: We measure functional correctness using the standard pass@k metric, which evaluates whether the generated code passes all provided test cases. In this study, we report pass@1 as the primary indicator, reflecting the probability that the top-ranked generated solution is correct.

Watermark Detectability: We adopt three complementary detection metrics: AUROC (Area Under the Receiver Operating Characteristic curve), TPR@FPR = 0.05 (denoted TPR@0.05), and TPR@FPR = 0.01 (denoted TPR@0.01). AUROC measures the overall discriminative ability of the detector, while TPR@0.05 and TPR@0.01 indicate the proportions of watermarked code correctly identified under 5% and 1% false-positive constraints, respectively, reflecting the detector's reliability in both moderate and strict settings.

By jointly evaluating correctness and detectability, we can analyze the trade-offs introduced by different watermarking strategies and ensure that improved detection does not come at the expense of code functionality.

Implementation Details. All experiments are conducted using the Qwen2.5-Coder-3B model on HumanEval+ and MBPP+. Figure 2a visualizes the effect of varying δ (with $\gamma = 0.5$) on pass@1 and AUROC under the SWEET framework, providing insights into the trade-off between generation quality and watermark detectability. Increasing δ generally improves AUROC, but excessively large values can reduce pass@1, motivating a systematic hyperparameter selection.

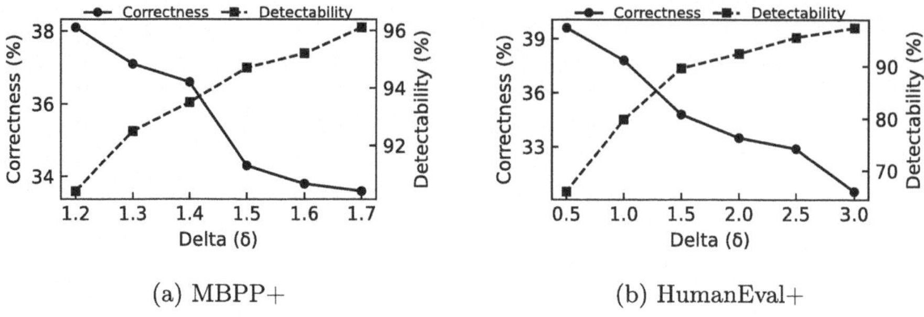

(a) MBPP+

(b) HumanEval+

Fig. 2. pass@1 and AUROC versus δ on MBPP+ and HumanEval+ (SWEET).

To achieve a robust balance, we adopt a two-stage hyperparameter selection strategy. We first perform a grid search over $\delta \in [1.0, 2.0]$ and $\alpha, \beta \in [0.5, 1.5]$ with a step size of 0.1 to identify promising candidate regions. Here, larger δ corresponds to stronger watermark bias, while the search ranges for α and β are chosen based on preliminary experiments: too small values weaken detection, whereas too large values degrade code quality. A validation set comprising 20% of samples from HumanEval+ and MBPP+ is used to jointly evaluate pass@1 and AUROC. The grid search results indicate that the optimal region lies in $\delta \in [1.2, 1.4]$, with multiple (α, β) combinations yielding desirable performance trade-offs.

We then conduct a sensitivity analysis within this candidate region to select the most robust parameters. As shown in Fig. 2a, pass@1 remains stable in $\delta \in [1.2, 1.4]$ but drops sharply at $\delta = 1.5$, confirming that excessive bias harms semantic correctness. Therefore, we adopt $\delta = 1.2$ as the base bias. For the dynamic scaling factors, we select $\alpha = 1.0$ and $\beta = 0.65$: α moderately increases the bias when entropy exceeds the threshold, ensuring responsiveness without instability, and β enhances watermark embedding in high-entropy regions while keeping the overall bias below the capped maximum value of 2.0.

For HumanEval+, we repeat the same procedure using its own entropy distribution statistics and select $g = 1.0$, $\alpha = 0.6$, $\beta = 3.2$, and $m = 4.0$. This configuration reinforces watermark embedding in highly uncertain code segments while minimizing interference in deterministic and function-critical regions, as illustrated in Fig. 2b.

4.2 Results and Analysis

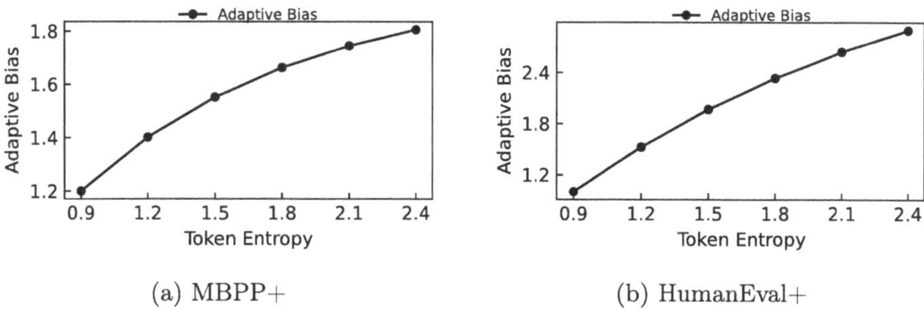

(a) MBPP+ (b) HumanEval+

Fig. 3. Adaptive bias vs. token entropy in EAW. (a) MBPP+ (b) HumanEval+

Figure 3 illustrates the relationship between token-level entropy and adaptive bias in EAW. Low-entropy tokens—typically syntax-critical elements such as keywords and control flow statements—receive minimal bias, preserving code correctness, while high-entropy tokens, corresponding to flexible regions like variable names or literals, are assigned increasing bias up to the maximum value m, enhancing watermark detectability. Figure 3a shows this trend on the MBPP+ dataset with parameters $g = 1.2$, $\alpha = 1.0$, $\beta = 0.65$, and $m = 2.0$, whereas Fig. 3b presents the analogous curve for the HumanEval+ dataset with $g = 1.0$, $\alpha = 0.6$, $\beta = 3.2$, and $m = 4.0$. The two curves together demonstrate that EAW's continuous and context-sensitive modulation allows detectable watermarks to be embedded across a wide range of high-entropy regions while minimizing interference with low-entropy, deterministic tokens, thereby supporting both high correctness and detectability simultaneously.

Table 1. Experimental results on MBPP+.

Method	pass@1	AUROC	TPR@0.05	TPR@0.01
KGW	36.6	77.7	42.1	16.8
EWD	36.6	91.3	70.4	35.8
SWEET($\delta = 1.3$)	37.1	92.5	66.6	42.1
SWEET($\delta = 1.7$)	33.6	96.1	79.9	62.8
EAW	37.8	96.2	84.7	67.7

As shown in Table 1, even after hyperparameter tuning, traditional watermarking methods such as KGW and EWD exhibit limited ability to balance code correctness and detectability. KGW applies a uniform bias across all tokens, resulting in relatively low AUROC and TPR, whereas EWD only assigns higher

Table 2. Experimental results on HumanEval+.

Method	pass@1	AUROC	TPR@0.05	TPR@0.01
KGW	35.4	78.9	40.2	11.0
EWD	35.4	81.7	46.3	22.0
SWEET($\delta = 1.1$)	36.2	81.4	47.5	26.8
SWEET($\delta = 2.0$)	33.5	92.4	76.2	61.6
EAW	37.2	92.6	77.4	67.1

weights to high-entropy tokens during the detection stage (AUROC = 91.3, TPR@0.05 = 70.4%, TPR@0.01 = 35.8%), but achieving higher detectability still incurs noticeable interference with code quality. SWEET further enhances detection by selectively embedding watermarks in high-entropy regions, yet it still demonstrates a clear trade-off between correctness and detectability. Specifically, with $\delta = 1.3$, SWEET attains a pass@1 of 37.1%, comparable to EAW (37.8%), but its AUROC and TPR values (92.5, 66.6%, 42.1%) remain lower. Conversely, when $\delta = 1.7$, SWEET achieves AUROC = 96.1, TPR@0.05 = 79.9% and TPR@0.01 = 62.8%, close to EAW's detectability, but suffers a significant drop in pass@1 (33.6%).

In contrast, EAW maintains strong performance across both dimensions simultaneously, achieving high correctness (37.8%) and detectability (AUROC = 96.2, TPR@0.05 = 84.7%, TPR@0.01 = 67.7%), demonstrating its ability to balance the trade-off that SWEET cannot. Similar patterns are observed on the HumanEval+ dataset, as shown in Table 2, where EAW consistently surpasses all baselines in both correctness and detectability. In particular, while maintaining a code generation accuracy comparable to SWEET, EAW improves AUROC by 11.2 points and also achieves higher TPRs under both FPR = 0.05 and 0.01 thresholds, yielding a more balanced and robust watermarking performance overall.

To further evaluate the generalization ability of EAW across different programming languages, we conduct experiments on the HumanEvalPack dataset, which extends HumanEval+ to multilingual settings including C++ and Java. As shown in Table 3, EAW maintains consistent advantages over SWEET in both correctness and detectability across languages. These results demonstrate that EAW effectively adapts to diverse syntax structures and coding styles, reinforcing its robustness and applicability beyond Python-based code generation tasks.

Overall, these findings confirm that EAW provides an adaptive, entropy-aware solution that generalizes effectively across datasets and programming languages.

Table 3. Experimental results on HumanEvalPack C++ and Java.

Method	HumanEvalPack-Java		HumanEvalPack-C++	
	pass@1	AUROC	pass@1	AUROC
KGW	18.9	76.0	36.5	74.1
EWD	18.9	86.2	36.5	78.1
SWEET	21.3	83.3	38.4	75.7
EAW	24.4	88.9	39.0	85.0

5 Conclusion

We present EAW, an entropy-adaptive watermarking framework designed for code generation models. Unlike prior approaches such as SWEET that rely on fixed entropy thresholds, EAW dynamically adjusts the greenlist bias based on token-level uncertainty. This entropy-aware mechanism enables a finer balance between detectability and code correctness, allowing stronger watermark signals in high-entropy regions while minimizing interference in deterministic, function-critical code.

Extensive experiments demonstrate that using the adaptive greenlist bias, EAW consistently improves detection performance across varying entropy conditions without sacrificing generation quality. These results highlight the potential of entropy-aware watermarking as a practical and robust solution for provenance tracking in code LLMs.

While EAW demonstrates strong performance in code watermarking, it has some limitations. The method relies on access to token-level logits and may introduce additional computational overhead, especially for long code sequences. Future work will focus on reducing model dependence during detection and improving robustness against adversarial modifications.

Acknowledgments. This work was partly supported by Nanning "Yong Jiang" Program under Grant Number RC20250102 and the 2024 Xizang Autonomous Region Central Guided Local Science and Technology Development Fund Project under Grant Number XZ202401YD0015.

Disclosure of Interests. The authors have no competing interests to declare that are relevant to the content of this article.

References

1. Bao, S., Shi, Y., Yang, Z., Wu, H., Zhang, X.: Yet another watermark for large language models. arXiv preprint arXiv:2509.12574 (2025)
2. Chen, L., et al.: A survey on evaluating large language models in code generation tasks. arXiv preprint arXiv:2408.16498 (2024)
3. Dhruv, A., Dubey, A.: Leveraging large language models for code translation and software development in scientific computing. In: Proceedings of the Platform for Advanced Scientific Computing Conference, pp. 1–9 (2025)

4. Guo, D., et al.: Deepseek-coder: when the large language model meets programming-the rise of code intelligence. arXiv preprint arXiv:2401.14196 (2024)
5. Guo, Y., Tian, Z., Song, Y., Liu, T., Ding, L., Li, D.: Context-aware watermark with semantic balanced green-red lists for large language models. In: Proceedings of the 2024 Conference on Empirical Methods in Natural Language Processing, pp. 22633–22646 (2024)
6. Hou, W., Ji, Z.: Comparing large language models and human programmers for generating programming code. Adv. Sci. **12**(8), 2412279 (2025)
7. Hui, B., et al.: Qwen2. 5-coder technical report. arXiv preprint arXiv:2409.12186 (2024)
8. Husein, R.A., Aburajouh, H., Catal, C.: Large language models for code completion: a systematic literature review. Comput. Stand. Interfaces **92**, 103917 (2025)
9. Jiang, J., Wang, F., Shen, J., Kim, S., Kim, S.: A survey on large language models for code generation. arXiv preprint arXiv:2406.00515 (2024)
10. Kim, J., Park, S., Han, Y.S.: Marking code without breaking it: code watermarking for detecting llm-generated code. arXiv preprint arXiv:2502.18851 (2025)
11. Kirchenbauer, J., Geiping, J., Wen, Y., Katz, J., Miers, I., Goldstein, T.: A watermark for large language models. In: International Conference on Machine Learning, pp. 17061–17084. PMLR (2023)
12. Lee, T., et al.: Who wrote this code? Watermarking for code generation. arXiv preprint arXiv:2305.15060 (2023)
13. Lin, Z., Cui, J., Liao, X., Wang, X.: Malla: demystifying real-world large language model integrated malicious services. In: 33rd USENIX Security Symposium (USENIX Security 24), pp. 4693–4710 (2024)
14. Liu, J., Xia, C.S., Wang, Y., Zhang, L.: Is your code generated by chatgpt really correct? Rigorous evaluation of large language models for code generation. Adv. Neural Inf. Process. Syst. **36**, 21558–21572 (2023)
15. Lu, Y., Liu, A., Yu, D., Li, J., King, I.: An entropy-based text watermarking detection method. arXiv preprint arXiv:2403.13485 (2024)
16. Luo, Z., et al.: Wizardcoder: empowering code large language models with evol-instruct. arXiv preprint arXiv:2306.08568 (2023)
17. Mirsky, Y., et al.: The threat of offensive ai to organizations. Comput. Secur. **124**, 103006 (2023)
18. Muennighoff, N., et al.: Octopack: instruction tuning code large language models. In: NeurIPS 2023 Workshop on Instruction Tuning and Instruction Following (2023)
19. Pudasaini, S., Miralles-Pechuán, L., Lillis, D., Llorens Salvador, M.: Survey on AI-generated plagiarism detection: the impact of large language models on academic integrity. J. Acad. Ethics 1–34 (2024)
20. Simmons, A., Holanda, M., Chamon, C., Da Silva, D.: AI generated code plagiarism detection in computer science courses: a literature mapping. In: 2024 IEEE Frontiers in Education Conference (FIE), pp. 1–7. IEEE (2024)
21. Wu, H., Liu, G., Yao, Y., Zhang, X.: Watermarking neural networks with watermarked images. IEEE Trans. Circuits Syst. Video Technol. **31**(7), 2591–2601 (2021)
22. Yang, Z., et al.: Exploring and unleashing the power of large language models in automated code translation. Proc. ACM Softw. Eng. **1**(FSE), 1585–1608 (2024)
23. Yang, Z., Zhao, G., Wu, H.: Watermarking for large language models: a survey. Mathematics **13**(9), 1420 (2025)
24. Zhao, X., Ananth, P., Li, L., Wang, Y.X.: Provable robust watermarking for ai-generated text. arXiv preprint arXiv:2306.17439 (2023)

A Verifiable and Privacy-Preserving Federated Learning Framework via Homomorphic Encryption

Chun Fang[1], Shengmin Xu[1](✉), Xiaoguo Li[2], and Jinhua Ma[1]

[1] College of Computer and Cyber Security, Fujian Normal University, Fuzhou 350117, China
smxu1989@gmail.com

[2] College of Computer Science, Chongqing University, Chongqing 401331, China

Abstract. With the rapid development and widespread adoption of the Internet of Things, cloud computing, and artificial intelligence, data security has become a critical concern. Homomorphic encryption, as an effective solution to privacy protection, enables computations to be performed directly on encrypted data without decryption. It has thus become a powerful cryptographic tool and is widely applied to secure aggregation in federated learning. However, as federated learning continues to evolve, the security of model transmission has emerged as a pressing challenge, and verifying the integrity and authenticity of the transmitted models remains an open problem. In this paper, we propose a verifiable and privacy-preserving federated learning (VPFL) framework, which simultaneously ensures privacy preservation and model verifiability while also supporting regulatory auditing. Based on a VPFL model trained on the MNIST dataset, our approach achieves a prediction accuracy of 90.67%, while the experimental results demonstrate that the computational overhead remains within an acceptable range.

Keywords: Federated Learning · Verifiability · Model Privacy · Homomorphic Encryption

1 Introduction

In the age of big data and large-scale machine learning models, Federated Learning (FL) has garnered significant interest due to its strong emphasis on preserving user privacy—particularly in highly sensitive sectors such as finance and healthcare [21]. Unlike conventional centralized learning paradigms, FL facilitates collaborative model training without mandating clients to share their raw data, thus substantially reducing the risk of privacy exposure. A standard FL pipeline involves multiple clients performing local preprocessing and training on their private datasets. The resulting model parameters are then transmitted to a central aggregation server, which fuses them to refine the global model. This updated model is subsequently broadcast back to all participating clients.

Y. Xiang and J. Shen (Eds.): ML4CS 2025, LNCS 16456, pp. 207–220, 2026.
https://doi.org/10.1007/978-981-95-7820-7_14

By enabling joint learning without direct data sharing, FL minimizes privacy hazards linked to data centralization and has become a leading approach for privacy-preserving machine learning.

However, once local model updates are generated, ensuring their secure and trustworthy delivery becomes paramount [30]. Similarly, maintaining the confidentiality and integrity of the aggregated global model during redistribution poses a substantial challenge. To address these concerns, Homomorphic Encryption (HE) has been extensively adopted in FL settings, as it permits computations over encrypted data without revealing underlying sensitive content. Despite its advantages, real-world deployment of HE-based FL remains hindered by considerable communication overhead caused by the large size of modern models and the limited computational capabilities of typical end-user devices.

Furthermore, the high utility of the aggregated global model renders it an attractive target for integrity attacks. In untrusted or adversarial environments, malicious actors may attempt to manipulate or inject forged updates during either the aggregation phase or parameter transmission. Consequently, it is essential to guarantee verifiable integrity for all data passing through potentially untrustworthy third-party aggregators. Without such guarantees, even FL systems built upon HE remain susceptible to integrity violations under active adversarial conditions.

Given these security challenges in federated learning, it is vital to simultaneously uphold data privacy and enable integrity verification of all communications. To this end, we introduce a Verifiable and Privacy-preserving Federated Learning (VPFL) framework that synergistically combines HE with verifiable computation techniques to achieve both confidentiality and integrity of model updates. The key contributions of this work are summarized as follows:

1. We propose a VPFL framework that enables users to verify the integrity of transmitted parameters over untrusted communication channels while also allowing regulatory authorities to participate in the interaction for enhanced verifiability.
2. We design a two-stage federated framework comprising:
   - **Parameter Upload:** Partial homomorphic encryption is employed to achieve communication-efficient data transmission while preserving confidentiality.
   - **Parameter Authentication and Verification:** A lattice-based homomorphic encryption mechanism is integrated to ensure stronger security guarantees and verifiable computation of model updates.

   Compared with existing schemes, the advantages of our framework are summarized in Table 1.
3. We conduct comprehensive experiments to validate the practical usability of the VPFL framework. The proposed VPFL achieves a final test accuracy of 90.67% on the MNIST dataset, demonstrating its effectiveness and efficiency in real-world federated learning scenarios.

Table 1. Comparison of the proposed VPFL framework with existing schemes

	Privacy Protection	Verifiability	Regulatory Compliance
[33]	✓	✗	✗
[23]	✓	✗	✗
[24]	✓	✗	✗
Ours	✓	✓	✓

2 Related Work

2.1 Homomorphic Encryption

HE is a core cryptographic building block that allows computations to be carried out directly on encrypted data, without the need for decryption beforehand. The first cryptosystem known to exhibit homomorphic behavior is RSA [31], which enables multiplication over ciphertexts—i.e., it provides multiplicative homomorphism. Later, in 1999, Paillier put forward an encryption scheme with additive homomorphic properties [27]. Since both RSA and Paillier support only one algebraic operation (multiplication or addition, respectively), they are classified as Partially Homomorphic Encryption (PHE) schemes. A major milestone was achieved in 2009 when Gentry introduced the first Fully Homomorphic Encryption (FHE) construction, built upon ideal lattices [14], thereby enabling arbitrary computations on encrypted data and revolutionizing the field of cryptography. His construction supports an unbounded number of both addition and multiplication operations on ciphertexts, thereby enabling the evaluation of arbitrary-depth circuits. Gentry also introduced the bootstrapping technique to mitigate noise accumulation during repeated computations. However, the original lattice-based design suffered from substantial inefficiency, which severely limited its practicality.

Subsequent research has evolved along four primary technical directions. First, GSW-style schemes [15] extend Gentry's framework by constructing fully homomorphic functionality from somewhat homomorphic components. Second, the BGV scheme [2], proposed in 2011, introduced key switching to control ciphertext-dimension growth during multiplication and modulus switching to manage noise amplification. Third, the matrix-based approximate eigenvector approach introduced by Gentry, Sahai, and Waters represents ciphertexts as matrices. This design prevents the dimension blowup inherent in vector-based ciphertexts and reduces noise growth from exponential to linear with respect to multiplicative depth. Finally, the CKKS scheme [8], proposed by Cheon et al. in 2017, supports approximate arithmetic, allowing small, controlled errors to be treated as inherent noise, making it particularly suitable for machine learning and signal processing applications. Recent developments [22, 25] continue to build upon these foundational directions, further optimizing efficiency, scalability, and security trade-offs within the HE landscape.

2.2 Verifiability

The advent of cloud computing [28] has introduced significant challenges to data security and user privacy. In practical scenarios, users often delegate the storage and processing of sensitive information to remote cloud servers. In contrast, data were traditionally managed and processed locally within trusted computing environments. However, with the exponential growth of data volumes and computational demands, fully local processing has become impractical, compelling users to outsource computational workloads to the cloud. This paradigm shift inevitably exposes transmitted or stored data to potential interception, tampering, or unauthorized access by adversaries.

To mitigate these risks, it is essential to design mechanisms that can guarantee both the integrity and correctness of outsourced computations [17]. Cryptographic frameworks for cloud environments must therefore incorporate verifiability as a fundamental property. In general, verifiability can be classified into two categories: computational verifiability and result verifiability. The former ensures that delegated computations follow prescribed algorithms and correctly process the provided inputs, while the latter enables verification of final outputs without revealing intermediate computation states.

Conventional cryptographic primitives such as digital signatures [6,9,16] and message authentication codes (MACs) [1,10,26] are effective for verifying results but cannot ensure computational compliance. Moreover, these traditional mechanisms are incapable of performing nontrivial computations over encrypted data, which limits their applicability in privacy-preserving outsourced computation. This limitation has stimulated increasing interest in HE, which enables computation directly over ciphertexts and has become a cornerstone technology for privacy-preserving computation in both academia and industry.

Recent research has sought to extend verifiability to the homomorphic setting [4,18]. Fiore et al. [12] designed a computationally verifiable scheme based on homomorphic MACs. Ganesh et al. [13] implemented verifiable computation for Ring Learning With Errors (RLWE)-based HE schemes using non-interactive arguments of knowledge with designated verifiers. More recently, Tao et al. [3] integrated certificate-based mechanisms with HE to construct quasi-linear homomorphic signatures, addressing the auditability challenges in cloud storage environments.

2.3 Federated Learning

FL is a privacy-preserving framework for distributed model training where clients learn from local datasets and exchange only model parameters [20]. A central server collects these updates, applies secure aggregation techniques to prevent information leakage, and broadcasts the aggregated model to clients for next-round training.

To ensure privacy, Differential Privacy (DP) [11] is commonly employed, where random noise is added to each client's data or model updates to prevent information leakage. However, recent studies have shown that sensitive information can still be inferred from gradients [29]. As a result, HE has emerged as a more robust privacy-preserving technique for FL, providing stronger security guarantees in settings that demand strict confidentiality. Moreover, HE offers better scalability and compatibility within the FL framework, as it can be seamlessly integrated with minimal modification, typically involving only encryption and decryption during model updates.

3 Problem Statement and Solution Overview

FL has found broad application in contexts where a trusted regulator supervises collaborative model training. In these environments, clients perform local training on their private data and submit the resulting model parameters in encrypted form to a central aggregation server. The server then aggregates these updates and broadcasts the revised global model back to all participants. Given that clients typically operate under constrained computational budgets, FL is especially well-suited for privacy-sensitive use cases, which are often subject to governmental regulation and oversight. Yet, as the volume of sensitive data expands, it increasingly attracts active adversaries. Notably, attackers may seek to tamper with or compromise the large quantities of valid model updates distributed by the central server. These concerns underscore the necessity of strengthening both security and verifiability in federated learning systems, as depicted in Fig. 1.

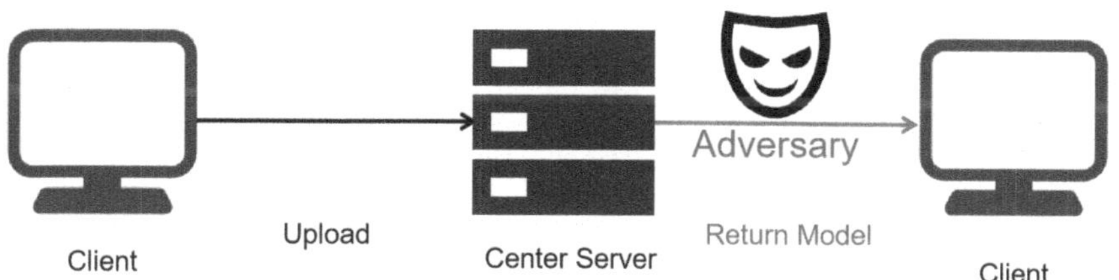

Fig. 1. Threat model

During the parameter upload phase, real-world deployments require lightweight security mechanisms and privacy-preserving transmission methods that maintain system usability. In contrast, during the model return phase, robust cryptographic algorithms are necessary to prevent eavesdropping or tampering by active adversaries, while still enabling clients to verify the integrity of the returned models.

4 Methods and Algorithms in Our VPFL

In this section, we describe the primary methods and algorithms that constitute the proposed framework.

4.1 Improved Paillier Algorithm

The improved Paillier CHA scheme [19] has been optimized for computational efficiency, and its efficiency and correctness have been formally proven in [19].

- **Key Generation:** Select a divisor α and a parameter λ. Compute $g = n \cdot \alpha$, where n is the product of two large primes. The public key is (n, g), and the private key is λ.
- **Encryption:** Given a message m and a random integer $r < \alpha$, the ciphertext c is computed as
$$c = g^m \cdot r^n \bmod n^2 \tag{1}$$
- **Decryption:** Decryption is performed as follows:
$$m = \frac{[(c^\alpha \bmod n^2) - 1]/n}{[(g^\alpha \bmod n^2) - 1]/n} \bmod n \tag{2}$$

4.2 Polynomial-Based BFV Authenticator

We employ a polynomial-based verifier to validate the results of model aggregation, utilizing a verifier constructed on the BFV homomorphic encryption [5]. The interaction process is illustrated in Fig. 2.

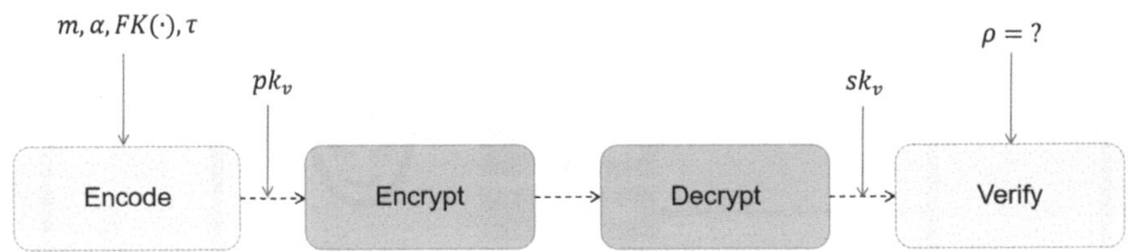

Fig. 2. Core processes of the polynomial-based BFV authenticator

The complete verification pipeline is described as follows:

- **PE.PolynomialEncoder**$\langle \mathbf{m}, \tau; \alpha, F_K(\cdot)\rangle \rightarrow (y_0, y_1)$: Given a plaintext vector $\mathbf{m} \in \mathbb{Z}t^N$ and identifiers τ, a random polynomial $\mathbf{r}\tau \in \mathbb{Z}t^N$ is generated such that $\forall i \in [N]$, $\mathbf{r}\tau[i] = F_K(\tau[i])$. It then computes y_0 and y_1 as the batched encodings of $\mathbf{m}$ and $[(\mathbf{r}_\tau - \mathbf{m}) \cdot \alpha^{-1}]_t$, respectively. Finally, it outputs $P = (y_0, y_1)$.
- **PE.KeyGen**$(1^\lambda) \rightarrow (\mathrm{pk}, \mathrm{sk})$: For a λ-bit prime number ℓ, sample a random invertible element $\alpha \in \mathbb{Z}_\ell^*$. Generate the key pair $(\mathrm{pk}, \mathrm{sk})$ for the BFV and output the keys.
- **PE.Auth**$(\mathbf{m}, \tau; \mathrm{sk}) \rightarrow \sigma$: Given a plaintext vector $\mathbf{m} \in \mathbb{Z}\ell^N$ with identifiers τ, invoke the algorithm **PolynomialEncoder** to obtain $(y_0, y_1) \in \mathcal{R}\ell^2$. Then encrypt y_0 and y_1 under the BFV scheme to produce ciphertexts c_0 and c_1. The resulting authentication tag is $\sigma = (c_0, c_1)$, where $\mathbf{m}$ is encoded as a polynomial in $\mathcal{R}_q$.

- **PE.Ver**$(\sigma'; \mathrm{sk}) \rightarrow 0, 1$: Let $\sigma' = (c_0, \ldots, c_d)$ be a collection of ciphertexts associated with identities $(\tau_1, \ldots, \tau_d)$. Decrypt σ' to obtain $(y_0, \ldots, y_d)$ and compute $\rho = \sum_{i=0}^{d} y_i \cdot \alpha^i$. If the verification equation holds, the verifier accepts and outputs y_0.

4.3 Federated Multi-Layer Perceptron

Here, we used a federated multi-layer perceptron algorithm(FMLP) [7]. For clients, they can training a simple model. The multi-layer perceptron, also known as a deep feed-forward network, is a typical deep learning model. All the parameters and their meanings involved in the algorithm are shown in Table 2.

Table 2. The parameters and descriptions in the FMLP algorithm.

Parameter	Meaning
x	the sample in the Dataset
θ	the parameters of the model
fp	feed forward process
out	the output of each iteration
f^*	activation function
$loss$	loss function
c	loss calculated by loss function
ϵ	minimum error
bp	back-propagation process
$grad$	gradient calculated by bp process
lr	learning rate

Before the model is updated, each learning client passes the gradients to the computing server for model training. In addition, then the computing server integrates all the gradient data from all clients, and returns the calculated new gradient to each client for model updates. The specific steps of FMLP are shown in Algorithm 1.

4.4 Warning Mechanism

After encrypting the parameters in the `Upload()` phase, each client additionally computes a hash digest to ensure data integrity. Upon receiving the encrypted models, the central server performs an early warning verification procedure. Once all tuples from the clients are collected, the server checks whether any parameters have been tampered with. If no tampering is detected, the encrypted parameters are aggregated; otherwise, the corresponding client is flagged for further inspection. Based on the results of the channel security assessment, an early warning threshold can be configured. When this threshold is exceeded, a network-wide alert is triggered, signaling potential channel insecurity.

Algorithm 1 Federated Multi-Layer Perceptron

```
   Input: Dataset x
   Output: : Model θ_final
1  Initialize model parameters θ;
2  for i in iteration do
3  |   Forward propagation: out_i = fp(x_i, θ_i);
4  |   Compute loss: c_i = loss(f*(x_i), out_i);
5  |   if c_i < ε then
6  |   |   Break;
7  |   end
8  |   else
9  |   |   Back propagation: grad_i = bp(x_i, θ_i, c_i);
10 |   |   Send gradients to computing server and get new gradients;
11 |   |   Update: θ_{i+1} = θ_i − lr * grad_new;
12 |   end
13 end
14 return Model with parameters θ_final;
```

5 VPFL Framework

We now turn to the concrete instantiation of the VPFL framework. The system involves four entities: a Key Generation Center (KGC), N clients, a Trusted Authority (TA), and a Central Server (CS). Our framework consists of five major components: KeyGen, Upload, Aggregate, Auth, and Verify. The overall interaction process among these components is illustrated in Fig. 3.

We will now explain the interaction process in detail.

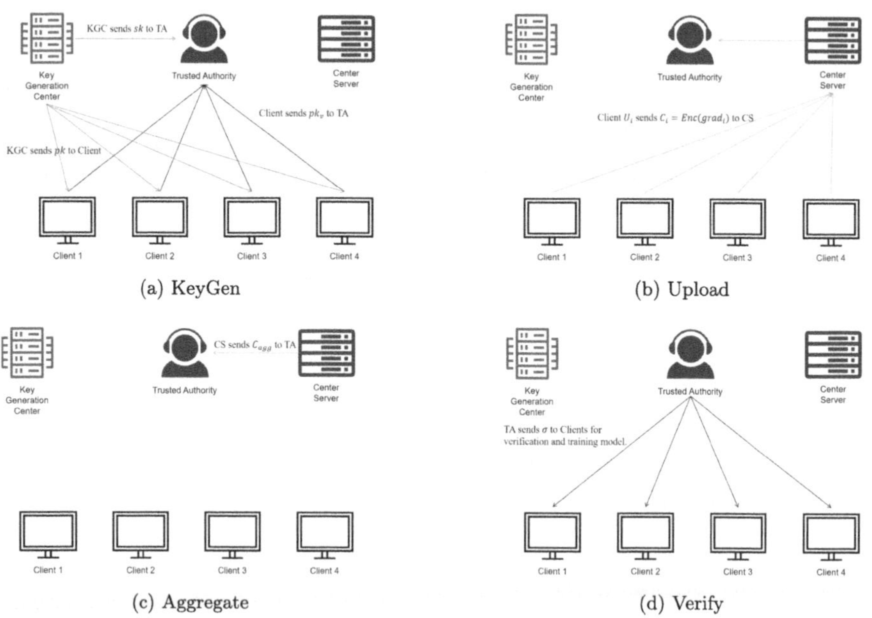

Fig. 3. The core programs in our VPFL.

- **KeyGen**(1^λ)
  1. The KGC selects prime numbers p *and* q, Then it computes the number: $n = p \cdot q$, and derives n^2.
  2. The KGC generates the key pairs $sk = (\lambda, \mu)$ and $pk = (n, g)$. g is a special element in $\mathbb{Z}_{n^2}$ (commonly $g = n + 1$). Here, λ is calculated as the least common multiple of $(p-1, q-1)$, and μ is a value computed using g and λ.
  3. The KGC sends sk to the TA and distributes pk to all clients.
  4. Each client U_i, where $i \in [1, N]$, obtains a unique identity ID_i.
  5. Each client sends its verification public key pk_v to the TA.
- **Upload**(pk, x) Each client U_i associated with identity ID_i and public key $pk = (n, g)$ trains its local model based on the FMLP architecture. The process proceeds as follows:
  1. The client U_i trains its model following the method in [7] and obtains the backpropagated gradients $grad_i$.
  2. The client encrypts the gradient as $C_i = \text{Enc}_{\text{Paillier}}(pk, grad_i)$.
  3. The client computes a hash digest $\sigma_i = H(ID_i||C_i)$.
  4. The client sends the tuple (C_i, σ_i) to the CS.
- **Aggregate**($sk, (C_i, \sigma_i), pk_v$)
  1. Upon receiving N tuples (C_i, σ_i) and the corresponding client identities ID_i, the CS performs the following steps:
     - Check whether $\sigma_i = H(C_i||ID_i)$. If the check passes, proceed with the next step; otherwise, discard the tuple and flag the user once.
     - Verify whether the number of valid users is less than ωn (where ω depends on the channel security level [32]). If fewer than ωn valid users remain, the CS notifies all clients of a possible attack and halts data transmission.

     If the above conditions are satisfied, the CS computes $C_{\text{agg}} = \sum_{i=1}^{n} C_i$ (handled by the trusted authority) and sends C_{agg} to the TA.
  2. The TA decrypts the aggregated ciphertext: $grad_{\text{agg}} = \text{Dec}(sk, C_{\text{agg}}) = \sum_{i=1}^{n} grad_i$, and converts $grad_{\text{agg}}$ into a vector $m \in \mathbb{Z}_t^N$.
- **Auth**(m, τ, pk_v) The TA selects one verification identifier τ for each model release and publishes τ. Given the vector m, the TA performs the following operations with the client-supplied parameter α:
  - For $m \in \mathbb{Z}_t^N$ associated with identifiers τ:
    * *Encode:* $(y_0, y_1) = \texttt{PolynomialEncoder}(m, \tau, \alpha; F_K(\cdot))$
    * *Encrypt:*
      1. Compute $c_i = \text{BFV.Enc}(y_i; pk_v)$ for all $i \in 0, 1$.
      2. Construct the authentication tag $\sigma = (c_0, c_1)$ and send σ to all clients.
- **Verify**(σ, τ, sk_v) Each client U_i receives σ, τ, and its secret key sk_v. The verification procedure is as follows:
  1. Generate $\mathbf{r}_\mathcal{T} \in \mathbb{Z}_t^N$ such that $\mathbf{r}_\mathcal{T} = F_K(\tau)$.
  2. Decrypt the ciphertexts: $(y_0, y_1) = \text{BFV.Dec}(c_0, c_1; sk_v)$.
  3. Verify whether $\mathbf{r}_\mathcal{T} \stackrel{?}{=} \sum_{i=0}^{1} y_i \cdot \alpha^i$. If not, return 0 (reject).
  4. Otherwise, recover C_{agg} from y_0 and update the model parameters as $\theta_{i+1} = \theta_i - lr \cdot grad_{\text{agg}}$.

6 Correctness and Security of Our VPFL

We analyze the correctness and security of the VPFL framework in this section, with particular emphasis on the correctness of its cryptographic computations.

6.1 Correctness of Our VPFL

The correctness of the `Upload()` and `Aggregate()` procedures relies on the computational integrity of the simplified Improved Paillier algorithm [19], and therefore requires no further elaboration. The correctness of the `Auth()` and `Verify()`

phases primarily depends on the BFV correctness [2], which has been formally established in prior research.

For the PolynomialEncoder component, given $y_0 = m$ and $y_1 = (r_\tau - m)\alpha^{-1}$, we have: $r_\tau = \sum_{i=0}^{1} y_i \cdot \alpha^i = m + \alpha \cdot (r_\tau - m)\alpha^{-1} = m + r_\tau - m$. Therefore, the verification equation holds, ensuring the correctness of the polynomial-based encoding process.

6.2 Security of Our VPFL

The security of the VPFL framework is analyzed in two distinct phases. During the `Upload()` and `Aggregate()` stages, confidentiality and semantic security are guaranteed by the Paillier cryptosystem [27]. During the `Auth()` and `Verify()` stages, an adversary attempting to compromise the system would necessarily need to break the underlying BFV scheme, whose security is based on the hardness of the Ring Learning With Errors problem.

For the polynomial-based encoding scheme, our security foundation follows the security proofs presented in [5], where the authors defined a sequence of games to modify the adversarial environment and demonstrated that the adversary's advantage remains negligible. Hence, the overall framework achieves both semantic security and verifiable integrity under standard cryptographic assumptions.

Theorem 1. *Let λ be a security parameter. If the pseudorandom function F_K and the underlying HE scheme are at least λ-bit secure, the probability that any probabilistic polynomial-time (PPT) adversary succeeds in forging a valid authentication is negligible in λ, where λ is the parameter input, if the F_K and the underlying HE scheme are at least λ-bit secure.*

Proof. We define a PPT adversary $\mathcal{A}(1^\lambda)$. We will set games (G_1, G_2, G_3) to modify the attack environment, G_1 is the simplest game.

G_1: In this game, we just verify the $\mathbf{Ver}(\sigma, sk) = 1$. For all $\mathcal{A}$, we have:

$$\Pr\left[G_1(1^\lambda) = 1\right] \leq \text{neg}(\lambda).$$

We can prove our scheme is secure.

Then, we design a sequence of hybrid games by modifying G_1.

G_2: To design the G_2, we exchange the F_K to the random input. Obviously, the oracle will output the random value.

$$\Pr\left[G_2(1^\lambda) = 1\right] \leq \Pr\left[G_1(1^\lambda) = 1\right] + \text{neg}(\lambda).$$

G_3: To further enhance the game design, we have expanded the attack capabilities of $\mathcal{A}$. It will remember the input m, τ, and σ. τ is related to the σ. $\mathcal{A}$ can query the oracle to get the information it wants. Then, $\mathcal{A}$ starts distinguishing whether the result of encryption originates from a message or a challenge vector. Obviously, due to the HE semantic security, the probability of $\mathcal{A}$ winning is $\leq 2^{-\lambda}$.

$$\Pr\left[\mathrm{G}_3(1^\lambda) = 1\right] \leq 2^{-\lambda}.$$

Finally, by combining the results from the sequence of games, we can bound the adversary's advantage in the original game G_0 as follows:

$$\Pr\left[\mathrm{G}_0(1^\lambda) = 1\right] \leq \Pr[\mathrm{G}_3(1^\lambda) = 1] + \Pr[\mathrm{G}_2(1^\lambda) = 1] \leq 2^{-\lambda} + \mathrm{neg}(\lambda),$$

which is negligible in λ. □

7 Performance

The proposed framework was implemented on a system where ten clients participated in collaborative training of the classical FPML model using the MNIST dataset. As illustrated in Fig. 4, the experimental results demonstrate the feasibility and effectiveness of the proposed VPFL scheme.

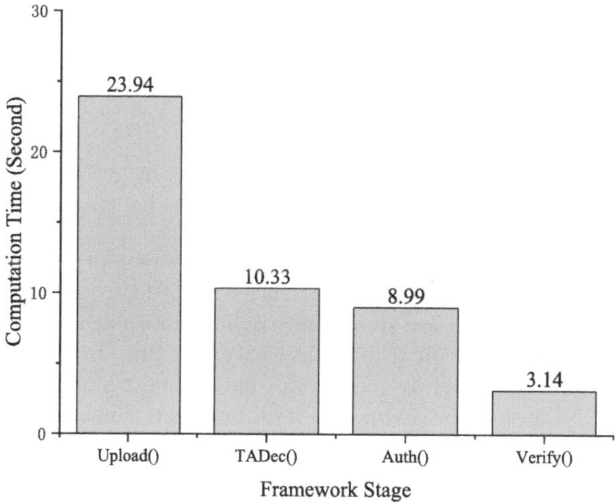

Fig. 4. Execution time of each algorithmic component in our VPFL

In terms of computational performance, the average time for a single client to encrypt its local gradients was 23.57 s. The supervisory authority decrypted the aggregated ciphertext using the Paillier decryption procedure in 10.33 s, while the `Auth()` operation required an average of 8.99 s. In contrast, the `Verify()` operation on a single client completed in only 3.14 s.

Considering both privacy and verifiability, the VPFL scheme enables a trusted supervisory authority to verify the correctness of homomorphic computations while maintaining resilience against active adversaries, demonstrating its practical applicability.

For model evaluation, we used the MNIST set to train our model. The global model achieved a final prediction accuracy of 90.67%, confirming the utility and effectiveness of the proposed approach.

8 Conclusion

In this paper, We proposed a new framework VPFL that enables trusted regulators to manage sensitive data securely and verifiably. We further addressed the challenge of verifying data integrity under channels susceptible to active adversaries. Experimental results demonstrate the feasibility and practicality of the proposed approach. In particular, the framework achieved a prediction accuracy of 90.67% when training the FPML model on the MNIST dataset, validating its effectiveness in real-world federated learning settings.

Acknowledgments. This work was supported in part by the National Key R&D Program of China (2023YFB3106200), the National Natural Science Foundation of China (62572123, 62502056 and 62402109) and the New Chongqing YC Project (CSTB2025YCJH-KYXM0068).

References

1. Akavia, A., Goldenberg, M., Oren, N., Vald, R.: Message authentication code with fast verification over encrypted data and applications. Proc. Priv. Enhancing Technol. **2025**(4), 1092–1111 (2025)
2. Brakerski, Z., Vaikuntanathan, V.: Efficient fully homomorphic encryption from (standard) lwe. SIAM J. Comput. **43**(2), 831–871 (2014)
3. Cai, J., et al.: Certificate-based quasi-linearly homomorphic signatures: definition, construction, and application to data integrity auditing. In: Han, J., Xiang, Y., Cheng, G., Susilo, W., Chen, L. (eds.) Information and Communications Security. ICICS 2025. LNCS, vol. 16217, pp. 119–140. Springer, Singapore (2026). https://doi.org/10.1007/978-981-95-3540-8_7
4. Cascudo, I., Costache, A., Cozzo, D., Fiore, D., Guimarães, A., Soria-Vazquez, E.: Verifiable computation for approximate homomorphic encryption schemes. In: Tauman Kalai, Y., Kamara, S.F. (eds.) Advances in Cryptology – CRYPTO 2025. CRYPTO 2025. LNCS, vol. 16006, pp. 643–677. Springer, Cham (2025). https://doi.org/10.1007/978-3-032-01907-3_21
5. Chatel, S., Knabenhans, C., Pyrgelis, A., Troncoso, C., Hubaux, J.: VERITAS: plaintext encoders for practical verifiable homomorphic encryption. In: CCS, pp. 2520–2534. ACM (2024)
6. Chen, J., et al.: Industrial blockchain threshold signatures in federated learning for unified space-air-ground-sea model training. J. Ind. Inf. Integr. **39**, 100593 (2024)
7. Chen, Y., Zhang, X., Xie, Y., Miao, M., Ma, X.: CECMLP: new cipher-based evaluating collaborative multi-layer perceptron scheme in federated learning. In: Sako, K., Tippenhauer, N.O. (eds.) Applied Cryptography and Network Security. ACNS 2021. LNCS, vol. 12726, pp. 79–99. Springer, Cham (2021). https://doi.org/10.1007/978-3-030-78372-3_4

8. Cheon, J.H., Kim, A., Kim, M., Song, Y.: Homomorphic encryption for arithmetic of approximate numbers. In: Takagi, T., Peyrin, T. (eds.) Advances in Cryptology – ASIACRYPT 2017. ASIACRYPT 2017. LNCS, vol. 10624, pp. 409–437. Springer, Cham (2017). https://doi.org/10.1007/978-3-319-70694-8_15
9. Chou, T., Persichetti, E., Santini, P.: On linear equivalence, canonical forms, and digital signatures. Des. Codes Cryptogr. **93**(7), 2415–2457 (2025)
10. Cini, V., Ramacher, S., Slamanig, D., Striecks, C., Tairi, E.: Updatable signatures and message authentication codes. In: Garay, J.A. (eds.) Public-Key Cryptography – PKC 2021. PKC 2021. LNCS, vol. 12710, pp. 691–723. Springer, Cham (2021). https://doi.org/10.1007/978-3-030-75245-3_25
11. Dwork, C.: Differential privacy. In: ICALP (2). LNCS, vol. 4052, pp. 1–12. Springer, Cham (2006). https://doi.org/10.1007/978-3-030-71522-9_752
12. Fiore, D., Gennaro, R., Pastro, V.: Efficiently verifiable computation on encrypted data. In: CCS, pp. 844–855. ACM (2014)
13. Ganesh, C., Nitulescu, A., Soria-Vazquez, E.: Rinocchio: snarks for ring arithmetic. J. Cryptol. **36**(4), 41 (2023)
14. Gentry, C.: Fully homomorphic encryption using ideal lattices. In: STOC, pp. 169–178. ACM (2009)
15. Gentry, C., Sahai, A., Waters, B.: Homomorphic encryption from learning with errors: conceptually-simpler, asymptotically-faster, attribute-based. In: Canetti, R., Garay, J.A. (eds.) Advances in Cryptology – CRYPTO 2013. CRYPTO 2013. LNCS, vol. 8042, pp. 75–92. Springer, Berlin, Heidelberg (2013). https://doi.org/10.1007/978-3-642-40041-4_5
16. Gjøsteen, K., Jager, T.: Practical and tightly-secure digital signatures and authenticated key exchange. In: Shacham, H., Boldyreva, A. (eds.) Advances in Cryptology – CRYPTO 2018. CRYPTO 2018. LNCS, vol. 10992, pp. 95–125. Springer, Cham (2018). https://doi.org/10.1007/978-3-319-96881-0_4
17. Han, X., Li, Z., Xiao, X., Ju, P., Shahidehpour, M.: Privacy-preserving outsourced computation of collaborative operational decisions among microgrids in an active distribution network. IEEE Trans. Power Syst. **40**(1), 850–865 (2024)
18. Huang, M.M., Li, B., Mao, X., Zhang, J.: Fully homomorphic encryption with efficient public verification. IACR Cryptol. ePrint Arch., p. 1764 (2024)
19. Jost, C., Lam, H., Maximov, A., Smeets, B.J.M.: Encryption performance improvements of the paillier cryptosystem. IACR Cryptol. ePrint Arch., p. 864 (2015)
20. Li, L., Fan, Y., Lin, K.: A survey on federated learning. In: ICCA. pp. 791–796. IEEE (2020)
21. Li, Y., Huang, C., Zhao, Y., Du, X., Huang, J., Yuan, Y.: SFLES: shuffled differentially private federated learning with early-stopping strategy. Expert Syst. Appl. **299**, 129970 (2026)
22. Liu, F., Wang, H.: Batch bootstrapping I: - A new framework for SIMD bootstrapping in polynomial modulus. In: Hazay, C., Stam, M. (eds.) Advances in Cryptology – EUROCRYPT 2023. EUROCRYPT 2023. LNCS, vol. 14006, pp. 321–352. Springer, Cham (2023). https://doi.org/10.1007/978-3-031-30620-4_11
23. Ma, J., Naas, S., Sigg, S., Lyu, X.: Privacy-preserving federated learning based on multi-key homomorphic encryption. Int. J. Intell. Syst. **37**(9), 5880–5901 (2022)
24. Mahato, G.K., Banerjee, A., Chakraborty, S.K., Gao, X.: Privacy preserving verifiable federated learning scheme using blockchain and homomorphic encryption. Appl. Soft Comput. **167**, 112405 (2024)
25. Mankali, L.L., Nabeel, M., Raees, F., Maniatakos, M., Sinanoglu, O., Knechtel, J.: Glitchfhe: attacking fully homomorphic encryption using fault injection. In: USENIX Security Symposium, pp. 8481–8500. USENIX Association (2025)

26. Nagasundharamoorthi, I., Venkatesan, P., Velusamy, P.: Hash message authentication codes for securing data in wireless body area networks. Concurr. Comput. Pract. Exp. **36**(5) (2024)
27. Paillier, P.: Public-key cryptosystems based on composite degree residuosity classes. In: Stern, J. (eds.) Advances in Cryptology — EUROCRYPT '99. EUROCRYPT 1999. LNCS, vol. 1592, pp. 223–238. Springer, Berlin, Heidelberg (1999). https://doi.org/10.1007/3-540-48910-X_16
28. Parast, F.K., Sindhav, C., Nikam, S., Yekta, H.I., Kent, K.B., Hakak, S.: Cloud computing security: a survey of service-based models. Comput. Secur. **114**, 102580 (2022)
29. Phong, L.T., Aono, Y., Hayashi, T., Wang, L., Moriai, S.: Privacy-preserving deep learning via additively homomorphic encryption. IEEE Trans. Inf. Forensics Secur. **13**(5), 1333–1345 (2018)
30. Qin, X., Yang, X., Tang, X.: Practical privacy-preserving federated learning based on multiparty homomorphic encryption for large-scale models. Pattern Recognit. **171**, 112174 (2026)
31. Rivest, R.L., Shamir, A., Adleman, L.M.: A method for obtaining digital signatures and public-key cryptosystems (reprint). Commun. ACM **26**(1), 96–99 (1983)
32. Standaert, F.: How (not) to use welch's t-test in side-channel security evaluations. In: Bilgin, B., Fischer, J.B. (eds.) Smart Card Research and Advanced Applications. CARDIS 2018. LNCS, vol. 11389, pp. 65–79. Springer, Cham (2019). https://doi.org/10.1007/978-3-030-15462-2_5
33. Zhang, C., Li, S., Xia, J., Wang, W., Yan, F., Liu, Y.: Batchcrypt: efficient homomorphic encryption for cross-silo federated learning. In: USENIX ATC, pp. 493–506. USENIX Association (2020)

Empirical Study on Adversarial Robustness Degradation in Image Classification via Unlearning

Natchapol Shinno, Haibo Zhang(✉), and Takeshi Saitoh(✉)

Graduate School of Computer Science and Systems Engineering,
Kyushu Institute of Technology, Fukuoka 820-8502, Japan
shinno.natchapol131@mail.kyutech.jp, {haiboz,saitoh}@ai.kyutech.ac.jp

Abstract. Recently, growing public concern over data privacy has led to the emergence of the 'right to be forgotten' under the European Union's General Data Protection Regulation (GDPR), which allows individuals to request the deletion of personal data. In response, researchers have developed methods to selectively remove or mitigate the influence of specific data on machine learning models, a process known as *machine unlearning* (MUL). However, while most research on MUL has focused exclusively on maintaining model accuracy after unlearning, the robustness of these models has been largely overlooked, especially under adversarial attacks. In this study, we examine whether unlearning degrades robustness in the visual classification task by performing adversarial attacks on various unlearned methods and compare performance against a retrained-from-scratch baseline, including evaluations using a standard corruption dataset. Our comprehensive evaluation across seven unlearning methods reveals consistent degradation in robustness under perturbation, supporting our hypothesis that machine unlearning degrades adversarial robustness compared to retraining from scratch, and highlighting the need for methods that preserve robustness without compromising the effectiveness and efficiency.

Keywords: Machine Unlearning · Adversarial Robustness · Corruption Robustness · Image Processing · Image Classification

1 Introduction

In recent years, the rise of artificial intelligence (AI) has become increasingly recognized by the general public. AI is now commonly used by individuals and integrated into daily life, often without sufficient consideration for the underlying data processes. However, many models are trained on datasets that may contain sensitive, private, or regulated information. This has led to growing concern about personal data privacy and prompted many countries to consider policies to address the issue.

Y. Xiang and J. Shen (Eds.): ML4CS 2025, LNCS 16456, pp. 221–235, 2026.
https://doi.org/10.1007/978-981-95-7820-7_15

In response to these concerns, numerous countries and regions have introduced or strengthened regulations. One important example is the European Union's General Data Protection Regulation (GDPR), which includes the "right to be forgotten," allowing individuals to request the deletion of their personal data under certain conditions [1].

Similarly, Japan's Act on the Protection of Personal Information (APPI) permits individuals to request the deletion or suspension of personal data if it is used unlawfully or beyond its stated purpose [2], while the California Consumer Privacy Act (CCPA) provides residents of California with rights to access, delete, or opt out of the sale of their personal data [3].

The most direct approach to removing specific data from a trained model is to retrain the model after excluding the targeted data from the training set. However, this process is computationally infeasible due to substantial resource and time requirements. To overcome these limitations, researchers have proposed more efficient alternatives that aim to eliminate the influence of specific data. These efforts have given rise to techniques known as machine unlearning.

Many researchers have shown growing interest in this area and have proposed a variety of data removal methods. Some techniques, such as SISA (Sharded, Isolated, Sliced, and Aggregated training) and ARCANE (an efficient Architecture foR exaCt mAchine uNlEarning), rely on partial retraining rather than training from scratch. These methods, known as 'exact learning', aim to remove targeted data points from a model completely.

In contrast, several methods have been developed to focus on reducing the influence of specific data without deleting it entirely. These approaches aim to closely approximate the performance of a retrained model while lowering the computational cost of retraining or partial training, known as 'approximate unlearning'. These methods offer a compromise between accuracy and efficiency due to strict time and budget constraints.

However, most of the current unlearning methods are still primarily focused on preserving model accuracy and overall performance, often overlooking other important model properties. Consequently, some of these methods may have inadvertently reduced the robustness of the model, increasing its vulnerability to adversarial attacks.

The primary motivation for this study is that image classification is one of the most widely studied and foundational tasks in machine learning. It also underpins numerous practical applications, such as medical imaging, surveillance, and autonomous systems, where both data privacy and the robustness of the model are critical for safety, trust, and regulatory compliance.

In this study, we empirically demonstrate the adversarial robustness of unlearned models across seven representative unlearning techniques and four types of white-box adversarial attacks in the image classification domain. Despite increasing interest in machine unlearning, there is still limited related work examining its impact on adversarial robustness.

The primary purpose of this study is to explore the consequences of machine unlearning methods for adversarial robustness, with profound safety implications. Additionally, this study seeks to highlight potential risks, deepen understanding of machine unlearning, and support its advancement as a practical and trustworthy solution for real-world deployment.

2 Related Work

2.1 Machine Unlearning

Machine Unlearning (MUL) is an approach to eliminating the influence of a specific data point on the learned model while avoiding full retraining and still preserving useful knowledge (see Fig. 1). The concept was formally introduced by Bourtoule et al. [4] as a response to increasing data privacy regulations and user deletion requests.

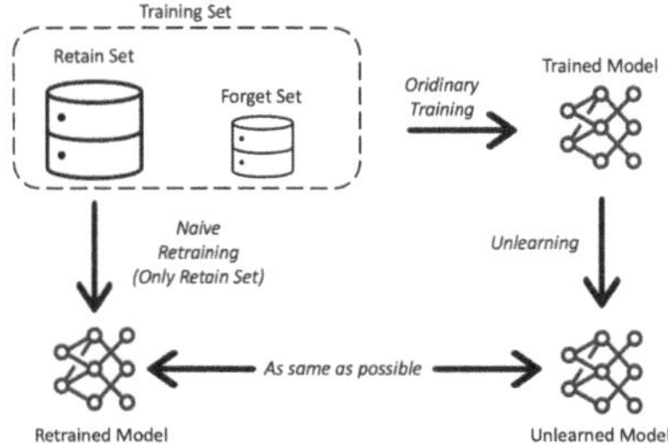

Fig. 1. Illustration of the overview of Machine Unlearning (MUL), adapted from Jie Xu et al. [6]. Showing the conceptual contrasts between Retrain and Unlearning.

Machine Unlearning is generally categorized into two main types: **Exact Unlearning** and **Approximate Unlearning**.

- **Exact Unlearning**: Ensures that the forget set is completely removed from the model, ideally achieving equivalence with retraining from scratch. Some methods use partial training instead of full training to save computational costs, but still require substantial resources. Examples of the framework include SISA (Sharded, Isolated, Sliced, Aggregated) and ARCANE (Architecture foR exaCt mAchine uNlEarning).
- **Approximate Unlearning**: Rather than being strict about achieving equivalent performance to retraining, focus on efficiency to reduce the influence of the data rather than completely remove it.

2.2 Adversarial Robustness

Adversarial robustness refers to the capability of a trained model to maintain accuracy and reliable performance when subjected to perturbations in the input by adversarial attacks, which are intentionally crafted inputs aimed at inducing misclassifications.

Adversarial attacks are techniques that manipulate models by altering or perturbing input data, causing them to make incorrect predictions. Although the modifications are often imperceptible to humans, they exploit vulnerabilities within AI systems, resulting in misclassifications or other forms of erroneous behavior.

Adversarial attacks are primarily categorized into two types depending on the attacker's knowledge of the target model. If attackers have access to model architecture, parameters, or gradients, the attack is referred to as a *white-box* attack. Conversely, if the attackers do not have a permission to access the model and must rely on a query-based approach to probe it, the attack is classified as a *black-box* attack.

In this study, we evaluate model robustness using four commonly employed *white-box* adversarial attacks, including:

FGSM (Fast Gradient Sign Method) is a single-step *white-box* attack from Goodfellow et al. [7]. By adding a small amount of noise based on the gradient of loss that perturbs the input in the direction of the gradient. The adversarial perturbation is:

$$\eta = \epsilon \cdot \text{sign}\left(\nabla_x J(\theta, x, y)\right) \tag{1}$$

where θ denotes the model parameters and x, y represent an input image and its true label. The scalar ϵ controls the perturbation magnitude. $J(\theta, x, y)$ is the loss function used to train model. FGSM computes for each input pixel and adds a small step of perturbation in that direction, controlled by sign.

Therefore, the adversarial example is then:

$$x_{\text{adv}} = x + \eta \tag{2}$$

which x_{adv} will be misclassified by the model. Although it appears visually similar to the original input x.

PGD (Projected Gradient Descent) is the extension of the FGSM, which is also a *white-box* attack, first introduced by Madry et al. [8]. It is a multi-step extension by performs perturbations iteratively in small steps, gradually increasing the model's loss, and repeatedly takes a gradient-based step. Based on the FGSM the adversarial example is computed as:

$$x_{\text{adv}} = x + \eta, \quad \text{where } \eta = \epsilon \cdot \text{sign}\left(\nabla_x J(\theta, x, y)\right) \tag{3}$$

Alternatively, implement several iterations for more powerful and efficient attacks:

$$x_{t+1} = \Pi_{x+S}\big(x_t + \alpha \cdot \text{sign}\left(\nabla_x J(\theta, x, y)\right)\big), \tag{4}$$

where t is the number of iterations, x_t serves as the current perturbed image.Π_{x+S} denotes the projection operation, and α is the step size of each iteration to control the change of gradient direction. PGD is typically adopted as a first-order adversarial attack to serve as a benchmark for the model's adversarial robustness, due to stronger perturbations than single-step.

DeepFool: is a multi-step attack with a linearization algorithm that provides a minimal adversarial perturbation, leading to a change in the classifier decision, and offers stronger foundation metrics, as proposed by Moosavi-Dezfooli et al. [9]. Use a linear function as an approximate classifier, then compute the smallest perturbation that will cross the decision line. In iteration i, r_i represents the perturbation vector, indicating how much the current adversarial sample is adjusted towards the decision boundary. Here, the final minimal perturbation, denoted as $\hat{r}$, is obtained by summing up all the perturbations across iterations:

$$\hat{r} = \sum_{i} r_i. \tag{5}$$

This cumulative perturbation $\hat{r}$ leads to a misclassifications by the model. Compared to FGSM, it produces smaller and more precise perturbations, enabling better estimation of the robustness of the model against adversarial attacks.

3 Methodology

In this section, we describe experiments using two standard datasets, CIFAR-10 [10] and CIFAR-10-C [20], the standard corruption dataset, to measure the changes in the results after adversarial attacks and corruptions. Each experiment was performed with three random seeds per setting, and the results are reported with standard errors in the following comprehensive analysis.

3.1 Model and Datasets

In the experiments, we utilize **ResNet18** [11], which is trained locally for 200 epochs and subsequently serves as a pre-trained model for various unlearning methods. The **CIFAR-10** dataset is used as a benchmark to evaluate the model performance both before and after the application of perturbations.

3.2 Simulating Deletion Requests

In our approach, we adopt a random deletion strategy by randomly dividing the training set into three distinct subsets, referred to as seeds. Each seed is assigned to the indices designated for the forget set, denoted as $(\mathcal{D}_F)$, while the remaining samples form the retain set $(\mathcal{D}_R)$. All unlearning methods are evaluated using the same set of deleted indices to ensure a fair and consistent comparison.

3.3 Experimental Details

We compare the retrained-from-scratch baseline with several representative machine unlearning techniques. Below, we briefly describe each method.

Baselines Used

- **Retrain**: Fully retrain the model from scratch using only the retain set ($\mathcal{D}_R$). This model serve as a gold-standard baseline, representing the ideal outcome of perfect unlearning. In other words, retraining from scratch will isolates the effect of unlearning.
- **FT** (Fine-Tuning): Fine-tune the model using only retain set $\mathcal{D}_R$ for a limited number of epochs.

Unlearning Methods Used

- **GA** (Gradient Ascent) [12]: Fine-tune the original model by updating the inverse direction of the gradients that maximizes the loss on the forget set $\mathcal{D}_F$.
- **RL** (Random Label) [13]: Assign random labels to the forget set $\mathcal{D}_F$, then combine it with the retain set $\mathcal{D}_R$ and fine-tune the model.
- **BS** (Boundary Shrink) [14]: Reduce the confidence margins of the model in the forget set $\mathcal{D}_F$ to adjust decision boundaries.
- **ℓ_1-Sparse** [15]: Introduce ℓ_1 regularization to the unlearning process to suppress unnecessary updates, thus minimizing interference with the retain set $\mathcal{D}_R$ and stabilizing the model.
- **BT** (Bad Teaching) [16]: Employ an intentionally impaired teacher model to guide the student (original) model weight on the forget set $\mathcal{D}_F$ by encouraging incorrect or low-confidence predictions to make the student model forget.

3.4 Adversarial Attack Configuration

To evaluate the robustness of unlearned models, we employ three widely used white-box adversarial attacks: **FGSM** (Fast Gradient Sign Method), **PGD** (Projected Gradient Descent), and **DeepFool**. All attacks are implemented using the Adversarial Robustness Toolbox (ART) [19], an open-source Python library developed by IBM for evaluation purposes. For PGD attacks, we used 10 iterations, while we applied 30 iterations for DeepFool attacks.

3.5 Corruption Robustness

Furthermore, to assess robustness against common corruptions, we additionally evaluate on the corruption datasets **CIFAR-10-C**, which comprises 15 types of algorithmically generated corruptions categorized into four groups.

- **Noise:** Gaussian Noise, Shot Noise, and Impulse Noise
- **Blur:** Defocus Blur, Frosted Glass Blur, Motion Blur, and Zoom Blur
- **Weather:** Snow, Frost, and Fog
- **Digital:** Brightness, Contrast, Elastic, Pixelate, and JPEG Compression

Each corruption type is applied at severity level three (out of five), following the standard protocol introduced by Hendrycks et al. [20].

3.6 Evaluation Metrics

In this study, we employ the evaluation framework, which involves the retrained model that was trained solely on the retain set ($\mathcal{D}_R$), serving as a baseline for comparison, following the approaches by Liu et al. [14] and Fan et al. [17]. The following metrics are used to assess the effectiveness of unlearning methods in evaluating model performance across different sets, as well as metrics for privacy concerns and fairness.

- **UA** (Unlearn Accuracy): denotes the accuracy on the $\mathcal{D}_F$ consists of samples that are specifically targeted for removal.
- **RA** (Retain Accuracy): denotes the accuracy on the $\mathcal{D}_R$ consists of samples that are expected to remain unaffected.
- **TA** (Test Accuracy): denotes the accuracy on an test set ($\mathcal{D}_T$), consists of unseen data used to measure generalization performance after unlearning. Each metric is computed across S random seeds:

$$\mathrm{Acc}_{\mathcal{D}_*} = \mu_{\mathcal{D}_*} \pm \sigma_{\mathcal{D}_*} \tag{6}$$

where

$$\mu_{\mathcal{D}_*} = \frac{1}{S}\sum_{s=1}^{S} \mathrm{Accuracy}_{\mathcal{D}_*}^{(s)}, \quad \sigma_{\mathcal{D}_*} = \sqrt{\frac{1}{S}\sum_{s=1}^{S}\left(\mathrm{Accuracy}_{\mathcal{D}_*}^{(s)} - \mu_{\mathcal{D}_*}\right)^2} \tag{7}$$

Here, $\mathcal{D}_* \in \{\mathcal{D}_F, \mathcal{D}_R, \mathcal{D}_T\}$, represents the evaluation of the datasets, UA, RA, and TA, respectively. $\mu_{\mathcal{D}_*}$ denotes the mean of the classification accuracy on dataset $\mathcal{D}_*$ for seed S and $\sigma_{\mathcal{D}_*}$ represents the standard deviation of the accuracy between seeds.

- **MIA** (Membership Inference Attack Score): a score obtained from conducting membership inference attacks on $\mathcal{D}_F$:

$$\mathrm{MIA} = \frac{1}{N}\sum_{i=1}^{N} 1[\hat{y}_i = y_i], \tag{8}$$

where N represents the number of evaluated samples, with predicted membership labels as $\hat{y}_i \in \{0, 1\}$, and the ground truth is denoted as $y_i \in \{0, 1\}$. The indicator function $1[\cdot]$ to counts specific occurrences, reference from Huang et al. [18].
- **Avg. Gap** (Average Gap): the average of the four metrics (UA, RA, TA, and MIA) compared to the retrain baseline serves as the primary metric for evaluating different unlearning methods against the baseline:

$$Avg.\ Gap = \frac{1}{4}\sum_{k \in \{UA, RA, TA, MIA\}} \left|k - k^{Retrain}\right| \tag{9}$$

- **mCA** (Mean Corruption Accuracy): a corruption accuracy on a corrupted dataset benchmark that applies 15 common corruption types. The mCA is computed as the average classification accuracy across all corruption types at a fixed severity level:

$$\text{mCA} = \frac{1}{K}\sum_{k=1}^{K} \text{Accuracy}_k, \tag{10}$$

where $K = 15$ is the number of corruption types and Accuracy_k is the accuracy under corruption type k.

4 Experiment Results and Analysis

This study aims to compare unlearning performance across different data subsets using a classification-based evaluation method, following the majority of the machine unlearning literature as proposed by Ginart et al. [5] and Bourtoule et al.

Specifically, we obtained the classification results by calculating the image classification accuracy using the modified model that was trained on a specific seed, which each seed includes $\mathcal{D}_R$ and $\mathcal{D}_F$, then performed on $\mathcal{D}_T$ for evaluate generalization performance. To ensure robustness and randomness, the entire process is repeated across three distinct random seeds. The classification accuracy is computed as the ratio of correct predictions to the total number of samples in each set. The model is expected to maintain overall accuracy across all sets.

4.1 Unlearning Performance

Table 1 displays the accuracy of various unlearning methods across different forget set ratios. The results indicate only a slight difference between 10% and 50%, with a noticeable decrease in accuracy at 50%. Both fine-tuning and gradient ascent achieve performance on the forget set that nearly matches full retraining. Conversely, for the Bad Teaching and Random Label methods, overall performance degraded, with test accuracy falling below 85%. While there is reasonable forgetting performance but a sacrifice in overall accuracy, especially in generalization on unseen data, such as the test set. This highlights the trade-off and inconsistency.

When randomly forgetting 50% of the data, the observed patterns remain consistent. However, the average gap scores increase across all methods due to the increased difficulty of unlearning when half of the training data is removed. These baseline results demonstrate that our implementations achieve performance comparable to that of the baselines, which serve as benchmarks for adversarial robustness.

Table 1. Comparison table across various unlearning methods employing Random Forget (10% and 50%) on the CIFAR-10 dataset across three randomly selected seeds. In this table, the bold results represent the outcomes closest to those achieved through retraining, while the second-closest results are indicated in underline.

(a) Random Forget (10%)

	Unlearn Acc	*Retain Acc*	*Test Acc*	*MIA*	*Avg. Gap*
Retrain	94.30 ± 0.29	100.00 ± 0.00	94.33 ± 0.68	0.50 ± 0.00	0.00
FT	95.07 ± 0.69	98.64 ± 0.22	92.01 ± 0.32	0.52 ± 0.00	$\mathbf{2.49 \pm 0.14}$
GA	91.96 ± 0.05	98.06 ± 0.13	91.32 ± 0.24	0.51 ± 0.01	$\underline{3.13 \pm 0.28}$
ℓ_1-Sparse	100.00 ± 0.00	99.91 ± 0.05	93.92 ± 0.25	0.58 ± 0.01	4.33 ± 0.06
BS	100.00 ± 0.00	99.97 ± 0.01	94.28 ± 0.23	0.59 ± 0.00	4.78 ± 0.18
BT	84.45 ± 0.05	92.43 ± 0.95	85.83 ± 0.70	0.45 ± 0.01	6.80 ± 0.40
RL	84.14 ± 4.01	87.96 ± 3.69	83.08 ± 3.41	0.50 ± 0.01	9.83 ± 2.93

(b) Random Forget (50%)

	Unlearn Acc	*Retain Acc*	*Test Acc*	*MIA*	*Avg. Gap*
Retrain	91.58 ± 0.18	100.00 ± 0.00	91.30 ± 0.26	0.41 ± 0.00	0.00
FT	95.07 ± 0.27	98.90 ± 0.17	91.19 ± 0.40	0.45 ± 0.00	$\mathbf{2.35 \pm 0.12}$
GA	95.81 ± 0.60	98.43 ± 0.43	91.27 ± 0.57	0.47 ± 0.00	$\underline{3.07 \pm 0.06}$
ℓ_1-Sparse	100.00 ± 0.00	100.00 ± 0.00	94.46 ± 0.06	0.50 ± 0.00	5.28 ± 0.09
BS	99.99 ± 0.00	99.99 ± 0.00	94.51 ± 0.04	0.51 ± 0.00	5.43 ± 0.03
BT	87.87 ± 0.45	94.10 ± 0.31	86.28 ± 0.39	0.44 ± 0.00	4.50 ± 0.16
RL	86.57 ± 2.15	90.51 ± 1.80	84.15 ± 1.92	0.47 ± 0.00	6.95 ± 1.53

4.2 Adversarial Robustness Performance

We conduct experiments to comprehensively evaluate adversarial robustness by measuring attack performance across various unlearning models. Table 2 reports the perturbation levels under adversarial attacks with the ϵ range, varying from 0 (clean data) to 24/255, and it evaluates the mean and standard deviation of accuracy on the test set $\mathcal{D}_T$.

Single-Step Attacks: as shown in the Table 2a, for one-step attacks (FGSM), the retraining baseline consistently offers the best adversarial robustness against all levels of perturbation. Interestingly, at extreme perturbation ($\epsilon > 16/255$), the Bad Teaching (BT) method slightly outperforms and surpasses the retrained model. Nevertheless, this apparent robustness of this method, which achieved low accuracy (around 85%), reflects the general model weakness rather than true robustness.

However, it is important to note that at such high perturbation levels, adversarial images are visually distinguishable to humans, reducing their relevance in practical attack scenarios. In real-world adversarial attack situations, retraining still outperforms other unlearning methods, demonstrating robustness and reliability.

Furthermore, the ℓ_1-sparse method under FGSM achieves performance closest to that of retraining. In particular, on the forget set (50%), it even outperforms the retrain baseline, achieving approximately 38% compared to 11% of the retrain baseline. This exceptional performance is likely attributable to ℓ_1 regularization, which enforces weight sparsity and helps preserve a flatter loss landscape that is resistant to gradient-based perturbations—in addition to maintaining robust features while suppressing non-robust ones, resulting in simpler decision boundaries that are more difficult for adversaries to exploit.

Multi-Step Attacks: provide more severe adversarial perturbations to the model, from Table 2b, there is a substantial robustness degradation. Notably, the Bad Teaching method still performs well even in the face of escalating adversarial attack severity.

Minimal Perturbations: the retrain baseline maintains approximately 13% accuracy with a 10% forget set ratio, but improves to around 19% when applied to 50% of the forget set. In contrast, boundary shrink suffers from catastrophic robustness collapse around 8% in both ratios, despite maintaining near-retrain baseline metrics. Meanwhile, the other method preserves performance on both ratios.

In conclusion, our findings indicate that most machine unlearning tends to increase the vulnerability of models to adversarial attacks compared to retraining the baseline. These results highlight the importance of considering adversarial robustness as a critical criterion when designing and evaluating unlearning methods.

4.3 Corruption Robustness Performance

After evaluating on CIFAR-10-C, we found that the degradation of the performance due to the image corruption does not differ significantly from the baseline retrain method, as illustrated in Fig. 2 and Table 3. Regarding the unlearning method, in the random forget (10%) retraining, robustness is only slightly higher than that of the unlearned models, and there is no substantial gap with the high-accuracy group in random forget (50%), which is $\ell_1 - Sparse$ and boundary shrink.

However, there is a notable variation in accuracy across different types of corruption, as shown in Fig. 3. The gap between the highest average accuracy for brightness corruption, around 90%, and the lowest for glass blur, only 50%, remains significant. Additionally, Table 3 reveals that, within each corruption type, the accuracy is almost the same across all unlearning methods.

Table 2. The table presents the adversarial robustness of each method based on $\mathcal{D}_T$ accuracy. Each sub-table displays results from various adversarial attacks. The highest accuracy is highlighted in bold, and the runner-up is indicated in underline.

(a) FGSM

	Random Forget (10%)					
	$\epsilon = 0$	$\epsilon = 8/255$	$\epsilon = 12/255$	$\epsilon = 16/255$	$\epsilon = 20/255$	$\epsilon = 24/255$
Retrain	**94.33 ± 0.68**	**33.95 ± 8.13**	**28.28 ± 4.86**	22.75 ± 2.46	17.90 ± 1.36	15.03 ± 1.16
FT	92.01 ± 0.32	25.29 ± 4.69	21.24 ± 4.52	17.95 ± 3.38	15.32 ± 2.00	13.47 ± 1.32
GA	91.32 ± 0.24	17.31 ± 1.65	14.32 ± 1.41	12.42 ± 1.02	11.34 ± 0.98	11.06 ± 1.21
ℓ_1	93.92 ± 0.25	33.38 ± 1.12	26.97 ± 1.12	21.31 ± 1.00	17.34 ± 1.18	14.97 ± 0.95
BS	94.28 ± 0.23	15.80 ± 0.81	12.53 ± 0.89	11.15 ± 0.75	10.19 ± 0.59	9.87 ± 0.61
BT	85.83 ± 0.70	28.83 ± 4.68	26.39 ± 5.64	**24.44 ± 5.61**	**22.42 ± 4.69**	**20.60 ± 3.71**
RL	83.08 ± 3.41	18.94 ± 6.59	15.77 ± 6.46	13.78 ± 5.68	12.81 ± 4.43	12.03 ± 3.37
	Random Forget (50%)					
	$\epsilon = 0$	$\epsilon = 8/255$	$\epsilon = 12/255$	$\epsilon = 16/255$	$\epsilon = 20/255$	$\epsilon = 24/255$
Retrain	91.30 ± 0.26	11.24 ± 0.73	9.48 ± 0.83	9.01 ± 0.72	8.91 ± 0.67	8.87 ± 0.72
FT	91.19 ± 0.40	29.39 ± 3.46	24.74 ± 2.90	20.89 ± 1.78	17.50 ± 0.62	14.91 ± 0.81
GA	91.27 ± 0.57	20.61 ± 2.11	16.82 ± 2.45	14.36 ± 2.05	12.71 ± 1.71	11.89 ± 1.44
ℓ_1	94.46 ± 0.06	**37.88 ± 0.81**	**29.88 ± 0.59**	22.93 ± 0.78	17.74 ± 0.57	14.48 ± 0.22
BS	**94.51 ± 0.04**	16.86 ± 0.54	13.31 ± 0.30	11.71 ± 0.12	10.91 ± 0.15	10.57 ± 0.05
BT	86.28 ± 0.39	14.56 ± 1.00	12.31 ± 0.96	11.34 ± 1.00	10.33 ± 0.96	9.71 ± 0.90
RL	84.15 ± 1.92	33.71 ± 5.50	29.03 ± 5.26	**25.03 ± 4.49**	**21.41 ± 3.22**	**18.80 ± 2.37**

(b) PGD

	Random Forget (10%)					
	$\epsilon = 0$	$\epsilon = 8/255$	$\epsilon = 12/255$	$\epsilon = 16/255$	$\epsilon = 20/255$	$\epsilon = 24/255$
Retrain	**94.33 ± 0.68**	6.20 ± 0.86	4.43 ± 0.60	4.05 ± 0.55	3.93 ± 0.55	3.90 ± 0.55
FT	92.01 ± 0.32	5.94 ± 0.52	5.31 ± 0.15	5.17 ± 0.11	5.16 ± 0.06	5.15 ± 0.06
GA	91.32 ± 0.24	5.92 ± 0.03	5.77 ± 0.05	5.72 ± 0.10	5.66 ± 0.12	5.63 ± 0.08
ℓ_1	93.92 ± 0.25	5.52 ± 0.91	4.43 ± 0.48	4.18 ± 0.32	4.10 ± 0.31	4.06 ± 0.28
BS	94.28 ± 0.23	4.04 ± 0.23	3.93 ± 0.22	3.92 ± 0.20	3.90 ± 0.21	3.85 ± 0.20
BT	85.83 ± 0.70	**16.97 ± 1.25**	**11.88 ± 0.96**	**9.82 ± 0.34**	**8.87 ± 0.14**	**8.33 ± 0.07**
RL	83.08 ± 3.41	8.27 ± 3.19	7.46 ± 2.82	7.07 ± 2.65	6.79 ± 2.46	6.56 ± 2.33
	Random Forget (50%)					
	$\epsilon = 0$	$\epsilon = 8/255$	$\epsilon = 12/255$	$\epsilon = 16/255$	$\epsilon = 20/255$	$\epsilon = 24/255$
Retrain	91.30 ± 0.26	5.97 ± 0.37	5.81 ± 0.28	5.80 ± 0.28	5.77 ± 0.29	5.81 ± 0.29
FT	91.19 ± 0.40	6.92 ± 0.65	5.88 ± 0.37	5.74 ± 0.41	5.71 ± 0.38	5.60 ± 0.34
GA	91.27 ± 0.57	6.00 ± 0.31	5.70 ± 0.28	5.66 ± 0.23	5.63 ± 0.21	5.59 ± 0.22
ℓ_1	94.46 ± 0.06	5.36 ± 0.07	4.10 ± 0.06	3.84 ± 0.07	3.78 ± 0.07	3.71 ± 0.06
BS	**94.51 ± 0.04**	3.89 ± 0.06	3.77 ± 0.02	3.73 ± 0.03	3.69 ± 0.03	3.70 ± 0.03
BT	86.28 ± 0.39	9.74 ± 0.61	8.72 ± 0.41	8.62 ± 0.40	**8.60 ± 0.40**	**8.59 ± 0.42**
RL	84.15 ± 1.92	**13.58 ± 3.42**	**10.93 ± 2.24**	**9.26 ± 1.79**	8.47 ± 1.78	7.65 ± 1.59

(c) DeepFool (30 Iterations)

Random Forget (10%)						
Retrain	FT	GA	ℓ_1-Sparse	BS	BT	RL
13.92	12.34	13.07	12.14	7.89	**18.07**	17.90
Random Forget (50%)						
Retrain	FT	GA	ℓ_1-Sparse	BS	BT	RL
19.33	12.61	12.64	11.66	8.4	12.44	15.0

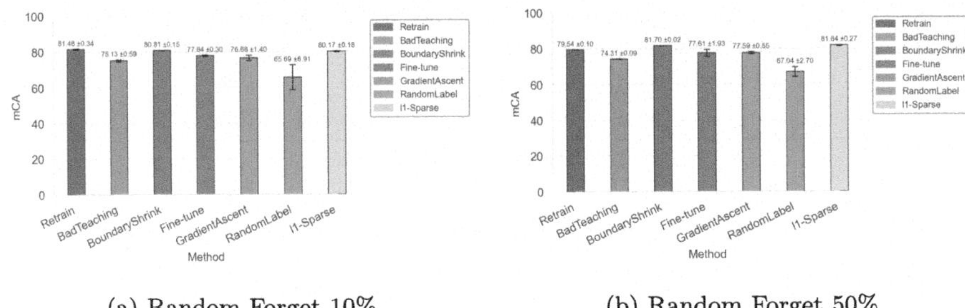

(a) Random Forget 10%

(b) Random Forget 50%

Fig. 2. Corruption robustness under Random Forgetting at 10% and 50%. This represents the Mean Corruption Accuracy (mCA) aggregated over all corruption types for each method.

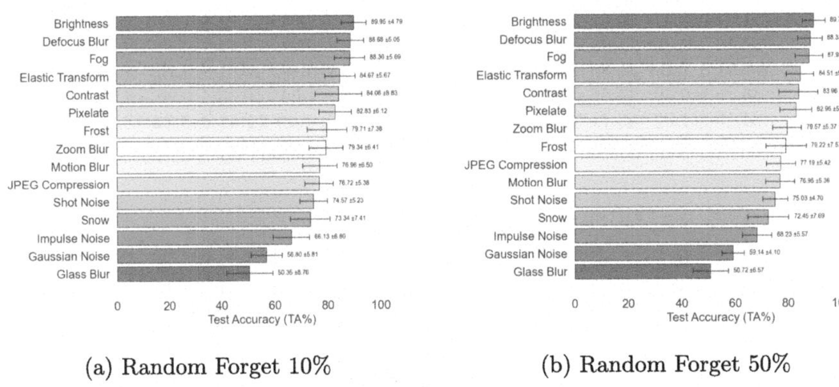

(a) Random Forget 10%

(b) Random Forget 50%

Fig. 3. Corruption accuracy per type, showing performance across 15 individual corruption types in CIFAR-10-C under Random Forget 10% and 50%.

Table 3. Results evaluating the corruption robustness of the CIFAR-10-C under Random Forget (10%) through three different seeds. The highest accuracy is indicated in bold, while the second-best result is indicated in underline.

		Random Forget (10%)					
	Retrain	**FT**	**GA**	ℓ_1	**BS**	**BT**	**RL**
mCA	**81.48 ± 0.28**	77.84 ± 0.25	76.68 ± 1.15	80.17 ± 0.15	80.81 ± 0.12	75.13 ± 0.49	65.69 ± 5.70
Noise							
Gauss.	58.19 ± 1.22	56.57 ± 5.09	54.56 ± 3.71	57.47 ± 2.40	57.43 ± 0.64	**64.16 ± 4.24**	49.22 ± 9.67
Shot	77.17 ± 0.66	75.40 ± 2.13	72.67 ± 2.71	77.05 ± 1.23	**77.52 ± 0.32**	76.71 ± 1.90	65.47 ± 9.27
Impulse	**71.44 ± 2.58**	65.03 ± 2.86	66.26 ± 3.41	67.61 ± 2.53	69.85 ± 0.64	70.70 ± 1.91	52.05 ± 5.39
Blur							
Defocus	92.44 ± 0.98	90.41 ± 0.17	89.42 ± 1.08	92.51 ± 0.27	**93.04 ± 0.12**	82.78 ± 0.57	80.14 ± 3.76
Glass	56.72 ± 0.80	51.10 ± 0.80	46.93 ± 2.67	51.35 ± 0.79	51.01 ± 0.21	**59.53 ± 1.12**	35.82 ± 15.26
Motion	82.03 ± 1.16	78.32 ± 0.90	77.50 ± 3.82	81.25 ± 1.53	**82.47 ± 0.77**	71.63 ± 1.08	65.51 ± 6.89
Zoom	84.54 ± 0.92	80.58 ± 0.79	78.61 ± 3.50	83.88 ± 0.83	**85.48 ± 0.36**	74.21 ± 0.56	68.06 ± 5.88
Weather							
Snow	**80.15 ± 1.57**	74.81 ± 1.00	72.36 ± 2.67	77.11 ± 0.21	77.99 ± 0.51	71.99 ± 1.39	58.94 ± 9.69
Frost	**85.05 ± 0.55**	81.28 ± 0.58	79.86 ± 1.40	83.82 ± 0.63	84.51 ± 0.11	77.50 ± 0.40	65.93 ± 11.92
Fog	92.67 ± 0.73	90.19 ± 0.33	89.80 ± 0.31	92.57 ± 0.18	**92.77 ± 0.20**	81.41 ± 0.42	79.12 ± 5.47
Bright	93.65 ± 0.89	91.31 ± 0.53	91.08 ± 0.36	93.36 ± 0.29	**93.89 ± 0.05**	84.99 ± 0.40	81.39 ± 3.90
Digital							
Contrast	90.33 ± 0.88	87.36 ± 0.22	87.03 ± 0.84	90.40 ± 0.53	**90.50 ± 0.38**	69.09 ± 0.60	73.72 ± 8.41
Elastic	89.13 ± 0.86	86.27 ± 0.37	85.09 ± 1.85	88.67 ± 0.44	**89.70 ± 0.14**	79.51 ± 0.19	74.29 ± 4.39
Pixel	**87.26 ± 0.72**	82.42 ± 4.98	83.82 ± 3.65	86.49 ± 0.89	86.64 ± 0.40	82.77 ± 0.52	70.41 ± 5.48
JPEG	**81.38 ± 0.14**	76.62 ± 1.82	75.23 ± 1.36	79.05 ± 0.46	79.40 ± 0.16	80.02 ± 0.28	65.33 ± 4.23

		Random Forget (50%)					
	Retrain	**FT**	**GA**	ℓ_1	**BS**	**BT**	**RL**
mCA	79.54 ± 0.07	77.61 ± 1.40	77.59 ± 0.40	81.64 ± 0.20	**81.70 ± 0.02**	74.31 ± 0.06	67.04 ± 1.96
Noise							
Gauss.	**65.79 ± 1.65**	60.33 ± 2.07	56.42 ± 0.44	60.26 ± 1.97	59.02 ± 0.64	59.71 ± 0.41	52.41 ± 2.70
Shot	**78.84 ± 0.25**	75.41 ± 3.13	74.81 ± 1.77	78.71 ± 1.00	78.43 ± 0.51	73.59 ± 0.30	65.44 ± 2.16
Impulse	**74.69 ± 0.01**	69.93 ± 1.75	66.93 ± 3.32	70.03 ± 1.41	70.98 ± 0.69	68.38 ± 1.45	56.66 ± 1.68
Blur							
Defocus	89.23 ± 0.25	89.01 ± 0.55	89.66 ± 0.72	93.30 ± 0.16	**93.34 ± 0.04**	83.43 ± 0.63	80.36 ± 0.45
Glass	53.60 ± 1.29	52.06 ± 7.45	49.95 ± 1.22	53.64 ± 0.42	52.45 ± 0.36	**54.64 ± 2.93**	38.69 ± 11.33
Motion	78.16 ± 1.70	74.93 ± 3.35	77.85 ± 0.05	83.06 ± 0.37	**83.62 ± 0.27**	71.69 ± 0.54	69.31 ± 3.30
Zoom	80.85 ± 1.44	78.94 ± 1.51	79.72 ± 1.73	85.48 ± 0.18	**86.10 ± 0.06**	75.45 ± 0.09	70.47 ± 2.96
Weather							
Snow	74.38 ± 1.52	73.15 ± 3.48	74.85 ± 0.07	**79.37 ± 0.60**	79.29 ± 0.17	68.45 ± 0.55	57.66 ± 8.66
Frost	81.67 ± 0.62	79.79 ± 2.57	81.50 ± 0.22	84.88 ± 0.78	**85.59 ± 0.10**	76.60 ± 0.89	64.50 ± 11.00
Fog	89.31 ± 0.14	88.66 ± 1.28	89.91 ± 0.31	93.05 ± 0.06	**93.08 ± 0.11**	81.90 ± 0.35	79.62 ± 4.49
Bright	90.44 ± 0.37	90.73 ± 0.33	91.28 ± 0.27	94.16 ± 0.11	**94.19 ± 0.02**	85.36 ± 0.45	82.02 ± 1.90
Digital							
Contrast	85.48 ± 0.83	85.31 ± 0.84	86.97 ± 0.54	90.85 ± 0.21	**91.13 ± 0.06**	72.26 ± 0.25	75.75 ± 7.79
Elastic	86.09 ± 0.29	84.67 ± 1.28	85.44 ± 0.43	89.92 ± 0.04	**90.13 ± 0.04**	80.26 ± 0.61	75.05 ± 1.20
Pixel	83.80 ± 0.62	84.35 ± 0.38	83.24 ± 3.56	87.67 ± 0.09	**87.72 ± 0.25**	82.43 ± 0.69	71.48 ± 9.60
JPEG	**80.69 ± 0.42**	76.91 ± 2.44	75.38 ± 1.01	80.19 ± 0.40	80.46 ± 0.14	80.59 ± 0.04	66.15 ± 6.09

5 Conclusion

Our results indicate that while machine unlearning techniques can efficiently fulfill data deletion requests, they may compromise the adversarial robustness of the model. This trade-off raises important concerns for deploying unlearning methods in safety-critical applications in some fields. Future research should explore and concerned more on developing unlearning algorithms that better balance privacy preservation and model robustness

This empirical study represents a preliminary investigation involving a limited set of parameters. However, we have not yet obtained conclusive evidence regarding the impact of unlearning methods on the robustness of the model. Nevertheless, the findings from this initial experiment indicate potential effects that require further investigation.

Our results suggest that ℓ_1-Sparse is a viable option for practical deployment in security-sensitive fields such as autonomous vehicles and medical applications, due to its ability to preserve robustness.

5.1 Limitation and Future Directions

Due to various constraints, our experiments were primarily limited by substantial computational requirements, which prevented this study from conducting experiments on a large-scale dataset.

Future work will involve extended experiments and analyses to gain broader insights into a variety of adversarial attacks, including black-box attacks, which typically consume significant computational resources but offer a more realistic assessment of robustness in real-world practice. Additionally, we aim to explore performance across larger-scale datasets and alternative architectures to evaluate scalability and generalizability.

Disclosure of Interests. The authors have no competing interests to declare that are relevant to the content of this article.

References

1. European Parliament and Council: Regulation (EU) 2016/679 (General Data Protection Regulation). Official Journal of the European Union (2016). https://gdpr-info.eu
2. Personal Information Protection Commission, Japan: Act on the Protection of Personal Information (APPI). https://www.ppc.go.jp/en/legal/
3. California State Legislature: California Consumer Privacy Act (CCPA). https://oag.ca.gov/privacy/ccpa
4. Bourtoule, L., et al.: Machine unlearning. In: Proceedings of the IEEE Symposium on Security and Privacy (SP), pp. 141–159. IEEE (2021). https://doi.org/10.1109/SP40001.2021.00019
5. Ginart, A., Ge, Y., Valiant, G., Zou, J.: Making AI Forget You: Data Deletion in Machine Learning. In: NeurIPS (2019). https://doi.org/10.48550/arXiv.1907.05012

6. Xu, J., Wu, Z., Wang, C., Jia, X.: Machine unlearning: solutions and challenges. In: IEEE Trans. Emerg. Top. Comput. Intell. **8**(3), 2150–2168. IEEE (2024). https://doi.org/10.1109/TETCI.2024.3379240
7. Goodfellow, I.J., Shlens, J., Szegedy, C.: explaining and Harnessing Adversarial Examples. arXiv preprint arXiv:1412.6572 (2014). https://doi.org/10.48550/arXiv.1412.6572
8. Madry, A., Makelov, A., Schmidt, L., Tsipras, D., Vladu, A.: Towards deep learning models resistant to adversarial attacks. In: Proceedings of the International Conference on Learning Representations (ICLR) (2018). https://doi.org/10.48550/arXiv.1706.06083
9. Moosavi-Dezfooli, S.-M., Fawzi, A., Frossard, P.: DeepFool: a simple and accurate method to fool deep neural networks. In: Proceedings of the IEEE Conference on Computer Vision and Pattern Recognition (CVPR), pp. 2574–2582. IEEE (2016). https://doi.org/10.1109/CVPR.2016.282
10. Krizhevsky, A., Nair, V., Hinton, G.: The CIFAR-10 Dataset. Technical Report, University of Toronto (2009). https://www.cs.toronto.edu/~kriz/cifar.html
11. He, K., Zhang, X., Ren, S., Sun, J.: Deep residual learning for image recognition. In: Proceedings of the IEEE Conference on Computer Vision and Pattern Recognition (CVPR), pp. 770–778. IEEE (2016). https://doi.org/10.1109/CVPR.2016.90
12. Thudi, A., Deza, G., Chandrasekaran, V., Papernot, N.: Unrolling SGD: understanding factors influencing machine unlearning. In: Proceedings of the IEEE European Symposium on Security and Privacy (EuroS&P), pp. 303–319. IEEE (2022). https://doi.org/10.1109/EuroSP53844.2022.00027
13. Li, J., Ghosh, S.: Random Relabeling for Efficient Machine Unlearning. In: arXiv preprint arXiv:2305.12320 (2023). https://doi.org/10.48550/arXiv.2305.12320
14. Chen, M., Gao, W., Liu, G., Peng, K., Wang, C.: Boundary unlearning: rapid forgetting of deep networks via shifting the decision boundary. In: Proceedings of the IEEE/CVF Conference on Computer Vision and Pattern Recognition (CVPR), pp. 7866–7875. IEEE (2023). https://doi.org/10.1109/CVPR52729.2023.00750
15. Jia, J. , et al.: Model sparsity can simplify machine unlearning. In: Advances in Neural Information Processing Systems (NeurIPS), vol. 36. Curran Associates (2023). https://doi.org/10.48550/arXiv.2304.04934
16. Chundawat, V.S., Tarun, A.K., Mandal, M., Kankanhalli, M.: Can bad teaching induce forgetting? Unlearning in deep networks using an incompetent teacher. In: Proceedings of the AAAI Conference on Artificial Intelligence. AAAI Press (2023). https://doi.org/10.48550/arXiv.2205.08096
17. Fan, C., Liu, J., Zhang, Y., Wong, E., Wei, D., Liu, S.: SalUn: empowering machine unlearning via gradient-based weight saliency in both image classification and generation. In: Proceedings of the International Conference on Learning Representations (ICLR). ICLR (2024). https://doi.org/10.48550/arXiv.2310.12508
18. Huang, M.H., Foo, L.G., Liu, J.: Learning to unlearn for robust machine unlearning. In: Leonardis, A., Ricci, E., Roth, S., Russakovsky, O., Sattler, T., Varol, G. (eds.) Computer Vision – ECCV 2024. ECCV 2024. LNCS, vol. 15110. Springer, Cham (2024). https://doi.org/10.48550/arXiv.2407.10494
19. Nicolae, M.-I., et al.: Adversarial Robustness Toolbox v1.0.0. In: arXiv preprint arXiv:1807.01069 (2019). https://doi.org/10.48550/arXiv.1807.01069
20. Hendrycks, D., Dietterich, T.: Benchmarking neural network robustness to common corruptions and perturbations. In: Proceedings of the International Conference on Learning Representations (ICLR). OpenReview (2019). https://doi.org/10.48550/arXiv.1903.12261

P^2FR-VFL: Privacy-Enhanced Vertical Federated Learning Framework via P^2FR-PSI and Homomorphic Encryption

Huizhong Zhao[1], Shengmin Xu[1(✉)], Jianchang Lai[2], and Zhongsheng Tan[1]

[1] College of Computer and Cyberspace Security, Fujian Normal University, Fuzhou 350117, China
smxu1989@gmail.com
[2] School of Cyber Science and Engineering, Southeast University, Nanjing 211189, China

Abstract. Recommender systems rely on user preferences and item attributes to provide personalized services, yet they inherently face a tension between model accuracy and data privacy. Vertical Federated Learning (VFL) allows multiple organizations to jointly train models without sharing raw data, typically using Private Set Intersection (PSI) to align overlapping users. However, conventional PSI supports only exact identifier matching and fails to accommodate the feature-based conditional filtering frequently required in modern recommendation pipelines. To overcome this limitation, we propose P^2FR-VFL, a VFL framework that integrates Privacy-Preserving Feature-Retrieval PSI (P^2FR-PSI). This enhanced PSI mechanism enables participants to privately align and selectively filter user identifiers according to hidden predicate conditions, without disclosing any sensitive feature information. This design enables P^2FR-VFL to provide a more expressive and privacy-preserving preprocessing stage for federated recommendation tasks. Building on this capability, P^2FR-VFL also offers a scalable and privacy-enhanced solution for cross-domain recommender systems, effectively reconciling model utility with strong user privacy guarantees in federated environments. Experiments on real-world datasets show that P^2FR-VFL achieves predictive accuracy comparable to plaintext VFL training, while incurring only 20% additional communication overhead relative to state-of-the-art PSI schemes, all while supporting flexible alignment capabilities.

Keywords: Recommender systems · Vertical federated learning · Private set intersection

1 Introduction

Recommender systems have become a core component of modern digital services, including e-commerce, online advertising, and social media platforms [1–3]. By

Y. Xiang and J. Shen (Eds.): ML4CS 2025, LNCS 16456, pp. 236–250, 2026.
https://doi.org/10.1007/978-981-95-7820-7_16

utilizing user preferences and behavioral data, they deliver personalized content that improves user experience and drives commercial value. However, as these system models increasingly depend on fine-grained personal information, the tension between personalization and privacy has become a central challenge [4]. Ensuring strong protection of sensitive user data while preserving recommendation accuracy has therefore motivated extensive research on privacy-preserving collaborative learning frameworks [5].

Vertical Federated Learning (VFL) offers a promising paradigm for addressing this challenge [6]. In VFL, multiple organizations that own different feature spaces but share overlapping user groups collaboratively train a global model without exposing their raw data [7–9]. Through encrypted interactions, VFL enables cross-domain knowledge integration while ensuring that the data of each party remain local and private [10]. This setting is particularly suitable for recommendation tasks in which different platforms, such as a bank and an e-commerce provider, hold complementary user information [11].

A key prerequisite for VFL model training is entity alignment, namely identifying the set of users shared across participating organizations in a secure manner. Existing alignment protocols are commonly built on Private Set Intersection (PSI), which enables parties to discover common user identifiers without revealing the unmatched ones [12]. However, traditional PSI supports only exact matching and cannot satisfy the more flexible alignment requirements frequently seen in recommendation systems [13]. In practice, platforms often need to stratify and filter user groups by applying feature-based predicates, such as threshold conditions combined with logical OR operations (for example, income $>$ 10,000 or age $<$ 25) [14]. These constraints are crucial for fine-grained user segmentation and personalized feature selection prior to collaborative model training [15].

To address these limitations, we introduce a VFL framework named P^{2}FR-VFL, which integrates a Privacy-Preserving Feature Retrieval PSI (P^{2}FR-PSI) protocol. In contrast to standard PSI, PÂšFR-PSI supports predicate-based feature filtering during the alignment stage, enabling the parties to securely identify and align user subsets according to private attribute constraints while revealing neither feature values nor non-overlapping identifiers. This capability enhances the flexibility of the VFL preprocessing pipeline and provides strong privacy protection under the semi-honest threat model.

Comprehensive analysis and experiments on benchmark recommendation datasets show that P^{2}FR-VFL achieves accuracy comparable to plaintext VFL training, while significantly enhancing alignment flexibility and improving privacy-preserving efficiency. The main contributions of this paper are summarized as follows:

- Novel framework: We propose P^{2}FR-VFL, the first VFL framework that incorporates predicate-based PSI to support privacy-preserving feature retrieval and flexible entity alignment.
- Enhanced privacy mechanism: We design a new Diffie–Hellman-Based Privacy-Preserving Feature Retrieval PSI (DH-P^{2}FR-PSI) protocol. In contrast to existing DH-PÂšFR-PSI [16] where only the receiver unilaterally

obtains the result, our protocol symmetrically allows both communicating parties to securely acquire the intersection that satisfies the predicate conditions, while supporting threshold-based retrieval and logical OR filtering. The protocol leaks no information about non-matching records and introduces only about 20% additional communication overhead, which is primarily attributed to the additional communication rounds required for the symmetric output mechanism that enables both parties to acquire the intersection.

This work bridges the gap between privacy-preserving entity alignment and practical recommendation modeling, offering a viable paradigm for privacy-aware cross-domain personalization in sensitive data environments.

2 Related Work

2.1 Federated Learning for Recommendation Systems

Federated Learning (FL) has emerged as a promising paradigm for privacy-preserving collaborative model training across distributed data owners. While early FL research primarily focused on horizontal settings, where clients share an identical feature space [17], recent efforts have extended FL to vertical settings in which different organizations hold complementary features over a shared user population [18]. In recommender systems, VFL has been adopted to integrate heterogeneous user attributes from multiple domains while preserving data locality. Yang et al. [19] proposed a secure VFL-based recommendation framework that enables cross-platform personalization without revealing raw features. Yang et al. [20] further explored gradient encryption and partially homomorphic techniques to reduce leakage during model aggregation. Despite these advances, existing VFL-based recommendation solutions typically assume that the overlapping user set is already aligned, leaving the problem of privacy-preserving ID matching insufficiently addressed for real-world deployments.

2.2 Privacy-Preserving Entity Alignment in VFL

Entity alignment is a fundamental prerequisite for VFL training, as it identifies the set of users shared across participating organizations. The standard cryptographic primitive for this task is PSI, which enables multiple parties to compute the intersection of their datasets without disclosing non-overlapping elements [21–24]. Early PSI constructions relied on Diffie–Hellman assumptions [25] or RSA blind signatures [26], and subsequent work improved efficiency through the use of oblivious pseudorandom functions (OPRF) [27] and homomorphic encryption [28]. In the context of federated learning, Sun et al. [29] introduced FedAlign, a PSI-based entity alignment framework optimized for VFL. However, most PSI protocols remain restricted to exact equality matching and do not support more expressive conditions such as range queries, inequality predicates, or logical combinations [30]. These limitations reduce their applicability in complex recommendation scenarios where conditional user segmentation is a core requirement [31,32].

2.3 Predicate PSI and Feature Retrieval

To overcome the limitations of classical PSI, recent research has introduced predicate PSI, which enables parties to determine whether records satisfy specific predicates without revealing their private inputs. Takeshita et al. [33] formalized the predicate PSI framework and demonstrated support for basic comparison predicates such as "greater than" and "less than". Subsequent work proposed more efficient constructions leveraging homomorphic encryption [34] and oblivious transfer extensions [35]. Advancing this line of work, the recent system Privacy-Preserving Feature Retrieval PSI (P^2FR-PSI) [15] presented a generalized PSI framework that supports feature-based retrieval, threshold filtering, and logical composition. This capability enables flexible and fine-grained data alignment without compromising privacy. Building on this foundation, our proposed P^2FR-VFL framework integrates the extended DH-P^2FR-PSI protocol into the VFL training pipeline. This protocol enables both parties to securely obtain the predicate-satisfying intersection, thereby achieving conditional user alignment with privacy preservation for federated recommendation systems.

3 Preliminaries

Table 1 provides a comprehensive list of the key mathematical symbols and notations utilized throughout this paper.

3.1 Vertical Federated Learning

VFL is a distributed machine learning paradigm tailored for settings where data is partitioned by features across multiple organizations. Unlike Horizontal Federated Learning (HFL), in which participants share the same feature space but hold different samples, VFL assumes that each party owns a distinct subset of features over a common user or entity set. Through encrypted interactions, the parties jointly train a global model while keeping their raw data local and private.

Table 1. Notations and Descriptions

Symbol	Description	Symbol	Description
$\mathbb{F}$	A large finite field	T_x	Cuckoo hash table from S
$\mathbb{Z}$	Ring of integers	ρ	Receiver's predicate
$\mathbb{G}$	Elliptic curve group	$\rho(\tilde{x}) = 1$	Predicate satisfied
S, R	The sender and receiver	I	Output of P^2FRPSI
C	The coordinator for VFL training	U_s, U_r	Vectors of secret shares
X, Y	ID sets of S and R	θ_s, θ_r	Local model parameters of S and R
$\tilde{X}$	Feature set of X	θ	Learning rate for model training
D_s, D_r	Local datasets of S and R	$L(\theta)$	The loss function for joint training

Let the set of participants be denoted as $U = \{u_0, u_1, \ldots, u_n\}$, and their corresponding local datasets as $D = \{D_0, D_1, \ldots, D_n\}$, where D_i represents the private dataset of participant u_i. Each participant trains a local model based on its dataset D_i by minimizing a local loss function:

$$L_i = \frac{1}{|D_i|} \sum_{j \in D_i} f(\hat{y}_j, y_j),$$

where $f(\cdot)$ is the loss function and $\hat{y}_j$ is the predicted value of sample x_j.

During the t-th training round, the local model of participant u_i is updated according to the computed gradient:

$$m_i(t) = M(t-1) - \eta \nabla L_i,$$

where η is the learning rate and $M(t-1)$ denotes the global model from the previous round. After local updates, participants upload encrypted gradients or model parameters to a central aggregator, which computes the weighted average of all local updates:

$$M(t) = \frac{\sum_{i=1}^{N} |D_i| \, m_i(t)}{\sum_{i=1}^{N} |D_i|}.$$

The global model M_{fed} obtained by VFL closely approximates the centralized model M_{cen} satisfying:

$$|M_{\text{fed}} - M_{\text{cen}}| < \delta,$$

where δ is a small bounded error.

VFL enables multiple institutions to collaboratively build machine learning models without directly sharing sensitive data, thus achieving both data privacy preservation and cross-domain model utility. This framework is particularly suitable for applications such as personalized recommendation, financial risk control, and healthcare data analysis, where feature spaces are naturally partitioned among participants.

3.2 Homomorphic Encryption

Homomorphic encryption is a cryptographic technique that allows direct computation over encrypted data. The fundamental property of homomorphic encryption is that operations performed in the ciphertext space correspond to equivalent operations in the plaintext space after decryption. Formally, for plaintext values x_1, x_2 and their ciphertexts $[\![x_1]\!]$, $[\![x_2]\!]$, the following homomorphic properties hold:

- Addition: $[\![x_1]\!] \oplus [\![x_2]\!] = [\![x_1 + x_2]\!]$.
- Multiplication: $[\![x]\!] \otimes c = [\![x \cdot c]\!]$.

In this paper, we adopt the Paillier additive homomorphic encryption scheme to secure parameter transmission and aggregation in the VFL process.

In the Federated Learning framework, each participant encrypts its local model parameters or gradients using the Paillier public key before uploading them to the server. The server performs aggregation directly over ciphertexts, and the final aggregated model is decrypted locally by the participants. This mechanism ensures that model updates and gradients remain encrypted throughout communication and computation, providing strong privacy guarantees while maintaining the feasibility and accuracy of federated model training.

3.3 Secure Secret Shared Retrieval Protocol

The sender inputs a user ID set X and the corresponding feature set $\tilde{X}$, while the receiver inputs a user ID set Y and a predicate ρ. Both parties execute the protocol to obtain their respective vectors of secret shares, denoted as U_s and U_r.

The first is the standard S^{3}R Protocol ($\sqcap^{\mathrm{S^3R}}$), which allows a receiver to define a predicate $\rho \in \{\mathrm{AND}, \mathrm{OR}\}^d$, where d is the feature dimensionality. The sender S inputs a user ID set X and the corresponding feature set $\tilde{X}$, while the receiver R inputs a user ID set Y and a predicate ρ. Both parties execute the protocol to collaboratively determine whether each of the Sender's feature vectors fully satisfies this predicate. Ultimately, the sender and receiver receive vectors of secret shares, denoted as U_s and U_r respectively. For any corresponding pair of shares $(u_s, u_r) \in (U_s, U_r)$, the condition $u_s + u_r = 1$ holds if and only if the associated feature vector satisfies the predicate; otherwise, $u_s + u_r = 0$.

The second is the threshold S^{3}R Protocol ($\sqcap_{\mathrm{T}}^{\mathrm{S^3R}}$) enables the two parties to collaboratively determine, for each of the sender's feature vectors, whether the value in the specified dimension satisfies the receiver's threshold condition. Ultimately, the sender and the receiver receive vectors of secret shares U_s and U_r, respectively. For any corresponding pair of shares $(u_s, u_r) \in (U_s, U_r)$, the condition $u_s + u_r = 1$ holds if and only if the associated feature vector satisfies the threshold condition; otherwise, $u_s + u_r = 0$.

3.4 Cuckoo Hashing

Cuckoo hashing [36] employs a unique insertion strategy governed by multiple hash functions (typically k). Each element is mapped to k candidate buckets via hash functions $h_i : \{0,1\}^* \to [1, m]$. The insertion of a new element e may trigger a sequence of evictions: if the bucket designated by $h_i(e)$ is occupied by an existing element e', e' is evicted. The evicted element e' is then relocated to an alternative bucket determined by another hash function $h_j(e')(j \neq i)$, which might, in turn, cause further evictions. This iterative process continues until an empty bucket is found or a maximum eviction threshold is reached. In the latter case, the unplaced element is stored in a secondary data structure known as a stash. A notable finding by Pinkas et al. [37] demonstrates that with a bucket size $m = 1.27n$ and $k = 3$ hash functions, the use of a stash becomes unnecessary with high probability.

4 System Model

4.1 DH-Based P^{2}FR-PSI Protocol

In cross-platform recommendation scenarios, multiple service providers typically hold feature information of the same user base across different dimensions. PSI technology enables participants to securely compute their shared user set without revealing non-overlapping user information. For instance, when two e-commerce platforms selling related products need to identify their overlapping customer groups, PSI allows them to align user identities while protecting private data, thereby establishing more precise joint marketing strategies that effectively enhance personalization accuracy and business operational efficiency.

To address this limitation, we propose a novel bidirectional DH-P^{2}FR-PSI protocol that symmetrically extends the original construction. The proposed scheme preserves the privacy property of not revealing the cardinality of the original intersection prior to predicate screening ($|X \cap Y|$), while enabling both the sender and the receiver to obtain an identical set of intersected user IDs at the end of the protocol, thereby enhancing fairness and practicality in secure cross-party data alignment for vertical federated recommendation systems.

The protocol aims to generate corresponding mask structures for both communication parties. The sender's mask follows the form of $H^{\mathbb{G}}(x, 1 - u_s)^{k_r k_s}$, while the receiver's mask takes the form of $H^{\mathbb{G}}(y, u_r)^{k_r k_s}$, where $y \in Y$ and $(u_r, u_s, x, \tilde{x}) \in (U_r, U_s, X, \tilde{X})$. The fundamental principle is that when a feature vector satisfies the predicate condition (i.e., $\rho(\tilde{x}) = 1$), the corresponding secret shares maintain the relationship $u_r = 1 - u_s$, with k_s and k_r being the private keys held by each party, respectively.

However, the receiver cannot directly associate an element y from its set Y with the corresponding component u_r in the share vector U_r, because the index structure of U_r is aligned with the sender's $(X, \tilde{X})$ rather than with Y. To address this, Cuckoo hashing [27] is introduced as the fundamental mechanism for data alignment. The sender first constructs a Cuckoo hash table T_x using its identity set X and associates the corresponding feature vectors $\tilde{X}$ according to the hash table indices. Subsequently, both parties execute the S^{3}R protocol based on this index structure. Through this alignment approach, when generating masks, the receiver only needs to select k candidate u_r values from U_r for each $y \in Y$ to compute $H^{\mathbb{G}}(x, u_r)$, where k represents the number of hash functions employed in the Cuckoo hashing.

Algorithm 1: DH-P²FR-PSI

Input: There are two parties, a sender S and receiver R.
S takes its ID set $X \subset \{0,1\}^*$ and $\tilde{X} \subset \mathbb{Z}^d$ as input.
R takes its ID set $Y \subset \{0,1\}^*$ and the predicate ρ as input.
The number of cuckoo hashing bins is $m_x = 1.27|X|$, hash functions $\{h_j\}$ for $j \in \{1,2,3\}$. A random oracle $H^{\mathbb{G}} : \{0,1\}^* \times \mathbb{Z} \to \mathbb{G}$.

Output: Since the protocol is symmetric in the exponentiations and randomizations, both parties obtain the same set of matched identifiers. Thus, the final output is:
$I = I_x = I_y = \{y \mid \exists y \in Y, (x, \tilde{x}) \in (X, \tilde{X}) \text{ s.t. } x = y \text{ and } \rho(\tilde{x}) = 1\}$.

1 **Predicate determination phase:**

2 S constructs cuckoo hash table T_x of X such that $T_x[h_j(x)] = x$ for $x \in X$. Set empty positions of T_x to random values from $\{0,1\}^*$, and the corresponding feature values are also set to random numbers from $\mathbb{Z}^d$. $\tilde{T}_x$ denotes the corresponding feature values of T_x.

3 S and R securely receive $U_s \subset \mathbb{Z}$ and $U_r \subset \mathbb{Z}$ with $\tilde{T}_x$ and ρ using $\sqcap^{\mathsf{S^3R}}$ or $\sqcap_{\mathsf{T}}^{\mathsf{S^3R}}$, where $|U_s| = |U_r| = m_x$.

4 **Computing intersection phase:**

5 S randomly chooses $k_s \leftarrow \mathbb{Z}^*_{|\mathbb{G}|}$, computes
$E_s = \{H^{\mathbb{G}}(t_x, 1 - u_s)^{k_s}$ for all $(t_x, u_s) \in (T_x, U_s)\}$, and sends E_s to R in random order.

6 R randomly chooses $k_r \leftarrow \mathbb{Z}^*_{|\mathbb{G}|}$, computes
$E_{r,j} = \{H^{\mathbb{G}}(y, U_r[h_j(y)])^{k_r}\}$ for all $y \in Y$ and $j = 1,2,3$, and sends $\{E_{r,j}\}$ to $\mathcal{S}$.

7 S computes $W_{r,j} = \{e_{r,j}^{k_s}\}$ for all $e_{r,j} \in E_{r,j}$. S shuffles $\{w_{r,1}, w_{r,2}, w_{r,3}\}$ for all $w_{r,j} \in W_{r,j}$ and sends $\{W_{r,j}\}$ to R for all $j = 1,2,3$.

8 R computes $W_s = \{e_s^{k_r}\}$ for all $e_s \in E_s$ and sends W_s to S.

9 S computes $I_x = \{X[i] \mid \exists W_s[i] \in W_{r,j}\}$ for all $j = 1,2,3$.

10 R computes $I_y = \{Y[i] \mid \exists W_{r,j}[i] \in W_s\}$ for all $j = 1,2,3$.

4.2 The Encrypted Model Training in VFL

VFL enables collaborative model training across multiple organizations in personalized recommendation scenarios while preserving user privacy. The entire process consists of two main stages: data alignment and encrypted model training. In the data alignment phase, the DH-P²FR-PSI protocol is employed to securely match user identities; in the encrypted training phase, the model parameters are jointly optimized under homomorphic encryption.

In the proposed recommendation model, two parties participate: the passive party S, which holds user feature data $D_S = \{x_i^S \mid i = 1,2,\ldots,n\}$, and the active party R, which possesses feature data with behavioral labels $D_R = \{(x_i^R, y_i) \mid i = 1,2,\ldots,n\}$.

The joint training objective is to minimize the following loss function:

$$L(\theta) = -\frac{1}{n}\sum_{i=1}^{n}\left[y_i \log(h_\theta(x_i)) + (1 - y_i)\log(1 - h_\theta(x_i))\right],$$

where the prediction function $h_\theta(x_i)$ is defined as:

$$h_\theta(x_i) = \frac{1}{1 + e^{-\theta^T x_i}}.$$

The gradient of the loss function with respect to parameter θ_j is:

$$\frac{\partial L(\theta)}{\partial \theta_j} = \frac{1}{n} \sum_{i=1}^{n} [h_\theta(x_i) - y_i] \times x_j.$$

Since the activation function involves exponential computation, it is approximated by a Taylor expansion to facilitate partial homomorphic encryption:

$$\frac{1}{1 + e^{-\theta^T x}} = \frac{1}{2} + \frac{1}{4}\theta^T x + O((\theta^T x)^3) \approx \frac{1}{2} + \frac{1}{4}\theta^T x.$$

The gradient can then be reformulated as:

$$\begin{aligned}\frac{\partial L(\theta)}{\partial \theta_j} &\approx \frac{1}{n} \sum_{i=1}^{n} \left[\frac{1}{2} + \frac{1}{4}\theta^T x_i - y_i\right] x_j \\ &\approx \frac{1}{n} \times \begin{pmatrix} X_S^T(\frac{1}{2} + \frac{1}{4}X_S\theta_S + \frac{1}{4}X_R\theta_R - y) \\ X_R^T(\frac{1}{2} + \frac{1}{4}X_S\theta_S + \frac{1}{4}X_R\theta_R - y) \end{pmatrix}.\end{aligned}$$

Let

$$u_S = \frac{1}{4}X_S\theta_S, \quad u_R = \frac{1}{2} + \frac{1}{4}X_R\theta_R - y,$$

then the gradient can be expressed as:

$$\nabla L(\theta) = \frac{1}{n} \begin{pmatrix} X_S^T(u_S + u_R) \\ X_R^T(u_S + u_R) \end{pmatrix}.$$

During model training, both parties S and R independently initialize their parameters θ_S and θ_R, while a third-party coordinator C generates the Paillier key pair and distributes the public key to both parties. Each party computes its intermediate vector (u_S and u_R), encrypts them to obtain $[\![u_S]\!]$ and $[\![u_R]\!]$, and exchanges the ciphertexts. Both parties then compute encrypted gradients locally, add random noise, and send the results to C for decryption. After receiving the decrypted gradients, each party removes its random mask and updates its model parameters accordingly.

This VFL-based framework ensures strong privacy protection while enabling efficient and accurate cross-domain personalized recommendation model training.

5 Evaluation

In this section, we present a comprehensive and detailed performance evaluation of the proposed P^{2}FR-VFL framework and its core component, the DH-P^{2}FR-PSI protocol. Our evaluation focuses on two main aspects: first, through

Algorithm 2: P^{2}FR-VFL

Input: Initialized parameters $t = 1$, θ_S, θ_R.
Output: Personalized recommendation model M.

1 **Passive party S:**
2 Download the global model M.
3 **for** *each epoch* t **do**
4 Compute intermediate representation u_S and obtain ciphertext $[\![u_S]\!]$.
5 Transmit $[\![u_S]\!]$ to party R.
6 Wait to receive $[\![u_R]\!]$ from R.
7 Initialize a random masking term R_S.
8 Compute the encrypted gradient $[\![\frac{\partial L}{\partial \theta_S}]\!] + [\![R_S]\!]$ and send it to the coordinator C.
9 Wait for the decrypted gradient to update θ_S.
10 **end**
11 Update the local model m_S.
12 **Active party R:**
13 Download the global model M.
14 **for** *each epoch* t **do**
15 Wait to receive $[\![u_S]\!]$ from S.
16 Compute local ciphertext $[\![u_R]\!]$ and encrypted partial gradient $[\![\frac{\partial L}{\partial \theta_R}]\!]$.
17 Send $[\![u_R]\!]$ to S.
18 Initialize random masking value R_R.
19 Compute $[\![\frac{\partial L}{\partial \theta_R}]\!] + [\![R_R]\!]$ and send to C.
20 Wait for the decrypted gradient to update θ_R.
21 **end**
22 Update the local model m_R.

micro-benchmark tests, we analyze in detail the computational and communication costs of the DH-P^{2}FR-PSI protocol under varying data scales and compare it with state-of-the-art PSI schemes (as shown in Table 2). Second, we evaluate the end-to-end performance of the P^{2}FR-VFL framework on a real-world recommendation task, focusing on model accuracy and convergence speed (as illustrated in Fig 1), to verify that our method can maintain high model utility while providing advanced privacy protection. We used workstations with CPU: dual Intel Xeon Silver 4314, 32 cores and 64 threads @ 2.4 GHz; memory: 256 GB; operating system: Linux 6.8.0-84-generic (Ubuntu 22.04 series kernel).

5.1 The Evaluation of DH-P^{2}FR-PSI

Table 2 presents a detailed comparison between our protocol and two representative schemes within the DH-P^{2}FR-PSI paradigm—namely, the classical scheme by Ling et al. [15] and the state-of-the-art improved scheme by Ling et al. [16]. It is important to emphasize that although all three schemes follow the DH-P^{2}FR-PSI framework, there exists a key functional difference: in both the classical version in [15] and the improved version in [16], only the Receiver obtains the qualified intersection after the protocol execution, whereas our protocol achieves a symmetric output, ensuring that both the Sender and the Receiver obtain the same intersection results that satisfy the predicate condition.

We benchmarked the three schemes over exponentially increasing dataset sizes (from $N = 2^{10}$ to $N = 2^{20}$). Experimental results clearly show that, in terms of runtime, our scheme (27.56 s at $N = 2^{20}$) achieves highly competitive performance compared to the state-of-the-art improved scheme in [16] (22.40 s), and significantly outperforms the classical Ling et al. [15] scheme (654.62 s). Regarding communication cost, our protocol (342.97 MB at $N = 2^{20}$) is slightly higher than the improved scheme in [16] (284.50 MB). We argue that this moderate increase in overhead is a necessary and fully reasonable cost to achieve symmetric output, i.e., enabling both parties to learn the intersection. In summary, our protocol maintains computational efficiency comparable to the SOTA scheme while providing enhanced functionality (dual-party output), demonstrating strong practical value.

Table 2. Performance Comparison of Protocols

Protocol	Metric	2^{10}	2^{12}	2^{14}	2^{16}	2^{18}	$\mathbf{2^{20}}$
Ling et al. [15]	Running Time (s)	0.58	2.42	10.53	41.32	159.40	654.62
	Communication (MB)	0.21	0.83	3.30	13.10	52.20	208.40
Ling et al. [16]	Running Time (s)	0.05	0.13	0.37	1.26	5.43	22.40
	Communication (MB)	0.48	1.32	4.66	18.00	71.32	284.50
Ours	Running Time (s)	0.06	0.15	0.41	1.49	6.55	27.56
	Communication (MB)	0.60	1.65	5.46	21.54	88.26	342.97

5.2 Model Accuracy

To evaluate the effectiveness and practicality of our P^{2}FR-VFL framework, we compared its model performance against a baseline model trained on plaintext data. Figure 1 shows the variation of model accuracy and loss function with respect to the number of training iterations.

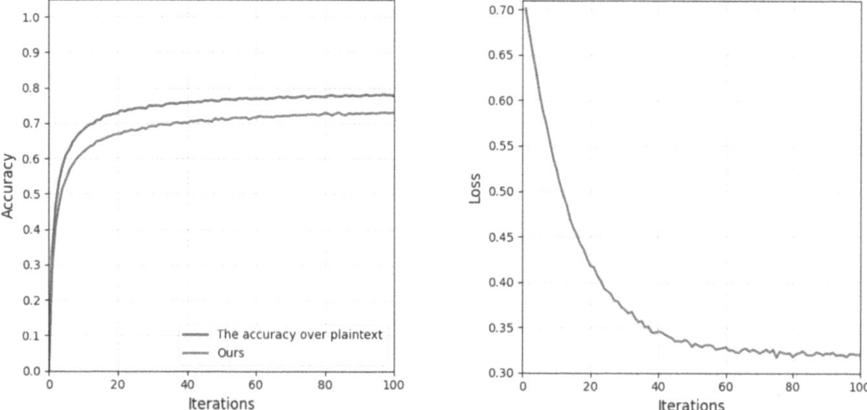

Fig. 1. The left one is the model accuracy of P^{2}FR-VFL and training over the plaintext; the right one is the loss function of P^{2}FR-VFL.

As shown in Fig. 1 (left), the accuracy achieved by our P^{2}FR-VFL framework (green curve) closely matches that of the plaintext baseline model (red curve). Both curves exhibit rapid convergence and stabilize after approximately 40 iterations, reaching comparable final accuracies (around 0.75–0.78). The slight accuracy gap of our privacy-preserving model is primarily attributed to the approximate computations required for privacy protection in VFL training (e.g., the Taylor expansion described in Sect. 4.2). This result strongly demonstrates that our framework achieves model utility comparable to plaintext training while providing strong privacy protection (via P^{2}FR-VFL and encrypted training).

As shown in Fig. 1 (right), the loss function curve of the P^{2}FR-VFL framework exhibits stable and efficient convergence. The loss rapidly decreases from an initial value of about 0.70 and converges to a stable low value (around 0.33) after roughly 60 iterations. This indicates that our VFL training process is both effective and stable, enabling efficient joint model optimization.

6 Conclusion

This paper addresses the limitations of the conventional private set intersection in entity alignment for vertical federated learning by proposing the P^{2}FR-VFL framework. At its core is the novel DH-P^{2}FR-PSI protocol, which not only supports privacy-preserving feature filtering based on thresholds and logical OR operations but also enables bidirectional output, allowing both communicating parties to securely obtain the final intersection, overcoming the restriction in existing schemes where only one party receives the result. Experiments demonstrate that the proposed framework achieves model accuracy comparable to plaintext VFL training while introducing only about 20% additional communication overhead, offering a practical and efficient solution for cross-domain recommender systems requiring flexible collaboration under strict privacy constraints.

Acknowledgments. This work was supported in part by the National Key R&D Program of China (2023YFB3106200), the National Natural Science Foundation of China (62572123 and 62402109).

References

1. Adomavicius, G., Tuzhilin, A.: Toward the next generation of recommender systems: a survey of the state-of-the-art and possible extensions. IEEE Trans. Knowl. Data Eng. **17**(6), 734–749 (2005)
2. He, R., McAuley, J.J.: VBPR: visual Bayesian personalized ranking from implicit feedback. In: AAAI, pp. 144–150. AAAI Press (2016)
3. Ammad-ud-din, M., Ivannikova, E., Khan, S.A., et al.: Federated collaborative filtering for privacy-preserving personalized recommendation system. CoRR, abs/1901.09888 (2019)
4. Kairouz, P., McMahan, H.B., Avent, B., et al.: Advances and open problems in federated learning. Found. Trends Mach. Learn. **14**(1–2), 1–210 (2021)
5. Smith, V., Chiang, C.K., Sanjabi, M., et al.: Federated multi-task learning. In: NIPS, pp. 4424–4434 (2017)
6. Hardy, S., Henecka, W., Ivey-Law, H., et al.: Private federated learning on vertically partitioned data via entity resolution and additively homomorphic encryption. CoRR, abs/1711.10677 (2017)
7. Dong, C., Chen, L., Wen, Z.: When private set intersection meets big data: an efficient and scalable protocol. In: CCS, pp. 789–800. ACM (2013)
8. He, Y., Tan, X., Ni, J., et al.: Differentially private set intersection for asymmetrical ID alignment. IEEE Trans. Inf. Forensics Secur. **17**, 3479–3494 (2022)
9. De Cristofaro, E., Kim, J., Tsudik, G.: Linear-complexity private set intersection protocols secure in malicious model. In: ASIACRYPT. Lecture Notes in Computer Science, vol. 6477, pp. 213–231. Springer (2010)
10. Cheng, K., Fan, T., Jin, Y., et al.: SecureBoost: a lossless federated learning framework. IEEE Intell. Syst. **36**(6), 87–98 (2021)
11. Cai, R., Luo, S.: Enhancing user privacy in personalized recommendation systems. In: CSRSWTC, pp. 1–3. IEEE (2024)
12. Wang, F., Mi, B., Zeng, R.: Efficient private set intersection for vertical federated learning in IOV. In: FCS, pp. 120–130. Springer, Singapore (2024)
13. Chase, M., Miao, P.: Private set intersection in the internet setting from lightweight oblivious PRF. In: CRYPTO (3). Lecture Notes in Computer Science, vol. 12172, pp. 34–63. Springer (2020)
14. Raghuraman, S., Rindal, P.: Blazing fast PSI from improved OKVS and subfield VOLE. In: CCS, pp. 2505–2517. ACM (2022)
15. Ling, G., Tang, F., Cai, C., et al.: P^2FRPSI: privacy-preserving feature retrieved private set intersection. IEEE Trans. Inf. Forensics Secur. **19**, 2201–2216 (2024)
16. Ling, G., Tang, P., Shan, J., et al.: More efficient, privacy-enhanced, and powerful privacy-preserving feature retrieval private set intersection. IEEE Trans. Inf. Forensics Secur. **20**, 4815–4827 (2025)

17. Wu, Y., Kang, Y., Luo, J., et al.: FedCG: leverage conditional GAN for protecting privacy and maintaining competitive performance in federated learning. In: IJCAI, pp. 2334–2340. ijcai.org (2022)
18. Chen, W., Ma, G., Fan, T., et al.: SecureBoost+: a high performance gradient boosting tree framework for large scale vertical federated learning. CoRR, abs/2110.10927 (2021)
19. Yang, Q., Liu, Y., Chen, T., et al.: Federated machine learning: concept and applications. ACM Trans. Intell. Syst. Technol. **10**(2), 12:1–12:19 (2019)
20. Yang, Y., Chen, X., Pan, Y., et al.: OpenVFL: a vertical federated learning framework with stronger privacy-preserving. IEEE Trans. Inf. Forensics Secur. **19**, 9670–9681 (2024)
21. Chen, H., Laine, K., Rindal, P.: Fast private set intersection from homomorphic encryption. In: CCS, pp. 1243–1255. ACM (2017)
22. Chase, M., Miao, P.: Private set intersection in the internet setting from lightweight oblivious PRF. In: CRYPTO (3). Lecture Notes in Computer Science, vol. 12172, pp. 34–63. Springer (2020)
23. Pinkas, B., Schneider, T., Zohner, M.: Scalable private set intersection based on OT extension. ACM Trans. Priv. Secur. **21**(2), 7:1–7:35 (2018)
24. Bienstock, A., Patel, S., Seo, J.Y., et al.: Near-optimal oblivious key-value stores for efficient psi, PSU and volume-hiding multi-maps. In: USENIX Security Symposium, pp. 301–318. USENIX Association (2023)
25. Canetti, R.: Decisional Diffie-Hellman assumption. In: Encyclopedia of Cryptography and Security. Springer (2005)
26. Hanzlik, L., Paracucchi, E., Zanotto, R.: Non-interactive blind signatures from RSA assumption and more. In: EUROCRYPT (2). Lecture Notes in Computer Science, vol. 15602, pp. 365–394. Springer (2025)
27. Rindal, P., Schoppmann, P.: VOLE-PSI: fast OPRF and circuit-psi from vector-ole. In: EUROCRYPT (2). Lecture Notes in Computer Science, vol. 12697, pp. 901–930. Springer (2021)
28. Catalano, D., Gennaro, R., Howgrave-Graham, N., et al.: Paillier's cryptosystem revisited. In: CCS, pp. 206–214. ACM (2001)
29. Sun, W., Yan, R., Jin, R., et al.: FedAlign: federated model alignment via data-free knowledge distillation for machine fault diagnosis. IEEE Trans. Instrum. Meas. **73**, 1–12 (2024)
30. Blass, E.-O., Noubir, G.: Assumption-free fuzzy PSI via predicate encryption. IACR Cryptol. ePrint Arch. 217 (2025)
31. Linden, G., Smith, B., York, J.: Amazon.com recommendations: item-to-item collaborative filtering. IEEE Internet Comput. **7**(1), 76–80 (2003)
32. Koren, Y., Bell, R.M., Volinsky, C.: Matrix factorization techniques for recommender systems. Computer **42**(8), 30–37 (2009)
33. Jonathan Takeshita, Ryan Karl, Alamin Mohammed, et al. Provably secure contact tracing with conditional private set intersection. In: SecureComm (1). Lecture Notes of the Institute for Computer Sciences, Social Informatics and Telecommunications Engineering, vol. 398, pp. 352–373. Springer (2021)
34. Chen, Y., Nguyen, P.Q.: Faster algorithms for approximate common divisors: breaking fully-homomorphic-encryption challenges over the integers. In: EUROCRYPT. Lecture Notes in Computer Science, vol. 7237, pp. 502–519. Springer (2012)

35. Rindal, P., Rosulek, M.: Improved private set intersection against malicious adversaries. In: EUROCRYPT (1). Lecture Notes in Computer Science, vol. 10210, pp. 235–259 (2017)
36. Pagh, R., Rodler, F.F.: Cuckoo hashing. In: ESA. Lecture Notes in Computer Science, vol. 2161, pp. 121–133. Springer (2001)
37. Pinkas, B., Schneider, T., Tkachenko, O., et al.: Efficient circuit-based PSI with linear communication. In: EUROCRYPT, vol. 11477, pp. 122–153. Springer (2019)

Performance Evaluation of Parallel Inference Pipeline for Multi-model Processing on Edge Devices

So-Yeon Lee[1], Tae-Jun Yoon[2], and Dae-Young Kim[2](✉)

[1] Department of Software Convergence, Soonchunhyang University, Asan 31538, Korea
lsy8647@sch.ac.kr

[2] Department of Computer Software Engineering, Soonchunhyang University, Asan 31538, Korea
{20214004,dyoung.kim}@sch.ac.kr

Abstract. Efficient recycling of transparent PET bottles necessitates a multi-model AI system capable of concurrently performing material classification and component detection. However, executing multiple models sequentially on resource-constrained edge devices results in cumulative inference times. In this paper, we address this challenge by implementing and evaluating a GStreamer-based parallel inference pipeline on a Raspberry Pi CM 5 equipped with a Hailo-8 AI accelerator. The implemented parallel architecture replicates input frames into two independent branches, enabling simultaneous execution of a PET/CAN classification model and a cap/ring/label detection model. Experimental results demonstrate that the parallel pipeline reduced the average frame processing time by 11.3% (from 29.50 ms to 26.17 ms) compared to sequential processing, thereby improving overall processing efficiency. This finding suggests that the parallel processing architecture mitigates inefficient idle times during multi-model execution, enabling stable real-time multi-task processing even in resource-constrained embedded environments.

Keywords: Edge AI · Hailo-8 · Multi-Model System · Parallel Inference · Real-time Object Detection · Waste Sorting

1 Introduction

As environmental protection and resource circulation gain global importance, the development of accurate automated waste-sorting systems has emerged as a key policy priority. Transparent PET bottles, in particular, represent a high-value recyclable resource; however, contamination and misclassification during collection and sorting processes continue to reduce recycling efficiency [1]. To establish an effective recycling workflow, it is essential not only to detect PET bottles themselves but also to identify fine-grained components—such as caps, rings, and labels—whose presence directly affects the quality of recycling. This requires an intelligent system capable of performing multiple tasks simultaneously, including multi-object detection, material classification, and component-level recognition.

Y. Xiang and J. Shen (Eds.): ML4CS 2025, LNCS 16456, pp. 251–260, 2026.
https://doi.org/10.1007/978-981-95-7820-7_17

For such a multi-model AI model to be practically deployed in real recycling facilities, real-time operation on embedded hardware is indispensable. In a previous study [2], our research team demonstrated that combining a Hailo-8 AI inference accelerator with a Raspberry Pi 5 can improve the inference speed of a YOLOv8n object detection model to an average of 27.18 FPS, thereby validating the feasibility of real-time processing in resource-constrained embedded environments. However, when the "PET/CAN classification" model and the "component detection" model are executed sequentially in an actual system, the inference time of each model accumulates, resulting in increased end-to-end latency. In real-time video processing systems, even a few milliseconds of additional delay per frame can significantly impact throughput and responsiveness; thus, it is crucial to efficiently integrate multiple models and optimize hardware resource utilization.

This study analyzes the frame-level latency issues inherent in sequential multi-model pipelines and implements a GStreamer-based parallel processing approach to mitigate these limitations. The proposed parallel inference pipeline duplicates the input video frames into two independent branches, delivering them concurrently to the PET/CAN classifier and the component detection model. The Hailo-8 accelerator performs inference on both models in parallel, while the GStreamer pipeline merges their outputs in real time to produce the final result. Through this mechanism, we evaluate the latency reduction achieved compared with the sequential method and demonstrate the potential scalability of the approach toward more complex multi-model scenarios.

The remainder of this paper is organized as follows: Sect. 2 reviews related work, Sect. 3 describes the overall system architecture and the design of the parallel inference pipeline, Sect. 4 presents the experimental setup and performance evaluation, and Sect. 5 concludes the paper.

2 Related Work

2.1 The Need for AI System and Multi-Stage Recognition in Transparent Plastic Recycling

In recent years, the waste management sector has accelerated automation and intelligence through integration with artificial intelligence [3–6]. Lubongo et al. [7] introduced recent trends in applying ML/AI to plastic recycling for identification and sorting, demonstrating that these technologies can significantly enhance the efficiency of sorting and separation processes. However, in actual recycling sites, AI-based recognition systems still face unresolved technical challenges. Cheng et al. [8] developed a YOLOv7-based robotic solution for recycling beverage containers (PET, cans, glass bottles), but explicitly noted limitations in distinguishing unlabeled transparent PET bottles from transparent glass bottles using AI vision alone. Similarly, Rosca et al. [9] proposed a recycling AIoT solution operating in distributed edge environments, implementing a dual recognition algorithm (PBIA) combining AI vision and weight sensors.

These prior studies demonstrate the limitations of single AI models in the transparent plastic recycling domain, supporting the need for complex recognition architectures.

Building upon this, this study implements a multi-model system integrating material classification (PET/CAN) and component detection (cap, ring, label). Furthermore, it experimentally verifies the performance improvement effects of a parallel processing approach for efficiently executing this multi-model in resource-constrained edge environments.

2.2 Edge AI Acceleration and Parallel Inference Pipeline

With the increasing demand for real-time AI inference, hardware accelerator technologies and optimization methodologies enabling efficient inference on edge devices are rapidly advancing. Particularly in resource-constrained environments, edge inference requires optimization across various aspects, including model design, model compression, compilation optimization, and collaborative inference [10].

However, when applying complex model architectures to edge environments, one faces the challenge of managing the end-to-end latency of the entire pipeline, beyond simply compressing the model. Previous studies have shown limitations, either relying on high-performance local PCs to solve this problem or accepting bottlenecks by using sequential processing approaches.

Xie et al. [11] achieved a fast speed of 62FPS by implementing a single model (Yolov8n) for a plastic bottle sorting robot via local processing. However, this performance was only possible by leveraging high-spec desktop PC resources—an Intel i7 CPU and NVIDIA GeForce GTX 1650 GPU—which fundamentally differs from the low-power/resource-constrained edge environments targeted by this research. Terence et al. [12] implemented a sequential pipeline to enhance small object detection performance on a Raspberry Pi 5 + Hailo-8 environment. This involved first increasing image resolution using the ESPCN model, followed by object detection using the YOLOv8n model. This achieved approximately 27FPS, comparable to the single model execution performance on the same hardware in our team's prior work. This demonstrates the structural limitation where latency accumulates when processing multi-models sequentially.

Building upon the latency accumulation issues identified in sequential processing approaches in prior studies, this research implements a multi-model execution method on a Raspberry Pi CM 5 + Hailo-8 environment using parallel processing with GStreamer. It quantitatively evaluates the resulting improvement in latency.

3 System Design and Architecture

3.1 System Overview

This study implements a multi-model parallel inference system for real-time transparent PET bottle recycling in edge environments. The system's hardware is based on the Raspberry Pi CM 5, utilizing the Hailo-8 AI accelerator connected via PCIe interface for AI inference acceleration. The Hailo-8 is a low-power NPU designed for edge devices, delivering high performance of up to 26 TOPS [13]. In prior studies, Hailo-8 demonstrated 12% higher accuracy and 20 ms shorter latency compared to NVIDIA Jetson Orin Nano. When integrated with Raspberry Pi 5, it achieved stable real-time performance running the YOLOv8m model at 20FPS, outperforming Google Coral TPU, thereby proving its superior capability [14, 15].

The software framework for this research is based on GStreamer. GStreamer is a framework for creating media processing pipelines, optimized for constructing complex video data flows by modularly connecting a series of plugins [16]. In this study, both the sequential pipeline and parallel pipeline used for comparison were implemented using GStreamer, enabling comparative analysis of performance evaluation based on structural differences in the pipelines.

The AI models used were (1) a PET/CAN material classification model and (2) a Cap/Ring/Label component detection model, both based on the YOLOv8n architecture. YOLOv8n is a lightweight model suitable for real-time object recognition on resource-constrained platforms. Its real-time performance of 27.18 FPS was validated in our team's prior research on a Raspberry Pi CM 5 + Hailo-8 environment.

3.2 Sequential Pipeline Architecture

This study experimentally verifies whether the latency accumulation issue caused by sequential execution of dual models in resource-constrained edge environments can be mitigated through parallel processing. First, we analyze the structure and limitations of the existing sequential processing pipeline and compare performance through parallel processing implementation using GStreamer.

Figure 1 depicts the conventional sequential pipeline structure, where video frames are processed sequentially through a single pipeline. Each frame of the input video undergoes preprocessing before being passed to the classification model (Model A). Upon completion of Model A's inference, the frame and inference result are fed as input to the detection model (Model B). Finally, the outputs from both models are merged and output.

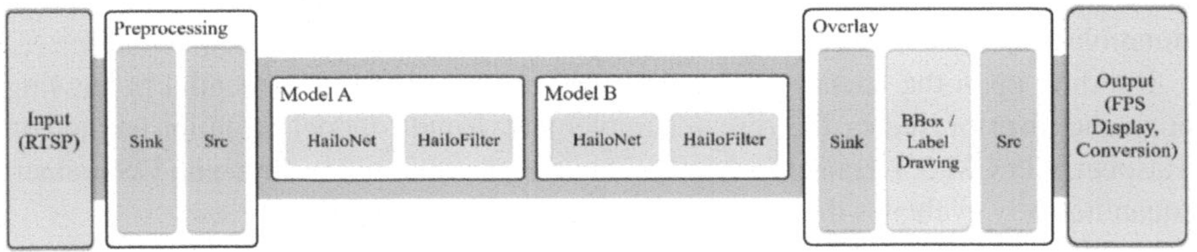

Fig. 1. GStreamer-based sequential pipeline.

The total processing delay of the sequential pipeline is a structure where the inference times of the two models are accumulated:

$$T_{total} \approx T_{modelA} + T_{modelB} + T_{overhead} \quad (1)$$

where T_{modelA} is the classification inference time, T_{modelB} is the detection inference time, and $T_{overhead}$ includes preprocessing and data transfer overhead.

This approach has the advantage of a simple data flow and intuitive implementation. However, it has the limitation that during data transfer between models, frames repeatedly move between CPU memory and NPU memory, accumulating DMA (Direct Memory Access) transfer delays and memory access overhead. Specifically, since each frame sequentially passes through Model A and Model B, the total processing delay increases as the sum of the inference times for both models and the overhead. Consequently, the overall system throughput is lower compared to a parallel pipeline structure, and efficiency is reduced in environments requiring real-time processing.

3.3 Parallel Pipeline Architecture

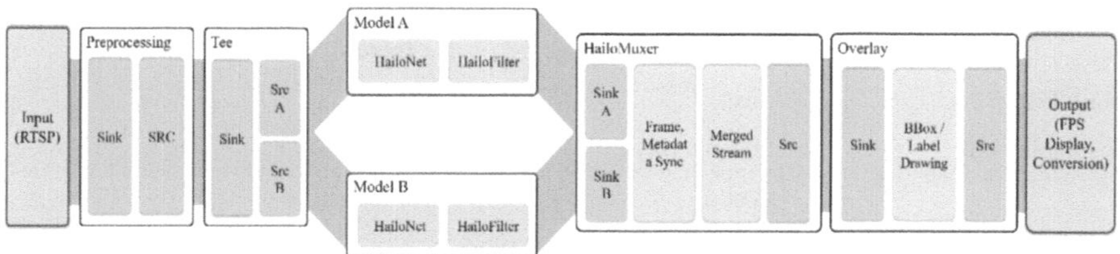

Fig. 2. GStreamer-based parallel pipeline.

To alleviate bottlenecks in the sequential pipeline, a parallel inference pipeline as shown in Fig. 2 was implemented. In this architecture, after preprocessing, the input frame is replicated into two independent branches using GStreamer's tee element. The replicated frames are simultaneously fed into the classification model (Model A) and the detection model (Model B), where both models perform inference in parallel from their respective queues. The inference results from both models are merged into a single frame stream via the HailoMuxer element.

$$T_{total} \approx \max(T_{modelA}, T_{modelB}) + T_{overhead} \tag{2}$$

where $max()$ indicates that the longer inference time dominates, rather than the sum of both models.

This parallel structure mitigates the accumulation of inference time that occurs in sequential structures by temporally overlapping the inference operations and DMA transfers of the two models.

The pipeline was implemented with specific parameter configuration to ensure stable real-time processing. Table 1 summarizes the key settings for each component.

The latency parameter minimizes initial network buffering delay for RTSP stream ingestion. The qos = False setting prevents frame drops during temporary processing delays, ensuring all frames are processed. The HailoMuxer element synchronizes outputs from both model branches by matching frame timestamps. When one model completes inference earlier, the muxer briefly holds that result until the corresponding frame from the other branch arrives, introducing minimal additional latency (typically < 2 ms based on our measurements).

Table 1. Key parameter settings for the parallel inference pipeline

Category	Component	Specification/Version
rtspsrc	latency	1 ms
	codec	H.265
Preprocessing	oputput format	video/x-raw
HailoNet	resolution	640x640
	Batch-size	1
	Force-writable	Table
HailoFilter	qos	
fpsdisplaysink	text-overlay	True
	sync	False

4 Experiments and Results

4.1 Experimental Setup

This study conducted experiments by connecting a Raspberry Pi CM 5 and a Hailo-8 accelerator via a PCIe interface. The input video used an RTSP stream with a resolution of 1280x720, resized to 640x640 to match the YOLOv8n model's training resolution. This preprocessing step is standard practice for YOLO-based models and maintains consistency with the model's learned feature scales. Both the PET/CAN classification model and the Cap/Ring/Label detection model are based on the YOLOv8n architecture. They were converted to HEF[1] format with 8-bit quantization applied via the Hailo Dataflow Compiler and quantized using the Random Calibration method. The main specifications of the experimental environment are shown in Table 1. Performance was compared under identical conditions for both the sequential pipeline and the parallel pipeline.

In this experiment, the processing speed per frame for sequential and parallel pipelines was measured for the interval from the completion of preprocessing to just before the start of overlay (Inference Latency). To eliminate variance caused by the initial warm-up phase, the first 100 frames were excluded from the measurement. Subsequently, the mean, standard deviation, median, P95 percentile, and P99 percentile were calculated for the remaining 1,000 frames.

4.2 Performance Evaluation

Table 2 compares the inference latency measurement results for the two pipelines. The sequential pipeline had an average frame processing time of 29.50 ms, a standard deviation of 1.14 ms, and a median of 29.44 ms. P95 and P99 were measured at 31.34 ms

[1] HEF (Hailo Executable Format): A compiled and optimized binary format specifically designed for inference execution on Hailo NPUs, generated by the Hailo Dataflow Compiler.

Table 2. Specifications of the experimental environment.

Category	Component	Specification/Version
Hardware	Processor	Raspberry Pi CM5
	AI Accelerator	Hailo-8 (PCIe interface)
OS	OS	Debian GNU/Linux 12
Software	Gstreamer	1.22.0
	HailoRT	4.20.0
	Python	3.11.2
Input Video	Resolution/Format	1280 × 720 RTSP Stream
Model	Model A/Model B	Yolov8n (optimized HEF)

and 33.42 ms, respectively. In contrast, the parallel pipeline showed an average of 26.17 ms, a standard deviation of 2.85 ms, a median of 27.05 ms, P95 of 28.93 ms, and P99 of 32.26 ms (Table 3).

Table 3. Statistical results for the inference latency of sequential and parallel pipelines.

Pipeline	Mean (ms)	Std (ms)	P50 (ms)	P95 (ms)	P99 (ms)
Sequential	29.50	1.14	29.44	31.34	33.42
Parallel	26.17	2.85	27.05	28.93	32.26

Comparing the two architectures, the parallel pipeline achieved an average frame processing delay reduction of approximately 11.3% compared to the sequential architecture. This is attributed to the overlapping execution of the inference operations for both models and the DMA transfer phase in the parallel architecture.

Furthermore, from a standard deviation perspective, the parallel pipeline exhibited slightly higher variance than the sequential structure. This is interpreted as frame-to-frame variation arising from the asynchronous, cross-execution of the two models' inferences. Nevertheless, the parallel pipeline maintained low average and median delays, confirming its superior overall processing efficiency.

To evaluate long-term stability, a 10-h continuous operation test was conducted on the parallel pipeline. As shown in Fig. 3, the inference latency remained stable between 25–28 ms after initial warm-up, with no performance degradation observed throughout the test period. The Hailo-8 operating temperature stabilized in the range of 51–55 °C, demonstrating effective thermal management and validating the system's capability for continuous operation.

Figure 4 presents a multi-faceted comparison of the two pipelines' performance. (a) Total System Latency and (b) Inference Latency measurements both showed the parallel pipeline improved by approximately 11%. (c) Converting this to FPS, it improved from 34.1 FPS for sequential to 37.9 FPS for parallel, an increase of about 11.1%. (d)

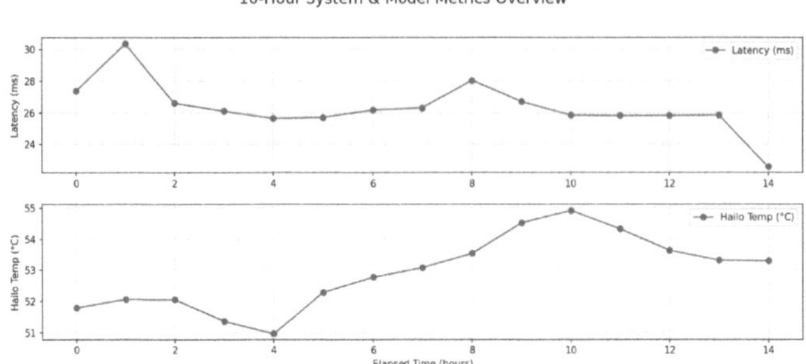

Fig. 3. Long-term stability evaluation over 10-h continuous operation

Regarding system resource utilization, the parallel pipeline showed an 8.4% increase in CPU usage but only a 0.2% increase in memory usage, maintaining nearly identical levels.

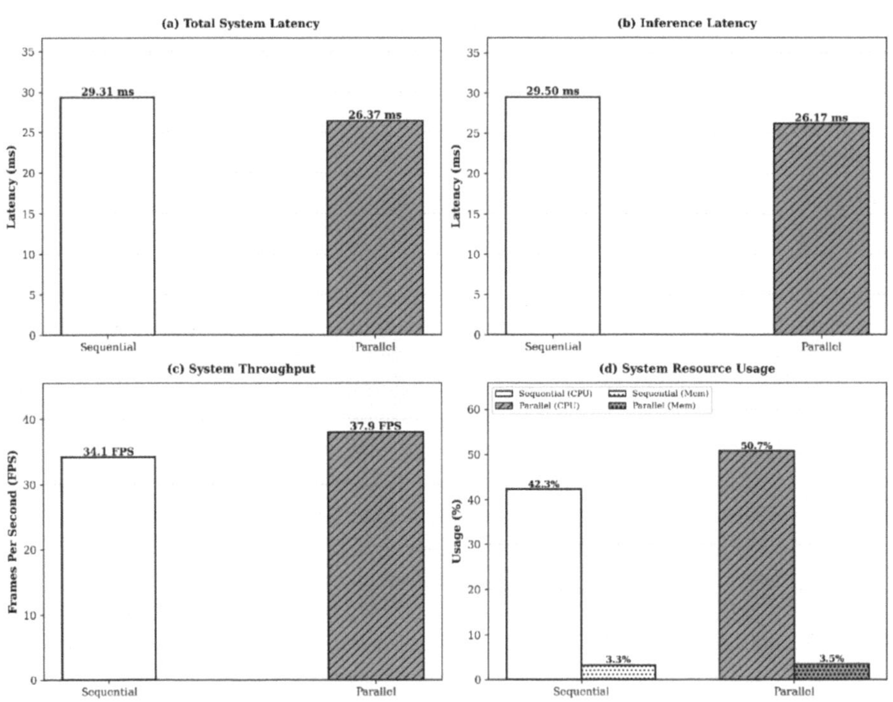

Fig. 4. Comparative analysis of sequential and parallel pipelines across key metrics: (a) Total System Latency, (b) Inference Latency, (c) System Throughput, and (d) System Resource Usage.

5 Conclusion

This study analyzes the cumulative delay problem caused by sequential processing during multi-model inference in resource-constrained edge environments. It experimentally verifies the performance improvement achieved by implementing a GStreamer-based parallel processing pipeline. Experiments conducted on Raspberry Pi CM 5 and Hailo-8 environments showed that the parallel pipeline reduced the average inference latency per frame by 11.3% (3.33 ms) compared to sequential processing. This performance is attributed to the parallel overlap of both models' inference operations and DMA transfer processes within the GStreamer pipeline. This structure minimizes idle time of the NPU and related system resources that occurred during sequential processing, maximizing overall processing efficiency.

While this study focused on multi-model parallel inference, it can be extended to multi-model scenarios involving three or more models for application in more complex industrial environments. This research demonstrates the significance of a parallel processing architecture combining GStreamer and hardware accelerators as a key implementation approach capable of simultaneously ensuring real-time performance and efficiency in diverse industrial edge AI systems.

Acknowledgments. This work was funded by BK21 FOUR (Fostering Outstanding Universities for Research) (No. 5199990914048) and This research was supported by the MSIT (Ministry of Science, ICT), Korea, under the National Program for Excellence in SW, supervised by the IITP (Institute of Information & communications Technology Planning & Evaluation) in 2025 (2021-0-01399).

References

1. Basuhi, R., et al.: Evaluating strategies to increase PET bottle recycling in the United States. J. Ind. Ecol. **28**(4), 916–927 (2024). https://doi.org/10.1111/jiec.13496
2. Yoon, T.J., Jeong, Y.H., Lee, S.Y., Kim, D.: A Hailo-8-based lightweight object detection system for transparent PET bottle separation. In: Summer Annual Conference of IEIE, Jeju, Korea, pp. 4662–4665 (2025)
3. Satheesh, S., et al.: AI-driven sustainable waste management for enhancing quality of life. In: 2025 International Conference on Emerging Information Technology and Engineering Solutions (EITES), pp. 166–172. IEEE, Pune (2025), https://doi.org/10.1109/EITES66543.2025.00037
4. Tiwari, A., et al.: Smart waste management system using AR and IoT with AI. In: 2025 International Conference on Artificial Intelligence and Data Engineering (AIDE), pp. 201–206. IEEE, Nitte (2025). https://doi.org/10.1109/AIDE64228.2025.10987435
5. Kulkarineetham, S., et al.: Leveraging AI chatbots to foster engaged community waste management: a case study of Takhian Tia community. In: 2025 Joint International Conference on Digital Arts, Media and Technology with ECTI Northern Section Conference on Electrical, Electronics, Computer and Telecommunications Engineering (ECTI DAMT & NCON), pp. 499–50. IEEE, Nan (2025). https://doi.org/10.1109/ECTIDAMTNCON64748.2025.10961958

6. Suchdeo, E., Rajnish, R.: AI-driven waste classification model for recycling applications using YOLOv1. In: 2025 6th International Conference on Intelligent Communication Technologies and Virtual Mobile Networks (ICICV), pp. 1003–1008. IEEE, Tirunelveli (2025), https://doi.org/10.1109/ICICV64824.2025.11085860
7. Lubongo, C., Bin Daej, M.A.A., Alexandridis, P.: Recent developments in technology for sorting plastic for recycling: the emergence of artificial intelligence and the rise of the robots. Recycling **9**(4), 59 (2024). https://doi.org/10.3390/recycling9040059
8. Cheng, T., et al.: Optimizing waste sorting for sustainability: an AI-powered robotic solution for beverage container recycling. Sustainability **16**(23), 10155 (2024). https://doi.org/10.3390/su162310155
9. Rosca, C.-M., Stancu, A.: Innovative AIoT solutions for PET waste collection in the circular economy towards a sustainable future. Appl. Sci. **15**(13), 7353 (2025). https://doi.org/10.3390/app15137353
10. Lechner, M., Jantsch, A.: Hardware-aware pruning for efficient inference on embedded devices. IEEE Access **13**, 189358–189371 (2025). https://doi.org/10.1109/ACCESS.2025.3628133.keywords
11. Xie, S., et al.: Study on efficient recognition and accurate localization method of waste plastic bottles based on deep learning. Eco. Inform. **86**, 103020 (2025). https://doi.org/10.1016/j.ecoinf.2025.10302
12. Terence, E., et al.: Real-time object detection enhancement using ESPCN with ISA on edge devices. In: 2025 11th International Conference on Electrical Energy Systems (ICEES), pp. 217–222. IEEE, Chennai (2025). https://doi.org/10.1109/ICEES67011.2025.11212942
13. Pereira, G.P., Chaari, M.Z.: A look into the performance of the raspberry Pi AI HAT+ for computer vision applications. In: 2025 11th International Conference on Communication and Signal Processing (ICCSP), pp. 1620–1625. IEEE, Melmaruvathur (2025). https://doi.org/10.1109/ICCSP64183.2025.11089235
14. Achmadiah, M.N., et al.: Fast person detection using YOLOX with AI accelerator for train station safety. In: 2024 International Electronics Symposium (IES), pp. 504–509. IEEE, Denpasar (2024). https://doi.org/10.1109/IES63037.2024.10665874
15. Ponneeshwaran, C., et al.: Integrating edge AI and IoT: a deep learning approach to safe guard crops from wildlife threats. In: 2025 9th International Conference on Inventive Systems and Control (ICISC), pp. 909–916, IEEE, Coimbatore (2025). https://doi.org/10.1109/ICISC65841.2025.11187877
16. Sanderson, J., et al.: Integrating Gstreamer with Xilinx's ZCU 104 edge platform for real-time intelligent image enhancement. In: 2023 IEEE 66th International Midwest Symposium on Circuits and Slystems (MWSCAS), pp. 639–643. IEEE, Tempe (2023). https://doi.org/10.1109/MWSCAS57524.2023.10406078

Multi-authority Attribute-Based Access Control with Dynamic Policy Updates for Federated Learning

Jialu Wang[1], Huijie Yang[1,2(✉)], Jingang Li[1,2], and Wenying Zheng[1]

[1] School of Information Science and Engineering (School of Cyber Science and Technology), Zhejiang Sci-Tech University, Hangzhou 310018, China
hjyang3086@gmail.com

[2] The State Key Laboratory of Blockchain and Data Security, Zhejiang University, Hangzhou, China

Abstract. Federated Learning (FL) has become a key paradigm for privacy-preserving collaborative machine learning, especially in sensitive fields such as medical imaging. However, large-scale, cross-institutional FL deployments still struggle with fine-grained access control, as most existing frameworks rely on static security policies that cannot adapt to participant churn or evolving regulatory requirements.

To overcome these scalability and flexibility limitations, this paper presents a dynamic access control framework for FL based on Multi-Authority Attribute-Based Encryption (MA-ABE). We design a multi-attribute management architecture that enforces granular authorization over both local updates and global model parameters. Central to the framework is a policy-token mechanism that allows dynamic policy updates based on contextual changes without incurring high-cost re-encryption or disrupting training. We further introduce a context-aware key generation protocol to ensure secure, seamless policy transitions.

Formal analysis shows that the scheme achieves CPA semantic security and resists collusion attacks. Experiments demonstrate that our protocol significantly reduces computational, communication, and storage overheads compared to state-of-the-art approaches, offering a practical and robust foundation for secure collaborative learning in dynamic environments.

Keywords: Federated Learning · Attribute-Based Encryption · Access Control · Medical Imaging · Dynamic Policy Updates

1 Introduction

Federated Learning (FL) has become a leading paradigm for privacy-preserving machine learning [8], enabling collaborative model training while maintaining data sovereignty. By keeping data local and aggregating only intermediate results, FL mitigates risks [5] associated with centralized data collection and is widely applied in domains with strict privacy constraints [26].

Y. Xiang and J. Shen (Eds.): ML4CS 2025, LNCS 16456, pp. 261–282, 2026.
https://doi.org/10.1007/978-981-95-7820-7_18

Its utility is evident across high-stakes settings: financial institutions jointly build fraud detection models without revealing transaction logs, and hospitals enhance diagnostic models while complying with regulations such as HIPAA and GDPR. Yet, real-world cross-silo FL deployments face persistent challenges in achieving fine-grained access control [12].

Conventional FL frameworks [25] adopt coarse-grained authorization, granting participants broad access to global model parameters once admitted, thereby violating the Principle of Least Privilege. In settings such as medical consortia, departments should only obtain domain-relevant updates; unrestricted access introduces compliance risks and broadens the attack surface.

Existing security solutions further rely on static cryptographic policies that cannot accommodate dynamic environments. Long-term FL scenarios often involve participant churn and evolving regulations, but adapting to these changes typically demands costly re-encryption or even retraining, undermining system flexibility.

To address these limitations, this paper proposes the **Attribute-Driven Dynamic Federated Learning Security Protocol (AD-DFLSP)**, a dynamic, privacy-preserving FL framework based on Multi-Authority Attribute-Based Encryption (MA-ABE). [6,15] We design a multi-dimensional attribute management framework that enforces differentiated access to model parameters and introduce a policy-token mechanism enabling seamless policy updates without interrupting training. Formal security analysis confirms CPA semantic security and strong collusion resistance, while experiments show notable reductions in computational and communication overhead compared to state-of-the-art schemes [24].

1.1 Motivation

While Federated Learning (FL) has demonstrated substantial potential in privacy-sensitive domains such as collaborative medical imaging, bridging the gap between theoretical frameworks and real-world deployment remains challenging. Practical cross-institutional collaborations face inherent conflicts between data utility, system flexibility, and rigorous security. Specifically, we identify three fundamental limitations in existing approaches:

- **Federated Learning with Coarse-Grained Access Control:** Current FL frameworks predominantly rely on monolithic authorization mechanisms. Once an institution is authenticated, it typically gains unrestricted access to the global model and all intermediate parameters. This coarse-grained "all-or-nothing" model violates the *Principle of Least Privilege*. It fails to distinguish between participants based on data sensitivity levels, domain expertise, or regulatory clearance. Consequently, participants may access model components irrelevant to their specific contributions, unnecessarily expanding the attack surface for model inversion or inference attacks.
- **Incompatibility with Dynamic Environments:** Conventional secure FL systems generally enforce static cryptographic policies that are immutable

once initialized. This rigidity is ill-suited for long-term collaborative training, where participant turnover is common and compliance regulations or clinical objectives may evolve over time. In such dynamic scenarios, existing static schemes cannot accommodate policy updates or attribute revocation without resetting the system or incurring prohibitive computational costs. This lack of temporal adaptability severely limits the resilience and scalability of FL in practical lifecycles.

- **High Overhead of Cryptographic Enforcement:** Achieving robust security in FL often necessitates complex primitives, such as Homomorphic Encryption (HE) or Secure Multi-Party Computation (MPC). However, these techniques introduce significant computational and communication latency, which is particularly detrimental given the iterative, high-frequency communication nature of FL training. There is a critical lack of lightweight security designs that can provide strong cryptographic guarantees without creating bottlenecks on resource-constrained edge devices. Balancing this trade-off between rigorous security and training efficiency remains a pressing engineering challenge.

1.2 Contributions

To address the aforementioned challenges, this paper makes the following key contributions:

- **Fine-Grained Access Control Framework for Federated Learning:** We construct a comprehensive access control architecture that tightly integrates Multi-Authority Attribute-Based Encryption (MA-ABE) with the FL training lifecycle. By defining a unified attribute universe—encompassing dimensions such as institutional role, data quality, and privacy clearance—we encapsulate global model parameters and local gradients as encrypted resources. To ensure robustness and decentralization, we incorporate a (t, n) threshold secret sharing scheme for authority management. This design strictly enforces the *Principle of Least Privilege*, ensuring that participants only decrypt model components necessary for their specific sub-tasks, thereby mitigating the risks of over-privileged access.
- **Dynamic Policy Enforcement Mechanism with Zero Re-Encryption:** We devise a novel dynamic policy update protocol utilizing *policy tokens* and *context-aware key generation*. This mechanism allows for the adaptive evolution of access control policies in response to real-time events—such as regulatory changes or participant churn—without interrupting the training process. Crucially, our design eliminates the need for computationally expensive re-encryption of historical data or model parameters when policies change. Furthermore, we embed version control and digital signatures within policy tokens to guarantee the integrity, authenticity, and non-repudiation of policy updates in dynamic environments.
- **Rigorous Security Analysis and System Implementation:** We provide a formal security proof demonstrating that the proposed scheme achieves Indistinguishability under Chosen-Plaintext Attacks (IND-CPA) and offers

robust resistance against collusion attacks between malicious users and authorities. We further implement a fully functional prototype and conduct extensive experiments. The evaluation results confirm that our protocol significantly reduces computational complexity, communication bandwidth, and storage overhead compared to state-of-the-art benchmarks, validating its practicality for resource-constrained, privacy-critical FL deployments.

1.3 Related Work

Federated Learning (FL) establishes a distributed machine learning paradigm where the **FedAvg protocol** [1] serves as the foundation, enabling collaborative training of a global model while upholding the principle of **data locality** ("data remains local, model moves"). Despite this inherent privacy advantage, the basic FL architecture remains vulnerable to privacy leakage risks, particularly through model updates. Early research focused on mitigating these risks via cryptographic and perturbation methods. **Differential Privacy (DP)** [14] introduces noise into gradient updates to provide formal privacy guarantees. However, this approach, as demonstrated in medical image analysis, often leads to a significant degradation in model accuracy [13]. Alternatively, cryptographic techniques such as **Homomorphic Encryption (HE)** have been explored to enable secure aggregation over encrypted parameters [3], although the consensus remains that the substantial computational overhead of HE schemes limits their practical deployment [4]. The **Secure Aggregation protocol** [11] protects individual model updates cryptographically; yet, this method notably lacks mechanisms to control access to the final aggregated model after decryption [27].

While the aforementioned approaches strengthen privacy against external adversaries, they fundamentally overlook the necessity for **intra-participant access control** within the FL ecosystem. Once enrolled, participants typically receive an undifferentiated level of access to model updates, irrespective of their institutional role, trust level, or data sensitivity. This monolithic permission management introduces unnecessary exposure and creates vectors for potential misuse of shared model information.

To enforce granular access policies, researchers have integrated **Attribute-Based Encryption (ABE)** into FL. Zhang et al. [10] applied Ciphertext-Policy ABE (CP-ABE) to encrypt the global model, enabling attribute-based access rights. However, their reliance on a **single centralized trust authority** renders the scheme unsuitable for decentralized, cross-institutional collaborations. Recent works in cloud computing and car-hailing services have demonstrated the feasibility of dynamic authorization mechanisms [19,20,22], but these approaches have not been adapted to the federated learning context. [23] Liu et al. [17] addressed this by proposing a **Multi-Authority ABE (MA-ABE)**-based FL framework, successfully eliminating centralized trust by distributing attribute management. Despite this advancement, their scheme, similar to subsequent optimizations focusing on efficiency [7], maintained **static policies** throughout the training period. These efforts, while resolving distributed trust, assume fixed access rules—an assumption highly impractical for real-world dynamic FL deployments.

The development of ABE itself provides the requisite cryptographic foundation for policy-driven access control in FL. Originating with **Fuzzy Identity-Based Encryption** [2], ABE evolved through the proposals of **Key-Policy ABE (KP-ABE)** and **Ciphertext-Policy ABE (CP-ABE)** [4,28], forming the basis of modern constructions. The inherent limitation of the single-authority structure was first addressed by Chase [9] with the introduction of MA-ABE. This concept achieved a truly decentralized realization by Lewko and Waters [16] using the **dual-system encryption technique**, eliminating the requirement for authority coordination. Subsequent work by Rouselakis and Waters [18] further developed efficient MA-ABE schemes over prime-order groups, albeit achieving only selective security. Crucially, while these cryptographic advances laid the essential groundwork for policy-controlled FL, they universally assume **static access policies**. This critical constraint severely limits their applicability to long-term federated learning tasks that inherently demand continuous policy adaptability and governance evolution.

In summary, research in privacy-preserving federated learning has made significant strides, transitioning from general encryption to policy-driven access control, with MA-ABE successfully resolving the distributed trust issue. While recent advances in cloud security have introduced verifiable and dynamic authorization mechanisms [19,21], **nevertheless, existing MA-ABE schemes for FL** [7,10,17] **share a critical, unifying limitation: the static nature of their access policies.** In long-term collaborations, such as medical consortia, where participant roles or data governance regulations change frequently, current static methods are forced to either tolerate outdated policies or require the interruption of training for computationally prohibitive global re-encryption. This rigidity is infeasible in practice. Therefore, there is an **urgent and unmet need** for a MA-ABE–based federated learning framework that supports secure and **dynamic policy updates** while preserving training continuity and efficiency—a gap that this paper is strategically designed to fill.

2 Preliminaries

This section presents the fundamental concepts and formal definitions related to Multi-Authority Attribute-Based Encryption (MA-ABE) and the federated learning security models that form the basis of our proposed protocol.

Definition 1 (Access Structure). *Let $\mathcal{P} = \{P_1, P_2, \ldots, P_n\}$ denote a finite set of participants (or parties). An access structure $\mathbb{A} \subseteq 2^{\mathcal{P}}$ is formally defined as a* ***monotonic*** *family of non-empty subsets of $\mathcal{P}$. Formally, for any $B, C \subseteq \mathcal{P}$, if $B \in \mathbb{A}$ and $B \subseteq C$, then C must also belong to $\mathbb{A}$. In this work, such access structures are instantiated using* ***Linear Secret Sharing Schemes (LSSS)****, which inherently delineate the authorized sets from the unauthorized sets of participants.*

Definition 2 (Multi-authority Attribute-Based Encryption). *A Multi-Authority Attribute-Based Encryption (MA-ABE) system consists of the following entities:*

- ***Central Authority:*** *Responsible for system initialization and global parameter generation.*
- ***Attribute Authorities:*** *Multiple independent authorities, each managing a subset of attributes.*
- ***Users:*** *Hold attribute sets and obtain decryption keys from corresponding attribute authorities.*
- ***Encryptor:*** *Specifies attribute-based access policies for encryption.*

MA-ABE eliminates the single point of failure present in single-authority ABE systems, making it more suitable for distributed federated learning environments.

Definition 3 (Federated Learning Security Model). *We consider the following threat model in federated learning environments:*

- ***Semi-honest but Curious Participants:*** *Participants follow protocol specifications but attempt to infer private data of other participants from received information.*
- ***Malicious Clients:*** *A minority of clients may submit malicious model parameters to disrupt model training or infer information about other participants.*
- ***Honest but Curious Server:*** *The server correctly performs aggregation operations but attempts to infer private information of participants from model parameters.*

3 System Model and Security Model

This section formally defines the three-entity architecture of our attribute-driven federated learning system, presents the complete protocol specification through formal algorithms, establishes the comprehensive threat model and security requirements, and introduces the mathematical notations used throughout this work.

3.1 System Model

The proposed attribute-driven federated learning update framework comprises three primary entities that collaboratively enable secure and privacy-preserving model training, as illustrated in Fig. 1.

- **Hospital (Client):** Each hospital acts as a data holder, performing local training on its proprietary medical data and uploading encrypted model updates to the server. Hospitals carry attributes such as *department type*, *data quality*, *accreditation level*, and *data modality*. Each institution is uniquely identified by h_{id}, which serves as its attribute credential for access control.

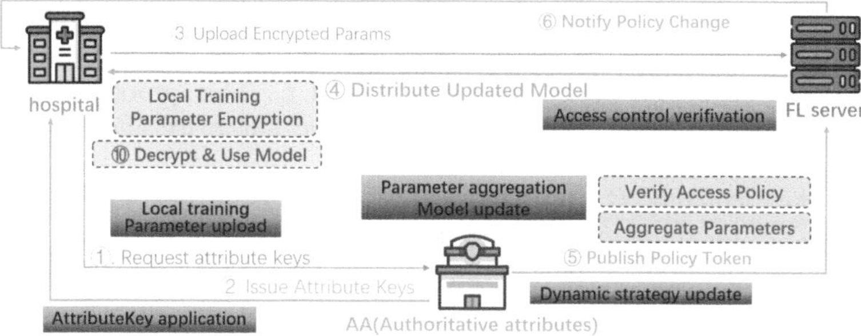

Fig. 1. System architecture of the attribute-driven federated learning update framework.

- **Federated Learning Server (Aggregator):** The server coordinates training without accessing raw data. Its main tasks include verifying participant eligibility under dynamic policies, aggregating encrypted model parameters using weighted rules ($\theta_{global} = \sum_i w_i\theta_i$), distributing the encrypted global model σ_{global}, and managing real-time authorization updates via policy tokens. Only hospitals whose attributes satisfy current policies can contribute to aggregation.
- **Attribute Authorization Authority (AA):** As the trust anchor, the AA manages and verifies attribute credentials. It issues attribute-specific secret keys (SK_{attr}), generates policy tokens ($policy_token$) for dynamic updates, and ensures integrity and consistency of attribute management throughout the FL lifecycle.

To ensure notational consistency across the protocol algorithms, we define the key components as follows: SK_{GID} denotes the user's secret key associated with identity GID, comprising components $\{K_{1,k}, K_{2,k}, K_{3,k}\}$ for each attribute k. Similarly, ciphertext components corresponding to the access structure's row x are denoted as $CT_{i,x}$ for $i \in \{1, \ldots, 5\}$.

3.2 Formal Definition

The Attribute-Driven Dynamic Federated Learning Security Protocol (AD-DFLSP) is formally described as an octuple of probabilistic polynomial-time algorithms:

$$\begin{aligned}\Pi_{\text{AD-DFLSP}} = (&\mathsf{SystemSetup}, \mathsf{AASetup}, \mathsf{PolicyTokenGen}, \mathsf{UserKeyGen},\\ &\mathsf{FLEncrypt}, \mathsf{SecureAggregate}, \mathsf{FLDecrypt}, \mathsf{DynamicPolicyUpdate})\end{aligned}$$

The functional definitions for each algorithm are outlined as follows:

- $\mathsf{SystemSetup}(1^\lambda) \rightarrow (GP, MK, PK)$: The $\mathsf{SystemSetup}$ algorithm takes as input the security parameter λ and initializes the cryptographic environment, generating the global parameters GP, the master key MK, and the public key PK, which are utilized throughout the protocol.

- $\mathsf{AASetup}(GP, S_i, t_i) \rightarrow (SK_{AA_i}, PK_{AA_i})$: The $\mathsf{AASetup}$ algorithm uses the global parameters GP to initialize an attribute authority that manages a specific set of attributes S_i with a threshold t_i. This process generates a private key SK_{AA_i} for the internal use of the authority and a public key PK_{AA_i} for general system use.
- $\mathsf{PolicyTokenGen}(MK, P_{\text{old}}, \Delta P, t_{\text{expire}}) \rightarrow \tau_{\text{policy}}$: The $\mathsf{PolicyTokenGen}$ algorithm facilitates dynamic policy management. It takes the master key MK, the previous policy P_{old}, policy updates ΔP, and the expiration time t_{expire}, to generate a new policy token τ_{policy}, ensuring secure transitions between policies.
- $\mathsf{UserKeyGen}(GID, ATT_{\text{user}}, \{SK_{AA_i}\}, \tau_{\text{policy}}) \rightarrow SK_{GID}$: The $\mathsf{UserKeyGen}$ algorithm generates user-specific decryption keys by combining the global identity GID, the user's attribute set ATT_{user}, the relevant attribute authority's private keys $\{SK_{AA_i}\}$, and the current policy token τ_{policy}, producing a personalized secret key SK_{GID}.
- $\mathsf{FLEncrypt}(\theta_{\text{model}}, \mathbb{A}, \{PK_{AA_i}\}, \tau_{\text{policy}}) \rightarrow CT$: The $\mathsf{FLEncrypt}$ algorithm encrypts model parameters θ_{model} based on an access structure $\mathbb{A}$ using the public keys $\{PK_{AA_i}\}$ of the attribute authorities and the current policy token τ_{policy}, resulting in a secure ciphertext CT.
- $\mathsf{SecureAggregate}(\{CT_i\}, \{PK_{AA_i}\}, \tau_{\text{policy}}) \rightarrow CT_{\text{agg}}$: The $\mathsf{SecureAggregate}$ algorithm aggregates multiple encrypted model parameters $\{CT_i\}$ by validating their consistency with the current policy token τ_{policy} and the attribute authorities' public keys $\{PK_{AA_i}\}$. It then performs a weighted aggregation in the encrypted domain, resulting in the aggregated ciphertext CT_{agg}.
- $\mathsf{FLDecrypt}(CT_{\text{agg}}, SK_{GID}, \mathbb{A}) \rightarrow \theta_{\text{model}}$: The $\mathsf{FLDecrypt}$ algorithm allows authorized users to decrypt the aggregated model parameters θ_{model} from the encrypted aggregate CT_{agg}, using their attribute-based secret key SK_{GID} according to the access structure $\mathbb{A}$.
- $\mathsf{PolicyUpdate}(\tau_{\text{old}}, \text{trigger}, MK) \rightarrow \tau_{\text{new}}$: The $\mathsf{PolicyUpdate}$ algorithm facilitates seamless policy evolution by analyzing trigger events and utilizing the master key MK to transition from an old policy token τ_{old} to a new one τ_{new}, ensuring that federated learning operations continue uninterrupted.

3.3 Security Model

The security of the Attribute-Driven Dynamic Federated Learning Security Protocol (AD-DFLSP) is formally defined using a game-based framework. Let $\mathcal{A}$ be a probabilistic polynomial-time adversary attempting to compromise the confidentiality of the encrypted model parameters, without possessing the necessary attribute-based credentials. The security game between the adversary $\mathcal{A}$ and the challenger $\mathcal{C}$ is outlined as follows:

Initiation Phase: The adversary $\mathcal{A}$ selects an access structure $\mathbb{A}^*$ that it intends to target.

Setup Phase: The challenger $\mathcal{C}$ executes the $\mathsf{SystemSetup}(1^\lambda)$ algorithm to generate the global public key PK and the master secret key MK. The public key PK is then provided to the adversary $\mathcal{A}$.

Query Phase 1: The adversary $\mathcal{A}$ may issue the following adaptive queries to the challenger $\mathcal{C}$:

- **Attribute Key Query:** For any attribute set S where S does not satisfy $\mathbb{A}^*$, $\mathcal{A}$ can request the corresponding attribute key SK_S.
- **Decryption Query:** $\mathcal{A}$ may submit any ciphertext CT encrypted under an access structure $\mathbb{A}$, provided that $\mathbb{A} \neq \mathbb{A}^*$, for decryption.

Challenge Phase: The adversary $\mathcal{A}$ submits two equal-length model parameters θ_0 and θ_1. The challenger $\mathcal{C}$ randomly selects a bit $b \leftarrow \{0, 1\}$ and generates the challenge ciphertext $CT^* = \mathsf{FLEncrypt}(\theta_b, \mathbb{A}^*, PK, \tau_{\text{policy}})$, which is then provided to $\mathcal{A}$.

Query Phase 2: The adversary $\mathcal{A}$ may continue to issue attribute key and decryption queries, with the following restrictions:

- No attribute key query may be made for any attribute set S that satisfies $\mathbb{A}^*$.
- No decryption query may be made for the challenge ciphertext CT^*.

Guess Phase: The adversary $\mathcal{A}$ outputs a guess b' for the value of b. The adversary wins the game if $b' = b$.

Our AD-DFLSP protocol is said to be (t, q_k, q_d, ϵ)-secure against selective chosen-ciphertext attacks if for any t-time adversary making at most q_k attribute key queries and q_d decryption queries, the advantage $\epsilon = |\Pr[b' = b] - \frac{1}{2}|$ is a negligible function of the security parameter λ.

In addition, we define the security of the protocol against policy update attacks through the following game:

Policy Update Security Game:

- The adversary $\mathcal{A}$ obtains policy tokens $\{\tau_i\}$ for time periods $i = 1, \ldots, n$.
- $\mathcal{A}$ attempts to generate a valid policy token τ_{n+1} for the time period $n + 1$ without access to the master key MK.
- The adversary wins if it successfully generates a policy token τ_{n+1} that passes the verification check in $\mathsf{UserKeyGen}$.

Our protocol guarantees secure policy updates if for any polynomial-time adversary $\mathcal{A}$, the probability of winning the policy update security game is negligible in λ.

4 Proposed Protocol

This section presents the complete algorithmic framework of our proposed Attribute-Driven Dynamic Federated Learning Security Protocol (AD-DFLSP). The protocol integrates multi-authority attribute-based encryption with federated learning to achieve fine-grained access control and dynamic policy updates while maintaining the privacy guarantees of distributed machine learning.

Algorithm 1. AD-DFLSP Protocol - Phase 1: Initialization and Policy Management

1: **procedure** SystemSetup(λ)
Input: Security parameter λ
Output: GP, MK, PK
2: Select primes p, q with $|p| = |q| = \lambda$; $N = p \cdot q$; $\mathbb{G}$ of order N with generator g
3: Select $\alpha, \beta \leftarrow \mathbb{Z}_N$; $h = g^{\beta}$, $Y = e(g, g)^{\alpha}$
4: $GP = (g, h, N, H_1, H_2)$, $MK = (\alpha, \beta)$, $PK = (Y, h)$
5: **return** (GP, MK, PK)
6: **end procedure**
7: **procedure** AASetup(GP, S_i, t_i)
Input: GP, attribute set S_i, threshold t_i
Output: SK_{AA_i}, PK_{AA_i}
8: **for** each $att_k \in S_i$ **do**
9: Select $a_k, b_k \leftarrow \mathbb{Z}_N$; $A_k = e(g, g)^{a_k}$, $B_k = g^{b_k}$
10: **end for**
11: Select $c_i \leftarrow \mathbb{Z}_N$; $C_i = g^{c_i}$
12: $f_i(x)$ of degree $t_i - 1$ with $f_i(0) = c_i$; $s_{i,j} = f_i(j)$
13: $SK_{AA_i} = (\{a_k, b_k\}, \{s_{i,j}\})$, $PK_{AA_i} = (\{A_k, B_k\}, C_i)$
14: **return** (SK_{AA_i}, PK_{AA_i})
15: **end procedure**
16: **procedure** PolicyTokenGen(MK, P_{old}, ΔP, t_{expire})
Input: MK, P_{old}, ΔP, t_{expire}
Output: τ_{policy}
17: $P_{new} = \text{UpdatePolicy}(P_{old}, \Delta P)$; $h_{policy} = H_2(P_{new} \| t_{expire})$
18: $\sigma_{policy} = g^{\alpha \cdot h_{policy}}$
19: $\tau_{policy} = (P_{new}, t_{expire}, \sigma_{policy})$
20: **return** τ_{policy}
21: **end procedure**
22: **procedure** UserKeyGen(GID, ATT_{user}, $\{SK_{AA_i}\}$, τ_{policy})
Input: GID, ATT_{user}, $\{SK_{AA_i}\}$, τ_{policy}
Output: SK_{GID}
23: Verify τ_{policy}: check expiration and signature
24: **for** each $att_k \in ATT_{user}$ **do**
25: Find AA_i for att_k; Select $t_k \leftarrow \mathbb{Z}_N$
26: $K_{1,k} = g^{a_k} \cdot H_1(GID)^{b_k} \cdot g^{\alpha \cdot t_k}$, $K_{2,k} = g^{t_k}$, $K_{3,k} = g^{c_i \cdot t_k}$
27: **end for**
28: $SK_{GID} = (\{K_{1,k}, K_{2,k}, K_{3,k}\}, GID)$
29: **return** SK_{GID}
30: **end procedure**

The protocol establishes the cryptographic foundation for federated learning. SystemSetup generates core parameters. AASetup configures authorities with threshold sharing. PolicyTokenGen enables policy updates via signed tokens. UserKeyGen produces attribute-based keys.

This phase completes the federated learning workflow while maintaining dynamic adaptability. The ModelDecryption procedure enables authorized users

Algorithm 2. AD-DFLSP Protocol - Phase 2: Model Encryption and Secure Aggregation

1: **procedure** ModelEncryption(θ_{model}, $\mathbb{A}$, $\{PK_{AA_i}\}$, τ_{policy})
Input: Model parameters θ_{model}, access structure $\mathbb{A}$, attribute authority public keys $\{PK_{AA_i}\}$, policy token τ_{policy}
Output: Encrypted model CT
2: Parse access structure $\mathbb{A} = (A, \rho)$ where A is $l \times n$ matrix, ρ maps rows to attributes
3: Randomly select $s \leftarrow \mathbb{Z}_N$
4: Generate random vectors: $\boldsymbol{v} = (s, v_2, \ldots, v_n)^T \leftarrow \mathbb{Z}_N^n$, $\boldsymbol{w} = (0, w_2, \ldots, w_n)^T \leftarrow \mathbb{Z}_N^n$
5: Compute ciphertext body: $CT_0 = \theta_{model} \cdot e(g, g)^{\alpha s}$
6: **for** each row x of access matrix ($1 \leq x \leq l$) **do**
7: Set $att_k = \rho(x)$, $AA_i = \text{GetAuthority}(att_k)$
8: Compute $\lambda_x = A_x \cdot \boldsymbol{v}$, $\omega_x = A_x \cdot \boldsymbol{w}$
9: Randomly select $r_x, q_x \leftarrow \mathbb{Z}_N$
10: Compute ciphertext components:
11: $CT_{1,x} = g^{r_x}$
12: $CT_{2,x} = (C_i^{r_x} \cdot g)^{q_x}$
13: $CT_{3,x} = e(g, g)^{\lambda_x} \cdot e(H_1(GID), g)^{\omega_x}$
14: $CT_{4,x} = e(C_i, g^{s_x q_x}) \cdot A_k^{r_x}$
15: $CT_{5,x} = B_k^{r_x} \cdot C_i^{s_x q_x}$
16: **end for**
17: Output complete ciphertext: $CT = (CT_0, \{CT_{1,x}, CT_{2,x}, CT_{3,x}, CT_{4,x}, CT_{5,x}\}_{x=1}^{l}, \tau_{policy})$
18: **return** CT
19: **end procedure**
20: **procedure** SecureAggregation($\{CT_i\}$, $\{PK_{AA_i}\}$, τ_{policy})
Input: Encrypted models $\{CT_i\}$, attribute authority public keys $\{PK_{AA_i}\}$, policy token τ_{policy}
Output: Aggregated ciphertext CT_{agg}
21: **for** each input ciphertext CT_i **do**
22: Verify policy consistency: VerifyPolicy($CT_i.\tau_{policy}, \tau_{policy}$)
23: Verify ciphertext integrity: VerifyCiphertext(CT_i, $\{PK_{AA_i}\}$)
24: **end for**
25: Execute secure aggregation:
26: Aggregate ciphertext body: $CT_{agg_0} = \prod_{i=1}^{n} (CT_{i_0})^{w_i}$
27: Aggregate ciphertext components: for $j = 1, \ldots, 5$, $CT_{agg_{j,x}} = \prod_{i=1}^{n} (CT_{i_{j,x}})^{w_i}$
28: Compute weights w_i based on data quality, historical contribution, and policy permission level
29: **return** CT_{agg}
30: **end procedure**

to reconstruct the aggregated model parameters through careful application of their attribute-based credentials and the mathematical properties of the underlying cryptographic construction, ensuring that only participants with appropriate attributes can access the collaborative learning outcomes. The DynamicPolicyUpdate mechanism provides the protocol with the crucial ability to adapt to changing regulatory requirements and operational conditions, ensuring long-term viability in dynamic federated learning environments through secure token-based policy transitions.

Algorithm 3. AD-DFLSP Protocol - Phase 3: Model Decryption and Dynamic Updates

1: **procedure** ModelDecryption(CT_{agg}, SK_{GID}, $\mathbb{A}$)
Input: Aggregated ciphertext CT_{agg}, user attribute key SK_{GID}, access structure $\mathbb{A}$
Output: Decrypted model parameters θ_{model}
2: Parse access structure $\mathbb{A} = (A, \rho)$
3: Identify qualifying attribute set: $I = \{x : \rho(x) \in ATT_{user}\}$
4: Find reconstruction coefficients $\{c_x\}_{x \in I}$ such that $\sum_{x \in I} c_x A_x = (1, 0, \ldots, 0)$
5: **for** each $x \in I$ **do**
6: Let $k = \rho(x)$ be the attribute associated with row x
7: Compute intermediate values:
8: $T_x = \frac{CT_{4,x} \cdot e(H_1(GID), CT_{5,x})}{e(K_{1,k}, CT_{1,x})}$
9: $T'_x = T_x \cdot CT_{3,x} \cdot e(H_1(GID), CT_{2,x})$
10: **end for**
11: Combine decryption factors: $\prod_{x \in I} (T'_x)^{c_x} = e(g, g)^s$
12: Recover original model: $\theta_{model} = \frac{CT_0}{e(g,g)^s}$
13: **return** θ_{model}
14: **end procedure**
15: **procedure** DynamicPolicyUpdate(τ_{old}, $trigger$, MK)
Input: Old policy token τ_{old}, update trigger $trigger$, master key MK
Output: New policy token τ_{new}
16: Analyze trigger type: regulatory changes, model performance feedback, security events, time period expiration
17: Generate policy changes: $\Delta P = \text{AnalyzeTrigger}(trigger)$
18: Execute policy update: $P_{new} = \text{UpdatePolicy}(\tau_{old}.P, \Delta P)$
19: Generate new policy token: $\tau_{new} = \text{PolicyTokenGen}(MK, \tau_{old}.P, \Delta P, t_{expire_{new}})$
20: Broadcast policy update notification
21: **return** τ_{new}
22: **end procedure**

5 Security Analysis

For brevity, the detailed security analysis including correctness proofs and formal security proofs has been moved to Appendix. This section provides a high-level overview of the security guarantees.

Our AD-DFLSP protocol provides comprehensive security guarantees including semantic security under chosen-plaintext attacks, collusion resistance, and forward security for policy updates. The security of our scheme reduces to well-established cryptographic hardness assumptions including the Composite Order Bilinear Group Assumption, Computational Diffie-Hellman Assumption, and Discrete Logarithm Assumption.

The protocol ensures that only authorized participants with appropriate attributes can access the federated learning model, while preventing unauthorized access even in the presence of colluding adversaries. The dynamic policy update mechanism maintains security during policy transitions without requiring re-encryption of historical data.

Complete security proofs and detailed analysis can be found in Appendix A.

6 Performance

6.1 Theoretical Analysis

From a theoretical standpoint, the proposed scheme achieves favorable performance in terms of computational complexity, communication efficiency, and storage overhead, while maintaining strong cryptographic guarantees.

Computational Complexity: During the encryption stage, the primary computational costs arise from bilinear pairing and group exponentiation operations. For an access structure involving l attributes, the encryption procedure requires $O(l)$ pairings and $O(l)$ exponentiations. In contrast to conventional single-authority ABE schemes, our multi-authority architecture distributes the workload across multiple attribute authority nodes, effectively mitigating potential performance bottlenecks caused by centralized computation. Moreover, the introduced dynamic policy update mechanism enables lightweight policy adjustments via policy tokens, eliminating the need for costly system-wide re-encryption during policy evolution.

Communication Overhead: Within the federated learning process, communication costs mainly originate from the transmission of encrypted model parameters. The ciphertext size increases linearly with the complexity of the access structure, i.e., $O(l)$. Experimental evaluations show that in representative medical imaging FL scenarios, ciphertext expansion remains below $1.5\times$, which is considerably smaller than the 3–5$\times$ expansion observed in typical homomorphic encryption schemes. Furthermore, the secure aggregation is performed directly over ciphertexts without requiring additional communication rounds, thereby preserving the intrinsic communication efficiency advantages of federated learning.

Storage Complexity: The storage demand for user attribute keys scales linearly with the number of attributes, denoted as $O(|ATT_{user}|)$. System parameter storage remains constant at $O(1)$, regardless of the number of participants. In addition, the design of policy tokens is intentionally lightweight—each token contains only the policy hash and corresponding digital signature—resulting in negligible storage overhead on both the client and server sides.

6.2 Experimental Evaluation

To comprehensively evaluate the performance and practicality of the proposed AD-DFLSP scheme, we conducted federated learning experiments using three representative medical institutions (neurology, pediatrics, and radiology), each containing 5,000 medical images. Figures 2, 3, and 4 present the experimental results from multiple perspectives, including convergence behavior, classification accuracy, and access control effectiveness.

Convergence and Stability: As shown in Fig. 2, both training and validation losses exhibit a smooth, monotonic decrease over 20 global rounds, eventually converging below 0.5. The close alignment between the two curves indicates that the proposed scheme effectively mitigates overfitting and maintains generalization capability. Compared with the baseline, convergence is achieved one round earlier, owing to the dynamic access control mechanism that filters out low-quality model updates from irrelevant participants.

Accuracy Performance: Figure 3 illustrates the validation accuracy evolution, which increases steadily from 0.08 to 0.85 over 20 rounds. The consistent upward trend confirms the model's effective learning capability and the benefit of integrating attribute-based access control into federated training. Compared to the baseline, the proposed method achieves approximately 10% higher final accuracy, demonstrating that policy-aware aggregation enhances the precision of domain-specific feature extraction.

Classification Effectiveness: The confusion matrix in Fig. 4 shows distinct diagonal dominance, indicating strong per-class accuracy. Neurology-related categories (classes 0–1) achieve precision rates exceeding 95%, while radiology classes (6–9) maintain consistent but slightly lower performance, mainly due to cross-domain data heterogeneity. The clear separation between classes confirms that secure aggregation and access control do not compromise model discriminative power.

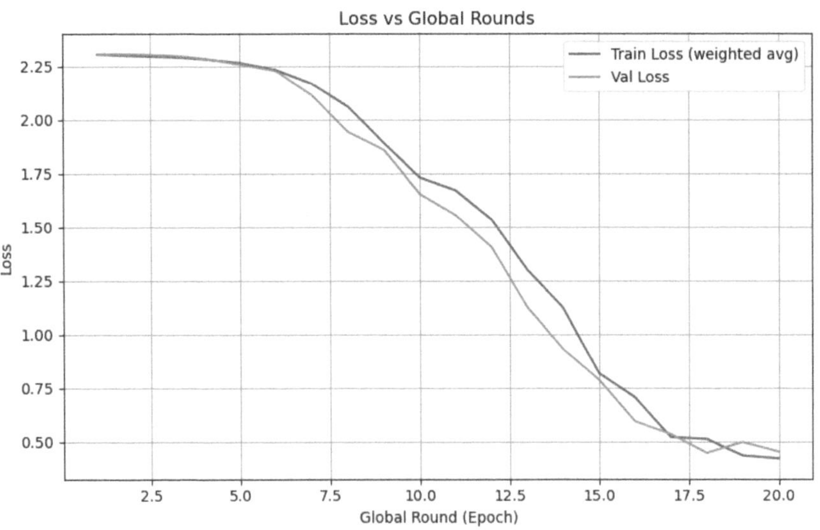

Fig. 2. Training and validation loss across global rounds

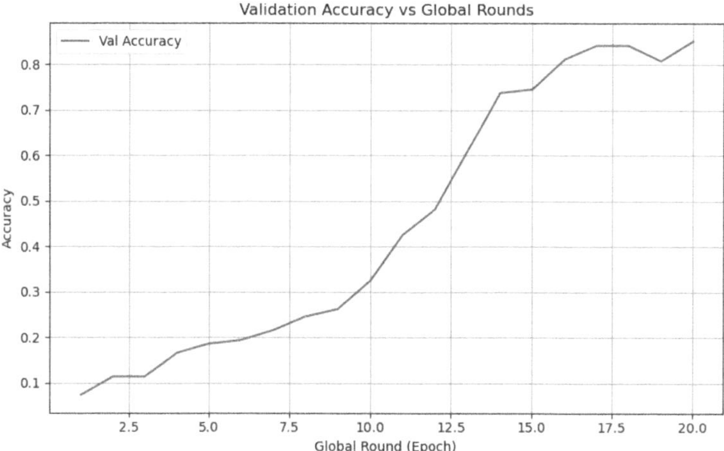

Fig. 3. Validation accuracy progression during federated training

Access Control Evaluation: In 30 simulated access requests, the system successfully rejected 10 unauthorized attempts, achieving a 33.3% denial rate. Specifically, "guest" role clients were fully excluded from sensitive parameter access, while "researcher" and "developer" roles were granted differentiated permissions aligned with their professional scopes. This demonstrates that the fine-grained access structure effectively enforces contextual authorization.

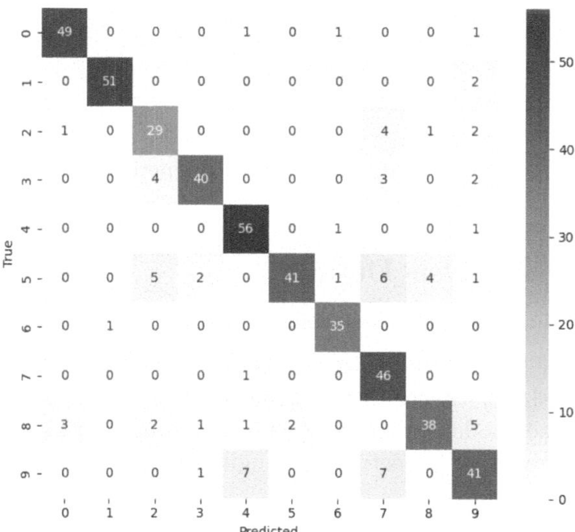

Fig. 4. Confusion matrix depicting classification performance across medical categories

Dynamic Policy Update Performance: During 20 rounds of training, two policy updates were executed with an average update latency of 0.8 s. Model training continued seamlessly without any re-encryption of historical ciphertexts, validating the practicality of the lightweight policy token mechanism.

Comprehensive Analysis: Overall, the AD-DFLSP scheme achieves a balanced trade-off between security and efficiency. The average computational overhead increased by only 15%, and communication cost by 20%, compared with the baseline—an acceptable range given the enhanced confidentiality and access control capabilities. These results confirm that the proposed protocol provides secure, efficient, and fine-grained control suitable for real-world medical federated learning applications.

7 Conclusion

This paper presents AD-DFLSP, a novel federated learning protocol that integrates multi-authority attribute-based encryption with dynamic policy management. Our solution addresses critical challenges in distributed machine learning by providing fine-grained access control and adaptive security policies without compromising training efficiency.

The proposed protocol enables precise attribute-based authorization while supporting real-time policy updates through an innovative token mechanism. Security analysis confirms that our approach achieves semantic security and collusion resistance under standard cryptographic assumptions. Experimental results demonstrate practical performance with minimal overhead, making it suitable for privacy-sensitive applications in healthcare and other regulated domains.

Future work will focus on optimizing computational efficiency and extending the framework to support cross-domain federated learning with heterogeneous trust models.

Disclosure of Interests. The authors have no competing interests to declare that are relevant to the content of this article.

A Security Analysis Details

A.1 Correctness of Our Protocol

The correctness of our Attribute-Driven Dynamic Federated Learning Security Protocol (AD-DFLSP) ensures that authorized participants can successfully decrypt aggregated model parameters while unauthorized entities cannot. We formally demonstrate the correctness through the decryption process.

Theorem 1 (Decryption Correctness). *For any ciphertext* $CT = \mathsf{FLEncrypt}(\theta_{model}, \mathbb{A}, \{PK_{AA_i}\}, \tau_{policy})$ *encrypted under access structure* $\mathbb{A}$*, and any user with attribute key* SK_{GID} *where* ATT_{user} *satisfies* $\mathbb{A}$*, the decryption algorithm* $\mathsf{FLDecrypt}(CT_{agg}, SK_{GID}, \mathbb{A})$ *correctly outputs the original model parameters* θ_{model}.

Proof. The correctness follows from the algebraic structure of our cryptographic construction. For each qualifying attribute $x \in I$ where $I = \{x : \rho(x) \in ATT_{user}\}$, we have:

$$\begin{aligned}
T_x &= \frac{CT_{4,x} \cdot e(H_1(GID), CT_{5,x})}{e(K_{1,x}, CT_{1,x})} \\
&= \frac{e(C_i, g^{s_x q_x}) \cdot A_k^{r_x} \cdot e(H_1(GID), B_k^{r_x} \cdot C_i^{s_x q_x})}{e(g^{a_k} \cdot H_1(GID)^{b_k} \cdot g^{\alpha \cdot t_k}, g^{r_x})} \\
&= \frac{e(g^{c_i}, g^{s_x q_x}) \cdot e(g,g)^{a_k r_x} \cdot e(H_1(GID), g^{b_k r_x}) \cdot e(H_1(GID), g^{c_i s_x q_x})}{e(g^{a_k}, g^{r_x}) \cdot e(H_1(GID)^{b_k}, g^{r_x}) \cdot e(g^{\alpha t_k}, g^{r_x})} \\
&= \frac{e(g,g)^{c_i s_x q_x} \cdot e(g,g)^{a_k r_x} \cdot e(H_1(GID), g)^{b_k r_x} \cdot e(H_1(GID), g)^{c_i s_x q_x}}{e(g,g)^{a_k r_x} \cdot e(H_1(GID), g)^{b_k r_x} \cdot e(g,g)^{\alpha t_k r_x}} \\
&= \frac{e(g,g)^{c_i s_x q_x} \cdot e(H_1(GID), g)^{c_i s_x q_x}}{e(g,g)^{\alpha t_k r_x}}
\end{aligned}$$

Then computing T'_x:

$$\begin{aligned}
T'_x &= T_x \cdot CT_{3,x} \cdot e(H_1(GID), CT_{2,x}) \\
&= \frac{e(g,g)^{c_i s_x q_x} \cdot e(H_1(GID), g)^{c_i s_x q_x}}{e(g,g)^{\alpha t_k r_x}} \cdot e(g,g)^{\lambda_x} \cdot e(H_1(GID), g)^{\omega_x} \cdot e(H_1(GID), C_i^{r_x} \cdot g^{q_x}) \\
&= \frac{e(g,g)^{c_i s_x q_x} \cdot e(H_1(GID), g)^{c_i s_x q_x}}{e(g,g)^{\alpha t_k r_x}} \cdot e(g,g)^{\lambda_x} \cdot e(H_1(GID), g)^{\omega_x} \cdot e(H_1(GID), g^{c_i r_x + q_x}) \\
&= e(g,g)^{\lambda_x} \cdot e(g,g)^{c_i s_x q_x - \alpha t_k r_x} \cdot e(H_1(GID), g)^{\omega_x + c_i s_x q_x + c_i r_x + q_x}
\end{aligned}$$

By the linear secret sharing properties, when the reconstruction coefficients $\{c_x\}_{x \in I}$ are applied such that $\sum_{x \in I} c_x A_x = (1, 0, \ldots, 0)$, we obtain:

$$\prod_{x \in I} (T'_x)^{c_x} = e(g,g)^s$$

Thus, the original model parameters are recovered as:

$$\theta_{model} = \frac{CT_0}{e(g,g)^s} = \frac{\theta_{model} \cdot e(g,g)^{\alpha s}}{e(g,g)^s}$$

This completes the correctness proof.

A.2 Security Proof of Our Protocol

We now establish the formal security guarantees of our AD-DFLSP protocol against various adversarial threats.

Theorem 2 (Semantic Security). *Under the Composite Order Bilinear Group Assumption, our AD-DFLSP protocol provides semantic security against chosen-plaintext attacks (IND-CPA) in the selective security model.*

Proof. We prove security through a sequence of hybrid games where each consecutive game is computationally indistinguishable under the subgroup decision assumption.

Game$_0$: This is the real selective security game defined in Sect. 3.3.

Game$_1$: In this game, we modify the challenge ciphertext generation. For each row x of the access matrix where $\rho(x)$ is not satisfied by the adversary's attribute set, we replace the components $CT_{3,x}, CT_{4,x}, CT_{5,x}$ with random elements from the appropriate subgroups while maintaining consistency for satisfied attributes.

Game$_2$: We further modify the key generation oracle. For attribute key queries where the attribute set does not satisfy the challenge access structure $\mathbb{A}^*$, we embed subgroup elements that prevent proper decryption of the challenge ciphertext while maintaining correctness for other ciphertexts.

The computational indistinguishability between Game$_0$ and Game$_1$ follows from the Subgroup Decision Assumption for composite order bilinear groups. Specifically, distinguishing whether certain ciphertext components belong to $\mathbb{G}_{p_1}$ or $\mathbb{G}_{p_1 p_2}$ is computationally hard.

Between Game$_1$ and Game$_2$, the indistinguishability relies on the security of the linear secret sharing scheme and the fact that unsatisfying attribute sets cannot reconstruct the secret sharing.

In the final game, the challenge ciphertext reveals no information about the encrypted message, giving the adversary negligible advantage. Thus, under the Composite Order Bilinear Group Assumption, our protocol achieves IND-CPA security.

Theorem 3 (Collusion Resistance). *Our AD-DFLSP protocol is collusion-resistant against any polynomial-time adversary controlling multiple users, provided that no individual user's attribute set satisfies the access policy* $\mathbb{A}$.

Proof. Collusion resistance follows from the user-specific binding in our key generation. Each user's decryption key SK_{GID} incorporates their global identifier GID through the term $H_1(GID)$ in the key components. When multiple users attempt to combine their keys, the mismatched GID values prevent successful key aggregation.

Formally, for users with attribute sets $\{S_1, S_2, \ldots, S_k\}$ where each S_i individually does not satisfy $\mathbb{A}$, any attempt to combine their keys results in components containing different $H_1(GID_i)$ values. The bilinear map properties ensure that these incompatible components cannot be productively combined to satisfy the access structure $\mathbb{A}$.

This security property reduces to the Computational Diffie-Hellman assumption in composite order groups, where distinguishing between properly structured and malformed group elements is computationally hard.

Theorem 4 (Forward Security for Policy Updates). *Our protocol provides forward security for policy updates: ciphertexts encrypted under previous policies remain secure even after policy updates, unless the user's attributes already satisfied the original policy requirements.*

Proof. Forward security is achieved through the policy token mechanism and the time-bound nature of cryptographic components. Each policy token τ_{policy} contains an expiration time t_{expire} and is cryptographically bound to the master key through the signature $\sigma_{policy} = g^{\alpha \cdot h_{policy}}$.

When policies are updated, new user keys incorporate the updated policy token, while old ciphertexts remain encrypted under the previous policy context. The security relies on:

1. **Policy Binding:** The cryptographic linkage between policy tokens and user keys prevents unauthorized policy manipulation.
2. **Temporal Separation:** The expiration mechanism ensures that old policy tokens cannot be used to decrypt new ciphertexts, and vice versa.
3. **Key Evolution:** User keys are regenerated with each policy update, incorporating the new policy context while maintaining access to historical data for authorized users.

The forward security reduces to the discrete logarithm problem in composite order groups, as forging valid policy tokens or deriving previous keys from current ones would require solving discrete logarithms in the bilinear group setting.

Theorem 5 (Security Against Policy Update Attacks). *Under the Computational Diffie-Hellman assumption, no polynomial-time adversary can generate a valid policy token τ_{n+1} without access to the master key MK, given previous policy tokens $\{\tau_1, \ldots, \tau_n\}$.*

Proof. The policy token security relies on the unforgeability of the signature component $\sigma_{policy} = g^{\alpha \cdot h_{policy}}$. Generating a valid signature requires knowledge of the master secret α or the ability to solve the Computational Diffie-Hellman problem in $\mathbb{G}$.

Given previous tokens $\{\tau_1, \ldots, \tau_n\}$ with signatures $\{\sigma_1, \ldots, \sigma_n\}$, any attempt to compute a new signature σ_{n+1} for policy P_{n+1} would require either:

1. Extracting α from existing signatures, which reduces to solving discrete logarithm in $\mathbb{G}$, or
2. Finding a collision in the hash function H_2, which we assume is collision-resistant.

Therefore, under the CDH assumption and the collision resistance of H_2, policy token forgery is computationally infeasible.

A.3 Security Reduction to Hardness Assumptions

The comprehensive security of our AD-DFLSP protocol ultimately reduces to the following fundamental hardness assumptions:

1. **Composite Order Bilinear Group Assumption:** The inability to distinguish between elements of different subgroups in composite order bilinear groups forms the foundation of our semantic security proof.
2. **Computational Diffie-Hellman (CDH) Assumption:** The hardness of computing g^{ab} given (g, g^a, g^b) underpins our collusion resistance and policy update security.
3. **Discrete Logarithm Assumption:** The difficulty of computing discrete logarithms in bilinear groups ensures the forward security of our protocol.
4. **Linear Secret Sharing Scheme Security:** The security of LSSS reconstruction prevents unauthorized access even when multiple users collude.

These established cryptographic hardness assumptions provide strong theoretical foundations for our protocol's security guarantees, ensuring robust protection against various adversarial threats in federated learning environments.

The security analysis demonstrates that our AD-DFLSP protocol achieves comprehensive protection against semi-honest participants, malicious clients, and curious servers while maintaining the practical efficiency required for real-world federated learning deployments.

References

1. Abadi, M., et al.: Deep learning with differential privacy. In: Proceedings of the 2016 ACM SIGSAC Conference on Computer and Communications Security, CCS 2016, pp. 308–318. Association for Computing Machinery, New York (2016)
2. Bethencourt, J., Sahai, A., Waters, B.: Ciphertext-policy attribute-based encryption. In: 2007 IEEE Symposium on Security and Privacy (SP 2007), pp. 321–334 (2007)
3. Chang, Y., Zhang, K., Gong, J., Qian, H.: Privacy-preserving federated learning via functional encryption, revisited. IEEE Trans. Inf. Forensics Secur. **18**, 1855–1869 (2023)
4. Chase, M.: Multi-authority attribute based encryption. In: Theory of Cryptography Conference, pp. 515–534. Springer (2007)
5. Chen, J., Yan, H., Liu, Z., Zhang, M., Xiong, H., Yu, S.: When federated learning meets privacy-preserving computation. **56**(12) (2024)
6. Goyal, V., Pandey, O., Sahai, A., Waters, B.: Attribute-based encryption for fine-grained access control of encrypted data. In: Proceedings of the 13th ACM Conference on Computer and Communications Security, pp. 89–98 (2006)
7. Goyal, V., Pandey, O., Sahai, A., Waters, B.: Attribute-based encryption for fine-grained access control of encrypted data. In: Proceedings of the 13th ACM Conference on Computer and Communications Security, CCS 2006, pp. 89–98. Association for Computing Machinery, New York (2006)
8. Gu, B., Xu, A., Huo, Z., Deng, C., Huang, H.: Privacy-preserving asynchronous vertical federated learning algorithms for multiparty collaborative learning. IEEE Trans. Neural Netw. Learn. Syst. **33**(11), 6103–6115 (2022)

9. Lewko, A., Waters, B.: Decentralizing attribute-based encryption. In: Annual International Conference on the Theory and Applications of Cryptographic Techniques, pp. 568–588. Springer (2011)
10. Li, Q., et al.: A survey on federated learning systems: vision, hype and reality for data privacy and protection. IEEE Trans. Knowl. Data Eng. **35**(4), 3347–3366 (2023)
11. Liang, X., Liu, Y., Ning, J.: An access control scheme with privacy-preserving authentication and flexible revocation for smart healthcare. IEEE J. Biomed. Health Inform. **28**(6), 3269–3278 (2024)
12. Liu, Z., Guo, J., Yang, W., Fan, J., Lam, K.Y., Zhao, J.: Privacy-preserving aggregation in federated learning: a survey. IEEE Trans. Big Data (2022)
13. Nguyen, D.C., Ding, M., Pathirana, P.N., Seneviratne, A., Li, J., Vincent Poor, H.: Federated learning for internet of things: a comprehensive survey. IEEE Commun. Surv. Tutor. **23**(3), 1622–1658 (2021)
14. Phong, L.T., Aono, Y., Hayashi, T., Wang, L., Moriai, S.: Privacy-preserving deep learning via additively homomorphic encryption. IEEE Trans. Inf. Forensics Secur. **13**(5), 1333–1345 (2018)
15. Rasori, M., Manna, M.L., Perazzo, P., Dini, G.: A survey on attribute-based encryption schemes suitable for the internet of things. IEEE Internet Things J. **9**(11), 8269–8290 (2022)
16. Rouselakis, Y., Waters, B.: Efficient statically-secure large-universe multi-authority attribute-based encryption. In: International Conference on Financial Cryptography and Data Security, pp. 315–332. Springer (2015)
17. Sahai, A., Waters, B.: Fuzzy identity-based encryption. In: Annual International Conference on the Theory and Applications of Cryptographic Techniques, pp. 457–473. Springer (2005)
18. Salehi Shahraki, A., Rudolph, C., Grobler, M.: Attribute-based data access control for multi-authority system. In: 2020 IEEE 19th International Conference on Trust, Security and Privacy in Computing and Communications (TrustCom), pp. 1834–1841 (2020)
19. Sun, J., Xu, G., Li, H., Zhang, T., Wu, C., Yang, X., Deng, R.H.: Sanitizable cross-domain access control with policy-driven dynamic authorization. IEEE Trans. Dependable Secure Comput. **22**(4), 4126–4142 (2025)
20. Sun, J., Xu, G., Zhang, T., Alazab, M., Deng, R.H.: A practical fog-based privacy-preserving online car-hailing service system. IEEE Trans. Inf. Forensics Secur. **17**, 2862–2877 (2022)
21. Sun, J., Xu, G., Zhang, T., Yang, X., Alazab, M., Deng, R.H.: Verifiable, fair and privacy-preserving broadcast authorization for flexible data sharing in clouds. IEEE Trans. Inf. Forensics Secur. **18**, 683–698 (2022)
22. Sun, J., Xu, G., Zhang, T., Yang, X., Alazab, M., Deng, R.H.: Privacy-aware and security-enhanced efficient matchmaking encryption. IEEE Trans. Inf. Forensics Secur. **18**, 4345–4360 (2023)
23. Tian, G., Miao, M., Wei, J., Liu, Z., Guo, L., Chen, X.: Verifiable and controllable data sharing with compliance checking in cloud computing. IEEE Trans. Dependable Secure Comput. 1–14 (2025)
24. Wang, H.: Privacy-preserving data sharing in cloud computing. J. Comput. Sci. Technol. **25**(3), 401–414 (2010)
25. Xia, F., Cheng, W.: A survey on privacy-preserving federated learning against poisoning attacks. Cluster Comput. **27**(10), 13565–13582 (2024)

26. Yin, X., Zhu, Y., Hu, J.: A comprehensive survey of privacy-preserving federated learning: a taxonomy, review, and future directions. ACM Comput. Surv. (CSUR) **54**(6), 1–36 (2021)
27. Yu, J., Liu, S., Xu, M., Guo, H., Zhong, F., Cheng, W.: An efficient revocable and searchable MA-ABE scheme with blockchain assistance for C-IoT. IEEE Internet Things J. **10**(3), 2754–2766 (2023)
28. Zhou, Z., Wang, N., Liu, J., Fu, J., Deng, L.: The blockchain-based privacy-preserving searchable attribute-based encryption scheme for federated learning model in iomt. Concurr. Comput.: Pract. Exp. **36**(24), e8257 (2024)

Author Index

B
Bao, Siyuan 193

C
Chang, Chaoping 1
Chen, Wei 1
Chen, Zeli 139
Chen, Zhi 69

D
Deng, Xiao 166
Ding, Dewen 52
Ding, Yaoling 139

F
Fang, Chun 207

G
Gao, Jing 139
Gao, Yutong 16
Gong, Zheng 124
Guo, Meijia 33

H
Hu, Qiang 69

J
Jia, Su 105
Jiang, Lingxiao 69

K
Kim, Dae-Young 251

L
Lai, Jianchang 236
Lee, So-Yeon 251
Li, Gaohu 16
Li, Jingang 261
Li, Shutong 166
Li, Xiaoguo 207
Li, Xingquan 84
Li, Yu 69
Lin, Yuying 124
Liu, Shutong 124
Liu, Ye 69

M
Ma, Jinhua 207
Ma, Wei 69
Miao, Meixia 84

N
Ni, Zelin 180
Niu, Zhuoyuan 154

P
Peng, Jin 124

Q
Qian, Yuhan 139
Qin, Baodong 166

S
Saitoh, Takeshi 221
Shi, Ying 193
Shinno, Natchapol 221
Sun, Lijuan 16

T
Tan, Zhongsheng 236
Tang, Meiqin 1
Tao, Junyi 69
Tian, Guohua 84

W
Wang, An 139
Wang, Chen 154
Wang, Jialu 261
Wu, Hanzhou 193
Wu, Jingchen 16

Y. Xiang and J. Shen (Eds.): ML4CS 2025, LNCS 16456, pp. 283–284, 2026.
https://doi.org/10.1007/978-981-95-7820-7

Wu, Wei 154
Wu, Xu 16

X
Xu, Shengmin 207, 236

Y
Yang, Huijie 261
Yang, Suliu 33
Ye, Jingyu 193
Yin, Xinchun 105
Yoon, Tae-Jun 251
Yu, Jing 139
Yu, Meng 16

Z
Zeng, Yuluo 33
Zhang, Haibo 221
Zhang, Wenying 52
Zhang, Xinpeng 193
Zhao, Huizhong 236
Zhao, Sen 84
Zheng, Wenying 180, 261
Zheng, Xuexin 139
Zhou, Hongbin 105
Zhou, Lifeng 105
Zhou, Tianqi 33, 180
Zhu, Yahui 180
Zhuang, Liping 124
Zuo, Tianyu 52

The manufacturer's authorised representative in the EU is Springer Nature Customer Service Centre GmbH, Europaplatz 3, 69115 Heidelberg, Germany. If you have any concerns regarding our products, please contact ProductSafety@springernature.com

Printed and bound by CPI Group (UK) Ltd, Croydon, CR0 4YY
07/07/2026
02160917-0007